Proceedings

D1496594

Tenth Workshop on
Parallel and Distributed Simulation

pads96

Proceedings

Tenth Workshop on
Parallel and Distributed Simulation

pads96

May 22-24, 1996 Philadelphia, Pennsylvania

Sponsored by

IEEE Computer Society Technical Committee on Simulation
ACM Special Interest Group on Simulation (SIGSIM)
Society for Computer Simulation

IEEE Computer Society Press
Los Alamitos, California

Washington • Brussels • Tokyo

IEEE Computer Society Press
10662 Los Vaqueros Circle
P.O. Box 3014
Los Alamitos, CA 90720-1264

Copyright © 1996 by The Institute of Electrical and Electronics Engineers, Inc.
All rights reserved.

IEEE Computer Society Press Order Number PR07539
IEEE Order Plan Catalog Number 96TB100048
ISBN 0-8186-7539-X (paper)
Microfiche ISBN 0-8186-7541-1
ACM Order Number 577960
ISSN 1087-4097

Additional copies may be ordered from:

IEEE Computer Society Press	IEEE Service Center	IEEE Computer Society	IEEE Computer Society
Customer Service Center	445 Hoes Lane	13, Avenue de l'Aquilon	Ooshima Building
10662 Los Vaqueros Circle	P.O. Box 1331	B-1200 Brussels	2-19-1 Minami-Aoyama
P.O. Box 3014	Piscataway, NJ 08855-1331	BELGIUM	Minato-ku, Tokyo 107
Los Alamitos, CA 90720-1314	Tel: +1-908-981-1393	Tel: +32-2-770-2198	JAPAN
Tel: +1-714-821-8380	Fax: +1-908-981-9667	Fax: +32-2-770-8505	Tel: +81-3-3408-3118
Fax: +1-714-821-4641	misc.custserv@computer.org	euro.ofc@computr.org	Fax: +81-3-3408-3553
Email: cs.books@computer.org			tokyo.ofc@computer.org

Editorial production by Penny Storms
Cover by Joseph Daigle / Studio Productions
Printed in the United States of America by KNI, Inc.

 The Institute of Electrical and Electronics Engineers, Inc.

Table of Contents

Keynote Address
Session Chair: Mary L. Bailey, University of Arizona, USA

Session 2: Techniques I: Load Balancing in Parallel Simulation
Session Chair: Stephen J. Turner, University of Exeter, UK

Session 3: Applications I: ATM and Network Simulation
Session Chair: Samir R. Das, University of Texas at San Antonio, USA

Session 4: Panel: PADS, DIS, and the DoD High Level Architecture:
What is PADS' Role?
Session Chair: Richard M. Fujimoto, Georgia Institute of Technology, USA

Invited Paper

Session 5: Techniques II: State-Saving and Synchronization in
Optimistic Simulation
Session Chair: Rajive Bagrodia, University of California at Los Angeles, USA

Preface

We are extremely pleased to welcome you to the tenth ACM/IEEE/SCS Workshop on Parallel and Distributed Simulation. Since 1985, PADS has been the premiere conference for original work in parallel and distributed simulation.

This year PADS is being held as part of the Federated Computing Research Conference (FCRC) in Philadelphia, Pennsylvania, May 21–24, 1996. FCRC brings together a spectrum of individual computing research conferences and workshops at a common site and time. We are proud to have our conference included among those participating in FCRC.

This year 43 papers were submitted to the conference for consideration. We continued the PADS tradition of double-blind reviews. Each paper was sent to three reviewers for comments. Of these papers 18 were chosen to be presented as full length papers, a 42% acceptance rate, and five were chosen to be presented as short papers.

At PADS one of the sessions has always been a panel discussion. This year we have invited Richard Fujimoto to present a paper to introduce the panel discussion topic, "PADS, DIS, and the DoD High Level Architecture: What is PADS' Role?"

As in the past, the program committee has selected one paper to receive the Best Paper Award. Each reviewer had the opportunity to nominate one or more papers. All of the nominated papers were reviewed again by a subcommittee which selected the award winner. The winner this year is "The APOSTLE Simulation Language: Performance Data and Granularity Control" by Paul Wonnacott and David Bruce. Congratulations Paul and David!

We would like to thank the members of the program committee and the other reviewers for helping to maintain the quality of this workshop.

Wayne Loucks   **Bruno Preiss**
Program Committee Co-Chairs

Committees

General Chair

Mary L. Bailey, *University of Arizona, USA*

Program Co-Chairs

Wayne M. Loucks, *University of Waterloo, Canada*
Bruno R. Preiss, *University of Waterloo, Canada*

Steering Committee

M.L. Bailey, *University of Arizona, USA*
A. Elmaghraby, *University of Louisville, USA*
R.M. Fujimoto, *Georgia Institute of Technology, USA*
C.M. Overstreet, *Old Dominion University, USA*
S.J. Turner, *University of Exeter, UK*
B.W. Unger, *University of Calgary, Canada*

Program Committee

D.K. Arvind, *Edinburgh University, UK*
R. Ayani, *Royal Institute of Technology, Sweden*
R. Bagrodia, *University of California at Los Angeles, USA*
R.D. Chamberlain, *Washington University, USA*
J.G. Cleary, *University of Waikato, New Zealand*
S.R. Das, *University of Texas at San Antonio, USA*
R.M. Fujimoto, *Georgia Institute of Technology, USA*
A.G. Greenberg, *AT&T Bell Labs, USA*
P. Heidelberger, *IBM T.J. Watson Research Center, USA*
D. Nicol, *College of William and Mary, USA*
V. Rego, *Purdue, USA*
J.S. Steinman, *Metron Incorporated, USA*
S.J. Turner, *University of Exeter, UK*
B.W. Unger, *University of Calgary, CA*
P.A. Wilsey, *University of Cincinnati, USA*

Reviewers

R. Ayani

R. Bagrodia

M.L. Bailey

P. Banerjee

L. Barriga

S. Bellenot

C.J.M. Booth

D.I. Bruce

R.D. Chamberlain

S. Chandrasekaran

Y.-A. Chen

J. G. Cleary

S.R. Das

E. Deelman

P.M. Dickens

A.S. Elmaghraby

R.M. Fujimoto

T.C. Hartrum

P. Heidelberger

K. Hering

C. Hirata

J. Jean

J. Keller

D. Kim

F. Knop

V. Krishnaswamy

A. Kumar

K. Kumaran

U. Legedza

M. Liljenstam

Y.-B. Lin

W.M. Loucks

B. Lubachevsky

E. Mascarenhas

T. Necker

D. Nicol

B.R. Preiss

T. Rauber

V. Rego

R. Ronngren

M. Rumekasten

J. Sang

F. Sarkar

W. Saunders

J. Steinman

A.R.W. Todesco

C. Tropper

S.J. Turner

B.W. Unger

D. West

P.A. Wilsey

L.F. Wilson

P. Wonnacott

Keynote Address

Ten Years of PADS: Where We've Been,
Where We're Going

R.M. Fujimoto, Georgia Institute of Technology, USA

Session Chair: Mary L. Bailey, University of Arizona, USA

Session 2

Techniques I: Load Balancing in Parallel Simulation

Session Chair
Stephen J. Turner, University of Exeter, UK

Experiments in Automated Load Balancing*

Linda F. Wilson

Institute for Computer Applications
in Science and Engineering
NASA Langley Research Center
Hampton, VA 23666–0001

David M. Nicol

Department of Computer Science
The College of William and Mary
P. O. Box 8795
Williamsburg, VA 23187–8795

Abstract

One of the promises of parallelized discrete-event simulation is that it might provide significant speedups over sequential simulation. In reality, high performance cannot be achieved unless the system is fine-tuned to balance computation, communication, and synchronization requirements.

In this paper, we discuss our experiments in automated load balancing using the SPEEDES simulation framework. Specifically, we examine three mapping algorithms that use run-time measurements. Using simulation models of queuing networks and the National Airspace System, we investigate (i) the use of run-time data to guide mapping, (ii) the utility of considering communication costs in a mapping algorithm, (iii) the degree to which computational "hot-spots" ought to be broken up in the linearization, and (iv) the relative execution costs of the different algorithms. We compare the performance of the three algorithms using results from the Intel Paragon.

1 Introduction

Discrete-event simulation can be used to examine a variety of performance-related issues in complex systems. Parallel discrete-event simulation (PDES) offers the potential for significant acceleration of solution time over sequential simulation. Unfortunately, high performance is often achieved only after rigorous fine-tuning is used to obtain an efficient mapping of tasks to processors. In practice, good performance with minimal effort is often preferable to high performance with excessive effort.

In a typical PDES, components of the system under examination are mapped into logical processes (LPs) that can execute in parallel. The LPs are distributed among the physical processors, and communication between LPs is accomplished by passing messages. There is a conflict between distribution for load balance and distribution for low communication costs. If LPs are distributed among the processors such that interprocessor communication is kept low, some processors may sit waiting for something to do while others are overloaded with work. At the other extreme, a "perfectly-balanced" workload may induce high communication costs. Thus, load-balancing strategies must find a compromise between distributing work evenly and minimizing communication costs.

Researchers have examined various load-balancing approaches for PDES (e.g. [1,3,4,7,8]). In many cases, load-balancing algorithms are designed for a particular class of simulation problems (e.g. digital circuit simulation). In other cases, application of the load-balancing algorithm requires significant modification of the user's simulation code. Our work focuses on load balancing for general-purpose simulations such that little modification of the user's code is required.

In earlier work [13], we described our early experiences in developing an automated load-balancing strategy for the SPEEDES simulation environment. In particular, we demonstrated that using run-time measurements, our automated load-balancing scheme can achieve better performance than simple allocation methods that do not use run-time measurements, particularly when large numbers of processors are used.

In this paper, we discuss experiments with three different mapping algorithms used in conjunction with our automated scheme. Section 2 presents background material on SPEEDES while Section 3 describes the load-balancing methodology and the three mapping algorithms. Section 4 presents results from two models simulated on the Intel Paragon and compares the execution times obtained by the models' default partitionings with those obtained by the different mapping

---

*This work was supported by the National Aeronautics and Space Administration under NASA Contract NAS1–19480 while the authors were in residence at the Institute for Computer Applications in Science and Engineering (ICASE), NASA Langley Research Center, Hampton, VA 23681. Professor Nicol's work was also supported in part by NSF Grant CCR-9201195.

algorithms. Section 5 discusses the issue of the execution times of the mapping algorithms. Section 6 presents our conclusions.

2 SPEEDES

SPEEDES (Synchronous Parallel Environment for Emulation and Discrete-Event Simulation) is an object-oriented simulation environment that was developed at the Jet Propulsion Laboratory [10]. Designed for distributed simulation, SPEEDES supports multiple synchronization strategies (including Time Warp, Breathing Time Buckets, and Breathing Time Warp) that can be selected by the user at runtime. In addition, SPEEDES provides a sequential simulation mode (with most of the parallel overhead removed) so that a particular simulation model can be executed serially or in parallel.

Developed using C++, SPEEDES uses an object-oriented computational model. The user builds a simulation program by defining simulation objects, object managers for those objects, and events. An object manager class must be defined for each type of corresponding simulation object. For example, in the SPEEDES model of the National Airspace System, an airport object class (AIRPORT_OBJ) must have a corresponding airport manager class (AIRPORT_MGR). The object managers are responsible for creating and managing the set of simulation objects. Thus, the user (through the object managers) is *completely responsible* for the mapping of the simulation objects to the processors.

While SPEEDES gives the user freedom to choose an appropriate mapping, it is quite likely that the user does not know *a priori* how to choose a good allocation of objects to processors. Most variations of the mapping problem are computationally intractable, so optimal mappings are extremely difficult to obtain. Furthermore, many users and potential users of PDES would prefer to let "the system" make such decisions, especially if the resulting performance is "good enough". In the next section, we present our methodology for automated load balancing in SPEEDES.

3 Automated Load Balancing

As discussed in [13], we modified SPEEDES to collect data on the workload characteristics of a simulation. Since each event is connected to exactly one simulation object, simulation objects determine the resolution of the partitioning. Thus, we collect computation data (number of events processed) for each object and communication data (number of messages sent) for each pair of simulation objects. The event

and message counts are collected and saved in data files during a single run of the simulation. Ultimately, we will use this data to govern dynamic load balancing based on run-time information. In this paper, we investigate the suitability of different algorithms for balancing computation and communication, with the expectation of embedding suitable candidates into a dynamic load-management system. Thus, at present, SPEEDES is instructed to collect the data (for one run) and use the data (in another run) through the use of run-time flags. The data is analyzed by a mapping algorithm that determines the load-balancing allocation of simulation objects to processors. In this paper, we experiment with three different mapping algorithms to examine the effectiveness of using run-time measurements in our automated load-balancing scheme. We also consider the execution costs of the algorithms themselves.

The first algorithm (LBalloc1) determines object placement based only on the computation weight of each object. Specifically, we use the longest-processing-time-first list scheduling algorithm in which the objects are ordered by decreasing computation weight and the heaviest unplaced object is placed on the processor with the lightest cumulative weight [2]. Notice that this approach concentrates on balancing the workload on the processors but ignores communication costs.

The second algorithm (LBalloc2, from [6]) arranges the LPs in a linear chain and then partitions the chain into as many contiguous subchains as there are processors, mapping one subchain per processor. The partition chosen minimizes the amount of work assigned to the most heavily-loaded processor, where the computation weight of a processor is the sum of measured computation weights of its LPs, and the computation weight of an LP is the number of committed events it executed.[1] Given a linear ordering, this optimization problem can be solved very quickly, e.g. in $O(PM \log M)$ time, where P is the number of processors and M the number of LPs.

However, choice of an optimal linearization of LPs is computationally intractable; choice of a "good" linearization remains an open research problem. One idea (used in LBalloc2) is to linearize so as to keep heavily communicating LPs close to each other in the chain, thereby increasing the chance that they will be assigned to the same subchain. This intuition is realized by a recursive heuristic which at the first step "pairs" LPs using a stable matching algorithm. Here

---

[1]Notice that the linearization approach will be useful in dynamic load balancing since it leads to incremental object migration.

the communication weight between two LPs is a measure of their attraction; a stable matching is one where if A and B are matched, and C and D are matched, it is not possible to break the matches and reassemble (e.g. A and C, B and D) and have higher attraction values for both matchings. Two LPs that are matched will be adjacent to each other in the linear ordering. We then merge matched LPs into super-LPs, and compute the attraction between two super-LPs as the sum of the attractions between LPs in the two super-LPs. Matching these, the sets of LPs represented in two matched super-LPs will be adjacent to each other in the linear ordering. This process continues until there is a single super-LP.

Using the communication weight between LPs as the base attraction function is suitable as long as there is only weak correlation between the communication between two LPs and their computation weights. However, many simulations have "hot spot" simulation objects that perform most of the work. Typically, the hot spots have large amounts of communication with other hot spots. Use of the communication weight as the attraction function can cluster the hot spots together, which results in poor load balancing.

For the third mapping algorithm (LBalloc3), we modified the linear chaining algorithm to discourage clustering of extremes: pairs of very heavy objects or pairs of very light objects. Basically, we want to encourage pairings in which the cumulative computation weight is close to the mean computation weight of all pairs (with non-zero attractions) while we discourage pairings with computation weights that are far from the mean. To accomplish this, the attraction (communication weight) between each pair of objects is scaled by a Gaussian function based on the pair's computation weight, relative to the weights of the other pairs (with non-zero attractions). The Gaussian is determined from the mean and variance of the paired computation weights, and the resulting scaling function has a value of one corresponding to the mean computation weight for all pairs with non-zero communication weights. For example, Figure 1(a) shows a plot of first-round communication and computation weights for all pairs with non-zero communication weights.[2] Figure 1(b) shows the corresponding scaling function, and Figure 1(c) shows the resulting scaled communication weights. Notice that this scaling will encourage pairings in which the resulting paired computation weight will be close to the mean while it discourages pairings far from the mean.

---

[2]This data comes from the DPAT algorithm, discussed in Section 4.

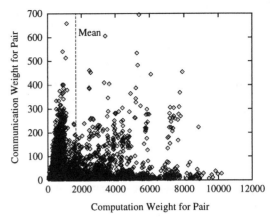

(a) Original Data

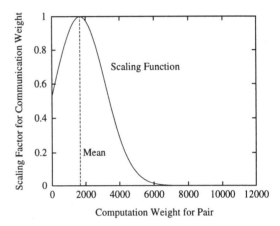

(b) Gaussian Scaling Function

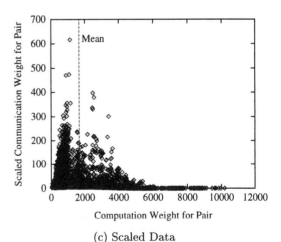

(c) Scaled Data

Figure 1: Scaling Communication Weights for the LBalloc3 Algorithm

While the automated load-balancing scheme can use any of the mapping algorithms to determine the allocation of simulation objects to processors, the SPEEDES user must choose to use that allocation when objects are created by the object managers. To assist the

6

user, we added three functions to SPEEDES: `LB_is_avail()`, `is_local_object(objnum)`, and `is_local_object(objname)`. The `LB_is_avail()` function is used to determine if the load-balancing data is available for use during this run (i.e. it was collected during a previous run). Thus, the user can write an object manager that uses a default mapping if data is not available and the load-balanced mapping if it is. The `is_local_object(objnum)` function is used to determine if the simulation object with global ID number `objnum` should be created on this node while `is_local_object(objname)` provides the same information based on a user-defined object name. Notice that the automated mapping will be inappropriate unless the global ID numbers and object names are consistent from one run to the next.

4 Results

We applied the three mappings in our automated load-balancing system to two simulation models: a fully-connected queuing network and the DPAT model of the National Airspace System [12]. In this section, we discuss the two models and present results from execution of the simulations on a 72-node Intel Paragon. Furthermore, we compare the results obtained from the three automated mappings with those obtained from the default partitioning.

4.1 Qnet Simulation

Queuing networks are often used as PDES benchmarks because they are commonly used in simulation studies, are relatively easy to program, and yet exhibit many of the difficulties experienced by more complex models [5]. Thus, it is reasonable to use a fully-connected queuing network (Qnet) as the first test of our automated load-balancing system.

The Qnet simulation contains 1600 fully-connected servers. Since a homogeneous network of queues is balanced naturally without sophisticated algorithms, we study a deliberately unbalanced network. We define 50 servers to be "hot spots", where the probability that a customer exiting a server goes next to a hot spot is 0.15. Furthermore, we give each server a neighborhood of up to 30 neighbors, where the probability that a customer exiting one server goes to a neighbor is 0.65.[3] Finally, a customer goes to a random queue with probability 0.10 and back to the same queue with probability 0.10.

For the Qnet simulation, the default mapping of simulation objects to processors is so-called *block* partitioning. Specifically, n objects are allocated to p

processors by placing the first (by global id) n/p objects on the first processor, the next n/p objects on the second processor, and so forth.

As we conducted our investigation, we were surprised to discover that in the SPEEDES implementation on the Intel Paragon, there is very little difference in the overall communication cost between placing two objects on the same processor or separating them.[4] As a consequence, any method that balances the workload well will perform well in this context. It is unrealistic to expect this to be true either on other architectures or with different simulation testbeds. For the purposes of exploring the effectiveness of the algorithms in such situations, we parametrically inflate the interprocessor communication costs by adding a timed delay to the posting of each interprocessor event.[5] For the Qnet simulation, we examined three different cases:

- Qnet #1: delay = 0 msec, 50 initial customers per server, simulated execution time = 1500 seconds

- Qnet #2: delay = 10 msec, 25 initial customers per server, simulated execution time = 250 seconds

- Qnet #3: delay = 15 msec, 25 initial customers per server, simulated execution time = 250 seconds.

To put these delays in perspective, the time required to execute a SPEEDES event on the Paragon is approximately 1 msec. Thus, the 10 and 15 msec delays represent the sorts of relative network delays one might see with medium-grained workloads running on a workstation cluster or fine-grained workloads on a large-scale parallel architecture.

For the simulations discussed in this paper, we used the optimistic Breathing Time Warp (BTW) synchronization protocol [9,11] that combines the Time Warp and Breathing Time Buckets protocols. At the beginning of each global virtual time (GVT) cycle, messages are sent aggressively using Time Warp. Later in the cycle, all messages are sent risk-free using Breathing Time Buckets. Two runtime parameters in SPEEDES determine the amount of risk in the BTW protocol: Nrisk and Nopt. For the first Nrisk events processed after the last GVT computation, messages are released immediately to the receiver (Time Warp). For the events from Nrisk to Nopt (where Nrisk < Nopt), event messages are cached locally and the event horizon is computed (Breathing Time Buckets).

The Breathing Time Warp parameters used for Qnet Simulation #1 were Nrisk = 1500 and Nopt =

---

[3]Note that if Server A is a neighbor of Server B, Server B is not necessarily a neighbor of Server A.

[4]This conclusion was driven by data obtained from several experiments. The reason for this is as yet unclear.

[5]To accomplish this, we modified SPEEDES to add a delay in the sending of each off-processor message.

3000. For Qnet Simulations #2 and #3, the parameters were Nrisk = 75 and Nopt = 150. These parameters were determined by conducting various runs of the Qnet simulation (using the default partitioning) on different numbers of processors. Overall, these parameters gave the shortest execution times.

Figure 2 presents results for Qnet #1. Notice that when eight or more processors are used, the automated load-balancing schemes give results that are noticeably better than the default partitioning, while the two linear-ordering mappings (LBalloc2 and LBalloc3)

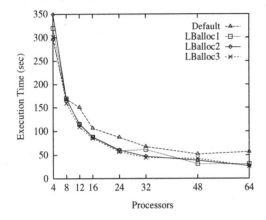

Figure 2: Results for Qnet #1 (delay = 0 msec)

give almost identical results. When four processors are used, LBalloc1 and the default partitioning yield the fastest execution time and yield significantly better performance than LBalloc2 and LBalloc3. This occurs because LBalloc2 and LBalloc3 are constrained somewhat from balancing load, based on their linear orders. Yet, with few processors the communication load is inconsequential compared to the computation load. The situation changes though as the number of processors is increased. The mappings that explicitly balance load are nearly identical in performance and leave the default performing rather poorly. Also, notice the relatively large difference between LBalloc2 and LBalloc3 at four processors. Here we see the effects of LBalloc2 naively clumping hot spots together in the linear order, making it harder to distribute the workload evenly. Surprisingly, the effects of this mishap are mitigated though by increasing the number of processors. However, for the case of four processors, the Gaussian-based weighting of communication costs in LBalloc3 significantly reduces the hot-spot clumping.

Figure 3 presents results for Qnet #2, where the sending of interprocessor messages is delayed by 10 msec. When four processors are used, the default and LBalloc1 yield mappings that are noticeably worse than those of the communication-sensitive mappers

LBalloc2 and LBalloc3. Specifically, LBalloc3 gives a 16% improvement over the default mapping while LBalloc2 provides an improvement of 11%. LBalloc1 yields an improvement (over the default mapping) of less than 2%. With larger numbers of processors, the

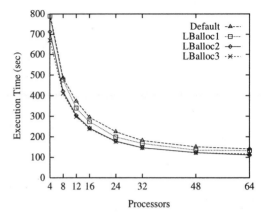

Figure 3: Results for Qnet #2 (delay = 10 msec)

results for LBalloc2 and LBalloc3 are very similar, and owing to their sensitivity to communication costs, are noticeably better than those for LBalloc1. With 32 processors, the execution times obtained using LBalloc2 and LBalloc3 are almost 20% less than the default execution time, while LBalloc1 improves the execution time by only 8%.

Figure 4 demonstrates the effect of even larger communication costs when large numbers of processors are used. When 24 processors are used, LBalloc3 is 10 seconds faster—about 5%—than LBalloc2, which indicates that some improvement was made by breaking up some of the hot spots. In general, there is little difference between LBalloc2 and LBalloc3. Both provide markedly better performance than either of the communication-cost insensitive mappings.

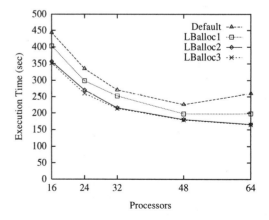

Figure 4: Results for Qnet #3 (delay = 15 msec)

4.2 DPAT: A Model of the National Airspace System

For the last several years, the MITRE Corporation has been studying the National Airspace System (NAS), which encompasses all commercial and general aviation air traffic in the United States [12]. On a typical day, the NAS consists of 45,000 to 50,000 flights from approximately 16,000 airfields. The commercial air traffic is handled by roughly 1000 airports while 80% of the general aviation traffic is handled by the top 500 airports. In addition to the airfields, the NAS contains 701 three-dimensional regions called sectors that cover the airspace between airports.

MITRE recently developed a PDES model of the NAS called DPAT (Detailed Policy Assessment Tool) that is used to examine the average delay encountered by aircraft under various weather and traffic conditions. As discussed in [12], the physical NAS system is a good candidate for PDES because the aircraft, air traffic controllers, and airports operate naturally in parallel.

The DPAT model contains SPEEDES simulation objects for 520 airports and 701 sectors. Events in the system include takeoffs, landings, and transfers of aircraft between sectors. Scheduling data from the Official Airlines Guide (OAG) is used to schedule commercial flights while general aviation flights are scheduled stochastically. Details of this model can be found in [12].

The DPAT simulation begins by reading in large files of flight and airplane data to initialize system parameters and schedule initial events. When we first executed DPAT on the Intel Paragon, we encountered severe performance problems due to memory paging. In particular, the aggregate size of the executable and data exceeded the roughly 23 MBytes per node of user-available memory. After discussing the problem with MITRE, we modified the program to use a subset of the aircraft data. This modification eliminated the memory problems (when multiple processors were used) without reducing the amount of computational work required.

The DPAT simulation organizes the airports and airspace sectors into geographic groupings called centers. For example, the La Guardia, Kennedy, and Newark airports in New York and New Jersey belong to a center that contains the airspace sectors around those airports. The Los Angeles and San Francisco airports belong to different centers because of the distance (and number of other airports) between them. These geographic centers form the basis for DPAT's default partitioning of simulation objects to processors.

Given that a flight must travel through contiguous sectors between airports, it is logical to assume that a geographical partitioning of the airports and sectors will reduce communication costs. The problem, however, is that the geographic distribution may not result in an even distribution of work. With DPAT, the airports and sectors are divided among 22 centers, where the "laziest" center is associated with 421 events and the busiest center has 20963. Even if more than 22 processors are used, only 22 will receive work. This center-based approach serves as the default mapping for DPAT.

We executed DPAT on the Intel Paragon using the default partitioning and the three automated algorithms. To determine the effect of interprocessor communication, we evaluated two scenarios:

- DPAT #1: delay = 0 msec

- DPAT #2: delay = 10 msec.

For consistency, all of the runs were initially taken with Nrisk = 250 and Nopt = 500, which were determined from the best timings of the default partitioning.

Figure 5 presents results for DPAT #1 in which no additional communication delays were added. Notice that LBalloc1 gives the best overall results while LBalloc2 and LBalloc3 give very similar results. Table 1 presents a comparison of LBalloc1 and LBalloc2 data for DPAT #1. Notice that the difference in their respective bottleneck weights (measured as the largest number of committed events executed on any processor) gradually increases with the number of processors. Furthermore, notice the dramatic difference between LBalloc1 and LBalloc2 in the total number of off-processor messages. In this case, the execution time corresponds directly with the maximum computation weight of a processor, and reducing the number of off-node messages has little or no effect. This data indicates that there is little difference in SPEEDES (on the Paragon) between the costs for on-processor and off-processor communication.

As mentioned earlier, we initially ran DPAT using Nrisk = 250 and Nopt = 500. When we added a communication delay of 10 msec, we had trouble running DPAT on large numbers of processors because the number of optimistically processed events grew much faster than the number of committed events, resulting in memory problems on the Paragon. Figure 6 presents results for the combinations that were able to run to completion using the initial parameters. In Figure 7, we present additional results that were obtained by modifying the parameters for runs with 32 or more processors. Specifically, we reduced Nrisk and Nopt until we could get all four versions to run for a

Table 1: Comparison of LBalloc1 and LBalloc2 for DPAT #1

# Proc.	Max. Comp. Weight[a]		Off-Node Messages		Exec. Time (sec)	
	LBalloc1	LBalloc2	LBalloc1	LBalloc2	LBalloc1	**LBalloc2**
4	121,474	121,538	179,222	54,510	221.8	**230.3**
8	60,739	61,241	205,711	74,075	126.3	**139.0**
12	40,496	40,818	228,322	85,096	99.9	110.8
16	30,374	30,787	235,065	102,734	84.1	95.0
24	20,253	20,682	261,144	113,984	71.6	77.4
32	15,194	16,009	285,942	141,032	64.7	70.1
48	10,142	10,732	334,786	175,977	57.4	59.4
64	7,611	8,446	388,998	218,582	54.1	57.5

[a]Computational workload is measured as the maximum number of committed events executed by any one processor.

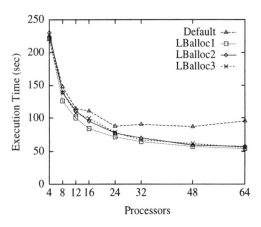

Figure 5: Results for DPAT #1 (delay = 0 msec)

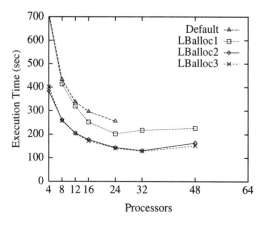

Figure 6: Results for DPAT #2 (delay = 10 msec)

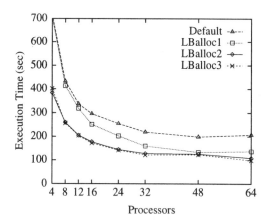

Figure 7: Results for Modified DPAT #2
(delay = 10 msec)

particular number of processors. For 32 and 48 processors, we used Nrisk = 250 and Nopt = 400. For 64 processors, we used Nrisk = 150 and Nopt = 200.

In Figures 6 and 7, the results obtained by LBalloc2 and LBalloc3 are significantly better than those obtained by LBalloc1 or the default (center-based) partitioning. When 24 processors are used, LBalloc2 and LBalloc3 yield execution times that are 44% faster than the default, while LBalloc1 provides an execution time that is only 20% faster. These results confirm the significance of minimizing communication when communication costs are high. Finally, notice that LBalloc3 has a slight advantage over LBalloc2 when large numbers of processors are used, probably because the hot spots are more evenly distributed among the processors.

5   Mapping Algorithm Execution Time

If we are to use any of these mapping algorithms at run-time, we must consider the costs of doing so. Towards this end we considered the execution time required to produce the mappings for LBalloc1, LBalloc2, and LBalloc3 on the DPAT benchmark (where approximately 1200 objects are mapped). More or less regardless of the number of processors targeted, LBalloc1 required 1/10*th* of a second, LBalloc2 required 3.5 seconds, and LBalloc3 required 7 seconds. Measuring the various contributions to this cost, we discovered that the dominant cost is due to pairings between simulation objects. If either method is to be implemented at run-time clearly more work is needed to intelligently cut down on the number of pairings considered, both from the point of view of computation time, and from the point of view of transporting the communication measurements to the processor responsible for executing the mapping routine. On the other hand, LBalloc1 is sufficiently fast to use at run-time, and requires much less information. At least for SPEEDES on the Paragon, LBalloc1 is clearly the mapping algorithm of choice. However, since the dominant cost of LBalloc2 and LBalloc3 is in the linearization (the workload balancing part is very fast), one might only consider the linearization part very infrequently, but balance workload more frequently (this is the approach used in [6]). It is also important to note that an execution time of 3–7 seconds is notable only in the context of repeated application at run-time. When used as we have—once, at initialization—it is a minor cost.

6   Conclusions

We have studied the suitability of various mapping algorithms for automated mapping of SPEEDES models. One algorithm, LBalloc1, is a well-known multiprocessor scheduling algorithm and ignores any information concerning communication costs between objects. LBalloc2 explicitly considers communication costs by constructing a linear ordering of objects wherein objects that communicate heavily tend to be close to each other in the ordering. The linear ordering is then partitioned subject to a constraint that only contiguous subchains be mapped to processors; subject to this constraint, we efficiently find the mapping that minimizes the computational workload of the most heavily loaded processor. LBalloc3 corrects the possibility of "hot spots" producing bad linearizations in LBalloc2.

Our experiences on a large queuing network model and on a realistic model of the National Airspace System show that for SPEEDES on the Paragon, LBalloc1 is clearly the mapping algorithm of choice. While it does not explicitly consider communication costs, there evidently is very little difference in SPEEDES on the Paragon between the cost of interprocessor and intraprocessor message passing. Furthermore, LBalloc1 is fast enough to be repeatedly called in a dynamic remapping context. However, whatever the cause of this lack of distinction between on-processor and off-processor messaging, one cannot expect it to hold true for other tools and/or other architectures. By artificially increasing the communication cost for interprocessor messages, we studied the benefit of LBalloc2 and

LBalloc3 in communication-sensitive contexts. While we did find instances where LBalloc3 improved upon LBalloc2, for the most part the differences were slight. However, in the presence of significant communication delays, they do both provide substantially better mappings than communication-blind mappings.

Currently, we are studying various issues in dynamic load balancing, such as how much data should be collected, how often should data be collected, and how often should the workload be rebalanced. We are also evaluating the concept of balancing the workload more frequently and recomputing the linearization less frequently. For future work, we will implement dynamic object migration in SPEEDES.

References

[1] J. V. Briner, "Parallel Mixed-Level Simulation of Digital Circuits Using Virtual Time", PhD Dissertation, Duke University, 1990.

[2] R. L. Graham, "Bounds on Multiprocessing Timing Anomalies", *SIAM Journal of Applied Mathematics*, Vol. 17, No. 2, pp. 416–419, March 1969.

[3] B. Nandy and W. Loucks, "An Algorithm for Partitioning and Mapping Conservative Parallel Simulation onto Multicomputers", *Proceedings of the 6th Workshop on Parallel and Distributed Simulation (PADS '92)*, pp. 139–146, January 1992.

[4] D. M. Nicol, "The Automated Partitioning of Simulations for Parallel Execution", PhD Dissertation, University of Virginia, 1985.

[5] D. M. Nicol, "Parallel Discrete-Event Simulation of FCFS Stochastic Queuing Networks", *Proceedings ACM/SIGPLAN PPEALS 1988: Experiences with Applications, Languages and Systems*, pp. 124–137.

[6] D. M. Nicol and W. Mao, "Automated Parallelization of Timed Petri-Net Simulations", *Journal of Parallel and Distributed Computing*, Vol. 29, No. 1, pp. 60–74, August 1995.

[7] P. L. Reiher and D. Jefferson, "Dynamic Load Management in the Time Warp Operating System", *Transactions of the Society for Computer Simulation*, 7(2):91–120, June 1990.

[8] R. Schlagenhaft, M. Ruhwandl, C. Sporrer, and H. Bauer, "Dynamic Load Balancing of a Multi-Cluster Simulator on a Network of Workstations", *Proceedings of the 9th Workshop on Parallel and Distributed Simulation (PADS '95)*, pp. 175–180, June 1995.

[9] J. Steinman, "Breathing Time Warp", *Proceedings of the 1993 Workshop on Parallel and Distributed Simulation (PADS '93)*, pp. 109–118, July 1993.

[10] J. Steinman, "SPEEDES: A Multiple-Synchronization Environment for Parallel Discrete-Event Simulation", *International Journal in Computer Simulation*, 2(3): 251–286, 1992.

[11] J. S. Steinman, C. A. Lee, L. F. Wilson, and D. M. Nicol, "Global Virtual Time and Distributed Synchronization", *Proceedings of the 9th Workshop on Parallel and Distributed Simulation (PADS '95)*, pp. 139–148, June 1995.

[12] F. Wieland, E. Blair, and T. Zukas, "Parallel Discrete-Event Simulation (PDES): A Case Study in Design, Development, and Performance Using SPEEDES", *Proceedings of the 9th Workshop on Parallel and Distributed Simulation (PADS '95)*, pp. 103–110, June 1995.

[13] L. F. Wilson and D. M. Nicol, "Automated Load Balancing in SPEEDES", *Proceedings of the 1995 Winter Simulation Conference*, pp. 590–596, December 1995.

Background Execution of Time Warp Programs *

Christopher D. Carothers and Richard M. Fujimoto
College of Computing
Georgia Institute of Technology
Atlanta, GA 30332-0280
chrisc,fujimoto@cc.gatech.edu

Abstract

A load distribution system is proposed to enable a single Time Warp program to execute in background, spreading over a collection of possibly heterogeneous workstations (including multiprocessor hosts), utilizing whatever otherwise unused CPU cycles are available. The system uses a simple processor allocation policy to dynamically add or delete hosts from the set of processors utilized by the Time Warp program during its execution. A load balancing algorithm is used that allocates logical processes (LPs) to processors, taking into account other computations executing on the host from the system or other user applications. A clustering mechanism is used to group collections of logical processes together, reducing process migration overheads and helping to retain locality of communication for simulations containing large number of LPs.

An initial, prototype implementation of the load distribution system is described that executes on a homogeneous network of Silicon Graphics workstations. Initial experiments indicate this approach shows promise in enabling efficient execution of Time Warp programs "in background" on distributed computing platforms.

1 Introduction

Many large-scale discrete event simulation computations are excessively time consuming, and are a natural candidate for distributed processing. Because of the large amount of computation required, and the availability of large networks of workstations, an attractive paradigm is to allow the distributed simulation to execute "in background," spreading across the available workstations in the network and making use of whatever otherwise unused CPU cycles are available. Because these computations should not degrade performance of interactive users or other higher priority computations, the distributed computation must be able to withdraw from any CPU on short notice if the need arises.

Time Warp is a well known synchronization protocol that detects out-of-order executions of events as they occur, and recovers using a rollback mechanism [10]. Time Warp has demonstrated some success in speeding up a variety of simulation applications, including combat models [17], communication networks [14], wireless networks [4], queuing networks [6], and digital logic circuits [1], among others. We assume that the reader is familiar with the Time Warp mechanism described in [10].

With few exceptions, most research on distributed simulation to date assumes the simulation program is allocated a fixed number of processors when execution begins, and has exclusive access to these processors throughout the lifetime of the simulation. Specifically, interference from other, external, computations is minimal, and no provisions for adding or removing processors during the execution of the simulation are made. In fact, in most experimental studies, one typically goes to great lengths to eliminate any unwanted external interference from other user and system computations in order to obtain performance measurements that are not perturbed by external workloads. While this paradigm makes perfectly good sense from an experimental standpoint, this "dedicated platform" scenario is often not the prevalent paradigm one encounters in practice. In particular, networks of desktop workstations and distributed compute servers consisting of collections of workstation-class CPUs interconnected through high-speed LANs have become prevalent. Despite the continual, reduced cost of computing hardware, shared use of computer resources will continue to be a common computing paradigm in the foreseeable future.

The goal of this study is to examine the "background" execution of Time Warp programs on distributed computing platforms in the presence of other external computations utilizing the same hardware resources, and to develop simple, but effective techniques to enable the Time Warp program to spread over the network and "soak up" whatever CPU cycles are available. Specifically, the background execution scheme must

- dynamically allocate additional CPUs during the execution of the distributed simulation as they become available and migrate portions of the distributed simulation workload onto these machines,

- dynamically release certain CPUs during the simulation as they become loaded with other, external, computations, and off-load the workload to the remaining CPUs used by the distributed simulation, and

- dynamically re-distribute the workload on the existing set of processors as some become more heavily or lightly loaded by changing, internal or externally induced workloads.

The last point, load distribution in the face of external computations, is particularly important for Time Warp because load imbalance can lead to very poor performance. The external workloads competing for the CPU with the Time Warp program may be user or system computations. A Time Warp program that is well balanced when executed on dedicated hardware may become grossly unbalanced when executed on machines with external computations from other users. Logical processes (LPs) that are mapped to heavily utilized processors will advance very slowly through simulated time relative to others executing on lightly loaded processors. This can

*This work was supported by U.S. Army Contract DASG60-95-C-0103 funded by the Ballistic Missile Defense Organization, and NSF Grant Number CDA-9501637.

cause some LPs to advance too far ahead into the simulation future, resulting in very long or frequent rollbacks. Thus, it is essential that any Time Warp simulation running in "background" take into account the other, external, workloads utilizing the same CPUs the Time Warp program is using.

The policies and mechanisms described here are intended to be used in large distributed simulation applications containing many logical processes, e.g., thousands or more. Because of the scale of these simulations, managing individual logical processes is too time consuming. Here, a clustering approach is used where LPs are organized into groups, and a group is the smallest unit that is moved between processors.

The next section describes related work concerning workload management of Time Warp programs. An approach to enable efficient background execution is then described. An implementation of the mechanism is discussed, followed by results from initial measurements of the prototype system.

2 Related Work

Background execution is essentially a load management problem. Traditionally, load balancing involves distributing the simulation workload across a fixed set of processors in order to minimize the elapsed time to execute the program. Here, the traditional load balancing problem must be extended in two ways. First, the load balancing mechanism must take into account dynamically changing external workloads produced by other computations. These external loads cannot be controlled by the load management software. Second, the set of processors that can be utilized by the distributed simulation expands and contracts during the execution of the program in unpredictable ways.

Optimistic synchronization mechanisms introduce new wrinkles to dynamic load management: high processor utilization does not necessarily imply good performance because a processor may be busy executing work that is later undone. Further, there is a close relationship between load management and the efficiency (e.g., amount of rolled back computation) of the synchronization mechanism, as discussed earlier. These factors necessitate development of new load management techniques specific to Time Warp. Thus, systems such as Condor [11] that distribute jobs onto networked workstations as background processes that "soak up" otherwise unused CPU cycles are not sufficient for Time Warp simulations.

Dynamic load management of Time Warp programs has been studied by others. Reiher and Jefferson propose a new metric called *effective processor utilization* which is defined as the fraction of the time during which a processor is executing computations that are eventually committed [15]. Based on this metric, they propose a strategy that migrates processes from processors with high effective utilization to those with low utilization. Reiher and Jefferson also propose splitting a logical process into *phases* to reduce the amount of process state that must be moved when an LP migrates from one processor to another, and present performance measurements of their scheme. Glazer and Tropper propose allocating virtual time-slices to processes, based on their observed rate of advancing the local simulation clock [8]. They present simulation results illustrating this approach yields better performance than the Reiher/Jefferson scheme for certain workloads. To our knowledge, this scheme has not been implemented on an operational Time Warp system. Goldberg describes an interesting approach to the load distribution that replicates bottleneck processes to enable

concurrent execution [9]. Time Warp is used to maintain consistency among the replicated copies.

None of these approaches address the question of background execution. The approach proposed here utilizes the ideas of not considering rolled back computation in deriving load balancing metrics, and workload allocation based on the rate of simulated time advance in developing an approach for background execution.

Burdorf and Marti [3] propose an approach to periodically compute the average and standard deviation of all the LP local clocks in the system. If the average local clock among the LPs mapped to a processor is greater than the system-wide average plus one standard deviation, it is concluded that this processor is advancing too rapidly through simulated time, so additional LPs are migrated to that processor to "slow it down." Specifically, the LP with the smallest local clock is moved. In addition, other LPs that have low virtual clocks (specifically, a local clock less than the system-wide average minus one standard deviation) are moved to the processor that has the LP with the largest local clock. Marti and Burdorf observe that this approach will balance the workload in the presence of external computations competing for the same processors.

Schlagenhaft et. al. [16] propose an approach to balance the load of a VLSI circuit application on a distributed Time Warp simulator in the presence of external workloads. They define an inverse measure of the load, called *Virtual Time Progress,* which reflects how fast a simulation process continues in virtual time. This approach has some similarities with ours, however neither their approach nor Burdorf's approach address the question of dynamically changing the set of processors utilized by the simulation.

The central contribution of the work described here is in devising and demonstrating an approach to enable efficient, background execution of Time Warp programs on networked workstations where the simulation is able to dynamically migrate over whatever CPUs are available to execute the simulation. A prototype system and initial performance measurements are described demonstrating the viability of this approach.

3 The Workload Management Policy

The load management policy used here consists of two components:

1. The *processor allocation* policy that defines the set of processors that may be used by the Time Warp program. In general, this *usable set* of processors will change dynamically throughout the execution of the distributed simulation.

2. The *load balancing* policy that migrates LPs between processors in the usable set. This policy must maintain efficient execution, in spite of dynamically changing external workloads in the processors in the usable set. It is assumed the Time Warp system has no control over these workloads, nor control over priority of execution in the operating system of these external computations relative to the Time Warp program.

Dynamic load distribution of individual LPs burdens simulations containing large numbers (say, thousands) of LPs. This is because a large number of entities must be considered by the load balancing algorithm, increasing the computation required for load distribution, and load balancing information that must be maintained. Further, because migrating each LP requires a certain amount of

```
Function DLMAnalyzeStatistics()
    For Each Processor, PE[i]
        if( PE[i] Is ACTIVE AND
            PE[i]'s Load Average > DeAllocThreshold )
            Set PE[i] to INACTIVE;
            UnLoad ALL Clusters From PE[i]
                to an ACTIVE Neighboring Processor;
            Set PE[i]'s PAT to INFINITY;
            NumActiveProcessors--;
        endif
        if( PE[i] Is INACTIVE AND
            PE[i]'s Load Average < AllocThreshold )
            Set PE[i]'s PAT to 0;
            NumActiveProcessors++;
        endif
    Done = FALSE;
    while( !Done )
        Compute PAT For All ACTIVE Processors by
            SUMMING the CAT values for each
            Processor's Assigned Clusters;
        Sort Processor Statistics Based on PAT;
        For Each ACTIVE Processor, PE[i]
            Sort PE[i]'s Cluster Statistics based
                on the Cluster's CAT;
        if( TryToOffLoad() == FAILED )
            Done = TRUE;
end DLMAnalyzeStatistics
```

Figure 1: Dynamic Load Management Algorithm.

```
Function TryToOffLoad()
    /* NOTE: PE[0..N-1] is SORTED from lowest */
    /*       to highest PAT values.           */
    /*       PE[NumActiveProcessors-1] is the */
    /*       ACTIVE PE with the highest PAT   */
    /*       value.                           */
    /*       PEs PE[NumActiveProcessors] ...  */
    /*       PE[N-1] are INACTIVE and have    */
    /*       PAT values set to INFINITY.      */
    highest = NumActiveProcessors-1;
    For All Clusters, c, assigned to PE[highest]
        For ALL ACTIVE Processors, PE[i], from 0
            to highest-1
            if( Moving Cluster, c, from PE[highest]
                to PE[i] reduces the difference in
                PAT values between PE[highest] and PE[i]
                AND the current PAT value difference >
                PAT_VALUE_TOLERANCE )
                Move Cluster c from PE[highest] to PE[i];
                return( SUCCEEDED );
            endif
    return( FAILED );
end TryToOffLoad
```

Figure 2: *TryToOffLoad* Algorithm.

overhead, independent of the "size" of the LP, migrating many LPs from one processor to another is less efficient than migrating a group of LPs as a unit. Here, LPs are first grouped (by the application) into *clusters* of LPs, and the cluster forms the atomic unit that can be migrated from one processor to another. In addition to reducing load management and process migration overhead, this approach will keep LPs that frequently communicate together, on the same processor, provided they are grouped within the same cluster.

3.1 Processor Allocation

The hardware platform is assumed to be a collection of possibly heterogeneous processors interconnected by a local area network (LAN). Individual *hosts* of this network may be single processor workstations or multiprocessors. The processor allocation software monitors the computation load assigned to each each processor and derives the *usable set* of processors that may be used by the Time Warp simulation. This usable set is passed to the load balancing policy for assignment of LP clusters to processors.

At present, a simple approach to processor allocation is used. A central process is responsible for monitoring the processors that *may* be used by the distributed simulation. This process executes periodically, at a user defined *scheduling interval* $T_{schedule}$. This process estimates the expected amount of CPU time that would be allocated to a Time Warp simulation if it were to execute on that host, based on the current workload of this host over the last schedule interval. A daemon-like process executes on each processor that is responsible for providing load information on that processor. If a processor is not in the current usable set and the expected CPU allocation (divided by $T_{schedule}$) is above a user defined threshold *AllocThreshold*, then the processor is added to the usable set. On

the other hand, if the processor is already included in the usable set, but the expected CPU allocation falls below a second user defined threshold *DeAllocThreshold*, then the processor is removed from the usable set. A straightforward extension of this approach is to allow external computations, e.g., created by the user that owns the CPU, to evict the distributed simulation when that user begins using the machine.

The expected CPU allocation is computed in one of two ways. If the processor is currently in the usable set, then the expected CPU allocation is simply the amount of CPU time the Time Warp program received on that processor during the last scheduling period. On the other hand, if the processor is not in the current usable set, the expected CPU allocation is computed from the processor's load average, obtained by a system call.

3.2 Load Balancing

The load balancing policy is responsible for assigning LP clusters to processors in the usable processor set. Like the processor allocation policy, the current implementation of the load balancing policy uses a central process that executes periodically every $T_{schedule}$ seconds to determine which clusters should be moved to another processor.

The load balancing policy attempts to distribute clusters across processors to equalize the rate of progress of each processor through simulated time, taking into account both the external (non-Time Warp) and internal (Time Warp) workloads assigned to each processor. The central metric that is used to accomplish this is the *processor advance time (PAT)*. The processor advance time indicates the amount of *wall-clock time* required for a processor to advance one unit of simulated time in the absence of rollback. By using wall-clock time rather than CPU time of the Time Warp simulation, the external workload on the processor is automatically taken into account. By only considering committed computation, rolled back computation is not allowed to be treated as additional computation load. The load balancing policy moves clusters from processors with large PAT values to those with lower values with the goal of minimizing the maximum difference between the PAT values in any two processors.

PAT values are easily measured for the current mapping of clusters to processors, as discussed below. In order to assess the effect of redistributing clusters, another mechanism is required to estimate how well (or poorly) the load will be balanced if a hypothetical move of cluster(s) between processors is performed. For this purpose, the *cluster advance time (CAT)* metric is defined. CAT is defined as the amount of computation required to advance a cluster one unit of simulated time, again in the absence of rollback. Unlike PAT, CAT is determined assuming an unloaded processor, so it is independent of the external workload assigned to the processor. In a heterogeneous computing environment, CAT for a single cluster will differ from one processor to another according to the processor's computation speed.

More precisely, we define:

1. $CAT_{c,i}$ is the estimated amount of computation time required by cluster c to advance one unit of simulation time on host i, measured in seconds. In the current implementation, this value is computed for a "standard" host processor by an estimate of the number of *committed* events processed over the last sample interval (recall load balancing decisions are made periodically) times the average amount of computation time required per event, divided by the net advance in simulated time achieved by the cluster over the sample period. An empirically derived scaling factor is used to convert this number between host architectures.

2. $TWFrac_i$ is defined as the fraction of the total CPU cycles that the Time Warp computation was allocated over the last scheduling interval. At present, this value is computed by dividing the amount of CPU time allocated to the Time Warp program over the last interval by the wall-clock time that elapsed over that time interval.

3. PAT_i is defined as CAT_i / $TWFrac_i$ where CAT_i is defined as the sum of all CAT values of clusters mapped, or hypothesized to be mapped, to processor i.

If cluster c is moved from processor i to processor j, then PAT_i is reduced by the amount $CAT_{c,i}$ / $TWFrac_i$ and PAT_j is increased by $CAT_{c,j}$ / $TWFrac_j$. The new PAT values reflect the expected wall-clock time for each processor to advance one unit of simulation time after the move is made.

In addition to balancing the workload, a second goal of the load balancing policy is to minimize the number of cluster moves required to achieve an acceptable load balance. This is accomplished by prioritizing clusters moves so that clusters with large CAT values are given precedence over cluster with smaller CAT values. Thus, the algorithm will attempt to move one cluster with large computation requirements rather than several clusters with small computation requirements, assuming the move results in a better load distribution.

In addition, load migration is only performed if the maximum difference in PAT values between any pair of processors exceeds a user defined tolerance. This avoids performing migrations when the benefit that can be realized by the migration is modest.

The load balancing algorithm attempts to minimize the maximum of $(PAT_i - PAT_j)$ over all i and j. The algorithm is shown in Figure 1. Processors added to the usable processor set are assigned a PAT value of zero, making them prime candidates for accepting new clusters. Conversely, processors removed from the usable set are assigned a PAT value of infinity. The algorithm repeatedly attempts to move cluster(s) from the processor containing the largest PAT value. Clusters on that processor are scanned in order of decreasing CAT value, in order to try to move large computation load clusters first to try to minimize the number of required migrations, as mentioned earlier. For each cluster, processors are scanned from low PAT values to high in order to locate a destination for the off-loaded workload. If moving the cluster will result in a reduction in the maximum difference between PAT values, the move is accepted, and the procedure is repeated. If subsequent moves fail to reduce the maximum difference in PAT values, the algorithm terminates and resumes when the next scheduling interval begins.

4 Implementation

An initial implementation of the background load management scheme has been developed. This implementation currently executes on networks of Silicon Graphics uniprocessor workstations. Extensions to multiprocessors and heterogeneous machines are under development. The Time Warp software executing on each processor was derived from a shared-memory multiprocessor-based implementation, and PVM is used for interprocessor communications, so it is anticipated that extension to multiprocessors and heterogeneous environments will be straightforward.

The same period ($T_{schedule}$) is used for both processor allocation and load redistribution decisions, and is a user defined parameter. The current implementation performs load management synchronously, i.e., a barrier is used to stop all processes. Once this happens, processor allocation and load redistribution decisions are made, migrations are performed, and then the simulation is allowed to resume execution.

A well known problem in migrating Time Warp LPs (and thus clusters of LPs) is the fact that each contains a large amount of state. Specifically, each LP maintains a history of state vectors, in case rollback is later required. While phases could be used to address this problem (see [15]), this necessitates implementation of a mechanism for rollbacks to span processor boundaries because a rollback may extend beyond the beginning point of a recently created phase. A simpler, though perhaps more radical, solution is to rollback the entire simulation computation to GVT if any load redistribution is to be performed. This makes migration of Time Warp LPs no more expensive than migrating non-optimistic computations because there is no need to migrate the history information. This approach also has the side effect of "cleaning up" overly optimistic computation. In this sense, this approach is not unlike the mechanism described in [12] which found such periodic, global rollbacks to be beneficial. Our initial experiments indicate that this mechanism provides a reasonably simple and efficient mechanism for reducing migration overhead.

To enable the shared memory Time Warp kernel to execute in a distributed environment and support dynamic load management several significant changes were made. First, an extra process is created on each workstation to manage all external communications. This process is called the *reflector thread*. Its tasks include the sending and receiving of all GVT, application defined and dynamic load management messages. Application messages or events are marshaled to the Time Warp kernel(s) that are executing on that local workstation via shared memory.

Another change was the piggy-backing of Mattern's GVT algorithm [13] on top of the existing shared memory GVT algorithm [7]. In this arrangement, Mattern's algorithm forces the shared memory algorithm to be executed on each workstation to determine its local virtual time. This information in-conjunction with a lower bound on all transit messages between consistent cuts is used to approximate GVT.

The last significant change was adding support for LP clustering and moving those clusters among the different workstations. To support clustering, a separate calendar queue [2] is used to store the pending set of events for each cluster of LPs. Before processing an event, the Time Warp kernel selects the cluster with the smallest time stamped event. Then that smallest time stamped event is dequeue from it's calendar queue and processed. The process of moving a cluster is accomplished by halting all Time Warp kernels from processing events and forcing all LPs in the system to roll back to GVT. The forced rollback is accomplished by placing a dummy event that has GVT as its time stamp in the message queue of every LP in the system. Once all rollback processing is complete, the moving of clusters between workstations is allowed to commence. Once cluster movement is accomplished the LP routing tables are updated to reflect the changes in LP and cluster locations.

The dynamic load manager (DLM) is implemented as a separate stand alone program that currently executes on its own machine. It was designed this way to provide a clean separation between the load management policy and the mechanism needed to support it. Moreover, this design simplifies the implementation by not having to integrate this functionality into the existing Time Warp kernel and has the capacity to work with any Time Warp system that uses PVM for external communications.

Upon receiving an update message from each workstation, the DLM analyzes the load statistics according to the previous mentioned algorithm. If any moves are necessary, the DLM broadcasts the *halt* message to all the workstations. Upon receiving the "halt" message, each workstation rolls back all LPs to GVT. When the *master* Time Warp workstation determines that all *client* Time Warp workstations have completed the force rollback, it sends a *halt complete* message to the DLM. After receiving the *halt complete* message, the DLM issues *move* messages to the appropriate workstations, which they process. When each move is complete the destination workstation sends a *move acknowledge* message to the DLM. After all *move acknowledge* message are received, the DLM broadcasts the *resume execution* message to all the workstations and event processing commences.

5 Experiments

Experiments were performed to evaluate the effectiveness of the load distribution system in (1) redistributing workload in the presence of external computations on a fixed set of host machines, and (2) being able to effectively redistribute the workload as the usable processor set changes. Controlled experiments were performed with artificial external application processes manually introduced before or during the execution of the Time Warp program.

The Time Warp application used in these experiments is a simulation of a personal communication services (PCS) network [4]. A PCS network [5] provides wireless

communication services for nomadic users. The service area of a PCS network is populated with a set of geographically distributed transmitters/receivers called *radio ports*. A set of radio channels are assigned to each radio port, and the users in the *coverage area* (or *cell* for the radio port) can send and receive phone calls by using these radio channels. When a user moves from one cell to another during a phone call a *hand-off* is said to occur. In this case the PCS network attempts to allocate a radio channel in the new cell to allow the phone call connection to continue. If all channels in the new cell are busy, then the phone call is forced to terminate. It is important to engineer the system so that the likelihood of force termination is very low (e.g., less than 1%). For a detailed explanation of the PCS model, we refer the reader to [4].

The PCS simulation is configured with 2048 Cells giving the simulation a total of 2048 LPs. These 2048 LPs are grouped into 64 clusters of 32 LPs each, and mapped to the processors such that the amount of remote communications is minimized. The completion time for a phone call was exponentially distributed with a mean of 3.0. The number of channels per cell is fixed at 10 and the number of portables per cell is fixed at 25. Each experiment processes between 47 and 67 million committed events.

The hardware platform includes 9 Silicon Graphics Indy Workstation interconnected through Ethernet. Here, one workstation executes the DLM process and the other eight execute the simulation. Each workstation has a single 200 MHZ, MIPS R4400 processor with 64 MB of RAM. In each experiment, we use the *best* static mapping of clusters to PEs that minimize the amount of remote communications. Each of the 8 simulation processors is initially assigned 8 clusters of LPs. The DLM update interval is set to approximately 50 seconds.

5.1 Time-Varying External Workloads

The first set of experiments evaluates the load management algorithm's ability to redistribute the Time Warp computation in the presence of a time-varying external workload. In these experiments, five external processes are initially added each to four of the eight simulation processors. The external workload then gradually increases and decreases over the period of 1 hour. This type of workload is one that a Time Warp simulation might encounter if it was part of federation of simulations sharing a common computing resource. For these experiments, thresholding is turned off and the set of usable processors remains constant for the life of the simulation.

Figure 3 shows how Time Warp with DLM performs over time in the presence of a time-varying external workload. The average load for the even and odd numbered processors is shown in Figure 3(a). The time-varying external workload induced on the even numbered processors causes the load average range from 3.7 to almost 9.0. The odd numbered processors have only the Time Warp simulation executing on them, making the load average 1.0. It is observed that the event rate over time (Figure 3(b)) remains fairly stable, despite the increasing external load on the even numbered processors. This stable event rate is attributed to the DLM moving the appropriate clusters off the loaded processors and unto the unloaded processors, as shown for PE's 0 (loaded PE) and 1 (unloaded PE) in Figure 3(c). The other even and odd numbered processors have a similar number of clusters assigned to them over time. In addition to the stable event rate, we observe that the number of rolled back events per second of wall-clock time, shown in Figure 3(d), actually decreases despite the steady increase in the external workload. Again, we attribute this decline in rolled back

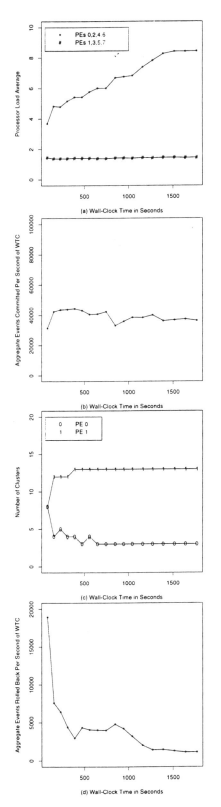

Figure 3: Trace of Time Warp performance using DLM in the presence of a time-varying external workload.

computation to the DLM making the right choice with respect to which clusters to move and where to move them.

Table 1 compares the execution time, efficiency (fraction of executed events that are eventually committed), and average rollback length with and without the load management scheme. Here it can be seen that DLM decreases the execution time of the simulation by 45%. We also observe higher efficiencies and shorter rollback distances for PCS simulation with DLM than without.

5.2 Changing the Usable Set of Processors

The next set of experiments are designed to evaluate the effectiveness of the algorithm in adapting to a different set of usable processors. Of particular interest is determining if the system can efficiently adapt to removing processors from the usable set due to excessive loads during the Time Warp execution and then re-allocates those processors when the external workload completes. In these experiments, a "spike" workload is added to four of the eight processor. This external workload is sufficient to cause the Time Warp simulation to vacate the four workstations. The *AllocThreshold* is set to 3.0 and *DeAllocThreshold* is set to 5.0 .

Figure 4 shows how Time Warp with DLM performs over time in the presence of the "spike" external workload. The average load for the even and odd numbered processors is shown in Figure 4a. The external workload induced on the even numbered processors causes the load average to rise from 1.0 to over 10.0. As in the previous experiment, the odd numbered processors have only the Time Warp simulation executing on them, making the load average 1.0. It is observed that the event rate over time (Figure 4b) is reduced from 80,000 to 20,000 as the external load is introduced. However, as the clusters assigned to even numbered processors are moved to the odd numbered processors (see Figure 4c), the event rate increases from 20,000 to 30,000. When the external load completes, the event rate rises back to 80,000 as the clusters are redistributed onto the even numbered processors. Underscoring the changes in the event rate over time, we observe that the number of events rolled back per second of wall-clock time, shown in Figure 4d, increase as the external workload is introduced, but then decrease as the clusters assigned to the overloaded (even numbered) processors are moved to the 4 unloaded (odd numbered) processors. As the external workload completes and the load average drops below the *AllocThreshold*, the events rolled back per second of wall-clock time re-increase. This increase is partially attributed to an increase in the rollback likelihood when moving from 4 to 8 processors given the same number of LPs. However, this explanation does not account for the events rolled back per second of wall-clock time being higher after the external load completes than before it was started. We believe the reason for this behavior is because the *best* static mapping which is initially used to assign clusters of LPs to processors is lost during cluster migrations. Because of this, more off-processor messages are being sent, which can lead to more rolled back computation. In the future, we plan to extend our dynamic load management algorithm to consider cluster-cluster affinity in making load distribution decisions.

Table 2 compares execution time, efficiency, and average rollback length for the PCS simulation with dynamic load management and thresholding when four of the eight processors incur a "spike" external workload. Here, it can be seen that DLM only slightly improves the execution time of the simulation. Similarly, we observe little difference in simulator efficiency and Time Warp with DLM actually yields a longer average rollback length. We be-

Simulation	Execution Time (sec)	Efficiency	Avg. RB Length
PCS With DLM	2096	82.42 %	41.30
PCS Without DLM	3835	53.10 %	53.33

Table 1: Performance comparison of PCS simulation with and without DLM for time-varying external workload.

Simulation	Execution Time (sec)	Efficiency	Avg. RB Length
PCS With DLM and Thresholding	1104	78.00 %	47.7
PCS Without DLM	1128	74.00 %	38.8

Table 2: Performance comparison of PCS simulation with and without DLM and thresholding in the presence of a "spike" external workload.

lieve the slower-than-expected execution time of the PCS simulation with DLM and thresholding is due to the extra overhead of considering inactive processors in the computation of GVT. By including inactive processors, the computation of GVT is slowed which increases the time between successive GVT approximations. A consequence of this is that the active processors exhaust their supply of memory before they exhaust the amount of optimism present in the application. Our Time Warp implementation manifests this phenomenon by exhibiting a large increase in what we term *aborted* events. An event is aborted if during processing it was unable to allocate a free event buffer during the scheduling of any subsequent events and must be reprocessed when a free event buffer becomes available. The number of aborted events can be viewed as a measure of how much time a processor is idle waiting for GVT to advance. In the presence of the "spike" external workload, we observe a sharp increase in *aborted* events as the the load was migrated off the 4 loaded processors, as shown in Figure 5, and continues as long as the external workload is executing. In our current uniprocessor implementation, every time the Time Warp process aborts an event it gives up the CPU to *reflector thread* allowing the immediate processing any GVT events in order to minimize the time between successive GVT approximations. Thus, each *aborted* event not only represents the wasted CPU time to process the event but also the overhead of a context switch to the *reflector thread* as well. By optimizing our GVT algorithm to not include inactive processors, we believe the execution time can be substantially improved.

6 Conclusions and Future Work

A load distribution system enabling background execution of Time Warp programs on distributed computing platforms is described. An implementation of this system on a network of workstations was realized and initial experiments indicate this approach shows promise in enabling efficient execution of Time Warp programs despite dynamically changing, externally induced workloads.

Work in refining and optimizing the performance of the load distribution system continues. Possible extensions include distribution of the load distribution software over multiple hosts, and asynchronous execution on the network of workstations. Another question is the determination of appropriate parameter settings to maximize performance as well refining the PAT metric to include cluster-cluster affinity (to minimize interprocessor traffic) and the processor's available memory resources.

Work is proceeding to extend the current implementa-

tion of the load distribution system to networks of heterogeneous workstations, including multiprocessor hosts. The distributed simulator already executes on Sun workstations, and multiprocessor Sparc machines, and an implementation on multiprocessor SGI machines is planned.

References

[1] J. Briner, Jr. Fast parallel simulation of digital systems. In *Advances in Parallel and Distributed Simulation.* volume 23, pages 71–77. SCS Simulation Series, January 1991.

[2] R. Brown. Calendar queues: A fast 0(1) priority queue implementation for the simulation event set problem. *Communications of the ACM*, 31(10):1220–1227, October 1988.

[3] C. Burdorf and J. Marti. Load Balancing Strategies for Time Warp on Multi-User Workstations. *The Computer Journal*, 36(2):168–176, 1993.

[4] C. Carothers, R. M. Fujimoto, and Y.-B. Lin. A case study in simulating pcs networks using time warp. In 9th *Workshop on Parallel and Distributed Simulation*, pages 87–94, June 1995.

[5] Cox, D. C. Personal Communications – A Viewpoint. *IEEE Communications Magazine*, 128(11), 1990.

[6] R. M. Fujimoto. Time Warp on a shared memory multiprocessor. *Transactions of the Society for Computer Simulation*, 6(3):211–239, July 1989.

[7] R. M. Fujimoto and M. Hybinette. Computing global virtual time on shared-memory multiprocessors. Technical report, College of Computing, Georgia Institute of Technology, August 1994.

[8] D. W. Glazer and C. Tropper. On process migration and load balancing in Time Warp. *IEEE Transactions on Parallel and Distributed Systems*, 3(4):318–327, March 1993.

[9] A. Goldberg. Virtual time synchronization of replicated processes. In 6th *Workshop on Parallel and Distributed Simulation*, volume 24, pages 107–116. SCS Simulation Series, Jan. 1992.

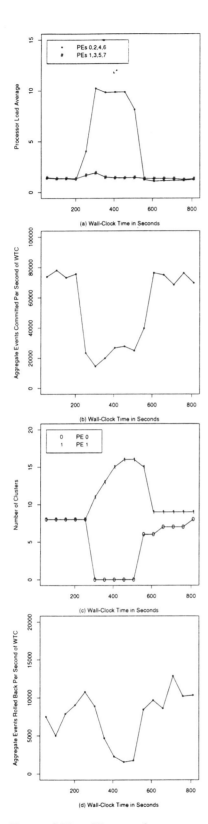

(a) Wall-Clock Time in Seconds

(b) Wall-Clock Time in Seconds

(c) Wall-Clock Time in Seconds

(d) Wall-Clock Time in Seconds

Figure 4: Trace of Time Warp performance using DLM with thresholding in the presence of a "spike" external workload.

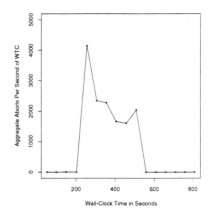

Wall-Clock Time in Seconds

Figure 5: Trace of aborted events in the presence of a "spike" external workload.

[10] D. R. Jefferson. Virtual time. *ACM Transactions on Programming Languages and Systems*, 7(3):404–425, July 1985.

[11] M. Litzkow and M. Livny. Experience with the condor distributed batch system. In *IEEE Workshop on Experimental Distributed Systems*, October 1990.

[12] V. K. Madisetti, D. A. Hardaker, and R. M. Fujimoto. The mimdix operating system for parallel simulation and supercomputing. *Journal of Parallel and Distributed Computing*, 18(4):473–483, August 1993.

[13] F. Mattern. Efficient distributed snapshots and global virtual time algorithms for non-fifo systems. *Journal of Parallel and Distributed Computing*, 18(4):423–434, August 1993.

[14] M. Presley, M. Ebling, F. Wieland, and D. R. Jefferson. Benchmarking the Time Warp Operating System with a computer network simulation. In *Proceedings of the SCS Multiconference on Distributed Simulation*, volume 21, pages 8–13. SCS Simulation Series, March 1989.

[15] P. L. Reiher and D. Jefferson. Dynamic load management in the Time Warp Operating System. *Transactions of the Society for Computer Simulation*, 7(2):91–120, June 1990.

[16] R. SchlagenHaft, M. Ruhwandl, C. Sporrer, and H. Bauer. Dynamic Load Balancing of a Multi-Cluster Simulation on a Network of Workstations. In 9th *Workshop on Parallel and Distributed Simulation*, volume 24, pages 175–180. IEEE, July 1995.

[17] F. Wieland, L. Hawley, A. Feinberg, M. DiLorento, L. Blume, P. Reiher, B. Beckman, P. Hontalas, S. Bellenot, and D. R. Jefferson. Distributed combat simulation and Time Warp: The model and its performance. In *Proceedings of the SCS Multiconference on Distributed Simulation*, volume 21, pages 14–20. SCS Simulation Series, March 1989.

The Dynamic Load Balancing of Clustered Time Warp for Logic Simulation

Hervé Avril *and *Carl Tropper*
School of Computer Science
McGill University, Montréal, Canada H3A 2A7
Email : herve@cs.mcgill.ca, carl@magic.cs.mcgill.ca

Abstract

We present, in this paper, a dynamic load balancing algorithm developed for Clustered Time Warp, a hybrid approach which makes use of Time Warp between clusters of LPs and a sequential mechanism within the clusters. The load balancing algorithm focuses on distributing the load of the simulation evenly among the processors and then tries to reduce inter-processor communications. We make use of a triggering technique based on the throughput of the simulation system. The algorithm was implemented and its performance was measured using two of the largest benchmark digital circuits of the ISCAS'89 series. In order to measure the effects of the algorithm on workload distribution, inter-processor communication and rollbacks, we defined three distinct metrics.

Results show that by dynamically balancing the load, the throughput was improved by 40 to 100% when compared to Time Warp. Throughput is the number of *non rolled-back* message events per unit time.

When the algorithm tried to reduce inter-processor communication, rollbacks were substantially reduced. Nevertheless, no substantial improvement was observed on the overall simulation time, suggesting that load distribution is the most important factor to be taken into consideration in speeding up the simulation of digital circuits.

1 Introduction

Logic simulation poses a severe challenge to the PDES community due to the fine granularity of the computation, the very large number of basic elements, and the low level of circuit activity. Two different classes of algorithms are commonly employed to solve the synchronization problem of parallel simulation: the conservative approach introduced by Chandy, Misra [5], and Bryant [3], and the optimistic approach pioneered by Jefferson [9]. Conservative algorithms must either prevent or detect and break deadlocks. As for optimistic algorithms, processes must roll back to cancel

---

*also with the Hutchison Avenue Software Corporation, Montréal, Canada

wrong computations. Furthermore, memory management [6] and instability [11] are two fundamental problems of the Time Warp paradigm.

In an attempt to accommodate the low level of circuit activity, a hybrid approach, Clustered Time Warp (CTW) [1], was developed. CTW makes use of Time Warp between clusters of LPs and uses a sequential algorithm within the clusters. In CTW, several clusters can reside on the same processor, but a single cluster cannot be split among different processors. Three checkpointing algorithms were developed and represent a different memory vs. execution time trade-off.

Empirical results [13], have shown that a very strong locality exists in digital circuits, suggesting that historical information can be used to improve the mapping of the simulated model onto processors. In this spirit, we feel that the use of a dynamic load balancing technique can substantially improve the performance of logic simulations. Furthermore, the fact that CTW groups LPs into clusters makes the load balancing mechanism easier to implement since instead of having to deal with individual LPs, only clusters are considered.

Our dynamic load balancing algorithm attempts to evenly distribute the load among the processors. We believe the most important factor in load balancing of parallel VLSI simulations is keeping the processors as busy as possible, even at the expense of increased inter-processor communications and rollbacks. We provide evidence to support this contention later in the paper.

The remainder of the paper proceeds as follow. Section 2 discusses related results, while section 3 describes our algorithm in detail. Section 4 describes our experiments, and the concluding section follows.

2 Related results

In [12], Nicol and Reynolds present a statistical approach to dynamically partition a circuit and to map it to a set of processors. In their approach, a work graph is created to describe the precedence relations between the nodes. Edges in the work graph are weighted depending on the communication delays between the nodes and their overlap. If over a clock cycle, the time region of the activity of two nodes overlap, parallelism can be achieved by mapping these two nodes on two different processors. Given the work graph, the authors partition the nodes into clusters by using a min-cut clustering algorithm based on Losen's approach [10]. The complexity of their algorithm is $O(E.(N-K).log_2(N-K))$ where N is the number of nodes in the work graph, E is the number of edges and K is the number of partitions. Their empirical results are positive. Nevertheless, the tests were done on a single 64-gate circuit and the authors assumed networks having no directed cycles. Because of the small size of the model, the lack of other tests, and the restrictions put on the connectivity graph of the circuit, it is extremely difficult to extrapolate the results to large sequential circuits.

Reiher and Jefferson introduce in [14] a new metric called the *effective utilization* which is "the proportion of work that is effective". The authors define effective work as the "work that will not be rolled back". Based on this metric, their load balancing algorithm moves logical processes from processors which are doing a lot of effective work to other processors which are doing little effective work. The performance results presented in the paper were obtained from running two typical benchmark simulations. One was a battlefield simulation, from which they obtained an improvement of 25% of the total simulation time by using their load balancing algorithm. The other model was a simulation of two-dimensional frictionless pucks moving and colliding on a table. Since the number of pucks used was quite high relatively to the number of processors, the simulation was naturally balanced and very little improvement was observed.

Burdorf and Marti [4] present a dynamic load balancing algorithm which executes on their Lisp-based Time Warp system running on a network of workstations. Their approach was motivated by the fact that users may load the workstations while a simulation was taking place, hence the need to move objects around to give the users a higher priority on computing resources. They chose the simulation time (Local Virtual Time) as a metric based on the assumption that rollbacks are extremely costly since they undo work which must be redone afterwards. Therefore, the main purpose of their algorithm is to reduce the variance between the objects' simulation times. By moving on the same processor objects which are far ahead in time and objects that are far behind, the authors believe that objects will synchronize with each others and less rollbacks will occur, hence speeding up the simulation. In their performance results, they find a five to ten times performance improvement over a simulation which does not use a dynamic load balancing strategy.

Glazer [7] [8] presents a dynamic load balancing strategy based on time slices. A time slice is a metric proportional to the ratio of the amount of computation time required by a process over its simulation advance. Once the time slice lengths are derived, processes are allocated to processors in an attempt to equalize the load on each processor. Three simulation models were constructed to represent different classes of simulation: a pipeline model, a hierarchical network model and a distributed network model. These models were ran on PARALLEX, a simulated multi-processor environment and the experimental results show that speedups ranging from 12% for the pipeline model up

to 49% for the distributed network model were observed. Rollbacks were also decreased during the load balancing process, up to 50%.

In [15], the authors present a method for dynamic load-balancing for a simulator whose logical processes are grouped into clusters and which runs on a network of workstations. They introduce the Virtual Time Progress (VTP) which reflects how fast a simulation process continues in virtual time. Load imbalance is translated into a variation between the VTPs of the processors. By moving one or more clusters during the execution of the simulation, the load is balanced by trying to get all of the VTPs to be approximately the same value. Their results are quite encouraging since on a circuit of around 10,000 gates, they obtain a simulation runtime about 20% smaller than the time needed for the same simulation without load balancing. Nevertheless, only two workstations were used for the simulation and only one circuit was tested, so it is difficult to draw any general conclusion from these performance results.

A number of the existing load balancing strategies we have described above base their decision to invoke the load balancing algorithm on the progress of virtual time in real time. In the domain of logic simulation, the computational granularity is fine and is approximately the same at all of the LPs. Furthermore, the level of circuit activity is low. Consequently, we have decided to emphasize the role of the load in our dynamic load balancing algorithm and we have not used any virtual time metric.

3 The Algorithm

In this section, we describe our dynamic load balancing algorithm in detail.

3.1 Workload distribution

Due to the fine computational granularity of logic simulation, we need a metric to measure the load that is easy to compute and does not create too much overhead. We define the *load of a cluster* to be the number of events which were processed by its constituent logical processes since the last load balance in the simulation. This includes the rolled back events as well as the stragglers. Each processor also computes its load, which is the sum of the loads of all the clusters hosted by that processor. The load balance is improved by moving clusters from overloaded to underloaded processors. Given the load information of the clusters and the processors, our algorithm iteratively chooses the most loaded and the least loaded processors (respectively P_{heavy} and P_{light}). The load difference $\delta Load$ of both processors is then calculated. $\delta Load/2$ represents the load that must be transferred from P_{heavy} to P_{light} so that both are likely to have the same workload once the transfer has been performed. Since we want to move as few clusters as possible, we will choose the cluster whose load is the closest to $\delta Load/2$, and assign it to P_{light}. The load of P_{heavy} and P_{light} are then updated and the same procedure is executed iteratively.

In the current implementation of Clustered Time Warp, a processor called the *pilot* is dedicated to collecting statistics and other types of information from the processors involved in the simulation. In order to simplify the implementation, we assigned the load balancing task to this processor. Processors periodically send their load information to the *pilot* by piggybacking it on the GVT token.

3.2 Inter-Processor communication

Delays created by inter-processor communications may play an important role in determining the execution time of a parallel simulation. Consequently, we extend our algorithm to incorporate the communication factor. Instead of directly picking up the most heavily loaded cluster C_{heavy} in processor P_{heavy}, we will consider all the clusters whose load is close to that of C_{heavy}. We say that two clusters have approximately the same load when their difference is less than a certain tolerance. In our implementation, a tolerance of 10% was used. Then for each of these clusters, we evaluate the change that would occur in inter-processor communications if it is moved to any of the lightly loaded processors. The move that minimizes communication is then chosen.

Moving a cluster C_k from processor P_i to processor P_j is likely to alter the amount of communication between these two processors. It may worsen the situation since other clusters in P_i which are communicating with C_k will have to send events over the network. On the other hand, the situation is also improved since clusters in P_j which were communicating with C_k will not need to send messages over the network anymore. Therefore the overall change in communication load is:

$$\delta IPC(C_k, P_i, P_j) = \sum_{\forall C_n \in P_j} ICC(C_k, C_n) - \sum_{\forall C_m \in P_i} ICC(C_k, C_m)$$

where $ICC(C_a, C_b)$ is the number of messages exchanged between clusters C_a and C_b. The number of messages is calculated over a certain period of time which must be long enough so that the measure can be considered as reliable. In the case of logic simulation, this period of time must include the processing of at least one input vector so that all parts of the circuit have a chance to be activated. Since the load balancing algorithm is not activated until the whole system becomes stable, several input vectors which would have already been processed.

3.3 Pseudocode

Input: Π is the set of all processors.

Output: C_{move} is the cluster to move.
P_{dest} is the destination processor of C_{move}.

```
begin
(1)   P_dest ← ∅
(2)   C_move ← ∅
(3)   select P_light ∈ Π | Load(P_light) = Min_{P_i∈Π}(Load(P_i))
(4)   select P_heavy ∈ Π | Load(P_heavy) = Max_{P_i∈Π}(Load(P_i))
(5)   δLoad ← Load(P_heavy) − Load(P_light)
(6)   let Γ_c ⊂ P_heavy | ∀C_i ∈ Γ_c ⇒ Load(Ci) < δLoad/2
(7)   select C_heavy ∈ Γ_c | Load(C_heavy) = Max_{C_i∈Γ_c}(Load(C_i))
(8)   for each C_i ∈ Γ_c | Load(C_i) ≈ Load(C_heavy)
(9)     for each P_j ∈ Π | Load(P_heavy) − Load(P_j) > 2.Load(C_i)
(10)      if δIPC(C_i, P_heavy, P_j) < δIPC(C_move, P_heavy, P_dest)
(11)         P_dest ← P_j
(12)         C_move ← C_i
          endif
        endfor
      endfor
end.
```

3.4 Triggering the load-balancing algorithm

Once a move has been decided upon, the loads of the two processors involved in the transfer are reevaluated. Then a decision process is started to find what cluster to move and where to move it. This procedure will converge to a better mapping of clusters, but not necessarily to the optimal one. This process can be repeated until the estimated workload distribution cannot be improved upon. Nevertheless, this procedure would not be very realistic for two main reasons. First, there is no control over the number of moves. Second, even though the processors' loads are reevaluated each time a move has been decided upon, the newly evaluated loads do not necessarily reflect the actual resulting load of the processors, mainly because the loads of the other processors have changed. Therefore, an iterative method was used. At each step of the load-balancing algorithm, only a certain number of clusters will be allowed to move. Then the system waits until the following two conditions are satisfied before triggering other moves:

- The cost of moving the clusters has been amortized by the resulting speed-up.

- New up-to-date measures are available.

Our load-balancing triggering mechanism is based on the *throughput* of the simulation system, defined as the number of *non rolled-back* message events per unit time. The throughput does not include anti-messages. In the domain of logic simulation, we feel that the throughput is a better measure of the overall speed of the simulation than the GVT advance. This is because the GVT advance is more dependant then the throughput on the nature of the model and its behavior. A large advance in GVT can be achieved by processing a small number of events.

Since the throughput fluctuates over time, a least-square approximation is used to obtain the general trend of throughputs, expressed by a first-degree equation. The system is considered stable when the coefficients obtained from the approximation do not vary by more then 5%. In our implementation, a throughput

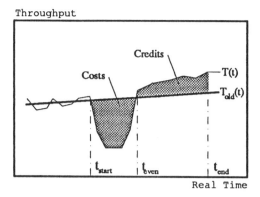

Figure 1: Throughput during a transfer

point is calculated every 3 seconds, the least-square approximation spans 6 points.

When a move is initiated at real time $t = t_{start}$, the throughput of the system tends to decrease since processors are spending their time transferring clusters. Then, once the operation is completed, the throughput increases, reaches its original value at $t = t_{even}$ which is equivalent to the break-even time (as defined in [15]). The throughput finally reaches a stable value larger than that previous to the transfer. Figure 1 depicts this situation.

Triggering the load balancing mechanism each time the stability is detected might actually decrease the overall speed of the simulation, even if the final throughput is higher than the previous one. As we have seen, moving clusters around has a cost in terms of throughput which is represented by the shaded area in the interval $[t_{start}, t_{even}]$ in figure 1. On the other hand, the transfer has the benefit of ultimately increasing the overall throughput of the system by an amount equal to the area above the interval $[t_{even}, t_{end}]$. If the next load balancing mechanism is triggered before the gain in throughput is equal to the cost of the transfer, the overall speed of the simulation might actually decrease. As a consequence, before launching the next load-balancing mechanism, we wait at least until the following condition is satisfied:

$$\int_{t_{start}}^{t_{end}} T(t) = \int_{t_{start}}^{t_{end}} T_{old}(t)$$

where $T_{old}(t)$ is the approximation of the throughput before the transfer and $T(t)$ is the actual throughput.

Observations have indicated that as the simulation progresses, the improvements become less significant and the period between each balancing adjustment grows longer. Once the cost of moving clusters does not improve the throughput so as to "pay back" the cost of the transfers, the load balancing mechanism is halted.

3.5 Metrics

To measure the effect of the load balancing mechanism, we define three metrics which depict different characteristics of the simulation system.

3.5.1 β: Workload distribution

To measure the quality of the load-balance, we define β as the ratio of the standard deviation of the processor loads to the maximum load observed. The lower that β is, the more equally the load is distributed.

$$\beta = \frac{1}{Load_{max}} \sqrt{\frac{\sum_{i=0}^{n-1} \left(Load(P_i) - \overline{Load}\right)^2}{n-1}}$$

where $n = |\Pi|$ and Π is the set of all processors,

$$Load_{max} = Max(Load(P_i)) \; \forall P_i \in \Pi \text{ and}$$

$$\overline{Load} = \frac{\sum_{i=0}^{n-1} Load(P_i)}{n}$$

3.5.2 γ: Inter-processor communication

We define γ as being the ratio of the number of events exchanged between processors (C_{ipc}) to the number of events exchanged between clusters (C_{total}). The lower that γ is, the lower is the inter-processor communication.

$$\gamma = C_{ipc}/C_{total}$$

3.5.3 ρ: Cancelled computation

ρ is defined as the ratio of the number of events rolled back ($E_{cancelled}$) to the total number of events processed ($E_{processed}$). The lower that ρ is, the less computation is cancelled.

$$\rho = E_{cancelled}/E_{processed}$$

The three metrics β, γ, and ρ are measured over the same period of time as the throughput and only their mean calculated over the six previous points is considered.

4 Implementation and Experiments

4.1 Implementation

In Clustered Time Warp, each gate of a digital circuit is modelled by a Logical Process. LPs are then grouped into clusters which are in turn mapped onto processors. Several clusters may reside on the same node, but a single cluster cannot be split among different processors.

Three checkpointing algorithms were developed for CTW:

- **CRCC** Clustered Rollback, Clustered Checkpoint.

- **LRCC** Local Rollback, Clustered Checkpoint.

- **LRLC** Local Rollback, Local Checkpoint.

Each of these techniques offers a different memory vs. execution time trade-off [1]. CRCC is the least expensive in terms of memory, and LRLC is the least expensive in terms of time. In our experiments, we make exclusive use of LRCC since it offers an intermediate choice for both of these characteristics.

Cluster sizes in the range of 50 to 200 gates were experimented with. Since little difference was observed between these sizes, we present the results for 100 gates. We used a string partitioning algorithm, because of its simplicity and especially because results have shown that it favors concurrency over cone partitioning [2].

The dynamic load balancing algorithm was implemented on top of Clustered Time Warp and run on a BBN Butterfly GP1000 multiprocessor [1]. The implementation of message passing in the simulation is *independent of the shared memory of the Butterfly*. Consequently our results will apply to distributed memory architectures.

Moving a cluster from one processor to another is a 2-phase operation. First, the sending processor encodes the data structure of the cluster into a message and then sends it to the receiving processor. While the transfer is taking place, events are still sent to the original processor which stores them in a forward list. Once the transfer is over, the second phase of the transfer starts. The receiving processor sends an acknowledgment to the sending one which then sends it the forward list and broadcasts to all the other processors the new location of the cluster. Even though routing tables are updated immediately, due to variable communication delays it is still possible for a processor to receive messages for a cluster that has been moved away. In this case, the message is simply forwarded to the correct processor.

4.2 Experiments

We conducted a series of experiments in order to determine how well our dynamic load-balancing algorithm performs when compared to Time-Warp. We also tried to measure the effects of load distribution, inter-processor communication and rollbacks on the overall performance of the simulation. The circuits used in our study are digital circuits selected from the IS-CAS'89 benchmarks. For the sake of the clarity, we only present the results obtained from simulations of two of the largest circuits (table 1) since they are both representative of the results which we obtained with other circuits and they have characteristics which result in two different behaviors.

First of all, we analyzed the effect of workload distribution without considering inter-processor communications and rollbacks. To this end, a series of simulations were ran on 20 processors, with pure Time Warp (TW), with Clustered Time Warp (CTW), and with CTW using our load balancing technique (BCTW).

		inputs	outputs	flip-flops	total
C1	s38417	28	106	1,636	23,949
C2	s38584	12	278	1,452	20,995

Table 1: Circuits C1 (s38417) and C2 (s38584)

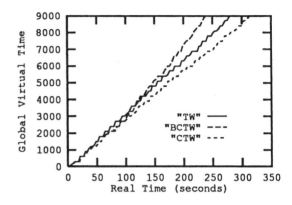

Figure 2: GVT Advance for C1

Each simulation consisted of the processing of about 500,000 events (cancelled events were not considered). Figures 2 and 3 show the progress of the Global Virtual Time versus the Real Time for C1 and C2 respectively, using TW, CTW and BCTW.

For both circuits, the figures clearly show that the total simulation time has been substantially decreased when load balancing was used. CTW is about 10% slower than pure TW for both circuits. This is due to the intrinsic properties of the LRCC algorithm used for CTW. LPs tend to roll back further in time when a straggler is detected since their checkpoint intervals tend to be larger than in Time Warp [1]. On the other hand, substantial memory savings are realized using

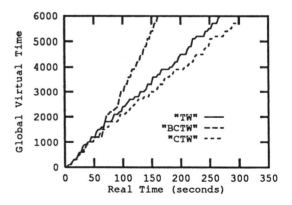

Figure 3: GVT Advance for C2

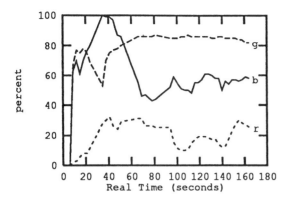

Figure 4: β, γ and ρ for C2

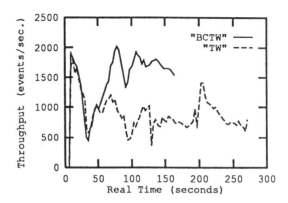

Figure 5: Throughput for C2

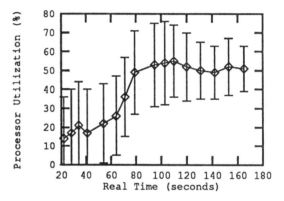

Figure 6: Mean and S.D. of the CPUs' activity for C2

LRCC.

When using Clustered Time Warp with our load balancing algorithm, we observe for C1 a decrease of about 15% of the simulation time compared to Time Warp and 25% compared to CTW without load balancing. For C2, the simulation was 40% shorter compared to TW. The reason why load balancing had a more pronounced effect on circuit C2 may be found in the locality of its activity. The same partitioning and the same mapping algorithm were used for both circuits. Nevertheless, the workload distribution of C2 at the beginning of the simulation was not as good as that of C1, which is caused by a stronger locality of the activity in C2. As a consequence, moving clusters out of the overloaded processors and assigning them to underloaded processors tends to speed up the whole simulation more effectively for C2.

Figure 4 shows the variation of the three metrics β (load imbalance), γ (inter-processor communication) and ρ (rollbacks) during the simulation run of C2 using the Clustered Time Warp engine along with the dynamic load balancing mechanism. The first transfer of clusters was triggered 21 seconds after the beginning of the simulation. For a period of about 10 seconds, overloaded processors are busy sending the states of the clusters and logical processes which have been assigned to underloaded processors. During this time, fewer messages are processed and generated, which is shown by the sudden decrease of gamma. As a direct consequence, underloaded processors have less to do, and since overloaded processors are still busy, the load imbalance gets worse, explaining the increase of β. Once clusters of LPs have been transferred, β starts to decrease to a value lower than that at the beginning of the simulation, indicating that the load balance is better. But this improvement has a cost both in inter-processor communications and rollbacks. We can observe that about 86% of the messages exchanged between clusters are sent over the communication network, instead of 77% previous to transfer. This increase was expected since loaded clusters have been more evenly distributed over the processors. Rollbacks also increase from about 10% before the transfer to about 20 to 30% after the transfer. Nevertheless,

despite the costs created by extra rollbacks and inter-processor communications, the overall throughput of the system increases. Even though the effect was less pronounced, we observed the same phenomenon for C1.

Figure 5 shows the impact of the load-balancing algorithm on the throughput of the system during the simulation of C2. We can notice that soon after the transfer of clusters are initiated, the throughput becomes smaller than that of Time Warp. Once the transfers are over, it becomes twice as large as that of Time Warp.

For each processor, we measured the activity, which is the percentage of time spent on computation during a fixed period of time. At different points in the simulation, we calculated the mean and the standard deviation of the processor activities. The results are given in figure 6 and they show that as the load balancing mechanism transfers clusters from overloaded to underloaded processors, the activity rises from 25% up to 60%, and the standard deviation decreases by about 40%. This proves that the computation load became more evenly distributed over the processors.

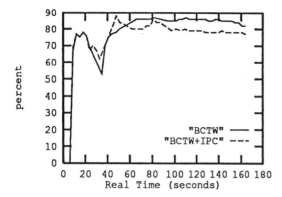

Figure 7: Effect on γ for C2 if IPC is minimized

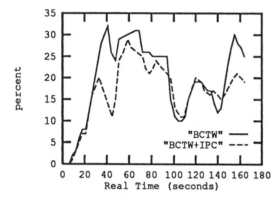

Figure 8: Effect on ρ for C2 if IPC is minimized

Similar results were obtained with C1, except for the fact that the throughput of the system did not increase as much as for C2. Instead of an increase of 100%, we observed an increase in the throughput of 40%. Note that C2 has a stronger locality of activity, which makes it easier for the load balancing algorithm to improve the overall throughput of the system.

If the load balancing mechanism tries to minimize inter-processor communications, we observe in figure 7 that γ could only be slightly decreased by about 5%. Figure 8 also shows that, on the average, the amount of computation cancelled by rollbacks has also been reduced, even though at some points, it is larger. Figure 9 shows for C2 the advance of the GVT versus real time for Clustered Time Warp with load balancing (BCTW), and Clustered Time Warp with load balancing considering inter-processor communication (BCTW+IPC). Even though we observe a small improvement of the total simulation time, it is obvious such an improvement is negligible when compared to that obtained with workload distribution alone.

Figure 10 shows the improvement of the throughput obtained by using the load balancing algorithm as

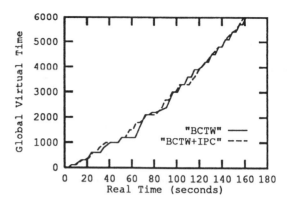

Figure 9: Effect on the GVT Advance for C2 if IPC is minimized

a function of the number of processors. We observe that as the number of processors increases, we obtain better performance. This is due to the fact that when a small number of processors are used, the load on the processors is much higher, thus leaving very little room to improve the load balancing. The improvement eventually levels off when the load is distributed among a large enough number of processors.

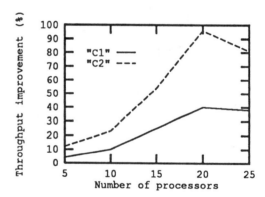

Figure 10: Improvement of the Throughput

5   Conclusion

We have described in this paper a dynamic load-balancing algorithm for Clustered Time Warp, a distributed logic simulator which makes use of Time Warp between clusters of LPs and a sequential algorithm within each cluster. The advantage of the clustering approach to load balancing is that instead of having to move individual LPs from one processor to another, clusters of LPs can be moved. We have also described a triggering technique based on the throughput of the simulation. Throughput is the number of *non rolled-back* message events per unit time.

We have shown that a substantial acceleration of the simulation speed can be obtained. Two circuits of more than 20,000 gates were tested and improvement of 40 and 100% were obtained for the throughput.

Finally, we have shown that the improvement that can be obtained by reducing rollbacks and interprocessor communications is limited and that *the focus should be on evenly distributing the workload over the processors so as to keep them as busy as possible.*

References

[1] Hervé Avril, Carl Tropper, "Clustered Time Warp and Logic Simulation", pp112-119, PADS'95

[2] J.V. Briner Jr., "Fast Parallel Simulation of Digital Systems", PADS'91, pp71-77

[3] R.E. Bryant, "Simulations of Packet Communication Architecture Computer Systems", T.R.-188, MIT, LCSi, 1977

[4] C. Burdorf, J. Marti, "Load Balancing Strategies for Time Warp on Multi-User Workstations", The Computer Journal, Vol.36, No.2, pp168-176, 1993

[5] K. Chandy, J. Misra, "Distributed Simulation: A Case Study in Design and Verification of Distributed Programs", IEEE Trans. Software Eng., S-5, pp440-453, Sept. 1979

[6] R.M. Fujimoto, "Parallel Discrete Event Simulation", CACM, Vol.33, No.10, pp31-53, 1990

[7] David M. Glazer, "Load Balancing Parallel Discrete Event Simulations", Ph.D. thesis, McGill University, 1993

[8] David M. Glazer, Carl Tropper, "A Dynamic Load Balancing Algorithm for Time Warp", pp318-327, Parallel and Distributed Systems, Vol.4, No.3, March 1993

[9] D.R. Jefferson, "Virtual Time", ACM Trans. Prog. Lang. Syst., Vol.7, No.3, pp404-425, July 1985

[10] S.L. Losen, "A Global Algorithm for the Multi-Partitioning of Graphs", M.Sc. thesis, University of Virginia, January 1985

[11] B. Lubachevsky, A. Schwartz, A. Weiss, "Rollback Sometimes Works... if Filtered", Proc.1989 Winter Simulation Conference, pp630-639, December 1989

[12] David M. Nicol, Paul F. Reynolds, Jr., "A Statistical Approach to Dynamic Partitioning", pp53-56, PADS'85

[13] B.L. Noble, R.D. Chamberlain, "Predicting the Future: Resource Requirements and Predictive Optimism", PADS'95, pp157-164

[14] Peter L. Reiher, David Jefferson, "Virtual Time Based Dynamic Load Management in the Time Warp Operating System", pp103-111, PADS'90

[15] R. Schlagenhaft, M. Ruhwandl, C. Sporrer, H. Bauer, "Dynamic Load Balancing of a Multi-Cluster Simulator on a Network of Workstations", pp175-180, PADS'95

Session 3

Applications I: ATM and Network Simulation

Session Chair
Samir R. Das, University of Texas at San Antonio, USA

Conservative Parallel Simulation of ATM Networks

John G. Cleary, Jya-Jang Tsai,
Department of Computer Science, University of Waikato, New Zealand.
email: {jcleary,jjtsai}@cs.waikato.ac.nz

Abstract

A new conservative algorithm for both parallel and sequential simulation of networks is described. The technique is motivated by the construction of a high performance simulator for ATM networks. It permits very fast execution of models of ATM systems, both sequentially and in parallel. A simple analysis of the performance of the system is made. Initial performance results from parallel and sequential implementations are presented and compared with comparable results from an optimistic TimeWarp based simulator. It is shown that the conservative simulator performs well when the "density" of messages in the simulated system is high, a condition which is likely to hold in many interesting ATM scenarios.

1 Introduction

ATM is a recent standard for broadband communications [3,7]. It is a rate independent system which uses fixed size (53 byte) *cells* for all transmission. The motivation of this work is the need to simulate large numbers of cells in ATM systems. Such simulations, which need to explicitly model the passage of cells through the fabric of switches and over the physical communications links, are particularly demanding for a number of reasons. There are indications that it is necessary to simulate in the order of 10^9 to 10^{12} cells in one run to measure some effects such as cell loss rates. Also the models of ATM at the individual cell level have very low compute grains. For example ATM-TN a detailed ATM model produced by the Telesim project [15] has average per simulation event granularities of 17 μseconds on a Sparc-2 55MHz CPU [11]. These granularities are close to the per event overheads that can be expected from sequential simulators. For example, the sequential simulator used to obtain the granularities has a measured per event overhead in the range of 11 to 18 microseconds (depending on the size of the event list).

The need for large numbers of high fidelity simulation events motivates the requirements for a high performance simulator. The low granularities imply that any simulator must be very efficient with per event overheads close to those of the best sequential simulators. Results reported later will show that expected simulation scenarios have significant available parallelism. Thus there is a strong motivation to construct parallel simulators to take advantage of this. The difficulty here is to keep the overheads low enough that the parallelism can be effectively used. To this end the conservative simulator is designed for a shared memory multiprocessor environment. This follows the lead of recent TimeWarp parallel simulators [8].

Any such simulation splits into two main parts: the models of the ATM switches, access points and links; and the models of the traffic generators. This paper is concerned mainly with the interior ATM objects and not so much with the traffic generators. There are two reasons for this: the ATM part is by far the most compute intensive; and it is more stereotyped and consistent than the generators.

ATM-TN is a generic cell-level ATM model [15]. The model deals with individual cells and passage through switches. As well it includes high-level models of TCP/IP, World-Wide-Web traffic, and self-similar traffic [1,2]. The current work is based around this model.

The proposed algorithm belongs to the class of conservative simulations. These, by definition, block until a process can ensure that it will not violate causality by processing the next event [10]. Nil messages, as proposed by Chandy and Misra [5,13], provide a method for communicating processes to exchange information regarding the lower bound on the time stamps of future messages. The effectiveness of nil messages depends greatly on the amount of lookahead available [9]. This is apparently application dependent [14,16]. In any case, the possible imposition of extra overhead by the use of nil messages has caused much criticism of the usefulness of such approaches.

Several mechanisms based on nil messages have been developed since it was first introduced. Chandy and Sherman [6] present an alternative. Instead of nil messages, a conditional message is sent to the receiving process only when the sender will otherwise become blocked. As long as there are (real) messages waiting in the receiver's input buffer, conditional events are not used. Also, Jha and Bagrodia [12] suggested a scheme combining the above approach and conventional nil messages. Cai and Turner [4] proposed a "carrier null message" approach. In this approach, an additional field is included to the nil message so that a process can identify a nil message initiated by itself. When such a message is detected, the blocking is ended. The effectiveness of this approach depends on how much earlier such a carrier can be detected compared to regular nil messages. Although performance speedup can be observed in certain cases with these approaches, the applicability of these to large complicated communication networks (eg ATM) remains unknown.

In the next section the simulation algorithm itself is described, together with both sequential and parallel implementations. Section 3 focuses on a key data structure and its optimisation. Section 4 considers the theoretical performance of the conservative simulator and compares this with event based simulators including TimeWarp. As well actual performance results from a toy problem on a distributed version of the conservative simulator are reported together with comparable results from a TimeWarp based simulator. Initial results from a full port of ATM-TN are also provided. The paper concludes with a summary.

2 Simulator

In the simulator all *processes* receive (0 or more) *input links* and generate (0 or more) *output links*. *Messages* are sent down links between processes. Each message has a *send* and *receive* time. The critical part of the proposed algorithm is that each time a process is executed it merges all its input lists and executes one *event* for each incoming message, this continues until one of the input links is empty where-upon the process *suspends*. Because the merge is done in time order the process suspends on the earliest empty link, the earliest time that a message can be received down that link is the process's *current time* (CT).

The generic simulation algorithm is:

```
while there are messages in system
    select next process to execute;
    while lowest time stamped
      incoming link has a message
      select lowest message;
      process message;
    end while;
    set current time of process to
      minimum time on any in-link;
    update last time on all outgoing
      links to minimum possible
      receive time of next message (will
      be ≥ current time + lookahead of
      link);
    suspend process;
end while;
```

This algorithm is different from many event driven simulators, in that, when a process is selected for execution it consumes all of its incoming messages before suspending. That is, scheduling is not done on an event by event basis. In the worst case no event will be executed when a process is selected, although the current time of the process may be advanced which will cause the time on the output links to also advance. Such an "empty" execution corresponds roughly to a nil message in a Chandy-Misra conservative simulator [5] and to the conditional messages used in [12]. Many algorithms are possible for selecting the next process to be executed. The aim is to minimise the cost of scheduling both by minimising the number of suspension/scheduling steps and by minimising the cost of suspension and scheduling.

It is assumed that the links are monotonic - that is messages are received in the order of their receive times which is the same order that they are sent (physically this can be interpreted as "messages cannot pass each other in the links"). Of concern is the *lookahead* of each link which is the minimum difference between the receive and send time of a message. This must be positive (it may be 0 in some cases), and in many interesting cases will be non-zero.

Consider a simulation model as a directed graph where the links are arcs and the processes are nodes. The arcs are labelled with the lookahead of the link. For any loop (sequence of nodes and arcs that arrives back where it starts) the *loop time* (LT) is the sum of the lookaheads along the loop. The *Minimum Lookahead Time* (MLT) for a link or process is the minimum LT of any loop which passes through the link or process. I will assume that no process (and by implication link) has a zero MLT. In particular all ATM models will be seen to have non-zero MLTs.

The algorithm above can be executed by randomly selecting a process, executing it, and then selecting the next process and so on. So long as this process is fair - that is every process is eventually selected for execution - then it is easily shown that the simulator will make progress (the GVT or minimum time of any unprocessed message in the system will increase). The problem is to minimise the overheads of suspension, that is, the aim is to maximise the number of events executed and minimise the number of suspensions.

2.1 Sequential Execution

The first (sequential) algorithm always schedules (one of) the processes with the smallest CT. In such a simulator the best that any process can do is to advance its simulation time by its MLT on each execution/suspension cycle[1]. If the MLT of the i'th process is given by MLT_i then a lower bound for the average number of suspensions per simulation time unit, C, will be:

$$C \geq \sum_i \frac{1}{MLT_i}$$

(2.1)

The process of scheduling on the basis of the CT is susceptible to many optimisations. Given that the processes can be scheduled at random, clearly scheduling on the basis of the CTs can be sloppy and still the algorithm will work. Note that selecting for execution on the basis of CT is different from using an event list (in particular, the times used for scheduling may correspond to no actual events in the system and the number of entries in the scheduling list is always equal to the number of processes in the system).

2.2 Static Schedules

Another possible algorithm is to have a loop in which each process is executed exactly once. This will clearly be sub optimal if the processes have differing MLTs - those with large MLTs will be executed too often. However, it seems that static schedules in which a process appears in inverse proportion to its MLT can approach close to the lower bound. The example systems in Figure 1 have close to optimum static schedules. In

Fig 1a the MLTs for the three processes are: A=1, B=2, C=3. From formula (2.1) the lower bound for the number of suspensions per unit of simulation time is C=1.83.. Using either of the static schedules below achieves C=2..:

    C B A A   C B A A ..

or

    C B A A B A   C B A A B A ..

For Fig 1b the MLTs are: A=1, B=3, C=3 and the optimum of C=1.67.. is actually attained by

    C B A A A   C B A A A ...

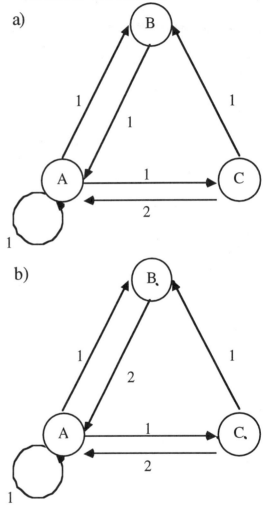

Figure 1. Example Process/Link Graphs.

Clearly the overheads of such static schedules can be made very small. It is not necessary to maintain an event list or any dynamic data structure. For small numbers of processes they could be directly compiled as an unrolled sequence of procedure calls.

---

[1]Consider the loop passing through the process that has the minimum LT. Assume that all the incoming links along the loop other than the one under consideration have minimum receive times that are infinite (or sufficiently far in the future that they do not contribute to the minimum). Then the minimum receive time on the incoming link will be equal to the sum of the lookaheads around the loop, that is, the MLT. It is this time that will limit the advance of the process when it is executed.

2.3 Parallel Execution

Consider a distributed system where the processes are each mapped to a processor. A static schedule can be followed locally on each processor. In the limit when each process is mapped to one processor the static schedule will be the repeated execution of the same process. In this case the process is effectively polling its input links.

For ATM systems this parallel case (with all processes mapped to their own processor) may be **more** efficient than the sequential one. The critical process, that is the one that on average runs the slowest may never suspend, as the other (lightly loaded) processes will run faster than the critical one and so the critical process will always have messages on all its input links. Thus the critical part of the computation will be essentially free from any suspension overheads, it will spend all its time executing in the user modelling code.

3 Link Data-structures

A key data-structure in any simulator based on these ideas is the one that holds the messages in the links. It should allow fast insertion and extraction of events and also be able to be shared between processes in a parallel system. The sharing is made easier by the fact that only two processes ever access the link - the sender and the receiver. The rest of this section consists of a series of refinements of an initial simple data structure. The refinements are designed to give greater efficiency and to provide effects such as bounding the time advance of the sending process. It is notable that the resulting data structure does not need any locking to work correctly, thus avoiding one important source of overheads.

3.1 Linked-list

Figure 2 gives a description and pseudo-code for a simple version of the link data structure. It uses single unidirectional pointers between the messages in the link together with two external pointers into the link: Top and Bottom.

This code works correctly even in the case where the sender and receiver are running in parallel. In this case Top is modified only by the sender and is read by the receiver. Bottom is used only by the receiver. To ensure correct parallel execution the order of assignments in send is important, in particular Top must be assigned after all the other fields have been set up. As well storing a pointer or a time-stamp must be an atomic operation.

3.2 Optimized

The first optimisation is to make the length of the list in the link constant. This achieves two things: it removes the overheads of allocating and deallocating links and it also allows the length of the list to be used as a flow control mechanism. For example, a process with no input links (a message generator) will have to suspend if its output links become full. Fixing the length allows the next fields to be initialised so that the list forms a circular loop and thus next need never be updated. There is one major change needed to the code for send to ensure that Top does not over-run Bottom (that is that too many messages are not inserted onto the link). This also means that the sender must be prepared to deal with the send function returning an indicator that the message cannot be sent - in this case the sender must suspend. The other code change is to initialise which now creates a fixed loop of links. This code works correctly in parallel.

The final optimisation is to put all the links adjacent to one another in a single block of memory. The main advantage of this is that it minimises cache misses when accessing the messages. The only code that needs to be changed is the initialise function (this is left as an exercise for the reader).

Two further refinements have been added to the implementation. First, links from an LP back to itself are treated specially - it is not necessary to delay on them when they are empty. Second, LPs forming a cycle of small LT can be clustered into a single LP. This optimisation has great impact on ATM-TN because a switch in ATM-TN is modeled by a number of LPs, which exchange control signals with small lookaheads forming low MLT loops.

4 Performance

4.1 Comparison With Event Driven Simulators

It is possible to make a simple comparison between the amount of computing expected in the type of conservative system outlined above and other event driven simulators such as TimeWarp. Let E be the maximum number of events possible in one (simulated) time unit, χ the cost of doing one suspension, ε the cost of executing one event and λ be a parameter that expresses the fraction of the maximum possible number of messages that are actually sent. Then the total cost of advancing one simulated time unit in the conservative scheme is given by the expression:

```
Top: pointer to next location to have a message stored;
Bottom: pointer to next message to be received;
structure link:
        time: receive time of message (or earliest time of next
                message if pointed at by Top);
        next: pointer to next message (undefined if
                pointed at by Top);
        data: user defined content of message (undefined if
                pointed at by Top);
end structure;
initialise: %Initialise link.
        t:= new link;
        t.time:=0;
        t.next := nil;
        Top:=t;
        Bottom:=t;
end initialise;
send(receive_time,next_time,msg): %Send a message.
next_time is the earliest possible receive time of the next message;
        Top.data:=msg;
        Top.time:= receive_time;
        t:= new link;
        t.time:= next_time;
        Top.next := t;
        Top:= t;
        send := true;
end send;
early_time(time): %Update earliest possible receive time:
        Top.time:= time;
%Receive a message - returns true if Bottom is left pointing at a valid message - in any
%case Bottom.time is left as the earliest time a message can arrive down the link;
receive:boolean;
        if Bottom = Top then
                receive:=false;
        else
                t:=Bottom;
                Bottom:=Bottom.next;
                deallocate t;
                receive:= boolean:(Bottom<>Top);
        end if;
```

Figure 2. Code for Link Datastructure.

$$t_c = \lambda \varepsilon E + \chi C$$

For an event driven system the cost is proportional only to the number of events:

$$t_o = \lambda \varepsilon E$$

Clearly as λ decreases the event driven system will eventually win out over the conservative as the costs of an event driven system are proportional to the number of events. The per event overheads of the conservative simulator will be inversely proportional to λ - an effect which is clearly seen in the empirical results below. This analysis is generous to real parallel event driven systems such as TimeWarp where the per event overheads will be higher than the conservative system because of the need to do state saving and rollback.

4.2 Empirical Results

The conservative simulator was implemented on a SPARC-1000 platform with 8 55MHZ Sparc processors. An initial series of experiments were conducted to collect performance measurements from the proposed mechanism in order to compare against a standard event list based sequential simulator, as well as a parallel simulator based on Time Warp. The benchmark used was a 4-dimensional hypercube communication network. Upon receiving a message, a node forwards the message, with an exponential delay with mean 1.2, to a neighbouring node. The selection of a destination node is random. The transit time on each link is set constant to 1.2 time units. As in ATM systems it is assumed that a message prevents another message being sent for one time unit. The experiments use various message populations, ranging from 1 to 1000. Thus the number of pending events per process will vary from 1/16 to 64.

The event granularity for the basic sequential simulation varied from 11 µsecs to 18 µsecs (for a large event list). It is difficult to separate the user code and the simulator overheads but the user code takes about 4 µsecs (mainly for random number generation). A spin-loop is also employed in some cases to investigate the impact of larger event grains.

The average execution time per event versus the message population is shown for a single processor in Fig. 4a. Following the theoretical predictions above, the execution time per event for the conservative simulator increases as the message popu lation decreases. The execution time for the sequential and TimeWarp simulators show an opposite trend increasing slightly as the message population increases - this is probably caused mainly by an increase in the size of the event list (the sequential simulator uses a splay tree and the TimeWarp simulator a calendar queue).

The other three subgraphs of Fig 4 show the overhead on 2, 4 and 8 processors. The performance of the conservative simulator improves smoothly in the parallel execution. Interestingly the TimeWarp simulator has difficulties at low message populations on the parallel runs. There has not been a chance to investigate this more closely but it may indicate the onset of some form of dynamic instability.

The results from the proposed mechanism are encouraging. Even at very low granularities the conservative mechanism shows speedup over a significant range of message populations. Preliminary estimates indicate that average message populations in ATM simulations will be well above the cross-over where the conservative system performs better than TimeWarp.

Fig. 5a shows the absolute speedup of the conservative simulator and Time Warp compared to the sequential simulator without any added granularity. Four different message populations, namely, 20, 100, 200 and 1000, were used. For large message populations, the proposed mechanism shows a speedup of 3.96 when running on 8 processors. Even with moderate message population, eg 100-200, the speedup observed on 8 processors is 2.82. Interestingly, the single processor

version of the distributed conservative algorithm shows a slow down of about 37% with a message population of 1000. In principle it should run at about the same speed as the sequential simulator (indeed a sequential implementation of the conservative simulator runs slightly faster than the standard sequential simulator for large message populations). The problem seems to lie in the implementation of the threads package on the Solaris operating system. This requires a system call to access memory which is local to a thread. The structure of the C++ system we are using forces such a call on every send. This seems to account for the slow down (investigations are proceeding on how to avoid this overhead).

In Fig. 5b-d, the same set of experiments are repeated, but with different event granularities. Each figure shows the speedup when a spin-loop of granularity around 10 µS, 100 µS, 1000 µS is added to each event (in addition to the original computation of the application). As seen from the figures, when the granularity increases, the speedup increases. Even with a small increase in event granularity (10µS), the speedup is elevated to about 4.91 on 8 processors when message population is high. Recent timing results on an implementation of the ATM-TN model indicates that the average event grains are about 17µS slightly higher than the grain used in Fig 5b. Time Warp also improves its performance drastically on larger event grains, leading to smaller differences between the two techniques. The results here are kind to TimeWarp in that the added compute grains include no provision for any additional state saving overhead.

4.3 ATM-TN Port

The full ATM-TN model has been ported to the a parallel version of the new simulator with encouraging preliminary results. A benchmark consisting of a perfect-port switch connecting three endnodes has been used to test the system. Two of the endnodes have an ethernet traffic source/sink modules running. The switch has three ports, at 45 Mbps each. The collected data in Table 1 shows that when the load on ethernet is low (λ=0.045), both the sequential simulator and the Time Warp simulator outperformed the conservative algorithm. However, as the ethernet load increased(λ=0.11 and 0.18), the execution time per event for the conservative simulator decreases greatly while the Time Warp based simulator and sequential simulators remain the same. The real strengh of the conservative simulator appears on executing on multiple processors. In one experiment, the speedup (vs. sequential simulator) on 4 processors is close to 2.5. Further experiments are planned for more realistic ATM networks. The following table shows the execution time per event (in µS) for the different simulators.

λ	con	con (4)	TW	TW (4)	Seq
0.045	32.02	15.69	40.16	27.22	25.37
0.110	26.53	12.01	42.40	27.06	25.52
0.180	24.74	11.80	42.15	26.97	28.07

Table 1. Execution Times for ATM-TN

5 Summary

A new shared memory based conservative simulator has been proposed and implemented. It is capable of exhibiting high efficiencies with overheads on a parallel implementation less than twice that for an optimised sequential simulator. It is well suited to its proposed domain of application in ATM models with its high efficiency overcoming problems of very low compute grain sizes. The parallel simulator compares well with a TimeWarp simulator over a wide range of parameters.

The conservative algorithm relies on a number of features of ATM networks to achieve good performance:

- all nodes (switches) have a small number of incoming and outgoing links;

- the capacity of links is limited by the (fixed) length of cells (this ensures a minimum lookahead for links);

- most "interesting" simulations will have links loaded close to capacity.

Clearly the algorithm is not universal as there will be problems where other mechanisms including TimeWarp will outperform it, however, it is well suited to ATM models and similar communications systems which are demanding and economically important.

Acknowledgments

This work was supported by grant 95-UOW-S14-4321 from the New Zealand Public Good Science Fund and by Science Applications International Corp. We would like to thank Xiao Zhonge and the rest of Telesim team for providing us with both sequential and parallel simulators and the ATM-TN model.

References

1. Arlitt, M., and Williamson, C.(1995a) *"A Synthetic Workload Model for Internet Mosaic Traffic,"* Proc. Summer Computer Simulation Conf., Ottawa, June.

2. Arlitt, M., Chen, Y., Gurski, R., and Williamson, C.(1995b) *"Traffic Modelling in the ATM-TN Telesim Project,"* Proc. Summer Computer Simulation Conf., Ottawa, June.

3. Boudec, J.L.(1992) *"The Asynchronous Transfer Mode: a Tutorial,"* Computer Networks and ISDN Systems, pp. 279-309.

4. Cai, W., and Turner, S.J.(1990) *"An Algorithm for Distributed Discrete Event Simulation,"* Proc. Distributed Simulation Conference, San Diego California, pp. 3-8, JanuaryJanuary.

5. Chandy, K.M., and Misra, J.(1979) *"Distributed Simulation: a case study in design and verification of distributed programs,"* IEEE Trans.Software Eng., **5**(5), pp. 440-452, September.

6. Chandy, K.M., and Sherman, R.(1989) *"The conditional event approach to distributed simulation,"* Proc. Distributed Simulation Conference, San Diego, California, pp. 93-99, March.

7. Comm. ACM.(1995) *"Special Edition on Issues and Challenges in ATM Networks,"* Comm. A.C.M., February.

8. Das, S., Fujimoto, R., Panesar, K., Allison, D., and Hybinette, M.(1994) *"A Time Warp System for Shared Memory Multiprocessors,"* Winter Simulation Conference, December.

9. Fujimoto, R.M.(1988) *"Performance measurements of distributed simulation strategies,"* Proc. Distributed Simulation Conference, San Diego, California, pp. 14-20, February.

10. Fujimoto, R.M.(1990) *"Parallel Discrete Event Simulation,"* Comm. A.C.M., **33**(10), pp. 30-53, October.

11. Jade Simulations International Corp.(1995) *"Deliverable for ATM-TN Performance Project,"* Science Applications Internationl Corp., August.

12. Jha, V., and Bagrodia, R.L.(1993) *"Transparent implementation of conservative algorithms in parallel simulation languages,"* Winter Simulation Conference, Los Angeles, pp. 677-686, December.

13. Misra, J.(1986) *"Distributed Discrete-Event Simulation,"* ACM Computing Surveys, **18**(1), pp. 39-65.

14. Nicol, D.M.(1988) *"Parallel discrete-event simulation of FCFS stochastic queuing networks,"* ACM SIGPLAN Notices, **23**(9), pp. 124-137.

15. Unger, B.W., Gomes, F., Zhonge, X., Gburzynski, P., Ono-Tesfaye, T., Ramaswamy, S., Williamson, C., and Covington, A.(1995) *"A High Fidelity ATM Traffic and Network Simulator,"* Winter Simulation Conference, Washington, D.C., December.

16. Wagner, D., and Lazowska, E.(1989) *"Parallel simulation of queuing networks: limitations and potentials,"* Proc. International Conf. on Measurement and Control, pp. 146-155.

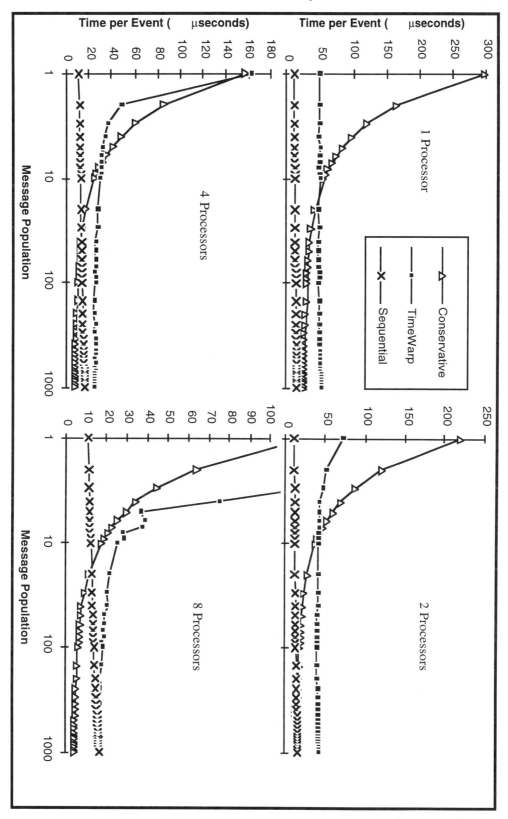

Figure 4. Event Overhead

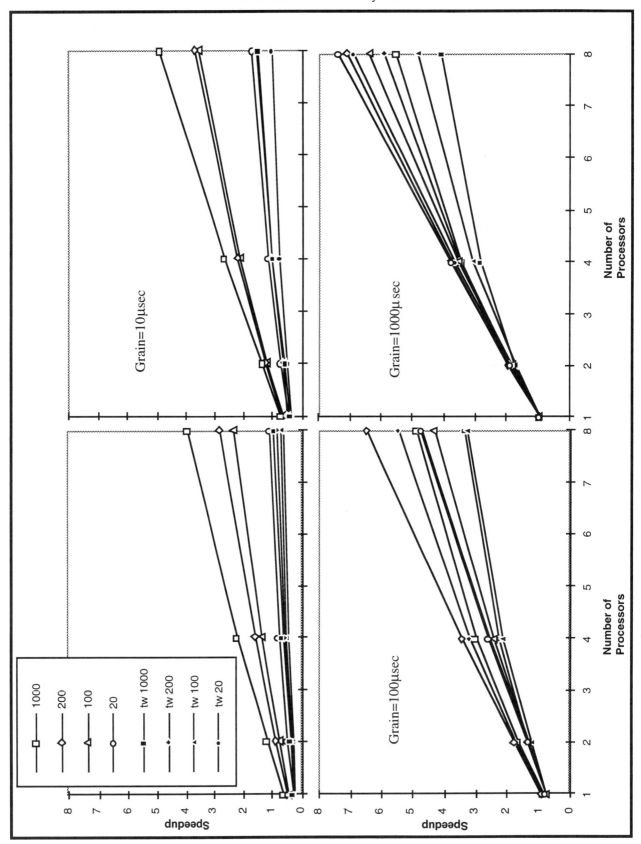

Figure 5.   Speedup

Massively Parallel Simulations of ATM Systems

Krishnan Kumaran*

Department of Physics
Rutgers University
Piscataway, NJ 08854

Boris Lubachevsky

Anwar Elwalid

Lucent Technologies
Bell Labs Innovations
600 Mountain Avenue
Murray Hill, NJ 07974

Abstract

We simulate models of ATM communication systems on a massively parallel SIMD computer. Fast simulations of ATM models are needed because the regimes of interest usually involve high volumes of traffic and low failure rates. Unexpected practical and theoretical difficulties, partly due to the massive parallelism and SIMD aspects, were encountered and we show how to cope with them. In a replica-parallel simulation of an ATM system, large variations in computed statistics are caused by small differences in the distribution of employed random number generators. A comparison of these distributions using a secondary statistical measure served to disambiguate the results. It was also found that time-parallel simulations of ATM systems with Markov sources can be efficiently performed using parallel prefix methods only when the sources have a small number of states, while more complex sources require end-state matching for efficient simulation. We discovered that, with the proper choice of initial state distributions and partial regeneration points, the time and memory requirements can be much improved. Our simulations were carried out on the MasPar MP-1216 system with 16,384 processors, which was compared against an SGI workstation. We achieved about $60\% - 70\%$ efficiency (speed-up of ≈ 35 compared to the ideal of ≈ 51).

---

*Work done while author was with AT&T Bell Labs, Murray Hill, NJ.

1 Introduction

A new communication technology, ATM systems, delivers high volume traffic with very low failure rates. Simulating an ATM model involves collecting statistics about rare "fault" events over long time periods with an enormous number of "normal" events. A single data point may require a week of serial processing on a fast workstation. Speeding up such simulations is an important task [1][3][6]. We present models of ATM and efficient techniques to simulating them on a massively parallel SIMD computer. During this research we encountered unexpected practical and theoretical difficulties, partly due to the massive-parallelism and SIMD aspects, and partly due to the fact that events of interest are rare.

Statistics of interest in our first model are obtained by an averaging which is performed over many short runs. This task easily lends itself to massively parallel processing via the obvious replication technique. The statistics produced in these simulations, however, deviated quite substantially from those found using other methods. The relative difference was not noticeable for the non-interesting cases of frequent "fault" events but was becoming intolerably large for the interesting cases of rare "fault" events. It was found out that the blame lies on the random number generator in our simulations. However, we could not substitute the generator without drastic performance degradation. We describe a method of comparing these results using secondary statistical measures and how we disambiguated and corrected the bias using the same generator.

Statistics of interest in our second model are obtained by an averaging which is performed over a single very long run. This task calls for a time-parallel technique [1] [5] [7]. We report three algorithms of simulating this model. The algorithms are presented in the order of increasing specialization to the simulated system properties. The last presented algorithm, most specialized, is based on end-state matching. It can be considered a continuous-time version of the discrete-time algorithm in [4]. The other two algorithms use parallel prefix method, amortization of overheads and partial regeneration. We considered these additional procedures because there are several important differences of our setup with that in [4]. Firstly, the bulk speed (along with the price) of our parallel computer is one-two order of magnitude lower than the speed of the computer employed in [4]. Secondly, there are substantial structural differences: our computer has a large number (16,384) of slow processors with relatively small memory and an SIMD mode of operation, while the simulation in [4] is arranged on a relatively modest number (32) of fast large-memory processors with an MIMD mode of operations. Thus, our task had stringent requirements for load-balancing and synchronization among processors; those were not the major issues in [4]. We discovered that an important feature that determines how easy or difficult would be to render the model time-parallel is the number of states of the simulated system.

We ran our parallel codes on a MasPar computer with the combined processor speed about 51 times higher than the speed of a SGI processor on which we ran their serial counterparts. The execution on a MasPar was 30-40 times faster than on an SGI which corresponded to $60\% - 70\%$ efficiency.

2 Replica-parallel simulation

The model and its simulation. The system (Fig. 1) consists of n independent traffic sources, each subjected to a leaky-bucket regulation mechanism (see details in [2]). A worst case (highest error rate for a given parameter set) scenario is pinpointed in [2] with each source having a traffic rate that is changing with time in a periodic fashion. The period begins with the source exhibiting a fixed rate during an *on* interval of length T_{on} followed by the no-traffic *off* interval of length T_{off}. Quantities T_{on}, T_{off} and the rate are common for all n sources and the only difference between the sources is the *phase*, i.e., the time when the period begins. The sum of rates of all the sources at each time instant is the rate of the *aggregate* source. Fig. 2 depicts examples of the aggregate source profile for different n. The incoming traffic is accumulated in the buffer from where it is "drained" by a single channel at a rate at most c, the channel capacity. The buffer has capacity $\bar{B}$, and incoming traffic that sees the buffer full is lost. The fraction of time when traffic loss occurs averaged over all possible phase configurations of the n sources is *loss probability*. In the averaging, the phase of source 1 is assumed 0 and the remaining $n - 1$ phases are distributed uniformly in the cube $[0, T]^{n-1}$ where $T = T_{on} + T_{off}$. Estimating the loss probability as the function of other parameters is the goal of the simulation.

To further simplify the model, we assume an infinite buffer and then determine the fraction of time when the buffer occupancy exceeds $\bar{B}$. This method has an advantage that the same set of sample paths can be used for different values of $\bar{B}$. A disadvantage is that the computed value is not exactly equal to the statistics sought. However, the approximation appears quite accurate and can be shown to yield the upper bound of the loss probability [2].

A serial simulation of this model consists of:

(a) sampling phases of $n - 1$ sources,

(b) constructing the sample aggregate rate source profile,

(c) computing the sample loss fraction.

The loss fraction sampled over many different runs is averaged to yield the sought loss probability. Note that if we begin the system trajectory with some system state (specifically, with some buffer occupancy level), we have to wait for the system to repeat a state twice with delay T between the state scans before being sure that the

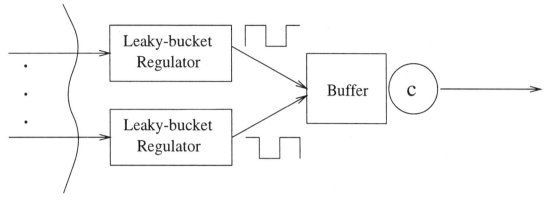

Figure 1: Regulated traffic into an ATM node.

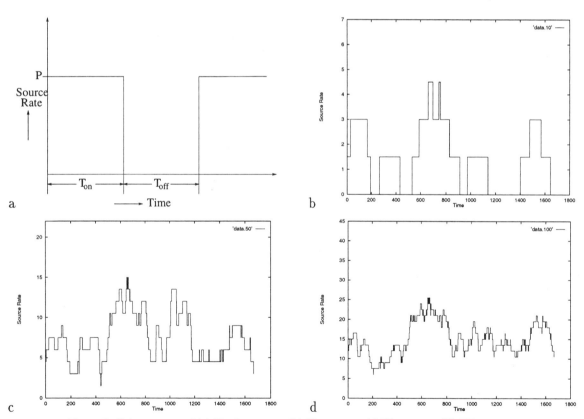

Figure 2: Rate process of (a) Single source, (b) 10 sources, (c) 50 sources, (d) 100 sources.

system has entered the periodic regime. Only after this repetition is detected we can make statistical measurements. It can be shown that if we begin with the zero buffer at time 0, then at the latest, by time T the system reaches such repeatable-with-delay-T state. Thus, statistics measured on the finite interval $[T, 2T]$ correctly represent the same statistics for the infinite trajectory. The algorithm easily lends itself to the replica-parallel execution by assigning different samples to different processing elements (PEs) of a parallel computer. Processing different samples happens to be uniform enough so that our SIMD machine, MasPar in one step efficiently computes $2^{14} = 16,384$ sample loss fraction estimates (it has so many PEs). Upon completion of a step, the scan-add operation averages the sample loss fraction over all samples made in this step. The steps are repeated, each time increasing the number of processed samples by 16,384, until satisfactory statistical quality of the total average is achieved. The efficiency of the parallel execution was at $60\% - 70\%$. The small degradation, as compared with the 100% efficiency, reflected the variability of processing time needed to simulate different number of events for different samples.

Wrong answers. We believed the problem was solved until we noticed a discrepancy between the estimates obtained by simulation on MasPar and the values that follow from a theoretical model [2]. Most unpleasantly, the relative discrepancy increased when the loss probability decreased and it became a several-fold ratio for the practically interesting case of the loss probability of the order of 10^{-8}. In view of the difficulty we attempted to vary the algorithm (a)-(c) and see if this would result in different answers. Thus, we considered two methods of sampling in (a) and computing the aggregate source rate profile in (b). Both methods employ sorted sequence (for $m = n - 1$)

$$ 0 < y_1 < y_2 < ... < y_m < 1 \qquad (1) $$

of random i.i.d. samples drawn from the uniform (0,1) distribution. Sequence (1) is used to generate random phases $t_i^{on} = T y_{i-1}$, of $m = n - 1$

sources, $i = 2, ... n$, relative to the phase of source 1, t_1^{on}, which was set to 0. The t_i^{on} are sorted to facilitate computation of the aggregate source profile in step (b). Sequence (1) is known as the m-dimensional order statistics for the uniform (0,1) distribution. Vector y_i, $i = 1, ... m$, is distributed uniformly in the simplex (1) with density $m!$

We varied the method of sampling the order statistics (1). In the first method, OS1, we proceeded literally according to the definition, that is, we sampled m uniform on (0,1) i.i.d. x_i, $i = 1, ... m$, and then sorted them to yield y_i, $i = 1, ... m$, as in (1).

In the second method, OS2, we sampled x_i, $i = 1, ... m$, as above, but instead of sorting them, we computed:

$$ y_m = (x_1)^{\frac{1}{m}}, \quad y_{m-1} = y_m(x_2)^{\frac{1}{m-1}}, ... $$
$$ y_i = y_{i+1}(x_{m-i+1})^{\frac{1}{i}}, ..., \quad y_1 = y_2 x_m \qquad (2) $$

Transformation (2) maps cube $(0,1)^m$ in the x_i-space onto simplex (1) in the y_i-space. The map is 1-to-1 with Jacobian equal to $\frac{1}{m!}$ identically for all vectors x_i, $i = 1, ... m$, in $(0,1)^m$. Because the random vector x_i, $i = 1, ... m$, is distributed uniformly in $(0,1)^m$ with density 1, the random vector y_i, $i = 1, ... m$, is distributed uniformly in simplex (1) with density $m!$, i.e., it is statistically identical to the vector of order statistics computed by method OS1.

Computational times of methods OS1 and OS2 were roughly equal: the extra expense in OS2 of floating-point operations in (2) balanced the extra expense of sorting x_i in OS1. Note that while the distribution of the order statistics (1) is well known (it is an instance of the Dirichlet distribution), we were not able to find in the literature our alternative method (2) of sampling this distribution, that avoids sorting. This alternative method happened to become a key element of resolving our difficulty. Table 1 presents the (estimates of the) loss probability obtained under the two methods. The relative difference between the answers increases with the decrease of the error rate. Because the equivalence of the methods is proven under assumption that the random

n	140	150	160	170	180	190
OS1, $P_l =$	5.777×10^{-8}	2.510×10^{-7}	8.942×10^{-7}	3.412×10^{-6}	1.236×10^{-5}	4.445×10^{-5}
OS2, $P_l =$	1.892×10^{-8}	5.563×10^{-8}	3.589×10^{-7}	1.779×10^{-6}	8.324×10^{-6}	3.519×10^{-5}

Table 1: Loss probability estimate P_l for different number of sources n, when using OS1 and OS2.

samples x_i are drawn independently from the uniform $(0,1)$ distribution, the discrepancy points to a fault in the random number generator. In both methods the x_i were generated by the same random number generator. This generator is specifically designed for SIMD computers and has been selected by the vendor of our MasPar computer for its computational efficiency. We did not have an option of replacing it by a custom-adjusted generator without drastically slowing down the computations.

Comparison. Thus, we decided to compare the two methods using a secondary measure, the distribution of the number n_{on} of sources that are *on* at a given instant, say at time T, excluding the non-random by convention source 1. This distribution can be easily computed: n_{on} is distributed on the segment $0 \le n_{on} < n$ binomially with probability weights

$$P_{n_{on}} = \frac{(n-1)!}{n_{on}!\,(n-1-n_{on})!}\,\left(\frac{T_{on}}{T}\right)^{n_{on}}\,\left(\frac{T_{off}}{T}\right)^{n-1-n_{on}} \tag{3}$$

The comparison was in favor of OS2 which generated the distribution virtually no different from that in (3), while the distribution generated by OS1 was noticeably different. A good agreement of the estimate of the loss probability obtained by simulation using method OS2 and the one that followed from the theoretical model in [2] also testified in favor of OS2. Thus, we concluded that we could trust method OS2, although the fact that transformation (2) makes the random number generator more accurate awaits a theoretical explanation.

3 Time-parallel simulation

The model and its serial simulation. As in the previous section, we consider an ATM system with n statistically independent *on-off* sources

multiplexed through a single buffered trunk of capacity c. Unlike the model in the previous section, the sources are Markovian. The time is continuous, and a source remains in an *on* or *off* state for a random, exponentially distributed time duration with mean α or β, respectively. As before, in all *on* states the traffic rate of an individual source is fixed. Without loss of generality, we assume this rate to be equal 1 for all sources. The aggregate source which has the traffic rate equal to the sum of the traffic rates of n sources corresponds to a Markov chain (birth-death process) with $n+1$ states. It follows that the sojourn time at state i, $i = 0, 1...n$, is random, exponentially distributed and that the cumulative traffic rate at state i is i. The rate of escaping state i (inverse of the mean sojourn time at state i) is $\frac{i}{\beta} + \frac{n-i}{\alpha}$. At the instant of escaping from state i, $1 \le i < n$, one of two states, $i-1$ or $i+1$, is chosen with rates in proportion $\frac{i}{\beta}:\frac{n-i}{\alpha}$. A transition from state 0 can be only to state 1 and from state n only to state $n-1$. The buffer occupancy level $B(t)$ within a sojourn period in state i is changing linearly with time, except for a lower bound of 0 (as before assuming the infinite buffer approximation):

$$B(t_0 + t) = max\{0,\ B(t_0) + (i-c)t\}, \tag{4}$$

When simulating this model serially, we successively generate random transitions and sojourn periods according to the rates and distributions specified and extend the trajectory one sojourn at a time.

Parallel prefix method. Consider time-parallel simulations of the described model on an SIMD parallel computer with M PEs. On each PE, we sample $n+1$ paths of the system starting from $n+1$ possible initial states $i = 0, 1...n$ for a fixed number of state transitions (sojourn periods) K. K is the same for all paths and all PEs. The sample paths are then sewn end-to-end, from PE1 to PE2 to PE3...to PEM, to form $n + 1$ long paths, one path for each starting state of PE1 (see Fig. 3). The sewing is done as follows. Each PEp maintains a map $label_p$:$\{0, 1, ...n\} \mapsto \{0, 1, ...n\}$, and a pointer $first(p)$ to another PE. Initially $label_p$ of PEp maps initial states of the Markov chain to the states that result from the K-step simulation by this PE and $first(p)$ is set to $p - 1$, i.e., it points to the previous PE ($first(1) = 0$ points to the "ground"). Then in synchrony with the other PEs, while $first(p) > 0$, each PEp executes:

$$label_p \leftarrow label_p \circ label_{first(p)}$$

$$first(p) \leftarrow first(first(p)).$$

Here $\circ$ is map composition: $(map1 \circ map2)(i) = map1(map2(i))$. It can be seen that $first(p) = 0$ at most after $\log_2 M$ steps for each PEp. (The obvious sequential method takes M steps to propagate the labels from PE1 to PEM.) Upon termination, we choose one path that starts with the accepted initial state, say, state 0, at the segment of PE1; this path ends in state $label_p(0)$ in PEp. Because only one path is finally used and because we are not concerned with the statistical dependence among the paths, two random numbers suffice to generate all the $n + 1$ state transitions and sojourn times at the kth transition, $k = 1, ...K$. Thus, we complete one round of calculations and produce a trajectory of KM state transitions. We can repeat these rounds, in each next round taking the initial state of PE1 to be the final state of PEM at the previous round and thus extending the generated system trajectory by KM transitions.

After we complete a KM-transition round, buffer occupancy profile is generated. An obvious sequential method takes M iterations, with PEp at iteration p computing the buffer occupancy for the pth segment of the trajectory. PEp idles until the the buffer occupancy at the beginning of the PE's segment is known which occurs only at the end of iteration $p - 1$. The parallel prefix method [5], instead, treats (4) as a linear recurrence and all PEs do useful work from the beginning even without knowing in advance the occupancy level

of the buffer. Specifically, (4) is rewritten as

$$\begin{pmatrix} B_{k+1} \\ 0 \end{pmatrix} = \begin{pmatrix} a_{k+1} & 0 \\ -\infty & 0 \end{pmatrix} \begin{pmatrix} B_k \\ 0 \end{pmatrix} \qquad (5)$$

where B_k is the buffer occupancy at the end of the kth sojourn period, $k = 1, 2, ...MK$, $a_k = (i - c)t$ assuming that the buffer is at state i in sojourn period k and the length of the period is t and where addition $\oplus$ and multiplication $\otimes$ are defined in an unusual fashion: $a \oplus b = max(a, b)$, $a \otimes b = a + b$. (Recurrences (4) and (5) are linear with respect to those $\oplus$ and $\otimes$, not to the usual ones.) We rewrite (5) in a compact form as $\mathcal{B}_{k+1} = \mathcal{M}_k \mathcal{B}_k$ and obtain

$$\mathcal{B}_k = \left\{ \prod_{j=1}^{k} \mathcal{M}_j \right\} \mathcal{B}_0 \qquad (6)$$

PEp is responsible for evaluating (6) for $k = (p - 1)K + 1, ...pK$. PEp begins by evaluating, in synchrony with the other PEs, the segment $\mathcal{N}_p = \mathcal{M}_{(p-1)K+1}\mathcal{M}_{(p-1)K+2}...\mathcal{M}_{pK}$ of the product in (6) for k=pK. The $\mathcal{N}_p$ is available for evaluation by PEp without exchanging data with other PEs because the evaluation only involves data that have been generated by PEp, e.g., a_j only for $j = (p - 1)K + 1, ...pK$. The resulting $2{\times}2$ matrix $\mathcal{N}_p$ has the bottom row $(-\infty, 0)$. The top row, e.g., in $\mathcal{N}_1$, contains elements that in a usual notation have the form $a_1 + a_2 + ... + a_K$ and $max\{0, a_K, a_K + a_{K-1}, ..., a_K + a_{K-1} + ... + a_2\}$. PE$p$ computes the top row elements in K steps and then in synchrony with the other PEs, while $first(p) > 0$, executes:

$\mathcal{N}_p \leftarrow \mathcal{N}_{first(p)}\mathcal{N}_p, \qquad first(p) \leftarrow first(first(p))$

Upon termination each PEp has in the updated $\mathcal{N}_p$ the full matrix product in (6) computed for $k = pK$. Multiplication of this final $\mathcal{N}_p$ on known vector $\mathcal{B}_0$ (that contains buffer occupancy at the last transition simulated in the previous round or the initial buffer occupancy for round 1) yields the buffer occupancies at the end of segments hosted by the PEs. Additional $K - 1$ processing steps done independently by each PE produce the buffer occupancy at each transition and - given a finite buffer size $\bar{B}$ - the estimate loss

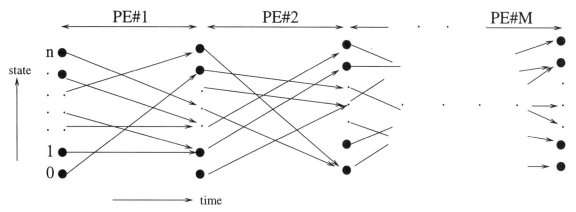

Figure 3: Sewing trajectories in the parallel prefix method.

probability on the PE's segment. Scan-add completes the task of estimating the loss probability on the entire KM-transition trajectory. Note that this method requires storage for the states and sojourn times of the path during each iteration, and also involves the overhead of generating $n+1$ paths while only one is finally used. It produces a single long simulation quite efficiently if n is small.

Regenerative simulation. In the method described above, PEs collect buffer occupancy statistics only *after* the entire trajectory of KM transitions is constructed and for that they must keep in their local memory the segments of the trajectory until the very end of the round; thus the length of simulation at one round is restricted by the available memory. We noticed that most of the time the buffer is, in fact, empty, owing to the fact that regimes of interest involve very low loss probabilities. This suggests an alternative way of simulating the described system on an SIMD computer with M PEs. As before, each PEp samples $n+1$ paths starting from $n+1$ possible initial states. However, unlike the previously described method, it is assumed that buffer is empty at the beginning of each path. The latter assumption allows the PE to collect the needed buffer occupancy statistics, together with the estimate of the traffic loss, "on the fly," as the trajectories are being generated, without waiting for the other PEs. Of course, each of the $n+1$ trajectories, generally, yields different values of the statistics. The im-

mediate advantage of the method is that the PE can forget the past states once the current state is generated and statistics for the current transition are updated. Hence, there is no upper bound on the length of the trajectory simulated by a PE in a round.

Specifically, the PE first generates (and collect the statistics on the way) the $n+1$ trajectories of K transitions each, same as in the method described above. Then, unlike the method described above, the PE extends those paths that have not happened to end at an empty buffer state after exactly K transitions. Usually there are only few of such paths as the buffer is empty almost all the time. Each extended path is being continued until the empty buffer state is reached. The resulted $n+1$ paths generated by a PE are not, generally, of the same length, and this is another distinction from the method described above. The sewing phase proceeds as above and produces the map *label*. Now each PEp knows which one, among the $n+1$ copies of statistics it has generated, has to be used. Namely, the one that corresponds to initial state $label_{p-1}(s)$ will be used by PEp if $p > 1$. As to PE1, it uses the one that corresponds to initial state s. Here either $s = 0$ if this is the first round or s is the last state from the previous round.

End state matching. When n is large, it is no longer economical for each PE to simulate $n+1$ distinct paths, of which only one is finally used. We thus use full-state matching. Each PEp generates only one trajectory, starting from a state $s(p)$ randomly chosen from a set S of initial states, until the initial state $s(p + 1)$ of $\text{PE}(p + 1)$ is reached. The algorithm is obvious. Advantageously, it avoids storing the entire trajectory by computing the statistics on line. Its possible disadvantage is disbalance of amount of work done by different PEs. If we require each PE to generate at least K transitions before attempting to match the state, then large enough K amortizes the disbalance.

To choose set S, we notice that the steady-state distribution of number n_{on} of sources that are *on*, given the probability $p_{on} = \frac{\alpha}{\alpha+\beta}$ of each separate source being in the *on* state is given by binomial distribution (3) where n is replaced with $n + 1$. We also have to substitute T_{on}/T with p_{on} and T_{off}/T with $1 - p_{on}$ in formula (3). Given a threshold P_* we choose $S = \{n_{on} : P_{n_{on}} \geq P_*\}$, where $P_{n_{on}}$ is computed by the appropriately updated formula (3). The starting states s are sampled in S with their relative weights as given by (3). We further require the buffer to be empty before matching the state. This further restricts the set of possible starting states, because the buffer cannot empty if the source rate exceeds the trunk capacity. Thus, only the states $s \leq c$ are considered. When the loss probabilities are low, the additional restriction is easily met, leading to considerable savings in time and memory.

A discrete-time version of end-matching simulation is discussed in detail by Fujimoto et al [4]. Set S consists of a single most likely state in [4] and the disbalance between different PEs executing different amount of work is not of a great importance as there are far fewer, but much faster processors than in our simulations. On account of the MIMD discipline in [4], the PEs that finish early do not need to wait for the slower ones. In our case, the disbalance was an important consideration. It was addressed by choosing a sufficiently large K so that each PE's segment must have at the least K transitions before testing the buffer-empty condition. Larger the K, more "amortized" is the disbalance. The fact, that the lengths of the paths were not restricted in this

method helped us to reduce the relative disbalance to a very low value.

4 Conclusion

We have presented our experiences with massively parallel simulations of ATM models, an endeavor in which few general methods are in existence. Certain problematic issues specific to massive parallelism and the SIMD nature of our simulations have been discussed, with possible recipes to overcome them. Further research aims at generalizing these techniques to wider classes of communication and queuing systems.

References

[1] K. M. Chandy and R. Sherman. Space-time and simulation. *Proceedings of the 1989 SCS Multiconference on Distributed Simulation*, pages 53–57, March 1989.

[2] Anwar Elwalid, Debasis Mitra, and Robert H. Wentworth. A new approach for allocating buffers and bandwidth to heterogenous, regulated traffic in an atm node. *IEEE Journal on Selected Areas in Communications*, 13(6):1115–1127, Aug. 1995.

[3] R. M. Fujimoto. Parallel discrete event simulation. *Commun. ACM*, 33(10):31–53, Oct. 1990.

[4] Richard M. Fujimoto, C. Anthony Cooper, and Ioanis Nikolaidis. Parallel simulation of statistical multiplexers. *32nd IEEE Conference on Decision and Control*, 1993.

[5] A. G. Greenberg, B. D. Lubachevsky, and I. Mitrani. Unboundedly parallel simulations via recurrence relations. In *Proceedings of the Conference on Measurement and Modeling of Computer Systems.*, pages 1–12, Boulder, Colorado, May 1990.

[6] F. J. Kaudel. A literature survey on distributed discrete event simulation. *Simuletter.*, 18(2):11–21, June 1987.

[7] Y.B Lin and E. A Lazowska. Time-division algorithm for parallel simulation. *ACM TOMACS*, 1(1):73–83, Jan. 1991.

Parallel Simulation of a High-Speed Wormhole Routing Network

Rajive Bagrodia, Yu-an Chen, Mario Gerla, Bruce Kwan,
Jay Martin, Prasasth Palnati, Simon Walton

Department of Computer Science
University of California, Los Angeles
Los Angeles, CA 90095

Abstract

A flexible simulator has been developed to simulate a two-level metropolitan area network which uses wormhole routing. To accurately model the nature of wormhole routing, the simulator performs discrete-byte rather than discrete-packet simulation. Despite the increased computational workload that this implies, it has been possible to create a simulator with acceptable performance by writing it in Maisie, a parallel discrete-event simulation language. The simulator provides an accurate model of an actual high-speed, source-routing, wormhole network (the Myrinet) and is the first such simulator.

The paper describes the simulator and reports on the performance of parallel implementations of the simulator on a 24-node IBM SP 2 multicomputer. The parallel implementations yielded reasonable speedups. For instance, on 12 nodes, the conservative algorithm yielded a speed-up of about 6 whereas an optimistic algorithm yielded a speed-up of about 4.

Keywords: *wormhole routing, parallel simulation.*

1 Introduction

The Supercomputer SuperNet (SSN) [10] is a hierarchical network prototype for supercomputer interconnection across campus and metropolitan areas. This project is ongoing at UCLA, the Jet Propulsion Laboratory, and The Aerospace Corporation. The goal of the project is to obtain a low-latency high-bandwidth interconnection network for supercomputers located in a metropolitan area (about 30 km apart). The hierarchical network architecture of SSN is illustrated in Fig. 1. At the lower level, we have a high-speed electronic mesh Local Area Network (electronic LAN) to which are connected the hosts of the network — workstations, supercomputers etc. At the higher level, we have an optical backbone network that interconnects several of these electronic LANs. The optical backbone network employs Wavelength Division Multiplexing (WDM) to exploit the vast bandwidth offered by the optical fiber medium.

The high-speed electronic network in SSN is a commercial product (Myrinet) that uses wormhole routing [13] to achieve very low latency. The optical backbone network also supports wormhole routing.

Other important features of the electronic LAN include source routing (the worm has the complete route to the destination when it leaves the source) and back-pressure flow control. These features are being extended to the optical backbone as well.

SSN is required to provide support for circuit-switched traffic, packet-switched traffic and multicasting (multipoint traffic). Of these, only support for packet-switched traffic is available in the electronic LAN testbed. A simulation testbed was developed for circuit-switched and multicast traffic using the Maisie simulation language. This paper describes the simulator and presents results of an experimental study on parallel execution of the model using both conservative and optimistic synchronization algorithms.

A number of previous studies have used parallel simulation to evaluate the interconnection of LANs and ATM LANs [7, 4, 12]. To the best of our knowledge this is the first parallel simulation of a wormhole-routing network. This is also among the few studies to directly compare the performance of conservative and optimistic algorithms for network simulation.

In section 2, we give a brief overview of SSN to describe the system that was modeled and simulated. In section 3, we discuss the simulation requirements and the various simulation platforms that were considered. We also compare the OPNET platform with sequential Maisie. In section 4, we present the topologies and parameters for the parallel simulations reported in this paper. Also, we discuss some of the model modifications required for the parallel implementation. In section 5, we report results from the parallel implementation of the SSN simulator for a 24-node shufflenet and an 8-node two-level SSN testbed topology. Finally, we present our conclusions in section 6.

2 Network architecture

The two-level hierarchical network architecture of SSN is shown in Figure 1. At the lower level, the host stations interface to the high speed electronic LAN. Using full-duplex point-to-point links, the cross-bar switches are interconnected to form the electronic LAN. At the higher level, we have an optical star network that interconnects several electronic LANs. The interface between the two different types of networks is provided by the Optical Channel Interface (OCI).

1087-4097/96 $5.00 © 1996 IEEE

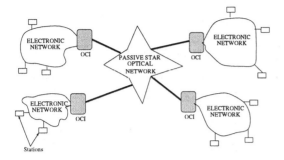

Figure 1: The two-level hierarchical network architecture of the Supercomputer SuperNet. One level is the High Speed Electronic LAN, the other is the Optical Star network.

2.1 High-speed electronic LAN

Host stations belonging to the electronic LAN are connected to the crossbar switches using full-duplex point-to-point links. An arbitrary topology can be created by interconnecting various crossbar switches as desired. The salient features of the high speed electronic LAN are:

- **Wormhole routing**: The traffic (both packet-switched and circuit-switched) in the network is sent from one host to another as worms (messages). Worms can vary in size from a few flits (flow-control digits) to several thousand flits[1]. Each switch forwards the worm without buffering it first. This means that the worm could stretch across several links and switches at the same time. The worm threads its way through the switches until it is switched to the destination host. If at any intermediate switch, the required output port for the worm is not available, the worm is blocked. Upon blocking, a worm holds the resources (buffers and network links) allocated to it so far. When the output port becomes available the worm continues its travel towards the destination. There is a possibility of deadlock in this scenario. A deadlock avoidance approach, namely, Up/Down routing (as in Autonet [15]) is used.

- **Source routing**: The header of each worm has a source route specified in it. The source route consists of the sequence of switch port numbers through which the worm must travel to get to its destination. It is assumed that the network has one or more Address Consultants which specify the source route upon request by the source station. Each switch is a complete crossbar without internal blocking. The worm is switched towards the output port specified in the header. Then, this port specification is removed from the header. Thus, at the next node, the head of the worm has the appropriate output port specification.

- **Backpressure flow control**: The input rate at a switch port may exceed the rate at which the worm leaves the switch if either the worm is blocked due to contention for an output port or when there is a

---

[1] In this paper, a flit is a byte. We will use flit and byte interchangeably.

speed mismatch in the rate at which the stations can receive worms. For this purpose, STOP and GO signals are used on the full-duplex links to exercise flow control on a link-by-link and byte-by-byte basis. Using this backpressure mechanism, the entire worm is frozen from the point of contention to the point of generation. This causes the resources allocated to the worm, namely, buffers and links at intermediate switches, to be 'frozen' as well.

For the SSN project, the high speed electronic LANs are the Myrinet LANs [3] that can sustain speeds of up to 640 Mbps over multiple twisted pair cables of length up to 82 ft (25 m). Myrinet LANs provide low-latency high-bandwidth interconnection using the features discussed earlier.

2.2 Optical network

The optical network has a broadcast-and-select star topology (using a passive star coupler) and provides (circuit-switched and packet-switched) service by configuring the network either as a single hop network or as a multihop network. The single hop network requires the use of tunable transmitters or receivers whereas the multihop network can be implemented by using only fixed tuned transmitters and receivers. For the SSN project, any virtual multihop topology can be configured on the optical star, since the OCI (described next) provides retunable transmitters and receivers.

2.3 Optical channel interface

The Optical Channel Interface (OCI) is custom-built hardware that acts as an interface between the electronic LAN and the optical network. The OCI–LAN interface supports the backpressure form of flow control used in the LAN. Each OCI is equipped with a fixed number of transmitters and receivers (tunable or fixed-tuned). The OCI also has processing power and thus, it can implement fairly sophisticated protocols, unlike the Myrinet switches, for which efficiency and cost considerations have precluded the use of more sophisticated algorithms. The OCI has a Myrinet interface at one end and an optical transmitter/receiver at the other. In between, there are some fairly large SRAM buffers and a processor.

3 The SSN simulator

3.1 Motivation

A primary goal of the SSN project is to provide support for packet-switching traffic, circuit-switching traffic with Quality of Service constraints and multicasting in the two-level network [10]. While the high-speed LAN is a commercial product, the wide area optical interconnection network is being constructed. There are a number of problems associated with using these testbeds for full evaluation of alternative protocols for determination of the most suitable one for each function. One problem is that the current hosts attached to the LAN (Sun SPARCstation 5) are incapable of stressing the network, since they cannot generate traffic at close to the LAN's capacity (640 Mb/s full duplex). Another problem is that we wish to evaluate network performance with a larger number of nodes than we currently possess, or would be practical to purchase. Thirdly, we wish to evaluate some protocol enhancements that do not currently exist: dividing single physical channels into several virtual channels for deadlock-free routing, an accelerated 'go' scheme for improved flow control, or an evaluation of deflection routing as a congestion control technique. If successful, these enhancements may be incorporated into future generations of the technology. Since analysis is impractical for many of our network models, we largely use simulation for our network performance evaluation.

Due to the previously listed reasons, a simulator for SSN was required to evaluate various protocols for the two-level network prototype. The simulator would measure such performance parameters as total network throughput and latency distribution. For circuit-switching schemes, the simulator would be used to evaluate circuit setup delays and delay jitter, as well as the impact of the circuit-switched service upon the packet-switched service.

An important consideration for the simulation model for SSN was the nature of flow control in wormhole-routing networks. Wormhole-routing networks have small buffers (called slack buffers) associated with each input port of the switch. In order not to overflow the buffers when a worm is blocked, backpressure flow control mechanism is employed. Unlike traditional packet-switched networks, the unit of flow control is the byte, not the packet. This is because the downstream end of a link can send a STOP command at any time, and the upstream end must halt transmission as soon as it receives this command. Thus, a worm can be stopped at any point within its length (the LAN uses byte-parallel transmission, so this means byte-granularity for stopping the worm). Further, the actual network inserts control symbols into the data traffic as and when desired. In order to accurately model this behavior, we use the byte as the discrete unit for simulation rather than the packet.

Since a flit-level simulation of SSN accurately reflects the actual testbed, any new protocols that are implemented and evaluated via simulation would be directly applicable to the testbed. For an example consider the provision of multicast service in the network. The protocol for this was first implemented and evaluated using the flit-level simulator, and then this code was used for providing the multicast service in the actual network. This ability to accurately test and implement protocols was also a contributing factor aiding in the choice of a flit-level simulator as opposed to a packet-level simulator.

3.2 Simulation platforms

Various platforms for the SSN simulator were investigated. An initial simulation was performed using the commercial simulation package OPNET [11] from Mil 3, Inc. The simulator implemented using the OPNET package offered flexibility and ease of statistics gathering using the OPNET tools. A major problem, however, is that OPNET is built around the *discrete-packet* paradigm. In order to implement a byte-level model, each byte of a worm in the LAN was modeled

as an OPNET packet. Different packet types were used to represent the head and tail bytes of a worm, and thus a byte-level model of a LAN packet was developed as a succession of OPNET packets. This sub-version of the OPNET paradigm led to long run times. Run times could be reduced by simulating at a coarser granularity but with reduced fidelity of the simulation model. Consequently inaccurate simulation results would be obtained.

The preceding reasons indicate that a general purpose discrete-event simulation language may be more suitable for a byte-level model. Further, to support the evaluation of networks with a large number of nodes, support for parallel execution of the models was desirable. For both these reasons, the Maisie language was considered as an alternative.

Maisie [2] is a C-based parallel language designed specifically for implementing simulators. Similar to other process-based simulation languages, Maisie allows the natural simulation of networks. A lightweight Maisie process, called an entity, maybe used to model network nodes such as hosts and routers. Maisie entities communicate via messages and the message passing between entities naturally models the network transmission between nodes. As most of the simulator code is ordinary C, the efficiency of the simulator is close to a simulator written in C, given the low overhead for context switching and message delivery in Maisie.

Another advantage of Maisie is its support for parallel execution [6]. Maisie is among the very few simulation languages that supports the execution of a discrete-event simulation model with multiple simulation algorithms, as well as providing constructs to reduce the simulation overheads with both conservative and optimistic parallel algorithms. A program written in Maisie is independent of any synchronization algorithm. When it is compiled, the analyst can indicate the specific simulation algorithm that is to be used to synchronize execution of the model: sequential, parallel conservative, or parallel optimistic. The compiler generates the appropriate code to interface the model with the corresponding run-time system: a splay-tree based implementation of the global event-list algorithm for the sequential implementation, a null-message or conditional event implementation of the parallel conservative synchronization algorithm[9], or a space-time implementation of the optimistic synchronization algorithm[1]. In this paper, we report on the performance of the Maisie model using conservative and optimistic synchronization algorithms.

3.3 Comparison of simulators

We now compare the performance of the OPNET and sequential Maisie simulators for the topology shown in Figure 2. In this topology there are two 8-port Myrinet switches (six of the ports are used) connected in a ring with four hosts attached to each switch. The Maisie simulator was developed after the OPNET simulator and is consequently more mature. The primary differences in the implementations are as follows:

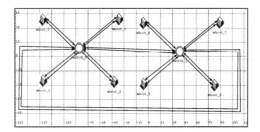

Figure 2: Topology of network simulated in Opnet.

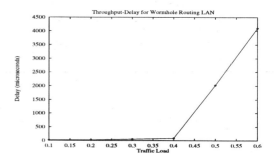

Figure 3: Simulation results

Load	OPNET (hours)	MAISIE (hours)	Factor (O/M)
0.2	19.46	2.89	6.73
0.4	16.02	1.70	9.42
0.8	9.88	0.933	10.59

Table 1: Simulation Run Times

- OPNET simulation transmits the control symbols using a separate control network. This explains the double connections between the different entities. The Maisie simulation handles the control symbols using the same network links as the data.

- OPNET simulation does not account for propagation delay. The Maisie simulation allows for any length propagation time and handles the buffers appropriately to support this feature.

- OPNET simulation assumes instant delivery of control symbols (no propagation delay or transmission delay). This simplifies buffer management at each switch. Maisie simulator allows for the transmission and propagation delays to model the real network.

- Traffic generation is done differently in each simulator. The OPNET simulator generates worms of a fixed size (128 bytes). These worms are grouped into a message that include multiple worms. The number of worms in each message follows a geometric distribution with a mean of 10. In contrast, the Maisie simulator generates messages whose length follows an geometric distribution with a mean of 1280 bytes. The messages are then broken down into smaller worms with length 128 bytes. The arrival process of messages for both simulators follow a Poisson distribution with varying rates depending on traffic load simulated.

Simulations were run for different network loads. Each simulation is run so that every host processes approximately 1200 message arrivals. The load is defined as the fraction of time each host spends transmitting a worm. The purpose of this set of simulations is to define the low latency region of operation for this particular wormhole routing LAN topology. From Figure 3, it is apparent that network users observe very low latency as long as the overall load for each host remains below 0.4.

Table 3.3 contains the execution times of the simulation runs. The 'Factor (O/M)' column lists the number of times longer the OPNET simulation run is compared with the Maisie simulation run. The OPNET simulator requires between 6 to 10 times more processing time. During higher loads, both simulators require less processing time because hosts begin dropping worms due to overloading of the network, causing the total number of events simulated in the system to

decrease. Indeed, as the load rises above 0.4, more blocking occurs and a larger fraction of the 1200 message arrivals are dropped at the host. Although the execution time decreases for both simulators, the relative performance of the Maisie simulator is better. One reason for this is that the OPNET simulator requires more processing overhead due to all the options it provides. The OPNET simulator allows for many features such as bit error rates, link failures, and other network attributes that are currently not of interest to our project. Unfortunately, these options must be handled even when they are not used. Consequently the OPNET simulator suffers.

3.4 Implementation of the simulator

A modular simulator of the SSN has been developed in Maisie to experiment with various routing, flow-control, and interconnection strategies in a hierarchical, reconfigurable network. The detailed model comprises more than 5000 lines of Maisie code. Innovative features of this simulator include a byte-level simulation model, potential for parallel execution and a scalable and modular design.

Each host of the high-speed LAN is modeled by a single Maisie entity. The OCIs are each modeled by a small number of entities — one for performing switching (routing) and one for each of the ports — to handle the greater functionality of the OCIs (See Fig. 4). When the simulator starts execution a single entity exists. This entity creates all the network entities and then suspends itself. Entity creation is thus performed only as part of the initialization phase leading to a static communication topology in the model.

The simulated worms are accurate down to the byte-level; the leading byte of the worm is stripped off as it passes through each switch, modeling the stripping off of source-route bytes in the actual network.

One important goal of the design was to achieve modularity. We wish to be able to substitute the modules representing network components, use such

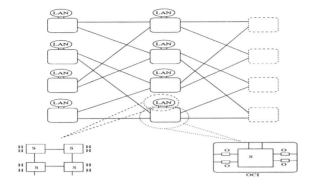

Figure 4: Components of Simulated Topologies: This figure shows an 8-node shufflenet. The first and third columns represent the same nodes. The 2×2 LAN with 8 hosts is attached to each node. The components of each node of the shufflenet are also shown. S denotes a switch entity, H denotes a host entity and O denotes the OCI entities (buffers plus transmission to optical backbone).

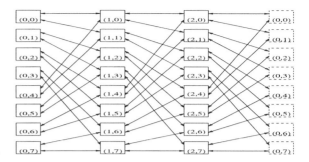

Figure 5: The 24-node bi-directional shufflenet topology. The first and last column represent the same nodes. Each node has the same composition as described in another figure.

components in future simulators, and so forth easily. This may be done in a straightforward manner under Maisie, because the code representing each such component is largely self-contained. The only interfaces to the rest of the code are those presented by the message-passing interface and the parameters supplied at initialization. With the freedom to use the full power of a C-like language we can make these interfaces only as complex as is necessary, unlike the situation with many simulation packages in which interfaces are predefined and must be complex in order to be flexible. Since each component is a true separate process (or several processes) there is no control flow into and out of it, making it simple to prepare such code in isolation.

The SSN simulator has a very flexible front-end that allows the specification of different topologies. The topology specifications are read in from a file and parsed to obtain necessary information.

4 Parallel implementation of simulator

We present the topologies and simulation parameters that were used for the parallel simulations reported in this paper. We also describe the model modifications that were required for the parallel implementation of the simulator.

4.1 Topologies for the parallel simulator

The SSN testbed is envisaged as an interconnection of high-speed LANs via an optical backbone on which a multihop topology is configured. We focus on the shufflenet multihop topology [8] for this paper. A shufflenet with $N = pk^p$ nodes has two parameters: p, which denotes the number of transmitter/receiver pairs of each node and k which denotes the number of columns in the shufflenet topology. We actually simulated a bi-directional version of the shufflenet topology, called the bi-directional shufflenet [14].

The first topology simulated was a 24-node bi-directional shufflenet (see Fig. 5) in which the nodes do not have a Myrinet LAN associated with them.

This experiment was designed to simulate large optical backbone topologies. The second topology simulated was an eight-node shufflenet with 2×2 Myrinet high-speed LAN with 8 nodes connected to each node. (See Fig. 4 for the 8-node shufflenet, the LAN attached to each node and a pictorial representation of the node.) We refer to this topology as the two-level model or the 8-cluster model. The main aims of this study were to evaluate the effect of different intra-LAN (intra-cluster) and inter-LAN (inter-cluster) traffic ratio on the running time of the simulation and the effect of different traffic loads on the improvement in parallel performance. These results would help in designing and running efficient future parallel simulations of large SSN testbed topologies.

4.2 Simulation model parameters

For the 24-node shufflenet, worm lengths were geometric with average worm length being 20 bytes. The transmission speed of the transmitters was assumed to be 1Gbps. The time to transmit one byte (i.e. 8 ns) was assumed to be our unit of time. The optical link lengths were assumed to be 0.1 mile (0.16 km) long. The resulting one-way propagation delay was a 100 time units (i.e. 80 ns). The slack buffers at the nodes were 5000 bytes.

For the two-level model evaluated in this paper, Up/Down deadlock-free routing was assumed. Two different traffic loads[2] were simulated — one in the low load region (0.05) and the second in the medium load region (0.15)[3]. The transmission speed of the transmitters (in the LAN as well as the optical backbone) was assumed to be 640Mbps. The time to transmit one byte (i.e. 12.5 ns) was assumed to be our unit of time. The optical link lengths were assumed to be 1 mile (1.6 km) long, while the Myrinet links were assumed to be 25m long[4]. The slack buffer in Myrinet was 80 bytes long. For the optical backbone, the slack buffer was 64K bytes.

---

[2]The load of the network is defined as the fraction of time that the host is busy transmitting worms.

[3]From earlier experiments, we know that shufflenet with Up/Down routing saturates at about 0.2 load.

[4]These parameters model the SSN testbed quite accurately.

4.3 Parallel model execution

This section presents our experiences with parallel execution of the model described in the previous section. The original Maisie model was developed without paying particular attention to concerns of eventual parallel model execution (in fact the initial model was developed by researchers who had little or no familiarity with parallel simulation). Parallel executions were explored only after the sequential model had been implemented and fully tested. In this section, we first describe the primary modifications that were made to the model to support parallel execution. The experience with parallelization of this model indicates that even though a language supports both sequential and parallel simulation algorithms, familiarity with parallel programming and parallel simulation is essential to exploit parallel execution of the model.

The experiments reported in this paper were executed on an IBM SP2 multicomputer. Each node of this architecture is a RS/6000 processor with 128MB of RAM and a peak rating of 225 Mflops. The interconnection bandwidth is 40Mbps and the hardware latency in the switch is 500 ns. Including software overheads, measurements show a minimum message latency of 30 μs.

4.4 Model modifications

In a sequential model, all entities are mapped to the same processor. In a parallel model, the target processor must be specified explicitly for each entity at the point at which the entity is created. Thus the first and perhaps most significant change to the sequential model is the assignment of entities among the processors. Depending on the application, the entity to processor assignment can have a major impact on parallel performance. The communication topology modeled in these experiments was a 24-node shufflenet, where each node has 4 neighbors. Each node of the topology is modeled by five different entities as described in the previous section, all of which were always mapped to a common processor. The model was partitioned by distributing the nodes uniformly among the processors where the nodes assigned to a processor were selected to minimize the number of edges that are cut. An alternative partitioning strategy was also used where nodes were assigned randomly to each processor. However, preliminary experiments indicated that the random partitioning always yielded worse performance, so this partitioning was not explored further.

The sequential model used dynamic data structures that were passed among entities (as message and entity parameters) using C pointer operations. The dynamic data structures were encapsulated into fixed sized array and record structures to support remote creation and communication.

The primary data structure used by the switch entity was a queue that is used to store the flits of an incoming worm; the flits are stored internally until the worm is forwarded on an out port. The maximum size of this data structure depends on the *load* on the network being simulated which is in turn determined by the frequency and the length of the worms transmitted in the simulation. The size of this data struc-

Load	0.1	0.2	0.3	0.4
Sequential_t(sec)	89	113	134	153

Table 2: Sequential execution time using global event list.

LOAD PROCESSORS	0.1	0.2	0.3	0.4
2	0.2	0.24	0.3	0.3
4	1.4	1.4	0.3	0.4
8	2.8	2.7	2.6	2.7
12	3.0	3.1	3.5	3.9

Table 3: Speedup for Optimistic Implementations

ture is particularly critical for optimistic executions as the checkpointing overheads are directly determined by the size of the entity state. Rather than assume a fixed size for all experiments, the model was modified to relate the size of the data structure directly to the *load* used in the specific experiment. Although this parameter may affect sequential performance (by increasing virtual memory references), the impact is much more significant for parallel model executions.

5 Results

This section presents the results of parallel execution of the simulator for the two topologies described earlier. The 24-node bi-directional shufflenet models an optical network; the two-level network architecture models an SSN testbed.

5.1 Optical network model

We first describe our experience with the parallel execution of the 24-node shufflenet model described earlier using both conservative and optimistic algorithms.

5.1.1 Optimistic implementation. A number of performance parameters must be tuned in optimistic runtime systems to reflect the characteristics of the specific application being simulated. The most important performance parameters include checkpointing frequency, the length of the time window used in optimistic executions of the model, the frequency of GVT computations, and the cancellation mechanism used during rollbacks (lazy or aggressive). Detailed experiments were executed to establish appropriate values for each of the preceding parameters. Empirically, we found a checkpointing frequency of 200 events and a time window of 200 simulation time units yielded the best execution time.

Lastly, because the primary task in the model was routing the incoming worm on an appropriate out port, and because the model used source routing where the entire route of the worm was computed at the source node (and thus unmodified by intermediate nodes), it was expected that lazy cancellation would considerably reduce the number of events that would need to be canceled following a rollback.

We now present the speedup obtained with the optimistic implementation. Table 2 presents the sequential execution time for the model as a function of the

Execution_t(sec)	84.6		
OVERHEAD	ave	max	min
Computation_t(%)	26.3	33.7	18.5
State-saving_t(%)	3.1	4.9	2.1
Blocking_t(%)	17.3	39.7	0
Msg_sending_t(%)	6.9	8.1	5.4
Msg_receiving_t(%)	16.1	33.3	11.9
Others (%)	21.3	25	19.9

Table 4: Overhead in the optimistic run-time for 12 nodes.

traffic load in the network. The traffic load was varied simply by changing the interarrival times of the worms at each node. As the load in the simulated network is increased, the absolute time for both the sequential and parallel implementations increases as expected due to the increase in the total number of events that must be simulated. The speedup obtained with the parallel implementation are presented in Table 3. For the 2-processor implementation, the parallel implementation actually runs slower due to the large overheads of message communication and optimistic synchronization. For similar reasons, a minimal speedup is observed for the 4-processor implementation. Although better speedups are observed for both 8 and 12 processor implementations, the overall level of improvement in performance is disappointing. Note that whereas for the 8-processor case, the speedups are approximately constant with the load factor, a gradual increase is observed for the 12-processor implementation. In general, we expect the speedup to improve as the load factor is increased as a higher load factor injects more traffic and hence increases the amount of computation in the model. We hypothesize that the increase is not visible in the case of 8 processors because the overall speedup is relatively small; an increase in the traffic may be coupled with an increase in the load imbalance in the model with the latter overshadowing the effects of an increase in the total amount of computation in the system. An analysis of the various components of the overhead corroborates this hypothesis as it indicated a wide range of blocking times among the different entities in the model — a clear indication of load imbalance. Finally, note that the each worm in the system injects significant computation in the model, as the transmission of each worm is simulated by a number of messages directly proportional to its length. However the computation can increase the load imbalance in the system as all of the computational load introduced by the worm is directed only towards the relatively small portions of the network traversed by the worm. Note that the load imbalance is likely to be exaggerated both for small load factors and for small number of processors.

The primary sources of overhead in the parallel execution are reported in Table 4. This is a measurement of the parallel execution with load equal to 0.4 on 12 processors. As the contribution to each of the categories differed across the various entities, the table indicates the average, maximum, and minimum contribution of each category to the total execution time. The major sources of overhead were the blocking time and message receive times, both of which also appeared to vary among the processors. The category called *others* includes miscellaneous runtime costs including the scheduler, context-switching time, experiment set-up and input/output times. Blocking time refers to the total time for which all entities on a given node were idle because no messages with timestamps in the time window were available. The receive time refers to the total time spent by entities on a processor in receiving incoming messages and inserting them in the appropriate queues. The variation in blocking times across the different processors indicates a severe imbalance in the distribution of computational load, which is partly responsible for the relatively low speedups that have been obtained. Experiments with different partitioning strategies are in progress to correct this imbalance.

5.1.2 Conservative implementation. We present the results of parallel model execution using conservative synchronization algorithms for the 24-node shuffle-net topology. The conservative algorithm used in this paper uses aggressive null message transmission. The implementation used to execute the programs reported in this paper has been described in [9]. Efficient conservative implementations of a model are typically easier to develop than optimistic ones. Other than the allocation of entities to processors which is needed for both conservative and optimistic algorithms, conservative implementations only require that the analyst express the lookahead [5] of each entity. As is well-known, a sufficient condition for progress is to ensure that every cycle in the communication graph has a non-zero lookahead. As the SSN simulator uses a static communication topology, the lookahead for the model could be expressed directly with appropriate use of the *lookahead* variable supported by Maisie [9]. The lookahead for each switch entity in this model is set to the delay experienced by each flit as it is transmitted over the network link (in other words for the purpose of computing lookahead, each link can be viewed as a FIFO server). For the optical network, this means that the value of the lookahead is high. Further as subsequent messages in a byte-level model have small timestamp increments, this yields a high lookahead ratio [5] for the switch entities in the model.

The Maisie program used to evaluate the conservative implementation was almost identical with the version used for the optimistic implementation. The only difference between the two programs was the specification of the lookahead for each entity and the specification of the communication topology in the model to avoid having to broadcast null messages.

We now examine the speedup obtained with the conservative implementation. Table 5 indicates the elapsed time for both sequential and parallel implementations as a function of the load factor. The sequential times reported in the table are not exactly the same as those reported in the previous section. The two sets of measurements were taken at different times in conjunction with running the optimistic and conservative algorithms respectively. The two sets

LOAD PROCESSORS	0.1	0.2	0.3	0.4
T_{seq}	86.3	110.0	132.0	149
T_{cons-1}	86.1	103	117.3	129.3
4	30.0	36.6	42.5	47.1
8	18.2	23.2	26.6	28.1
12	16.2	19.0	21.1	22.8

Table 5: Execution Time (seconds)

LOAD PROCESSORS	0.1	0.2	0.3	0.4
1	1.0	1.1	1.1	1.2
4	2.9	3.0	3.1	3.2
8	4.7	4.7	5.0	5.3
12	5.3	5.8	6.2	6.6

Table 6: Speedup for Conservative Implementations

	Intra-cluster Traffic	NUMBER OF PROCESSORS		
		GEL	1-cons	GEL/1-cons
L	12.5%	252.0	193.2	0.72
O	60%	231.8	177.8	0.71
W	80%	214.4	168.2	0.73
	100%	153.9	136.0	0.80
H	12.5%	391.0	282.3	0.76
I	60%	329.2	235.3	0.77
G	80%	292.5	214.1	0.78
H	100%	204.0	164.4	0.88

Table 7: Elapsed time on 1 processor

differ by less than 5% from each other and the difference is attributed to the measurement error that is unavoidable with measuring elapsed times on parallel architectures. Note that two sets of numbers are provided for the 1-node implementation: the first titled T_{seq} refers to the time that was measured using the sequential simulation algorithm that uses a global event-list (GEL) implemented as a splay tree. The second set of numbers titled T_{cons-1} were measured for the 1-node implementation that was executed using the conservative simulation algorithm. The reasons why sequential implementations using conservative algorithms sometimes perform better are also discussed subsequently in this section.

The speedup obtained with the conservative algorithm is presented in Table 6. We note that, as expected, for a given number of processors, the speedup increases monotonically with the load factor. Note that the improvement in speedup are relatively small when using few processors but is significant for the 12-processor implementation. This exactly follows the pattern observed with the optimistic implementations. Further, for a given load factor, the speedup improves significantly as the number of processors used in the simulation is increased. We note that the speedup achieved with our implementation of the conservative algorithms was considerably superior, for all configurations, as compared with our implementation of the optimistic algorithm. The primary reason for this appears to be the excellent lookahead ratio for the switch entities.

5.2 Two-level model

The next topology used in the simulation study was the two-level model that includes the LAN and the optical network. As the performance of the conservative algorithm was considerably better than that of the optimistic algorithms for the preceding model, this topology was executed only using the conservative algorithm.

The lookahead for the switch entities modeling the LAN was defined as discussed previously for the optical network. As the electronic LANs have lower communication latencies, the switch entities in that part of the model have lower lookahead and hence a worse Lookahead Ratio as compared with the optical network.

To establish a baseline performance for this model, the 8-cluster topology was executed on one processor of the IBM SP using a sequential simulation algorithm that uses a global event-list (GEL) implemented as a splay tree and also using a conservative synchronization algorithm (row marked 1-cons). As seen from the results in Table 7, the 1-processor conservative implementation was considerably more efficient than the global event-list implementation. The primary reason for this is that in the GEL implementation, all events are executed in strict timestamp order whereas in the conservative implementation, an entity can execute 'safe' events (i.e. all events that fall within its lookahead window) even if it means that some events at different entities are executed out of their strict timestamp order. If a large number of events are clustered around a small time interval across many entities (as is the case in byte-level models of wormhole routing protocols), the GEL implementation will require many more context-switches to process the same number of events than the conservative algorithm. Although context-switches are implemented efficiently in Maisie [2], the extremely large number of messages generated by the flit-level models impose a proportionately large number of context-switches in the GEL implementation leading to significantly worse performance.

As the percentage of network traffic that is intra-cluster is increased, we note that the performance of the GEL becomes somewhat closer to that of the conservative algorithm. Other things remaining the same, as the intra-cluster traffic is increased, more worms terminate within the cluster reducing the total number of events in the system. As the total number of events in the system decrease, the difference in context-switch times between the two implementations also decreases. Table 8 displays measurements on the number of events for each of the model parameters considered in this study for both low and high traffic scenarios. Note that, as expected, the configuration with the minimum number of total events

| Intra-cluster | NUMBER OF PROCESSORS | | | | TOTAL |
Traffic	GEL	1-cons	8	16	EVENTS
L 12.5%	6.0K	7.8K	39.2K	47.0K	1513K
O 60%	4.4K	5.7K	29.3K	34.0K	1018K
W 80%	3.3K	4.2K	25.4K	26.7K	713K
100%	3.3K	3.7K	21.5K	26.3K	502K
H 12.5%	9.5K	13.1K	69.4K	77.4K	3707K
I 60%	8.9K	12.5K	62.9K	71.9K	2933K
G 80%	7.7K	10.6K	57.5K	68.3K	2261K
H 100%	7.6K	9.4K	55.1K	70.1K	1550K

Table 8: Event Counts for Low and High Traffic Load

| Intra-cluster | NUMBER OF PROCESSORS | | |
Traffic	GEL/1-cons	8	16
L 12.5%	0.76	5.0	6.0
O 60%	0.77	5.1	5.9
W 80%	0.78	6.0	6.3
100%	0.88	6.3	7.1
H 12.5%	0.72	5.3	5.9
I 60%	0.71	5.0	5.8
G 80%	0.73	5.4	6.5
H 100%	0.80	5.9	7.4

Table 9: Speedups for Low and High Traffic Load

(502K events for low load with 100% intra-cluster traffic) also has the best GEL performance relative to the conservative implementation.

We now examine the speedups that were obtained with conservative implementations for the 8-cluster model using 8 and 16 processors. In the former case, each cluster was mapped to a unique processor; in the case of 16 processors, each cluster was further split into two parts, with the entities modeling each half mapped to a unique processor. For each experiment, we express speedup with n processors as the ratio of T_{cons-1}/T_{cons-n}; in other words the speedup is measured with respect to the 1-processor conservative implementation rather than with respect to the sequential implementation as the former is the more efficient 1-node implementation.

Table 9 shows the speedup as the percentage of intra-cluster traffic is increased from 12.5 (which corresponds to a situation where the destination host for a worm is chosen using a uniform probability distribution) to 100 (where all generated traffic must terminate at another host in the same cluster). The first graph shows speedups obtained with 8 and 16 processors for a relatively low traffic load factor of 0.05 and the second graph plots the speedup for similar configurations for a load factor of 0.15. Both tables also indicate the slowdown suffered by the GEL implementation as compared with the 1-node conservative implementation.

We first examine speedup as a function of the intra-cluster traffic. For the most part, the speedup tends to improve slightly as intra-cluster traffic is increased with this increase being most significant when all traffic is intra-cluster. An immediate explanation for this appears to be that as each cluster executes on its own processor, decreasing inter-cluster traffic (or increasing the percentage of intra-cluster traffic) reduces message traffic among the processors and hence improves performance. However, in conservative systems, the presence of a communication channel that carries low message traffic is typically expected to increase the number of null messages and eventually degrade parallel performance. Table 10 presents the average number of null messages sent by an entity for every event processed by that entity for each experiment. As seen

from the table, the number of null messages indeed increase as the percentage of intra-cluster traffic is increased. The explanation for the improved speedup lies in the excellent lookahead that is available for the optical network. (Recall that links in the optical network are 1.6 km whereas those in the Myrinet are only 25m.) Thus although the optical network links have less traffic for high intra-cluster traffic scenarios, their high lookahead combined with the reduced overhead for message transmission among remote entities leads to better relative performance for the parallel implementations.

For a given intra-cluster traffic load, there does not appear to be a strong correlation between speedup and load factor. This is particularly significant because the average number of null messages per event is almost 3 times larger for the high load factor case as compared with the corresponding low load factor scenario. Once again, the culprit turns out to be load imbalance: the increased traffic does not increase the computation in the model in a uniform manner. Rather computation is increased in selected parts of the network based on the route selected for the worm. Unlike the previous case, the high load scenario in this model corresponds to a load factor of only 0.15 which is not sufficient to increase the computation in the network in a uniform manner.

We note that the speedup does not increase significantly as we move from 8 to 16 processors, where each cluster of 4 switches is split among two processors. The maximum gain is for the situation where all generated traffic is intra-cluster. This is again expected because the lookahead defined for the switch entities in the LAN is considerably less than that for the switch entities modeling the optical network.

6 Conclusions

A byte-level simulator has been developed to study a number of protocol related issues in the design of SSN, a hierarchical network that uses wormhole routing. Commercial network simulators like OPNET were found to impose a sufficiently large overhead that rendered their run times (and memory requirements) untenable for evaluation of even relatively small networks. Instead the study explored the use of Maisie, a general purpose parallel simulation language to imple-

	Intra-cluster	NUMBER OF PROCESSORS		
	Traffic	GEL/1-cons	8	16
L	12.5%	0.47	0.70	0.71
O	60%	0.7	0.94	0.97
W	80%	0.99	1.2	1.25
	100%	1.53	1.47	1.65
H	12.5%	0.19	0.32	0.34
I	60%	0.24	0.38	0.41
G	80%	0.35	0.43	0.45
H	100%	0.48	0.48	0.56

Table 10: Null Messages per Event for Low and High Traffic Load

ment the simulator. The message-passing paradigm used by Maisie provided a natural and simple way to model such networks.

The simulator for SSN in Maisie has led to reasonable performance on sequential platforms. Parallel implementations of the simulator were explored on the IBM SP, a distributed memory multicomputer using both conservative and optimistic synchronization algorithms. The parallel implementations were used to execute two types of SSN models: smaller 2-level models which simulated both the local area networks (LANs) and the optical interconnects used to connect the LANs and large abstract models which simply modeled the optical interconnection network. The study concluded that conservative techniques were more effective in exploiting the parallelism in these models than optimistic techniques. The primary reason for this appears to be the relatively good lookahead in the models of the switch components, particularly for the optical interconnect. It is important to note that the existence of good lookahead in the model was not obvious due to the presence of cycles in the model.

To the best of our knowledge, this is the first byte-level simulation of a wormhole routing network and the first experimental study that directly compares the performance of a real world application at the language level with conservative and optimistic synchronization algorithms. We are continuing our investigations with the model to determine if there are specific model parameters where optimistic techniques will outperform conservative techniques.

Acknowledgments

This research was supported by the USDOD ARPA/CSTO (Contract DABT63-93-C-0055) under "The Distributed Supercomputer SuperNet – A Multi Service Optical Intelligent Network" project and the U.S. Department of the Air Force/Advanced Research Projects Agency ARPA/CSTO (Contract F-30602-94-C-0273), under "Scalable Systems Software Measurement and Evaluation" project. Thanks are extended to Vikas Jha for his help with the conservative implementations of the model. Thanks also to Monnica Terwilliger for her invaluable assistance in preparing the camera-ready copy.

References

[1] R. Bagrodia, K. M. Chandy, and W-L. Liao. A Unifying Framework for Distributed Simulations. *ACM Trans on Modeling and Computer Simulation*, October 1991.

[2] R. Bagrodia and W. Liao. Maisie: A Language for Design of Efficient Discrete-Event Simulations. *IEEE Transactions on Software Engineering*, April 1994.

[3] N. Boden et al. Myrinet: A Gigabit-Per-Second Local-Area Network. *IEEE Micro*, 15(1), February 1995.

[4] R. Earnshaw and A. Hind. A Parallel Simulator for Performance Modelling of Broadband Telecommunication Networks. In *1992 Winter Simulation Conference Proceedings*, pages 1365–1373, December 1992.

[5] R. Fujimoto. Lookahead in Parallel Discrete Event Simulation. In *International Conference on Parallel Processing*, August 1988.

[6] R. Fujimoto. Parallel Discrete Event Simulation. *Communications of the ACM*, 33(10):30–53, October 1990.

[7] A. Hajare. Simulating a Multiple Segment LAN. In 27th *Annual Simulation Symposium*, pages 89–98, April 1994.

[8] M. Hluchyj and M. Karol. Shufflenet: An Application of Generalized Perfect Shuffles to Multihop Lightwave Networks. *IEEE/OSA Journal of Lightwave Technology*, 9(10):1386–1397, October 1993.

[9] V. Jha and R. Bagrodia. Parallel Implementations of Maisie using Conservative Algorithms. In *Winter Simulation Conference*, December 1993.

[10] L. Kleinrock et al. The Supercomputer Supernet Testbed: A WDM Based Supercomputer Interconnect. *Joint issue of IEEE JSAC and IEEE/OSA JLWT*, 1995. To Appear in Special Issue on Multiple Wavelength Optical Technologies and Networks.

[11] MIL 3, Inc., 3400 International Drive NW, Washington, DC. *OPNET Modeler: Modeling Manual*, 1993.

[12] H. Mouftah and R. Sturgeon. Distributed Discrete-Event Simulation for Communication Networks. *IEEE Journal on Selected Areas in Communication*, 8(9):1723–1734, December 1990.

[13] L. Ni and P. McKinley. A Survey of Wormhole Routing Techniques in Direct Networks. *IEEE Computer*, 26(2):62–76, February 1993.

[14] P. Palnati, E. Leonardi, and M. Gerla. Bidirectional Shufflenet: A Multihop Topology for Backpressure Flow Control. In *Proceedings of 4th International Conference on Computer Communications and Networks*, pages 74–81, September 1995.

[15] T. Rodeheffer. Experience with Autonet. *Computer Networks and ISDN Systems*, 25(6):623–629, January 1993.

Session 4 — Panel

PADS, DIS, and the DoD High Level Architecture: What is PADS' Role?

Session Chair
Richard M. Fujimoto, Georgia Institute of Technology, USA

Invited Paper

Time Management in the DoD High Level Architecture

R.M. Fujimoto and R.M. Weatherly

Time Management in the DoD High Level Architecture

Richard M. Fujimoto
College of Computing
Georgia Institute of Technology
Atlanta, GA 30332-0280

Richard M. Weatherly
The MITRE Corporation
7525 Colshire Drive
McLean, VA 22102-3481

Abstract

Recently, a considerable amount of effort in the U.S. Department of Defense has been devoted to defining the High Level Architecture (HLA) for distributed simulations. This paper describes the time management component of the HLA that defines the means by which individual simulations (called federates) advance through time. Time management includes synchronization mechanisms to ensure event ordering when this is needed. The principal challenge of the time management structure is to support interoperability among federates using different local time management mechanisms such as that used in DIS, conservative and optimistic mechanisms developed in the parallel simulation community, and real-time hardware-in-the-loop simulations.

1. Introduction

The Defense Modeling and Simulation Office (DMSO), through its High Level Architecture (HLA) initiative, is addressing the continuing need for interoperability between new and existing simulations within the U. S. Department of Defense. The HLA seeks to generalize and build upon the results of the Distributed Interactive Simulation (DIS) world and related efforts such as the Aggregate Level Simulation Protocol (ALSP) [Wils94]. The HLA activity began in March 1995 with the goal of recommending an architecture to the Executive Council for Modeling and Simulation (EXCIMS) before the end of calendar year 1996. The EXCIMS in turn, after appropriate review, will recommend the architecture to the Under Secretary of Defense (Acquisition and Technology) for approval and standardization. Prototype demonstrations of the use of the architecture are scheduled to be completed in the summer of 1996. Information about the HLA concept and the DMSO Master Plan is available at http://www.dmso.mil.

The HLA consist of three parts: 1) rules governing certain characteristics of HLA-compliant simulations, 2) an object modeling scheme that describes the information of common interest to a group (called a federation) of cooperating simulations (federates), and 3) the Run-Time Infrastructure (RTI) that provides the software environment needed by the federates to exchange information in a coordinated fashion. The RTI is a special purpose distributed operating system that provides a variety of services, described below. The specification of these services is evolving through experimentation and can be found on the web server mentioned above. In this paper we describe the time management services. The principal challenge is to bring together, in a general and extensible way, the time management mechanisms used by several disparate communities including DIS, ALSP, and test and evaluation. Below, we briefly review key concepts in DIS and ALSP before describing the HLA.

"The primary mission of DIS is to define an infrastructure for linking simulations of various types at multiple locations to create realistic, complex, virtual `worlds' for the simulation of highly interactive activities" [DIS94]. A DIS exercise can be viewed as a collection of autonomous simulations each maintaining a virtual environment representing the portions of the battlefield relevant to the entities it is modeling. An exercise may include (1) human-in-the-loop elements such as tank or flight simulators, (2) computation only elements such as wargame simulations, and (3) live elements such as instrumented tanks. Time advances are paced by a real-time clock. State changes, e.g., firing a weapon, are broadcast as they occur. Each element determines what information is relevant to the entities it models and discards the rest. Messages are typically processed in receive order (not time stamp order) to reduce communication latency, sometimes leading to anomalies. Some temporal errors are acceptable because they will not be noticed due to limitations in human perception. Unreliable communication services are often used, again to reduce latency. See [DIS94] for an introduction to DIS, and [Fuji95] for a discussion contrasting DIS and parallel simulation research.

ALSP was designed to extend the DIS concept, and focused largely on combining separately developed wargame simulations into federations. Wargame simulations are often referred to as constructive or aggregated simulations because they model battlefield components at a higher, more aggregated level of abstraction, e.g., battalions or divisions rather than individual aircraft or tanks. A key distinction between ALSP and the training simulations used in DIS is ALSP federations require strict adherence to causality, i.e., simulation events must be processed in time stamp order. ALSP currently uses the Chandy/Misra/Bryant null message protocol to accomplish this [Chan79].

60

2. Overview of the HLA

Real-world entities are modeled in the HLA by objects. Each object contains an identifier, state, and a behavior description that specifies how the object reacts to state changes. The relationship of objects to one another is specified through (1) attributes that indicate those state variables and parameters of an object that are accessible to other objects, (2) association between objects (e.g., one object is part of another object), and (3) interactions between objects that indicate the influence of one object's state on the state of another object. A *federation object model (FOM)* specifies the common object model used by all federates.

Each object attribute has an owner that is responsible for updating the value of its attributes (e.g., position information). At any instant, there can be at most one owner of an attribute, however, ownership of the attribute may pass from one federate to another during an execution. Other federates *subscribe* to receive updates to attributes as they are produced by the owner.

The runtime component defines a set of services invoked by federates or by the Run-Time Infrastructure (RTI) during a federation execution. HLA runtime services fall into the following categories:

- *Federation management.* This includes services to create and delete federation executions, to allow federates to join or resign from an execution, and to pause, checkpoint, and resume an execution.
- *Declaration management.* These services provide the means for federates to establish their intent to publish object attributes and interactions, and to subscribe to updates and interactions produced by other federates.
- *Object management.* These services allow federates to create and delete object instances, and to produce and receive attribute updates and interactions.
- *Ownership management.* These services enable the transfer of ownership of object attributes during the federation execution.
- *Time management.* These services coordinate the advancement of logical time, and its relationship to wallclock time during the federation execution.

The remainder of this document is concerned with the time management services. See [DMSO96] for additional information concerning time management.

3. Time Management Interoperability

The RTI provides a base into which separately developed simulations can be "plugged in" to form large distributed simulations. A central goal of the high level architecture time management (HLA-TM) structure is to support interoperability among federates utilizing different internal time management mechanisms. Specifically, a single federation execution may include:

1. federates with different event ordering requirements, e.g., DIS and ALSP federates.
2. federates using different time flow mechanisms, e.g., timestepped and event driven mechanisms.
3. real-time (or scaled real-time) and as-fast-as-possible simulations; it is assumed that individual federates executing in conjunction with the RTI perform at least as fast as scaled wallclock time in federations requiring (scaled) real-time execution.
4. federates executing on parallel/distributed platforms using conservative or optimistic synchronization.
5. federates using a mixture of event ordering and transportation services, e.g., a DIS-like federate may use time stamp ordering and reliable message delivery for certain types of events, and receive-ordered, best-effort delivery for others. This facilitates gradual, evolutionary exploitation of previously unused HLA-TM services.

Time management transparency is important to achieve interoperability. This means the time management mechanism used within each federate is *not* visible to other federates.

4. Events, Messages, and Time

An execution can be viewed as a collection of federates, each performing a sequence of computations. Some of these computations are referred to as *events*, and some of these events are relevant to other federates. The RTI notifies other federates that have indicated an interest in an event by sending a *message* for each event notifying the federate the event has occurred. The time stamp of the message refers to the time stamp of the corresponding event. *Events* and *messages* are *not* synonymous; a single event typically produces many messages to notify other federates of the event. Lookahead constraints are also placed on events that are to be delivered in time stamp order, as discussed later. Federates need not schedule events in time stamp order. There are four types of events in the HLA: creation of a new object, deletion of an object, a state update, or an interaction.

Time in the system being modeled is represented in the HLA by a global *federation time axis*. The federation time axis is defined as a totally ordered sequence of values where each value represents an instant of time in the physical system being modeled, and for any two points T_1 and T_2 on the federation time axis, if $T_1 < T_2$, then T_1 represents an instant of physical time that occurs before the instant represented by T_2.

Two separate clocks are defined within each federate: *scaled wallclock time* is used to synchronize the execution with humans and live entities, and *logical time* is used to ensure that messages are delivered in a proper temporal sequence. Both represent points on the federation time axis. Scaled wallclock time is defined as offset + [rate *(wallclock time - time of last exercise start or restart)].*Wallclock time* is defined as a federate's measurement of true global time and is typically output from a hardware clock. If *rate* is k, scaled wallclock time advances k time faster than wallclock time. Non-real-time (aka as-fast-as-possible) executions set the rate factor to infinity.

Logical time is synonymous with "simulated time" in the parallel simulation literature, and is only relevant to federates that require that messages are not delivered to the federate "in its past," i.e., with time stamp smaller than the federate's current time. Federates must explicitly request advances in logical time. The requirement that messages are not delivered "in the past" only applies to messages that are not designated to be delivered in time stamp order. Federates not requiring this constraint (e.g., DIS federates) request a time advance to "infinity" at the beginning of the execution.

Federate time denotes the "current time" of the federate, and these two terms are used synonymously. Federate time is defined as scaled wallclock time or logical time of the federate, whichever is smaller. At any instant of an execution different federates will, in general, have different federate times.

5. HLA-TM Services

Time management is concerned with the mechanisms for controlling the advancement of time during the execution of a federation. Time advancement mechanisms must be coordinated with other mechanisms responsible for delivering information, e.g., to ensure messages are not delivered in a federate's past. Thus, the time management services must encompass two aspects of federation execution:

* *Transportation services:* Different categories of service are specified that provide different reliability, message ordering, and cost (latency and network bandwidth consumption) characteristics.
* *Time advancement services:* Different primitives are provided for federates to request advances in logical time. These primitives provide the means for federates to coordinate their time advances with the time stamp of incoming information, if this is necessary. The time advance mechanism in the RTI must accommodate both scaled real-time, and as-fast-as-possible executions.

5.1 Transportation Services

The different categories of transportation service are distinguished according to (1) reliability of message delivery, and (2) message ordering. With respect to reliability, *reliable message delivery* means the RTI utilizes mechanisms (e.g., retransmission) to increase the probability that the message is eventually delivered to the destination federate. This improved reliability normally comes at the cost of increased latency. On the other hand, the *best effort message delivery* service attempts to minimize latency, but with the cost of lower probability of delivery.

Message ordering characteristics specify the order and time at which messages may be delivered to federates and are central to the HLA time management services. A variety of services are provided to support interoperability among federates with diverse requirements. Five ordering mechanisms are currently specified in the HLA: receive, priority, causal, causal and totally ordered, and time stamp ordered. These provide, in turn, increased functionality but at increased cost.

The ordering mechanisms currently defined are:

* *Receive Order.* Messages are passed to the federate in the order that they were received. Logically, incoming messages are placed at the end of a first-in-first-out (FIFO) queue, and are passed to the federate by removing them from the front of this queue. This is the most straightforward, lowest latency ordering mechanism.
* *Priority Order.* Incoming messages are placed in a priority queue, with the message time stamp used to specify its priority. Messages are passed to the federate lowest time stamp first. This service does not prevent a message from being delivered in a federate's "past" (time stamp less than the federate's current time), but it is less costly in terms of latency and synchronization overhead than the time stamp ordered delivery mechanism. Priority order with best effort delivery may be used for federates where sequences of messages require ordering, but the increased latency associated with either reliable delivery or guaranteed order cannot be tolerated. For example, speech packets may utilize this service.
* *Causal order.* This service guarantees that if an event E "causally precedes" another event F, then any federate receiving messages for both events will have the message for E delivered to it before the message for F. For example, E and F might indicate firing a weapon, and the target being destroyed, respectively; if causal ordering is used, a federate observing both events will be notified of

the fire event before it is notified of the destroyed event.

The "causally precedes" relationship is identical to Lamport's "happens before" relationship [Lamp78]. This relationship is defined between a pair of actions A_1 and A_2, where an action is an event, and RTI message send, or an RTI message receive. This relationship (denoted $\rightarrow$) is defined as follows: (i) if A_1 and A_2 occur in the same federate/RTI, and A_1 precedes A_2 in that federate/RTI, then $A_1 \rightarrow A_2$, (ii) if A_1 is a message send action and A_2 is a receive action for the same message, then $A_1 \rightarrow A_2$, and (iii) if $A_1 \rightarrow A_2$ and $A_2 \rightarrow A_3$, then $A_1 \rightarrow A_3$ (transitivity).

- *Causal and totally ordered.* In the causally ordered service defined above, messages corresponding to events that are *not* causally related (referred to as concurrent events) may be delivered to federates in any order. The causal and totally ordered service extends causal ordering to guarantee that for any pair of concurrent events, messages for these events will be delivered to all federates receiving both messages *in the same order*, thereby defining a total ordering of events. This service is commonly referred to as CATOCS (causally and totally ordered communications support) in the literature (e.g., see [Birm91]).

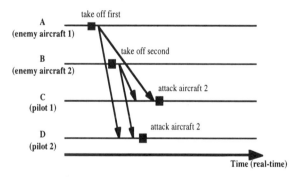

Figure 1. Scenario demonstrating causal and total ordering.

Figure 1 illustrates where CATOCS may be useful. Two federates (A and B) modeling enemy aircraft are taking off from an air field. Two pilots are assigned to intercept, with pilot 1 (federate C) given orders to attack the first enemy aircraft to take off, and pilot 2 (federate D) assigned to attack the second. Assume the "take-off" events are concurrent, e.g., the aircraft are taking off from different runways. Without total ordering, messages for the take-off events may arrive at the two federates in different orders. Figure 1 shows a scenario where pilot 1 incorrectly believes aircraft 2 took off first, while pilot 2 correctly believes

aircraft 1 took off first. The end result is both pilots attack aircraft 2! CATOCS would circumvent this anomaly by ensuring that both pilots see the same ordering of events. Both pilots may perceive an incorrect order (e.g., both might believe aircraft 2 took off first if the messages from Federate A are delayed), but the result of this error is likely to be less severe than having both pilots attack the same aircraft.

- *time stamp order (TSO).* Messages utilizing this service will be delivered to federates in time stamp order. Further, the RTI also ensures that no message is delivered to a federate "in its past," i.e., no TSO message is delivered that contains a time stamp less than the federate's current time. A conservative synchronization protocol is used to implement this service. All federates receiving messages for a common set of events will receive those messages in the same order, i.e., a total ordering of events is provided. The RTI provides a consistent tie breaking mechanism so messages containing identical time stamps will be delivered to different federates in the same order. Further, the tie-breaking mechanism is deterministic, meaning repeated executions of the federation will yield the same relative ordering of these events if the same initial conditions and inputs are used, and all messages are transmitted using time stamp ordering.

The relationship between causal and time stamp order is described in greater detail in [Fuji96]. The above orderings yield, in turn, successively stronger guarantees concerning message ordering, at the cost of increased latency, communication bandwidth, and in the case of time stamp ordering, constraints on scheduling events. Each federate may intermix different message ordering services for different types of information within a single federation execution. For example, periodic position updates may utilize a best effort, receive order category of service. These messages may be intermixed with messages for ordnance detonation events utilizing reliable, time stamp ordered delivery.

5.2 Object Management Services

The object management services include primitives to schedule and retract events, and primitives to receive messages. For example, **Update Attribute Values** and **Send Interaction** schedule events. The sender assigns a time stamp to the event to indicate when it is to occur, and specifies the category of transportation service (reliability and message ordering) that is to be used. The RTI delivers messages to the federate by invoking services that must be provided by the federate. Specifically, the RTI invokes the federate's **Reflect**

Attribute Values and **Receive Interaction** services to deliver messages denoting state changes and interactions.

Event retraction refers to the ability of a federate to retract or unscheduled a previously scheduled event. This is a common discrete-event simulation primitive often used to model interrupts and other preemptive behaviors. As discussed later, event retraction is also utilized by optimistic federates to implement anti-messages. The **Update Attribute Values** and **Send Interaction** services return an event handle that is used to specify the event that is to be retracted.

If the RTI at the destination federate receives a retraction request for an event that is not buffered in the RTI (e.g., because the corresponding message has already been forwarded to the federate), the retraction request is forwarded to the federate.

5.3 Lookahead

The time stamp order service requires specification of lookahead. Here, lookahead is defined as the minimum distance into the future that a TSO event will be scheduled. A lookahead value is associated with each federate. If the federate's lookahead is L, all TSO events must have time stamp of at least the federate's current time plus L.

Lookahead can change dynamically during the execution. However, lookahead cannot instantaneously be reduced. At any instant, a lookahead of L indicates to the RTI that the federate will not generate any event (using time stamp ordering) with time stamp less than C+L, where C is the federate's current time. If the lookahead is reduced by K units of time, the federate must advance K units before this changed lookahead can take effect, so no events with time stamp less than C+L are produced.

A federate's lookahead must be strictly greater than zero. This is necessary because if the RTI has advanced the federate's logical time to T, then (in most cases) it guarantees that all TSO messages with time stamp less than *or equal to* T have been delivered to the federate. This would be impossible to guarantee if lookahead were zero because a federate A at logical time T could schedule an event with time stamp T that is received by another federate B, which in turn schedules a second event also with time stamp T that is received by A, violating the guarantee that the RTI had delivered all TSO messages with time stamp T or less. The RTI will always use a small, nominal value for lookahead to circumvent situations such as this.

Lookahead restrictions must be applied to retracting previously scheduled events utilizing the time stamp ordered message delivery service if it is important that messages for retracted events never be passed on to other federates. Specifically, if the current time of a federate is T, and its lookahead is L, then the federate can only retract events containing time stamps greater than T+L. Messages for events containing a smaller time stamp may have already been passed to other federates.

It is possible that a message for a retracted event may be lost in the network, especially if best effort delivery is used. In this case, if the retract request was successfully delivered, the message for the retracted event will never appear, yet the retract request would still be passed to the receiving federate. Federates must be designed to allow for situations such as this. The RTI does guarantee that if a retraction request is forwarded to a federate, the retracted message will not be later delivered to the federate.

5.4 Time Advance Services

The time advance primitives serve several purposes. First, it provides a protocol for the federate and RTI to jointly control the advancement of logical time. The RTI can only advance the federate's logical time to T when it can guarantee that all TSO messages with time stamp less than or equal to T have been delivered to the federate. At the same time, the federate must delay processing any local event until logical time has advanced to the time of that event, or else it is possible it will receive a TSO message in its past.

The time management primitives also control the delivery of messages to the federate. TSO messages will not be delivered until the receiving federate has requested a time advance up to at least the time stamp of the message. In addition, the time management primitives provide information to the RTI that is used to synchronize the execution, as discussed below.

Two services for advancing logical time are defined: **Time Advance Request** and **Next Event Request**. Here, we assume these are invoked to request that all eligible messages are delivered to the federate. A provision is also provided to only deliver one message at a time. **Time Advance Request** is intended to be used by time-stepped federates, and **Next Event Request** by event-driven federates. Each invocation of either primitive eventually results in the RTI calling **Time Advance Grant** to indicate that logical time has been advanced, and all TSO messages with time stamp less than or equal to the grant have been delivered.

Time Advance Request with parameter t requests an advance of the federate's logical time to t. When used in a time-stepped simulation, t will usually indicate the time of the next time step. Invocation of this service implies that the following messages are eligible for delivery to the federate: (i) all incoming receive ordered messages, and (ii) all messages using other ordering services with time stamp less than or equal to t. The federate may simply note the occurrence of these events for later processing, or immediately simulate actions resulting from the occurrence of the events. When the RTI can guarantee that it has passed all TSO messages to the federate with time stamp less than or equal to t, logical time is advanced to t, and the RTI calls the federate's **Time Advance Grant** primitive. At this point, a time-stepped federate may proceed to simulate the next time step.

Next Event Request with time parameter t requests an advance of logical time to t, *or the time stamp of the next TSO message from the RTI*, whichever is smaller. When used in an event driven federate, t will usually indicate the time stamp of the next local event within the federate. After the primitive is invoked, the federate will either (i) deliver the next TSO message (and all other TSO messages containing exactly the same time stamp) if that message has a time stamp of t or less, and advance logical time to the time of that message, or (ii) not deliver any TSO messages and advance logical time to t. In either case, a **Time Advance Grant** is issued to indicate completion of the request. Other non-TSO messages may also be delivered as a result of invoking this primitive. If no TSO messages are delivered as a result of this request, this indicates to the federate that it may process its local event with time stamp t because no externally generated TSO messages with time stamp less than or equal to t are forthcoming.

In an as-fast-as-possible execution if a federate invokes **Time Advance Request** with parameter t, it unconditionally guarantees that it will not generate a TSO message at any time in the future with time stamp less than t plus that federate's lookahead. By invoking **Next Event Request** with parameter t, the federate is making a conditional guarantee that if it does not receive any additional TSO messages in the future with time stamp less than t, the federate will not later generate any TSO messages with time stamp less than t plus the federate's lookahead. This information is not unlike that used in the framework described in [Jha94].

It is noteworthy that as defined above, **Time Advance Request**, **Next Event Request**, and **Time Advance Grant** only pertain to the advancement of logical time. Wallclock time advances independent to the federate's actions (of course!). The **Time Advance Grant** call (or any action that advances logical time) will only be made after the RTI can guarantee no future messages will arrive with time stamp less than or equal to the federate's new logical time. The time required to make this advance depends on the performance of the synchronization protocol.

6. Synchronization Protocol

A conservative synchronization protocol implements the time stamp order message delivery service, and is used to advance logical time. The principal task of the protocol is to determine a value called LBTS for each federate, defined as a lower bound on the time stamp of future TSO messages that it will receive from other federates. Any TSO message with time stamp less than LBTS is eligible for delivery to the federate. The logical time of the federate cannot be advanced beyond LBTS. The specific synchronization protocol that is used is not visible to the federate to facilitate later inclusion of new protocols. Simulations that are dependent on the particular protocol that is used are considered non-HLA-compliant.

It is instructive to outline one *possible* implementation of the synchronization protocol. The following describes an implementation that is a variation of the well-known Chandy/Misra/Bryant "null message" algorithm. It is assumed that communications are reliable, and messages sent from one processor to another are delivered in the order that they were sent. This is important to prevent null messages from "passing" messages with smaller time stamps.

Federates are not constrained to send messages in time stamp order. Thus, the time stamp of incoming messages do not provide useful information that can be used by the synchronization protocol. Instead, null messages must be relied upon to carry all synchronization information.

LBTS for a federate F is computed as the minimum (current_time$_i$ + lookahead$_i$) computed over all other federates that send TSO messages to F. In an as-fast-as-possible execution, "current time" is identical to logical time, so LBTS can be maintained if each federate sends a null message each time it advances in logical time. However, in a real-time execution, current time advances with scaled wallclock time if logical time remains larger than scaled wallclock time. Further, DIS federates may not utilize logical time. Thus, it is not feasible to send a null message with each current time advance. This problem can be solved by observing that each federate can determine a lower bound on scaled wallclock time in each other federate provided the difference in wallclock values is bounded.

The synchronization protocol consists of two components: a sender and a receiver component. They operate as follows:

1. After each (local) logical time advance, the sender component transmits a null message to each destination to which it sends TSO messages with time stamp equal to the federate's current logical time, plus a lookahead value. This time stamp indicates a lower bound on the time stamp of any TSO message the federate will send in the future.

2. The RTI for each federate maintains a local bound for messages received from each source i called LB[i]. Upon receiving a null message for source *i*, the receiving RTI sets LB[i] equal to the time stamp of the null message. If this causes LBTS to change (increase; LBTS can never decrease), LBTS is also modified. This may, in turn, cause an increase in logical time, resulting in additional null messages.

3. In a real-time federation execution, each RTI also determines a lower bound on the wallclock time of neighboring federates (federates that send it messages) provided skew between the wallclock time of different simulations is bounded. This, along with lookahead information, enables the RTI to determine a lower bound on the time stamp of future TSO messages sent from other federates (even DIS federates) and can be used to set LB[i]. In general, LB[i] may be defined as the minimum of (1) the predicted real-time clock of simulation *i* plus its lookahead, and (2) the time stamp of the last null message received from simulation *i*.

7. Optimistic Time Management Services

The HLA-TM services described next are intended to enable optimistic federates to utilize HLA-TM services while still enjoying the advantages afforded by optimistic execution. These services *do not require all federates to support a rollback and recovery capability.* Indeed, it is envisioned that federations may include *both* optimistic and conservative federates within a single execution. Conservative federates not needing or desiring to utilize optimistic processing techniques may completely ignore the optimistic time management services with no ill effects.

An important goal of the optimistic time management services is to enable optimistic messages to be delivered to other optimistic federates (but not conservative federates). Thus, simple solutions such as requiring that the optimistic simulation *only* send messages that it can guarantee will not be later canceled are undesirable, because they do not fully exploit the potential offered by optimistic execution.

Several modest additions to the above services are used to support optimistic execution, as described below. These are collectively referred to as optimistic time management services. The discussion that follows only pertains to TSO messages.

1. Simulations may receive TSO messages *before* the RTI can guarantee that no smaller time stamped messages will be later received, i.e., before the RTI can guarantee time stamp ordered delivery.

2. An RTI primitive is provided for the federate to indicate to the RTI its logical time value, as discussed below.

3. The LBTS value is made available to the optimistic federate.

To illustrate how these services can be used by an optimistic simulation, the following outlines how a Time Warp [Jeff85] based simulation (TW) could be included in an HLA federation:

- The TW simulation uses the optimistic event facility to receive, and optimistically process events.

- Optimistically generated messages are transmitted through the RTI to other federates, the same as ordinary, non-optimistic messages. The RTI does not distinguish between optimistic and conservative events.

- The event retraction primitive provided by the RTI is used to cancel optimistic messages that later prove to be incorrect.

- If the canceled event has not been delivered by the RTI to the receiving simulation, annihilation happens within the RTI. If the message has already been delivered to the receiving simulation, the retraction request is forwarded to the simulation which must perform the cancellation itself, typically by performing a rollback in the receiving federate, possibly generating additional cancellation (retraction) requests.

- The RTI's conservative synchronization mechanism is used to prevent conservative federates from receiving optimistic messages. Specifically, the logical time of an optimistic federate is set equal to the GVT of the federate. Any event with time stamp less than GVT is guaranteed not to be prone to future rollbacks, and since events must be generated at least L time units into the future, where L is the lookahead, any event with time stamp less than GVT+L is guaranteed not to be subject to any future rollback. In effect, the GVT acts as the "local clock" for the TW federate from the perspective of the RTI. Lookahead is only used in the optimistic federate to enhance the performance of the GVT computation.

- Within the Time Warp simulation, GVT is computed as the minimum of the local GVT, and LBTS, provided by the RTI. This is because LBTS indicates a lower bound on the time stamp of any future TSO message, so it therefore provides a lower bound on the time stamp of any future rollback caused by receiving a message (or anti-message) in the federate's past.

A key property of this approach is it enables Time Warp federates to "plug into" the RTI, without any other federate (even optimistic ones) realizing there is an optimistic federate in the execution. The RTI allows for optimistic exchange of messages among optimistic federates, and at the same time, guarantees that optimistic messages are not released to conservative federates, all transparent to the federates participating in the execution. Further, no special GVT messages must be exchanged between optimistic federates, as the RTI automatically provides the information necessary for each optimistic federate to compute GVT locally. Finally, another attractive feature of this approach is it requires only modest modification of the "conservative" time management services already specified in the RTI.

One limitation of the above approach is it assumes a receive time stamp based definition of GVT. Some memory management protocols (e.g., Cancelback, message sendback) require a somewhat different definition of GVT. Some modifications to the above mechanism are required to support this alternate definition of GVT for optimistic federates using such techniques.

8. Conclusions

Thus far, research in the DIS and parallel simulation communities have proceeded largely independent of one another. Indeed, because of their different goals and requirements, there has been little reason for techniques in one domain to find application in the other. However, as DIS expands to encompass simulations requiring causality and event ordering, new opportunities arise for research in the parallel simulation community to have a large impact in future distributed simulation systems. The DoD High Level Architecture effort provides a framework into which research from the parallel simulation community can readily impact real-world systems.

9. Acknowledgments

The time management approach used in the HLA is the result of the collective efforts of many individuals, including Judith Dahmann, the technical lead of the HLA effort, and the members of the HLA time management working group. Individuals contributing to this design include David Bruce, Chris Carothers, Danny Cutts, Charles Duncan, Jerry Dungee, Jean Graffagnini, Richard Henderson, Jack Kramer, Michael Langen, Margaret Loper, Larry Mellon, Henry Ng, Ernie Page, Kiran Panesar, Les Parish, Dana Patterson, E. L. Perry, Jerry Reaper, Paul Reynolds Jr., Sudhir Srinivasan, Jeff Steinman, Bill Stevens, and Darrin West. Sudhir Srinivasan suggested inclusion of causal ordering in the HLA. Richard Fujimoto's work as chair of the HLA Time Management group was funded by the Defense Modeling and Simulation Office (DMSO).

10. References

[Birm91] K. Birman, A. Schiper and P. Stephenson, Lightweight Causal and Atomic Group Multicast, *ACM Transactions on Computer Systems,* 9(3): 272-314, August 1991.

[Chan79] K. M. Chandy and J. Misra, "Distributed Simulation: A Case Study in Design and Verification of Distributed Programs," IEEE Transactions on Software Engineering, SE-5(5), pp. 440-452.

[DIS94] "The DIS Vision, A Map to the Future of Distributed Simulation" Institute for Simulation & Training, Orlando FL, May 1994.

[DMSO96] Defense Modeling and Simulation Office, "HLA Time Management: Design Document," 1996.

[Fuji95] R. M. Fujimoto, "Parallel and Distributed Simulation," In 1995 Winter Simulation Conference Proceedings, pp. 118-125, December 1995.

[Fuji96] R. M. Fujimoto and R. M. Weatherly, "HLA Time Management and DIS," In 14th Workshop on Standards and Interoperability of Distributed Simulations, March 1996.

[Jeff85] D. R. Jefferson, Virtual Time, *ACM Transactions on Programming Languages and Systems,* 7(3): 404-425, July 1985.

[Jha94] V. Jha and R. Bagrodia, "A Unified Framework for Conservative and Optimistic Distributed Simulation," 1994 Workshop on Parallel and Distributed Simulation, pp. 12-19, July 1994.

[Lamp78] L. Lamport, Time, Clocks, and the Ordering of Events in a Distributed System, *Communications of the ACM*, 21(7): 558-565, July 1978.

[Wils94] A. L. Wilson and R. M. Weatherly, "The Aggregate Level Simulation Protocol: An Evolving System," In 1994 Winter Simulation Conference Proceedings, pp. 781-787, December 1994.

Session 5

Techniques II: State-Saving and Synchronization in Optimistic Simulation

Session Chair
Rajive Bagrodia, University of California at Los Angeles, USA

Transparent Incremental State Saving in Time Warp Parallel Discrete Event Simulation

Robert Rönngren, Michael Liljenstam
and Rassul Ayani
Email: parsim@it.kth.se
SimLab, Dept. of Teleinformatics
Royal Institute of Technology
SWEDEN

Johan Montagnat
Ecole Normale Superieure de Cachan
Cachan (Paris)
FRANCE

Abstract

Many systems rely on the ability to rollback (or restore) parts of the system state to undo or recover from undesired or erroneous computations. Examples of such systems include fault tolerant systems with checkpointing, editors with undo capabilities, transaction and data base systems and optimistically synchronized parallel and distributed simulations. An essential part of such systems is the state saving mechanism. It should not only allow efficient state saving, but also support efficient state restoration in case of roll back. Furthermore, it is often a requirement that this mechanism is transparent to the user. In this paper we present a method to implement a transparent incremental state saving mechanism in an optimistically synchronized parallel discrete event simulation system based on the Time Warp mechanism. The usefulness of this approach is demonstrated by simulations of large, detailed, realistic FCA and a DCA-like cellular phone systems.

1. Introduction

Many systems rely on the ability to rollback (or restore) parts of the system state to undo or recover from undesired or erroneous computations. Examples of such systems include fault tolerant systems with checkpointing, editors with undo capabilities, transaction and data base systems and optimistically synchronized parallel and distributed simulations. An essential part of rollback based systems is the underlying state saving mechanism. This mechanism should not only allow efficient saving of states, but also support efficient state restoration in case of rollback. The implementation of the state saving and restoration mechanism is in many systems transparent to the user. The reason for this is obvious: the user should not have to bother with the intricate details of this mechanism such as whether complete states are saved or only a list of changes to the state. In this paper we examine some issues regarding state saving mechanisms in an optimistically synchronized parallel discrete event simulation (PDES) system [9] based on the Time Warp synchronization mechanism [13].

The motivation for PDES is twofold: (i) to increase the execution speed; and/or (ii) to enable execution of larger simulation models compared to sequential DES. During the last decade, researchers have proved the efficiency of PDES methods in a number of application areas [6, 9, 11]. Today, very challenging simulation problems are common in the industry and the neces-

sary hardware for PDES is widely available, such as multi-processor workstations or reasonably efficient networks of workstations. Taking this into consideration one could expect PDES methods to be commonly used outside the PDES research community. This is however not yet the case [11]. One of the motivating factors for this is that very few, if any, PDES systems are sufficiently transparent. In most systems the user has to understand the underlying mechanisms and modify his (sequential) simulation code accordingly. This situation is by large a consequence of the quest for best possible performance. However, the execution of a simulation is only part of the simulation lifecycle [23]. Thus the performance gain from using a non-transparent PDES system is often outweighed by the additional time and effort that has to be spent in using the system.

In this paper we examine the possibilities to transparently implement incremental state saving in a PDES kernel based on Time Warp synchronization. The kernel is implemented in the C++ programming language. The rest of the paper is organized as follows. Section 2 describes several methods that have been proposed to reduce the state saving overhead in Time Warp. In Section 3 we describe the simulation kernel used in the experiments and in Section 4 a novel method to implement incremental state saving (ISS) in simulation kernels based on C++. This method has been implemented and tested in a cellular phone system simulator which is described in Section 5. Section 6 presents experimental results which show the impact on performance of the ISS method. Section 7 summarizes the contributions of the work presented in this paper.

2. State saving Issues in Time Warp

A PDES system can be expected to require significantly more memory than the corresponding sequential DES system to execute efficiently [20]. In the case of Time Warp based PDES a naive implementation can use an arbitrarily large amount of memory compared to the corresponding sequential system [18, 17, 19]. Since the motivation for PDES is to speed up the execution and/or enable the execution of larger simulation models it is essential to find mechanisms by which the state saving overhead can be reduced. We can distinguish between methods that: (i) reduce the amount of state information that is saved, thus reducing both execution time and memory consumption; and (ii) methods that can reclaim memory on demand, including memory of future objects (i.e. associated with events with timestamps greater than GVT [13]), limiting the maximum memory needed [14, 17]. In the following we concentrate on the former category.

2.1. State Saving Techniques in Time Warp

The simplest method for state saving in Time Warp is to copy the entire state of a logical process (LP) each time it executes an event message. This is often referred to as *copy state saving* (CSS). However, we can expect rollbacks to be relatively infrequent compared to ordinary event executions in most Time Warp based simulations [8]. Furthermore, a state of an LP can be regenerated from an earlier state by re-execution of intermediate events. Accordingly, an LP does not need to save (or checkpoint) its state at each event execution but can choose to checkpoint only every χ^{th} state [16]. This is referred to as *infrequent* (or sparse or selective) *checkpointing*. Several methods have been proposed by which LPs adaptively can select their checkpoint intervals χ [21, 12]. These methods can easily be made transparent to the user.

Many challenging simulations, such as battle field simulations or simulations of large communication systems, are characterized by LPs with very large states where only a fraction of the state is updated in each event execution. In such applications it may be inefficient or even infeasible to save copies of the complete state which can be in the order of hundreds of kilobytes [6]. In such applications it is often appropriate to use *incremental state saving* (ISS) [2, 4, 24, 25, 26], in which only the updated parts of the state are saved. Thus the state saving mechanism builds a chain of state changes. In case of rollback the state is restored by undoing these changes.

Few systems, if any, implement transparent ISS primarily due to problems associated with identifying which parts of the state that are updated and when. This could be accomplished by use of special purpose hardware [10] or by special purpose simulation languages with compiler support for ISS. However, due to cost issues, a majority of PDES systems are implemented on top of some general purpose programming language such as C or C++. Several of these systems implement ISS. The SPEEDES environment features several interesting and efficient techniques to implement ISS [24, 25]. Good performance results with ISS in the context of VLSI simulations [2] and simulations of large telecom networks [6] have been reported. ISS has also been implemented using persistent objects [4] in an interesting effort to achieve a transparent implementation of ISS. However, these implementations of ISS have the common denominator that they put the responsibility on the user of writing either special purpose code for the ISS or calling special functions when updating state variables or to explicitly save state variables that have been updated. If the user fails to supply the necessary code for ISS in these systems, the state restoration in case of rollback may be corrupted. This is likely to generate non-deterministic, erroneous, simulation results. Finding this type of programming errors is often hard, even for a user with a thorough understanding of the Time Warp mechanism. Hence, we conclude that it is essential that ISS can be implemented as transparently as possible to the user. The question is to which extent this is possible.

3. Parallel Simulation Kernel

The Parallel Simulation Kernel (PSK) used in this study is based on Time Warp synchronization and runs on shared memory multiprocessor workstations. It is written in C++ and uses static

assignment of the LPs to the processors, aggressive cancellation of events (i.e. events are cancelled as soon as an antimessage is received), and the direct cancellation optimization for shared memory machines described in [8]. The basic synchronization primitives (such as locks, and barriers) are supplied by the p4 macro library [3] making the PSK portable to a variety of multiprocessors. One modification has been made to this library, however, the queuing locks supplied in the package have been replaced by spin-locks.

3.1. PSK Structure

The PSK provides an application independent basis on top of which discrete event simulations can be built. The system is object oriented. When creating application specific logical processes the user inherits from a virtual LP class, see Figure 1. Associated with an LP is a *StateHandler* object which implements the state saving and restoration method. Through the StateHandler the LP object is able to save its state and to rollback to a previously saved state. These mechanisms are transparent to the user.

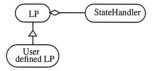

Figure 1. The LP inside the PSK

Each LP is also associated to an *Event Set* containing both executed and un-executed events and a *State Set* containing copies of old states to be used for state restoration purposes in case of rollback, Figure 2. When an event is executed, it usually modifies the LP state. Thus before an event execution the StateHandler constructs a data structure containing the information necessary to restore the old state and links it to the event.

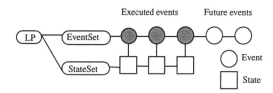

Figure 2. The events and the state set

In the case of incremental state saving, the data structure storing the state restoration information is a list of back ups of old values of state variables which have been modified in the execution of the event. In case of rollback, the StateHandler parses all executed events backward up to the rollback point. For each event in the rollback the StateHandler traverses the list of old state variable values in reverse order to restore the state.

4. Transparent Incremental State Saving

ISS can be implemented by identifying all updates to state variables at runtime and backing up the old values of the state variables before the state variable in itself is modified. In particular this could be implemented by changing the semantics of all side effect operators on state variables. In C++ it is possible to define data types and change the semantics of the operators on these data types by what is referred to as *operator overloading*. Thus, ISS can be implemented by creating special data types to encapsulate all state variables with overloaded operators that automatically perform the necessary ISS back up. Introducing special data types for state variables is not a severe limitation as many DES systems and most PDES systems require that the user declares his state variables so that they can be easily identified. Though this method may appear as straight-forward to implement there are several aspects of this approach which merit further attention.

4.1. Data Encapsulation

Only data which is part of the state of an LP should be backed up by the ISS mechanism. Hence, it is necessary to be able to distinguish between state variables and other variables. To solve this problem, a template class has been created to encapsulate any data type used to declare state variables, Figure 3. It is referred to as the State<> class.

```
template<class T> class State {
    public:
        ....          // overloaded operators
    private:
        T m_data;
};
```

Figure 3. The State class declaration

The user is required to declare his state variables as State<> encapsulated data. The declaration of a state variable of type integer:

```
int m_int;
```
is thus written as:
```
State<int> m_int;
```

This will create m_int as an object for which the operators are overloaded to backup the data by transparently calling a backup method of the StateHandler object. The state variable data is stored in the type int m_data data member of the State<> object.

4.2. Overloading Operators

The backup method must be called each time a state variable is modified. Thus any side effect operator must be overloaded. In C++ this includes the =, ++, --, +=, -=, *=, /=, %=, ^=, &=, |=, >>= and <<= operators. But to achieve complete transparency, all other operators on the State <> objects must be overloaded. This is to allow the user to write expressions such as: m_int + 2 or 2 + m_int or m_int + m_int which perform calls to:

```
operator+<int>(State<int>&, int);
operator+<int>(int, State<int>&);
operator+<int>(State<int>&, State<int>&);
```

The proposed State<> template, its associated operators and copy constructor provide the user with a transparent ISS mechanism for all simple data types, such as integers, floats etc. However, arrays and other compound data objects deserve special attention.

Some operators, such as the subscript([]) operator, may be overloaded using different prototypes. That is, the user can define compound classes for which he can overload the subscript operator to return an object of any type of data member. Hence, one

cannot make generic assumptions on the resulting type when applying subscript. Consequently, the State<> class cannot provide a generic subscript operator to ensure transparency. A simple solution is not to declare indexed state variables as State objects. Instead, each data member of indexed objects or classes should be State<> objects. This ensures that the state of the LP will be correctly backed up. An example illustrating this is found in Figure 4.

4.3. Initialization of Incremental State Saving

A problem related to automatic incremental state saving is how to initialize the state saving. When the LPs are created, their data is initialized, i.e. modified. These initializations will cause calls to the backup method of the StateHandler. This is not desirable since the simulation has not yet started and the StateHandler objects may not yet exist. Consequently, the proposed mechanism must be able to distinguish an initialization from an assignment, though both may use the same methods in C++.

In our PSK this has been solved by performing a call to the backup method through a pointer. When a State<> object is created, the pointer is set to a dummy backup method which does nothing. Consequently, backup calls performed during the initialization are harmless. When required, each LP enables the backup ability of all its internal State<> objects by changing the backup method pointer of these objects. To enable this, the State<> objects link themselves into a list accessible to the LP when they are created. Currently, the backup capability of the State<> objects of an LP is only enabled on the completion of the initialization of the LP. Hence, the state of an LP cannot be augmented after the initialization unless special provisions are made to enable their backup capabilities as these parts otherwise would not be backed up.

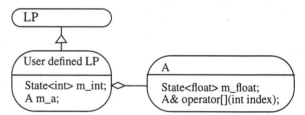

Figure 4. An example of correct data encapsulation in the proposed incremental state saving scheme

4.4. Temporary Objects

C++ compilers can sometimes create temporary objects automatically. Consider the example in Figure 4. If the user writes a statement like:

```
m_a = A();
```
a temporary object of type A is created on the stack, this object is copied to m_a and immediately deallocated from the stack. This could interfere with the incremental state saving mechanism if the temporary object contains State<> objects, in which case the temporary object would backup itself. This should not occur since the temporary object is not part of the LP state. Furthermore, it could cause the StateHandler to try to restore the state of non-existing objects in the case of rollback.

Two cases has to be taken into consideration. The temporary object could be created: (i) during the initialization phase; or (ii) after the initialization phase. In the first case the backup mechanism is not yet enabled but the temporary object will link itself to the LP list as described in Section 4.3. Since the temporary object will be deleted at the end of the LP creation, it should be unlinked from the linked list when its destructor is called.

If the temporary object is created during the execution it will not have its backup ability enabled. However, the State<> objects of the temporary object links and un-links to/from the list of State<> objects of the LP as described in Section 4.3. This could potentially be costly if the temporary object contains a large number of State<> objects. To prevent this a global variable is used as a flag which is set upon completion of the initialization. When created, a State<> object checks this flag to see if it should link to the list or not.

4.5. Pointers and Dynamic Memory Allocation

In a general case the state of an LP may contain pointers to data objects. These data objects could be dynamically allocated and deallocated. Our current implementation of ISS does not yet support these data types. In fact many PDES systems put the restriction that the state size of an LP has to be staticly defined. However, we will outline a possible solution to this problem which we intend to implement in a near future.

Integer arithmetic on pointers has to be supported. To guarantee transparency, operators acting both on State<> encapsulated pointers and integers should be overloaded in addition to the operators overloaded for non-pointer types. Since these operators do not exist for other objects than pointers, a template subclass of State<> will be declared, referred to as RefState<>. This will guarantee that pointers are correctly handled.

Transparent backup of dynamically allocated objects can be performed with the restriction that such objects only contain data members declared as State<> objects. To ensure that the backup capability of these objects are enabled, Section 4.3, the dynamically allocated object has to inherit from a base class where the constructor enables the backup capability. Furthermore, the method has to guarantee that a dynamically allocated object is not deallocated before it can be guaranteed that it will never be used in a rollback. For this purpose, the new and delete operators of the base class has to be overloaded. The base class contains a flag indicating if the user tried to delete the object or not. On a delete call, the memory block is not really deallocated, only the flag is set. The block can only be deleted in fossil collection and if it is tagged as deleted.

4.6. Memory Management Overhead

The proposed method for incremental state saving will cause the creation of backup objects each time a State<> variable is modified. Thus it is essential to have an efficient memory handler. We can expect that a majority of the data objects which will be backed up are small (such as 4-byte integers). Dynamically allocating and manipulating a large number of such objects in a list is not efficient. To alleviate this problem an improved memory manager for ISS has been introduced which treats backup objects containing less than 8-bytes of data (the size of a double

i.e. the biggest C++ built-in type) in a special way. The memory manager implements linked lists of arrays of update structures. Each update structure can hold backup data of up to 8-bytes length. When an event is executed the StateHandler will request arrays of update structures to store backups of state variables less than 8 bytes in from the memory handler on demand. Thus the linked list operations for small backup objects are replaced by incrementing an index in an array. This scheme also alleviates the problem of deallocating the backup structures at fossil collection. With this method all small backup objects can be deallocated efficiently by returning the update structure arrays to the memory handler. Only backup objects larger than 8 bytes are dynamically allocated and stored in the linked list.

4.7. Level of Transparency Achieved

The proposed mechanism is not completely transparent. In particular, the user has to explicitly declare state variables as State<> or RefState<> objects. In addition, some minor problems remain. The compiler is sometimes able to automatically cast from a user defined type T to a given type X, but not from State<T> to X, though a cast operator from State<T> to T is provided in the State<> class. Thus, the user might have to explicitly make some casts which were not previously needed.

The user should also be cautious when redefining the copy constructor or the assignment operator of compound classes used for state variables. If the user defines his/hers own copy constructor and/or assignment operator for such classes, he/she should call the copy constructor or assignment operator of all contained State<> declared objects.

The proposed method differs from what can be achieved by compiler based methods in that there is no way of preventing the user from, intentionally or not, bypass the backup mechanism by modifying State<> data through pointers.

5. The Cellular Phone Simulator

In this study we have tested our ISS implementation on a simulator of a cellular communication system. Good performance for parallel simulation of similar systems has been reported in e.g. [5]. Our simulator has previously been described in [15] and we will limit ourselves to describing some of its general properties.

5.1. The Cellular Phone Model

A cellular communication system is divided into a number of *cells*. To each cell a certain number of radio channels are allocated. Mobile Stations (MSs) residing in a cell can allocate any of the free radio channels allocated to the cell to send and receive phone calls. The same channel can be used in several cells that are sufficiently spaced apart since interference will be negligible.

When a mobile terminal moves from one cell to another it may become necessary to connect the MS to another base station, this is called a *handover*. If an attempt is made to make a call to or from a MS in a cell where there are no available channels, the call is *blocked*. If an ongoing call can not be handed over to a cell because there are no available channels it may be forced to terminate in which case the call is said to be *dropped*.

Radio channels can be allocated to cells staticly using Fixed Channel Assignment (FCA) or dynamically using some Dynamic Channel Assignment (DCA) scheme.

The simulation model consists of three submodels in a similar manner to the MaDRAS simulator [1]: the tele-traffic model, the mobility model, and the propagation model.

The teletraffic model describes the arrival process of new calls and their duration. The call arrivals form a Poisson process with a mean arrival rate λ, and exponential call duration with mean $1/\mu$. The mobility model describes the movements of the mobile stations (MSs). The propagation model describes distance dependent propagation loss using a statistical model for correlated log-normal shadow fading. The path losses at a specific position are regarded as constant over time, so that at a position p the gain from a transmitting station s is $G_{s,p}$ forming a two-dimensional matrix for each base station that describes the geography.

Each MS performs a "resource reallocation" procedure every 500 ms of simulated time. This procedure involves calculating the uplink and downlink Signal-to-Interference Ratio (SIR) and comparing it to a "least acceptable"-threshold to determine if the call should be dropped. Other BSs are also compared against the current connection and if another BS is found to be significantly better a handover is attempted. If a handover can not be completed due to lack of free channels the MS remains with the current connection.

Channel selection is done stochastically with equal probability among the available free channels on the BS. The uplink and downlink channels are changed at the same time and hence treated as one unit. Path losses are regarded as equal in both directions due to reciprocity. The radio channels are assumed to be orthogonal, so adjacent channel interference has been neglected.

The positions of the mobiles are updated every time there is new data to be read from the gain matrix, i.e. each mobile schedules a position update event for itself to occur when it has travelled the distance between two samples in the gain matrix. This event will cause the mobile to read the new radio gain from the matrix.

Each channel is a Logical Process (LP) in our model. There is also one generator LP that creates a mobile station when a new call arrives and sends it to the first channel assigned to it. Figure 5 shows an example of the communication patterns in the model. When a new call arrives to the system, a corresponding MS is created by the generator. After a BS has been selected, the new MS then proceeds to make its initial channel selection. A request is sent to all channels that are available on the selected BS to find out which channels are free at this time. One of the free channels is selected (if there is one, otherwise the call is blocked) and the MS object is sent to that channel. Similarly, when an MS decides to perform a handover to another BS a new set of requests are sent out to all channels available on the new BS and the selection is made. If no free channels are found and link quality is insufficient the call is eventually dropped. Requests made for the same channel from different MSs at the same simulation time is handled through an event priority scheme ordering the LPs so that one channel selection interaction is

always completed before the next request message is processed. A channel holds information about all entities (base stations and mobiles) communicating on that channel.

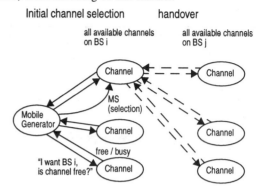

Figure 5. Basic communication pattern in the simulation model.

5.2. Characteristics of the models relevant to state saving issues

With each model we have simulated two scenarios: (i) a system of 7 cells; and (ii) a system of 67 cells. These scenarios are referred to as the small and large area respectively, where the larger area is closer to a realistic system. Radio signal propagation is described by a read only matrix which is 0.3 Mb for the small area and 27Mb for the large area.

Each event will only modify one mobile station out of all the connections contained in the Channel object. The size of the Channel state for the FCA case is 1720 bytes and one BS-MS connection is only 156 bytes. Furthermore, most events are simple position updates in which case only part of the BS-MS connection is modified. Hence, on average only about 2% of the state is updated in an event which makes incremental state saving seem like a good candidate as suggested in [6]. However, the state saving overhead is only a relatively small fraction of the total time to process an event due to the large event granularity. The mean event execution time is about 260 microseconds for the small area and 750 microseconds for the large area. The higher event execution time for the large area is primarily due to an increased cost for interference computations. The state size remains the same for both areas and the average time to save a state using copy state saving is about 140 microseconds. This means that for any improved state saving scheme (compared to pure copy state saving) we can at most cut the execution time by at about 45% for the small area and 15% for the large area by reducing the state saving overhead.

When using states sizes adjusted for a DCA model the situation becomes quite different. The mean event execution time increases slightly to about 430 microseconds for the small area and 830 microseconds for the large area, but the average state saving time increases to about 2200 microseconds for both models. This is due to a dramatic increase in state size for the Channel LP to 42776 bytes. The size of the BS-MS connection increases to 636 bytes. The most frequent events are still position updates. Consequently, the average fraction of the state updated in an event execution is even less for the DCA model than for the FCA model. In an average event execution less than 0.2% of the state is updated. The state saving overhead is quite severe when using copy state saving and in this case accounts for about 75 - 85 % of the total time to process an event. Thus, we hypothesize that the DCA models will benefit even more from ISS than the FCA model.

6. Experimental Results

In this study we have compared the impact of four different state saving mechanisms on the cellular phone simulator for the FCA and DCA models:

- Copy State Saving (CSS). The state of the LP is saved at each event execution.

- Sparse State Saving (SSS) with fixed state saving interval. The best state saving intervals were experimentally determined to be 5 for the FCA model and 10 for DCA model respectively.

- Transparent Incremental State Saving (TISS) which is the method described in this report.

- User dependant Incremental State Saving (UISS). This is a more conventional ISS method in which the user is required to explicitly call a backup function. The cellular phone models are such that only a well defined part of the state is updated on each event execution. Consequently, only a few calls to the backup function are necessary on each event execution.

An important aspect of the transparency achieved by the TISS method is that the *only* changes that had to be made to the user code of the simulation models was to declare the state variables as State<> objects. By defining a macro for the State<> declarations exactly the same code could be used for CSS, SSS and TISS. This has several important implications: i) it is of great value when selecting the appropriate state saving method for a particular application also making it possible to support a wider variety of applications with a single user interface to the simulation system; (ii) it forms a basis for building a system which automatically selects the best state saving method for individual LPs.

The experiments were performed on a SUN Sparcstation 10 with 4 processors, 128 Mb primary memory and 1 Mb cache per processor. The average rollback length, in these experiments, varies between 3 and 4.

6.1. Speed-up

The performance results in Figures 6 through 9 are shown as the relative speed of the proposed state saving algorithms compared to copy state saving. Figures 6 and 6 depicts the performance for the FCA model for small and large areas respectively. As predicted in Section 5.2 the improvement from reducing the state saving for this model would be limited to 15% for the large area and 45% for the small area. The performance results indicate that such improvements are possible with sparse state saving. To some extent the reduced memory consumption also results in improved performance of the memory system. Furthermore, the ISS methods are outperformed by the SSS method in these experiments. This is primarily due to the lower overhead in execution time for this method for the relatively small state sizes of this model.

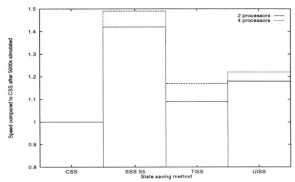

Figure 6. FCA model, small area simulated on 2 and 4 processors.

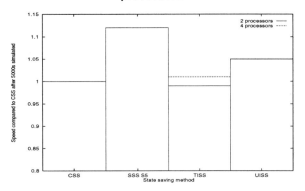

Figure 7. FCA model, big area simulated on 2 and 4 processors.

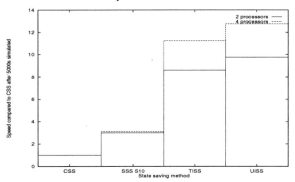

Figure 8. DCA model, small area simulated on 2 and 4 processors.

Figures 8 and 9 show the performance of the state saving algorithms for the DCA model. The DCA model differs from the FCA model in that the states of the LPs are significantly larger in the DCA model. Consequently, these figures reveal that the ISS methods perform significantly better than CSS and SSS. Furthermore, we see that there is a significant cost for the transparency of the TISS method compared to the UISS. We do, however believe that this cost is justified in most cases as it alleviates the user from the burden of having to explicitly deal with the underlying state saving mechanism. The speed-up achieved by the ISS methods are higher than what could be attributed to the reduction of the state saving overhead alone. Examining Figure 13 we see that this phenomenon is not due to an increased efficiency. We believe that the additional performance improvement mainly is caused by an improved locality which improves cache performance. This hypothesis is supported by the fact that the smaller model, for which the relative memory consumption reduction is larger, exhibits a larger improvement.

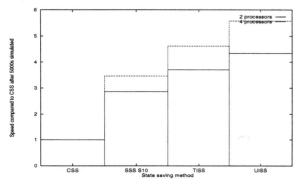

Figure 9. DCA model, big area simulated on 2 and 4 processors.

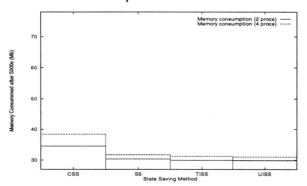

Figure 10. Memory consumption for the FCA model

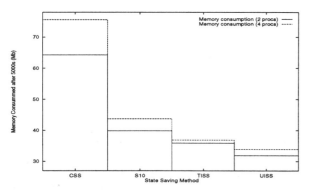

Figure 11. Memory consumption for the DCA model

6.2. Memory Consumption

Figure 10 and 11 show the memory consumption for the FCA and DCA models respectively for the large area. The memory consumption was recorded during long runs (5000 seconds of simulated time) for which the memory used by the simulator stabilized. In both models, the simulator first allocates a 27 Mb data structure to store the area simulated. Hence, only memory above 27 Mb is significant as far as state saving is concerned. These figures clearly show that both sparse and incremental state saving

can reduce the memory consumption significantly. UISS performs slightly better than TISS which is explained by the fact that while TISS saves several small pieces of the state UISS can save the same information as a single or a few larger pieces reducing the overhead.

6.3. Efficiency

Changes to one of the mechanisms in a Time Warp system can sometimes affect the optimistic synchronization substantially. This effect has been demonstrated for event list management [22] and other types of memory management policies [7]. Figures 12 and 13 show the impact of the state saving mechanism on the efficiency, defined as the ratio of committed events to executed events (committed events and events that are rolled back). These figures show that the state saving methods had little impact on the efficiency for these benchmarks.

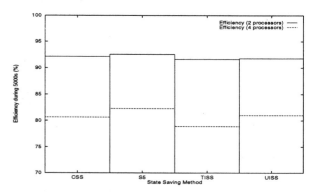

Figure 12. Efficiency of the state saving algorithms in the FCA model

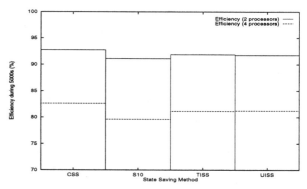

Figure 13. Efficiency of the state saving algorithms in the DCA model

7. Conclusions

Transparency of the state saving mechanism is essential for the acceptance of PDES methods by a wider audience as it relieves the user from the burden of having to understand and interact with an often intricate mechanism. In this paper we have discussed a method to implement incremental state saving in a Time Warp simulation system built on top of the C++ programming language. The method is based on the ability to overload operators in C++. The most prominent characteristics of this approach is that it achieves a high degree of transparency with acceptable overhead compared to a non-transparent implementation of ISS.

In the proposed method the *only* changes required to the users application code is to use special type declarations of the state variables. In particular, this allows the same user application code to be used regardless of whether the underlying state saving mechanism used is copy state saving, sparse state saving or incremental state saving.

The usefulness of the proposed method has been demonstrated by simulations of large realistic simulation models of cellular phone systems. The experimental results show that incremental state saving is important to achieve good performance in cases where the state vectors are large and only a small fraction of the state is updated on average. In some cases the execution time was reduced by more than an order of magnitude compared to conventional copy state saving.

In future systems we believe that the system should be able to select the best state saving method for individual LPs at run time. This will be facilitated if the state saving mechanism can be made transparent.

8. References

1. Andersin, M., Frodigh, M., Sunell K-E, "Distributed Radio Resource Allocation in Highway Microcellular Systems", Fifth WINLAB Workshop on Third Generation Wireless Information Networks, Rutgers University, New Jersey, -95

2. H. Bauer et al., "Reducing Rollback Overhead in Time-Warp Based Distributed Simulation with Optimized Incremental State Saving", Proceedings of the 26th Annual Simulation Symposium, pages 12-20, March 1993.

3. R. Butler, E. Lusk, "Monitors, messages, and clusters: the p4 parallel programming system", Parallel Computing, 20, April 1994

4. D. Bruce, "The Treatment of State in Optimistic Systems", Proceedings of the 9th Workshop on Parallel and Distributed Simulation (PADS95), pages 40-49, June 1995.

5. C. Carothers, R. Fujimoto and Y.-B. Lin, "A Case Study in Simulating PCS Networks Using Time Warp", 9th Workshop on Parallel and Distributed Simulation, Lake Placid, NY, 1995.

6. J. Cleary, F. Gomes, B. Unger, X. Zhonge and R. Thudt, "Cost of State Saving & Rollback", Proceedings of the 8th Workshop on Parallel and Distributed Simulation, Vol. 24, No. 1, pages 94-101, July 1994.

7. S.R. Das and R. F. Fujimoto. "A Performance Study of the Cancelback Protocol for Time Warp Parallel Simulation", Proceedings of the 1994 ACM SIGMETRICS Conference on Measurement and Modeling of Computer Systems. pages 201-210, May 1994.

8. R. Fujimoto, "Time Warp on a Shared Memory Multiprocessor", Transactions of the Society for Computer Simulation, Vol. 6, No. 3, pages 211-239, July 1989.

9. R. Fujimoto, "Parallel Discrete Event Simulation", Communications of the ACM, Vol. 33, No. 10, pages 30-53, October 1990.

10. R. Fujimoto. et al., "Design and Evaluation of the Rollback Chip: Special Purpose Hardware for Time Warp", IEEE Transactions on Computer, Vol. 41, No. 1, pages 53-64, January 1992.

11. R. Fujimoto, "Parallel Discrete Event Simulation: Will the Field Survive?", ORSA Journal on Computing, Vol. 5, No. 3, pages 213-230, Summer 1993.

12. J. Fleischmann and P. Wilsey, "Comparative Analysis of Periodic State Saving Techniques in Time Warp Simulators", Proceedings of the 9th Workshop on Parallel and Distributed Simulation (PADS95), pages 50-59, June 1995.

13. D. Jefferson, "Virtual Time", ACM Transactions on Programming Languages and Systems, Vol. 7, No. 3, pages 404-425, July 1985.

14. D. Jefferson, "Virtual Time II: Storage Management in Distributed Simulation", Proceedings of the 9th Annual ACM symposium on Principles of Distributed Computing, pages 75-90, August 1990.

15. M. Liljenstam, R. Ayani, "A Model for Parallel Simulation of Mobile Telecommunication Systems", To appear in Proceedings of the International Workshop on Modeling Analysis and Simulation of Computer and Telecommunication Systems (MASCOTS), San Jose, CA, February, 1996

16. Y.-B. Lin, B. R. Preiss, W. M. Loucks and E. D. Lasowska, "Selecting the Checkpoint Interval in Time Warp Simulation", Proceedings of the 7th Workshop om Parallel and Distributed Simulation (PADS93), pages 3-10, May 1993.

17. Y-B. Lin and B. Preiss, "Optimal Memory Management for Time Warp Parallel Simulation", ACM Transactions on Modeling and Computer Simulation, Vol. 1, No. 4, pages 283-307, October 1991.

18. B. D. Lubachevsky, A. Schwartz and A. Weiss, "Rollback sometimes works... if filtered", 1989 Winter Simulation Conference Proceedings, pages 630-639, December 1989.

19. B. D. Lubachevsky and A. Weiss, "An Analysis of Rollback-Based Simulation", ACM Transactions on Modeling and Computer Simulation, Vol. 1, No. 2, April 1991.

20. B. Preiss and W. M. Loucks, "Memory Management Techniques for Time Warp on a Distributed Memory Machine", Proceedings of the 9th Workshop on Parallel and Distributed Simulation (PADS95), pages 30-39, June 1995.

21. R. Rönngren and R. Ayani, "Adaptive Checkpointing in Time Warp", Proceedings of the 8th Workshop on Parallel and Distributed Simulation, pages 110-117, July 1994

22. R. Rönngren, R. Ayani, S. Das and R. Fujimoto, "Efficient Implementation of Event Sets in Time Warp", Proceedings of the 7th Workshop on Parallel and Distributed Simulation (PADS93), pages 101-108, May 1993.

23. R. G. Sargent, "Verification and Validation of Simulation Models", 1994 Winter Simulation Conference Proceedings, pages 77-87, December 1994.

24. J. Steinman, "SPEEDES: A Multiple-Synchronization Environment for Parallel Discrete-Event Simulation", International Journal in Computer Simulation, Vol. 2, No. 3, Pages 251-286, 1992.

25. J. Steinman, "Incremental State Saving in SPEEDES Using C++", Proceedings of the 1993 Winter Simulation Conference, pages 687-696, December 1993.

26. B. W. Unger, J. G. Cleary, A. Convington and D. West, "An external state management system for optimistic parallel simulation", Proceedings of the 1993 Winter Simulation Conference, pages 750-755, December 1993.

Automatic Incremental State Saving

Darrin West

Science Applications International Corporation

4301 N Fairfax Drive

Arlington VA 22203

west@jade.std.saic.com

Kiran Panesar

Georgia Institute of Technology

801 Atlantic Drive

Atlanta GA 30332-0280

panesar@cc.gatech.edu

Abstract

We present an Incremental State Saving technique for which the state saving calls are inserted automatically by directly editing the application executable. This method has the advantage of being easy to use since it is fully automatic, and has good performance since it adds overhead only where state is being modified. Since the editing happens on executable code, the method is independent of the compiler, and allows third party libraries to be used. None of the previous incremental state saving methods have both of these features. We find that it is beneficial to use Automatic Incremental State Saving if less than 15% of the state is modified in each event as compared to copy state saving. This technique allows us to efficiently parallelize existing simulations, and makes Time Warp more accessible to non-Time Warp experts.

1. Introduction

The efficiency with which Time Warp is able extract parallelism from a simulation problem is well recognized [4]. It is able to achieve these higher levels of efficiency by optimistically executing events without waiting to determine whether earlier events may arrive. Because of the risk that an earlier event may arrive, state saving must occur so that subsequent rollback may ensure a correct event execution order. The efficiency of the state saving technique has more dramatic effects on the performance of a Time Warp system than the cost of rolling back, since state saving occurs frequently on the critical path, and rollback rarely if ever occurs on the critical path of a parallel simulation.

If a simulation has a state saving cost which is so high that it completely dominates the event computation cost, it may be practically impossible to speed up the execution of that simulation. This is particularly likely in simulations with large states.

We examine various state saving techniques, focusing on both their performance and ease of use. We present an automatic incremental state saver which has reasonable execution costs and does not depend upon user intervention for correctness.

The new technique provides efficient, *fully automatic*, general purpose state saving to users of Time Warp systems. This will allow us to efficiently parallelize existing simulations (given sufficient intrinsic parallelism in the application) and create a parallel simulation product that is accessible to non-Time Warp experts.

2. State Saving

Saving the state of some process as it transitions through state changes can be done in one of several ways. The selection of the technique depends on the requirements on the use of the saved state and the burden of saving that state.

2.1 Checkpointing

One can perform a periodic state save by recording a full copy of the state of the process. This copy can be used to restore the state to what it was at the moment of the save, by overwriting the current state with the saved copy or by overwriting a pointer to the current state with a pointer to the saved state. The latter option is possible only if all application references to the current state are made indirectly through the pointer. This slightly increases the cost of access, and the complexity of the implementation.

Periodic state saving is often referred to as checkpointing, as the state of the process may only be restored to one of the checkpoints created by the full state copy. It is often used to reduce the cost of restarting a computation in the case of failure, since work prior to the checkpoint does not have to be reexecuted. In a Time Warp system, it is occasionally necessary to return a process to the point at which an erroneous event was executed. Therefore, in many Time Warp systems, checkpoints are taken prior to executing each event.

Checkpointing is efficient when used sparingly, thus reducing the overhead of checkpointing relative to the application computation. However, events, and thus checkpoints can occur very frequently in Time Warp systems. When the cost of full checkpointing is relatively high, such as when the state size is large, other state saving techniques must be considered.

It is possible to occasionally skip taking a checkpoint and its associated overhead, but this sometimes requires extra reexecution after restoring to the latest checkpoint prior to the erroneous event [10]. However, a method more widely recognized as having less overhead during forward computation is incremental state saving [13,16,17].

2.2 Incremental State Saving

Incremental state saving is defined as saving each change to the state as it occurs. A backtrace trail is created on which the old value of a variable is saved prior to overwriting the variable with a new value. This backtrace is used to restore the state of the process by restoring each saved variable value in the reverse order they were saved. The changes in the state associated with each event are saved, and the start of executing each event is marked in the backtrace. In a Time Warp system, this is done so that state changes can be undone should it be determined that an event was executed in the incorrect order.

The amount of space consumed by an incremental state save is proportional to the amount of state changed, but tends to have a larger multiple than a full state save, since location information is usually stored with each variable saved. The execution cost per variable saved is also higher than for a full state save, for the same reason. Thus there will be a tradeoff point at some fraction of the entire state that changed where incremental state saving will become more expensive than a full block copy state save.

If the same variable is changed multiple times during an event, this increases the per event cost of the technique. It is only necessary to save a variable once per event, since in Time Warp systems, the state is only restored to the beginning of an event execution. However, the cost of the test alone to detect prior incremental saving of a variable is often almost as expensive as just saving the variable without the test. Our current prototype does not have this optimization.

One tradeoff of using incremental state saving is that state restoration through a long backtrace trail can become expensive. However, in an evenly load balanced execution, this tends not to happen frequently.

3. Incremental State Saving Alternatives

One of the challenges to applying incremental state saving to a problem is identifying the places where state variables are modified. Refer to Figure 1 for the discussion that follows.

3.1 Manual Insertion

In general purpose computation, or in parallel simulation in particular, identifying each change of state is not as easy as transaction oriented applications such as data bases. One obvious solution is to provide a user with support functions which will save a variable, but are required to be inserted by hand. This is not a natural activity for the user who may be an application expert only, with no special understanding of state saving. It is an error prone approach, since if even a single variable change is not recorded, an inaccurate state restoration may result. Detecting this sort of error would be very difficult, and is amplified by the unusual circumstances surrounding the need to restore the state of the process (particularly if it was to recover from some other error). In general, it may not be possible for a user to perform this task, since third party software libraries may be used, to which the user has no source code access. Convincing the third party developer to make these changes is also extremely difficult.

3.2 Augmented Data Types

A second approach would be to provide primitive data types which are augmented with incremental state saving. This provides an opportunity to more efficiently save the state of variables of these types, in that only the semantic changes need to be saved. For example, a sorted list need not record changes in list pointers, but only the primitive operations which can be undone at a higher level of abstraction. More importantly, the user does not have to be aware of the state saving technology, since it is hidden inside the data types being used, and the type can be made to have a standard appearance. This technique is particularly easy when using an object oriented language that would allow the construction of objects with hidden state saving behavior and the external behavior and appearance of a primitive data type of the language. A related approach would be to use a preprocessor to scan the source code for variable changes and insert incremental state saving calls. However, this technique does not solve the problem of using third party software. It might use unmodified primitive data types that are not state saved.

3.3 Modified Compiler

A third alternative is to modify the compiler directly and have it recognize changes to variables [7]. The compiler is able to insert incremental state saving calls before each change to a variable. This technique provides the most promise for efficient state saving, as high level reasoning, such as data flow analysis, may be applied to avoiding unnecessary state saves. For example, if it is aware of the granularity of state restoration, it may also migrate what would be a series of state saves to one variable within a loop to a single state save prior to entering the loop. Again, this technique does not address the issue of third party libraries. If those libraries are not compiled with the modified compiler, they may contain non-state saved variable changes. A second problem with this technique is that of portability. Customers are rarely in the position to choose a compiler based on the capabilities of a single product such as the simulation kernel. It is also not feasible to modify several of the major compiler vendor's products to allay this difficulty, nor be able to track upgrades to those products.

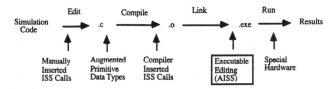

Figure:1 Incremental State Saving code may be inserted at various points in the
development cycle. Editing the executable offers several advantages over other methods.

3.4   Augmented Hardware

A fourth alternative would be to add special hardware that would appear to the application like regular memory, but could also incrementally state save the variables stored in that memory [5]. We would discount this sort of solution due to the cost of developing it, and since such a special purpose solution is also unattractive to a customer.

3.5   Automatic Incremental State Saving

We have developed a new technique that we call Automatic Incremental State Saving. In essence, we edit the already compiled executable code directly to insert the incremental state saving calls. The benefits are that the user does not have to make source code modifications, but simply executes the editing tool which automatically finds all instructions that change the state of a process. New assembly code is inserted prior the change which records the old value of a location prior to overwriting.

Inserting code requires updating of references to code that is relocated as a result. This includes relative and absolute jumps, as well as variables which record the address of instructions (e.g. function pointers or C++'s virtual functions). The addition of new code increases the code segment size, and may affect the location of a data segment if juxtaposed. References to these static data locations must also be edited.

In our experiments, we used the Wisconsin Architectural Research Tool Set (WARTS) [15] Executable Editing Library (EEL) [14]. EEL provides functions to search the code for state changing instructions, for inserting new code blocks (called snippets), and automatically making adjustments to any relocated code.

This editing technology is reliable and available. Other products which edit executable code include error detection software such as Purify[18] which instruments executable code such that illegal references to locations not restricted by the source language may be reported. Quantify[18] inserts code which allows effective instruction counting for purposes of accurate execution profiling. QPT [14] instruments code such that address traces can be recorded for use in parameterizing processor and cache simulators.

We have extended these notions to create traces of value changes to variables as they occur, for the purpose of backing out of those changes on demand.

To reduce the cost of the inserted state saving, we concentrate on saving only those variables that are necessary to reconstruct the state of the process at points to which a state restoration will occur. In Time Warp, that is just prior to executing an event. This allows us to ignore changes to registers and to automatic variables (those on the stack) that are not active at the beginning of an event. Process oriented implementations of Time Warp [11] would have to save automatic variables, since the stack for a process may exist at the beginning of an event. However, in event oriented implementations, the stack is empty at the beginning of an event.

We must also ignore changes to variables made within the Time Warp kernel. Operating system changes may not need to be recorded, nor changes in processes that cannot be rolled back (conservative, or interactive process). In general it may be necessary to provide to the user a technique whereby temporary variables can be identified, and incremental state saving instructions will not be inserted for their changes. However, in general it is impossible to do this perfectly except at run time, since some operations will be indirect and thus impossible to determine by static analysis of the code. This problem with indirection will result in extra state saving costs, not incorrectness.

The advantages to this technique are clear. Dependence on unreliable manual intervention is removed. Code written and compiled by a third party may now be state saved. It is not necessary to have access to the user's (and the third party's) compiler. As we shall see in the next section, the performance is reasonable, and may be improved by manual intervention if necessary for frequently accessed variables. This must be coordinated with the AISS mechanism so that it does not continue to save the optimized variable.

This technique provides efficient, automatic, general purpose state saving to users of Time Warp systems. We may be able to then efficiently parallelize existing simulations (given sufficient intrinsic parallelism in their application) and create a parallel simulation product that is accessible to non-Time Warp experts.

4.   Executable Editing

Executable editing is a powerful technique that has been successfully applied to program tracing, profiling [9], and debugging. To prove this technique's utility in incremental state saving, we have implemented a prototype using EEL, a package from University of Wisconsin. Here we present our experimental setup. We describe our Time Warp system, the word incremental state saver (WISS), and EEL. We also show how to recognize relevant write instructions, and how to instrument multiword stores. For each store instruction that changes simulation state, code is inserted that records a trace of the change in the WISS object.

4.1   Time Warp System

The automatic incremental state saver was implemented on TEMPO, a shared memory, multiprocessor, event oriented time warp [8] kernel developed at SAIC, in C++. Our kernel computes GVT using an asynchronous fossil collect scheme developed at GIT and uses direct cancellation [3]. A low water-high water scheme is used for buffer management [2]. The kernel supports at-GVT logical processes, and wide virtual time, a multifield timestamp designed for deterministic execution. A language layer, EvSim, provides a programming environment for developing parallel simulations.

4.2   Incremental State Saver

A Word Incremental State Saver (WISS) class defined in TEMPO maintains a trail of changes to the state of an LP [2]. Each change is recorded as an address and the previous four byte value at that address. The LP state is restored during rollback by traversing the history trail backwards and restoring the stored values at their corresponding addresses. Rollback is fast, since all changes are recorded in four byte chunks, and the size of restored data does not have to be checked on rollback. Space is reclaimed from the history trail during fossil collection by discarding all entries before GVT.

4.3   Executable Editing Library

Executable Editing Library (EEL) [9] is a machine independent executable editing package from the University of Wisconsin, a part of the Wisconsin Architectural Research Tool Set (WARTS). It was developed after experience with modifying code by hand in (QPT) [14] for performance monitoring of sequential computer programs.

Machine executables are modified by inserting, deleting or replacing code. The details of architecture and executable file formats are hidden to the extent possible. An executable is edited by opening it, breaking it up into routines, and editing each routine basic block by basic block. Inserted assembly code is encapsulated in snippets. A snippet contains arbitrary machine code, including branches to other parts of code. EEL recalculates branch offsets in the executable to account for the inserted snippet.

When a basic block is being edited, jump targets of newly inserted code may not be available, since code at the jump targets may not have been produced yet. EEL provides a callback mechanism that fills out the branch targets after all the code has been finally laid out and the branch targets are known. Callback does not alter the size of the executable.

Snippets are general purpose, and are customized according to the context in which they are inserted. The following example shows how a snippet for the Sparc architecture is customized. It is assumed that the reader is familiar with the Sparc architecture.

The following snippet is inserted into the Time Warp executable prior to each store instruction. As a convention in the Sparc architecture[12], registers O0..O5 pass function parameters, and registers I0..I5 hold return values. In this snippet the address of the store is calculated in register O1, and register O0 is loaded with the a pointer to the incremental state save object WISS. This information is utilized by the function that checkpoints the word. 1*, 2*, and 3* are labels utilized by EEL to refer to instructions during customization.

```
     .seg  "text"
          .global call_incr
call_incr:
1*        add %g1, 1, %o1        ! customize with
                                    store address, i_ptr
2*        ld [0x1 + %sp], %o0    ! first arg(reg
                                    o0) points to WISS object
3*        nop                   ! insert call to ISS here
```

Consider the following store instruction to be instrumented:

```
st %o0, [ %l0 + 0x68 ]
```

which stores register O0 at the effective address L0 + 0x68. To customize the above snippet for this store, the machine instruction at 1* is changed to the add instruction

```
add  0x68, %l0, %o1
```

so that register O1 holds the store address. The nop at 3* is changed to a call to the g++ mangled name save_word__15smtw_wissPi which is really int smtw_wiss::save_word(int *i_ptr).

The final snippet as inserted into the executable is:

```
 add  0x68, %l0, %o1
 ld  [ %sp + 0x48 ], %o0
 call  0x4fee8  <save_word__15smtw_wissPi>
```

Since code is inserted at arbitrary points in the executable, we have to be careful not to overwrite any live registers. In the above example, register O0 is live as it holds the value to be stored. It is overwritten by the snippet when it is used to pass the WISS pointer to the save_word function. Therefore it is necessary to save its contents before the snippet and restore them after. The temporary location to store register O0 is created on the execution stack by incrementing the stack pointer. Similarly, the WISS pointer is stored on the stack by incrementing the stack pointer by 8 bytes, and using the location at %sp+0x48. It is restored after the store. Since all stores in an event happen in the same stack context the stack does not change during an event. 16 words (i.e. 0x40 locations) on top of the stack are required by the Sparc architecture [12] to save the register window should an overflow occur.

4.4   Recognizing Writes

It is important to identify instructions that change state and ignore other instructions that do not. Checkpointing extra locations is not only bad for performance, but may be wrong too. Consider automatic variables which are allocated on the stack. Since the stack may not be the same during save and restore, saving that location is a recipe for disaster upon restoration.

Changes to simulation state are easily recognized by looking for store instructions. On the Sparc architecture, a RISC machine, memory is accessed only through load and store instructions. All changes to simulation state are done through store instructions.

However, not all store instructions change simulation state. Stores to automatic variables, and stores to save registers should be ignored for purposes of checkpointing. Loop counters, for example, need not be checkpointed. Such writes are easy to identify and ignore as all writes to them happen as an offset from the stack or frame pointer.

4.5   Other data types

TEMPO has a word (four byte) incremental state saver and AISS was built utilizing those calls. To incrementally state save other types of variables, it is a straightforward extension of the word based incremental state saver. For example, a double, which is 2 words, is compiled to machine instruction STD by gcc where as the Sparcworks compiler compiles it to two ST instructions. An STD to address x is instrumented to call the WISS twice, once at address x and second at address x+4. Floats and longs are one word, and there is no problem saving them as such.

	g++	Sparcworks
int, float	1 ST	1 ST
float	1 STF	1 STF
long long	1 STD, 2 words	2 ST
double	1 STDF, 2 words	2 STF

Table 1: SPARC Store instructions for C data types

The current implementation of our instrumenter has been tested for g++ and the Sparcworks compiler, two of the most popular compilers for Solaris platforms. It has been tested on optimized code as well.

We have tried to avoid any compiler specific design decisions. However, our AISS implementation depends on the compiler because of differing name mangling conventions. To port the AISS implementation to another compiler the new mangled name of the word incremental state saving function is used. This problem could be avoided in general by calling a non-C++ source code function, making the system more portable.

4.6   Function calls and libraries

One strength of executable editing is that functions called from the event handler can be identified and then instrumented for incremental state saving. It is quite easy and convenient then to develop application libraries without worrying about state saving. Executable editing will automatically insert calls to WISS where ever necessary. Functions called recursively from those functions will also be instrumented.

The danger is in over using this technique. These function calls may include system calls (e.g. malloc), library calls (e.g. sin), or Time Warp kernel calls (e.g. send). It is dangerous to instrument operating system calls or Time Warp kernel calls since these variables may not logically be part of the LP. To limit the functions that may be instrumented, several heuristics may be used. One such heuristic could be to limit the call tree by only editing application functions that contain a particular string or by ignoring specific functions that are known to cause problems. Another way of limiting state saving is to specify the bounds of memory from which state is allocated. Only locations inside those boundaries are state saved. The cost would be at runtime, where the effective address of every store is checked for the boundaries before state saving.

4.6   Optimizations

Since checkpointing happens at every store, it is executed frequently, and even small optimizations can have big payoffs. Currently a function call to the WISS function is inserted per store. It is slightly faster to insert the incremental state saving code itself, but it requires a few extra instructions. Since the inserted code refers to ISS data structures and the insertion happens after compilation and linking, those data structures would have to be global in the Time Warp kernel. This is not modular and against good programming practice. The option of inserting function calls is modular and allows us the capability to experiment with different state savers.

The following section describes the performance of our prototype.

5.   Experiments and Results

This section presents results that determine if automatic incremental state saving is fast enough to be practical. Our prototype is compared against other state saving schemes, and against other ISS implementations.

For each type of state saver described below, the overheads are measured. For different amounts of state accessed, the average time taken to process a simulation event is measured. As more state is accessed, the event processing takes longer since the store instructions themselves take time to execute. In incremental state saving, the time per event is proportional to the number of stores. The copy state save time is independent of the number of stores except for a small loop overhead. The point before which it is advantageous to use ISS rather than CSS is determined.

The experiments were conducted on a Sparc-20-514 with four 50 MHz SuperSPARC+ processors, each with 36K of first level and 1 Megabyte of second level cache. The experiments were run on a single processor with no other user load. They are then repeated on four processors to test parallel performance.

For the simulation application, we used the synthetic workload Phold [3] that models a closed queuing network. Servers are modeled as logical processes and jobs as messages. A FIFO queuing discipline is modeled. All our experiments were done with 16 logical processes and 256 messages. A server state size of 1K bytes is chosen because it is small enough to fit in first level cache and causes minimal paging activity. It is also big enough for copy state save overheads to be significant compared to other Time Warp overheads.

5.1   Kernels

Four types of Time Warp kernel with different state saving schemes were compared: no state save, copy state save, incremental state save and automatic ISS.

The first kernel is the simplest, and has no state saving scheme. This kernel is for academic interest only since Time Warp requires some sort of state saving during forward execution, and state restores during rollback. With this kernel we measure all Time Warp overheads other than SS overhead. In the other kernels these overheads are subtracted out to give us the state save overheads.

The second kernel does full copy state saves. A snapshot of the state is taken prior to processing an event. On rollback, state is restored by setting the state pointer to the snapshot at the time of the rollback. The amount of time spent in state saving is linear in state size (ignoring machine dependent effects like paging and caching). Restore on a rollback is fast as only a pointer has to be swapped.

The third kernel does automatic incremental state saves. We expect the overheads to increase with the amount of state saved on each event.

Finally the fourth kernel does incremental saves, but the calls are inserted manually instead of automatically. The inserted code is optimized during compilation and is therefore faster than code automatically inserted into the executable. We would like find out how significant this difference is, since the other ISS methods discussed earlier insert code before or during the compilation phase.

We also investigate the benefits of inlining the incremental state save code, instead of function calls.

5.2   Results

We find that automatic ISS is beneficial if less than 19% of the state is changed (Figure 2). We observe that it takes 0.71 ms to state save one 32 bit word. This is the slope of the Automatic curve in Figure 2. Out of this 0.18 ms per word, the slope of No-SS line, is required for loop overheads and for the write itself. Subtracting the two gives us an overhead of about 0.51 ms to state save one word in our kernel. We measure copy state saving overheads to be about 0.10 ms/word, or a copy rate of 38 MBytes/second.

Inlining the ISS function allows ISS to be used when less than 20% of the state is changed, slightly more than the 15% we get from function calls.

Method	Break even	Per word SS
AISS	15 %	0.51 ms
AISS Inlined	20 %	0.47 ms
Manual ISS	25 %	0.42 ms
Manual ISS Inlined	32 %	0.31 ms

Table 2: Summary of our results.

The manually inserted incremental state saver brings the ISS/CSS break even point to 25%, and saving one word overhead to 0.42 ms. The difference in the manually inserted code is better register usage due to compiler optimization. For automatic insertion, registers that are modified in the inserted snippet have to be saved and restored. The inserted snippet has seams of save and restore around it. On the other hand if the code is manually inserted and run through the compiler, the register allocator in the compiler is aware of the calls to incremental state saving, and the ISS code is seamlessly integrated.

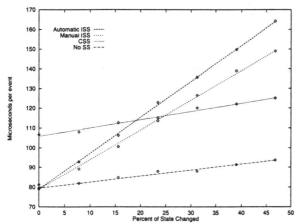

Figure 2: Event execution times with amount of state changed per event.

Inlining the manually inserted ISS code will increase the break even point to number to about 32%. Each store then takes about 0.31 µs. The savings come from one less function call, and better optimization, since the optimizer now has a chance to optimize the inserted code in the context of the event handler.

Similar per word saving costs and break-even points were observed for a state size of 2K. We checked the multiprocessor performance, and it is similar.

5.3 Comparison with previously reported results

Comparing our results with other implementations of ISS reported in [2] we find that our state saver performs comparably with other implementations. Of course our implementation has the aforementioned advantages of being fully automatic, compiler and library independent. A higher copy state time is reported in [2], which is more favorable relative to ISS. Consequently the reported break even points are higher. In addition since the ISS inserts in [2] are done before compile time they have the benefit of compiler optimization.

ISS Time	0.60 µs/word	0.53 µs/word
CSS Time	0.21 µs/word	0.10 µs/word
Break-even	35-55 %	20-35 %

Table 3: Comparison with a manual implementation.

6. Further Work

The difference in performance between our technique and manually inserted ISS calls is due to compiler optimization and better register usage. We want to find a way to run the optimizer over the inserted code to remove redundant register saves or in some other way reduce the overhead of the inserted code. Changes to the overhead of the ISS will improve the break-even point with respect to copy state saving and allow the efficient use of AISS in a wider envelope of applications.

We are in the process of measuring the performance of AISS on existing legacy simulations.

Executable editing combined with state saving is a powerful idea. This paper presents one application, i.e., Time Warp systems, but other uses can be thought of. This idea can be applied wherever state is saved, in transaction processing systems, source level debuggers, and editors. For debuggers one could imagine a system where a defect was detected using standard debugging techniques, but then having the ability to back step the execution of the defective process to see its state prior to the detected defect. For performance reasons it may not be possible to reconstruct the register values, as they change so frequently that even incrementally saving them might be too expensive, but all the memory locations could be thus tracked. State saving techniques have also been used in rollback recovery for distributed fault tolerance[19,20,21]. AISS may be used to automatically detect and log writes at a fine granularity.

7. Conclusion

The use of incremental state saving allows smaller granularity applications to be able to state save their variables and still obtain speedup in Time Warp. Traditionally this has required manual intervention. Automatic incremental state saving removes that requirement, while also allowing the use of third party libraries that novel compiler based techniques cannot address. We have shown that the performance of AISS is less than manual techniques, but still address a wide range of computational granularities in Time Warp. AISS also shows promise in other application areas, namely reversible debuggers, and distributed fault tolerance.

8.   Acknowledgment

This work was supported by Internal Research and Development funds at Science Applications International Corporation

9.   References

[1] C. D. Carothers, R. M. Fujimoto, Y-B. Lin, and P. England. Distributed simulation of large-scale pcs networks. In *Proceedings of the 1994 MASCOTS Conference*, January 1994.

[2] J. Cleary, F. Gomes, B. Unger, X. Zhonge, and R. Thudt. Cost of state saving and rollback. In *Proceedings of the 8th Workshop on Parallel and Distributed Simulation*, pages 94--101, 1994.

[3] R. M. Fujimoto. Time Warp on a shared memory multiprocessor. *Transactions of the Society for Computer Simulation* 6(3):211--239, July 1989.

[4] R. M. Fujimoto. Parallel discrete event simulation: Will the field survive? ORSA *Journal on Computing*, (3):213--230, summer 1993.

[5] R. M. Fujimoto, J. Tsai, and G. Gopalakrishnan. Design and performance of special purpose hardware for Time Warp. *Proceedings of the 15th Annual Symposium on Computer Architecture*, pages 401--408, June 1988.

[6] E. Gelenbe. On the optimum checkpoint interval. *Journal of the ACM*, 26(4):259--270, April 1979.

[7] Fabian Gomes. State saving and restoration experiments. http://bungee.cpsc.ucalgary.ca/GOMES/expts.html.

[8] D. R. Jefferson. Virtual time. ACM *Transactions on Programming Languages and Systems*, 7(3):404--425, July 1985.

[9] James R. Larus and Eric Schnarr. EEL: Machine-independent executable editing. *SIGPLAN Conference on Programming Language Design and Implementation*, June 1995.

[10] Y-B. Lin, B. R. Preiss, W. M. Loucks, and E. D. Lazowska. Selecting the checkpoint interval in Time Warp simulation. In *Proceedings of the 7th Workshop on Parallel and Distributed Simulation*, pages 3--10, May 1993.

[11] Baezner, D., Lomow,G., Unger, B. "Sim++: the Transition to Distributed Simulation," Proc. SCS Multiconference on Distributed Simulation, San Diego, California, January, 1990.

[12] Sparc International. The SPARC Architecture Manual, 1992. Version 8.

[13] Brian W. Unger, John G. Cleary, Alan Covington, and Darrin West. External state management system for optimistic parallel simulation. Winter *Simulation Conference Proceedings*, pages 750--755, 1993.

[14] James R. Larus, *Efficient Program Tracing*, IEEE Computer, 26(5):52-61, May 1993

[15] James R. Larus Wisconsin Architectural Research Tool Set. http://www.cs.wisc.edu/~larus/warts.html

[16] Jeff Steinman. Incremental State Saving in SPEEDES using C plus plus. *Winter Simulation Conference Proceedings*, pages 687-696, 1993

[17] Avinash C. Palaniswamy and Philip A. Wilsey. Analytical Comparison of periodic checkpointing and incremental state saving. *Proceedings of the 7 Workshop on Parallel and Distributed Simulation*, pages 127-134, 1993

[18] Pure Software Inc. HomePage. http://www.mwl.com/pure/

[19] B. Randell System Structure for software fault tolerance. *IEEE Transcations on Software Engineering* 1(2):220-232, June 1975.

[20] D. L. Russel State restoration in systems of communicating processes. *IEEE Transcations of Software Engineering*, 6(2):183-194, March 1980.

[21] R. Koo and S. Toueg. Checkpoint and rollback recovery for distributed systems. IEEE Transcations on Software Engineering,13(1):23-31, January 1987.

Author's Biographies

DARRIN WEST is a senior computer scientist with SAIC. He received his M.Sc. degree from the University of Calgary. His research interests include parallel simulation and distributed systems. Mr. West is currently principal investigator for the SAIC Tempo internal R&D program, and is a lead architect for the ARPA Synthetic Theater of War program.

Kiran Panesar is a PhD student at Georgia Institute of Technology. His research interests include high performance discrete event simulation, computer architecture, and operating systems. He received his MS degree from University of Maryland in 1991 and BE from University of Roorkee in 1989.

Reducing Synchronization Overhead in Parallel Simulation

Ulana Legedza *   William E. Weihl *

Large-Scale Parallel Software Group
MIT Laboratory for Computer Science
Cambridge, MA 02139

Abstract

Synchronization is often the dominant cost in conservative parallel simulation, particularly in simulations of parallel computers, in which low-latency simulated communication requires frequent synchronization. We present and evaluate **local barriers** and **predictive barrier scheduling**, two techniques for reducing synchronization overhead in the simulation of message-passing multicomputers. Local barriers use nearest-neighbor synchronization to reduce waiting time at synchronization points. Predictive barrier scheduling, a novel technique that schedules synchronizations using both compile-time and runtime analysis, reduces the frequency of synchronization operations. In contrast to other work in this area, both techniques reduce synchronization overhead without decreasing the accuracy of network simulation. These techniques were evaluated by comparing their performance to that of periodic global synchronization. Experiments show that local barriers improve performance by up to 24% for communication-bound applications, while predictive barrier scheduling improves performance by up to 65% for applications with long local computation phases. Because the two techniques are complementary, we advocate a combined approach. This work was done in the context of **Parallel Proteus**, a new parallel simulator of message-passing multicomputers.

1 Introduction

Software simulators are used in parallel computing for architecture design and application development. They are necessary because hardware prototypes of parallel computer architectures are time-consuming to build and difficult to modify. While sequential simulators have traditionally been used for this purpose, they tend to be slow and inadequate for detailed simulation of large systems. Consequently, parallelism is often used in an attempt to speed up simulations, as well as to accommodate the large memory requirements of simulated applications. Despite its benefits, parallel simulation introduces the need to periodically synchronize the simulating processors, for correctness. This synchronization introduces overhead that often dominates simulator execution time.

Synchronization is a particular problem in multicomputer simulators because accurate simulation of the fast networks found in parallel systems requires frequent synchronization. Less frequent synchronization leads to less accurate simulation, which is often undesirable. For example, accuracy is needed when modeling network contention, which, in turn, is useful in algorithm development. Also, accuracy in network simulation is necessary for testing and evaluating a network or network interface.

This paper describes *local barriers* and *predictive barrier scheduling*, two techniques for reducing synchronization overhead in simulations of message-passing multicomputers. Local barriers use nearest-neighbor synchronization to reduce waiting time at synchronization points. Predictive barrier scheduling, a novel technique that schedules synchronizations using both compile-time and runtime analysis, reduces the frequency of synchronization operations. Both techniques reduce synchronization overhead without decreasing network simulation accuracy.

We implemented local barriers and predictive barrier scheduling as part of Parallel Proteus, an execution-driven conservative parallel discrete-event simulator of message-passing multicomputers that is based on Proteus [6]. Experiments with Parallel Proteus on a CM-5 show that local barriers are effective at reducing overhead in simulations involving frequent communication, while predictive barrier scheduling is most effective for simulations in which communication is infrequent. Because the two approaches are complementary, we advocate a hybrid adaptive approach that dynamically chooses between the two techniques.

The following section provides background information on the types of multicomputers we are interested in simulating and on parallel simulation in general. Later sections discuss the problem of synchronization overhead in more detail, present and evaluate the local barrier and predictive barrier scheduling techniques, and discuss related work.

2 Background

This section describes the types of machines we want to simulate (the *target* architecture), overviews parallel simulation concepts and terminology, and explains the need for synchronization.

2.1 Target Architecture

Our research focuses on the simulation of large-scale, message-passing MIMD multiprocessors made up of independent processor nodes connected by an interconnection network (see Figure 1). The network consists of wires and switches. Each processor runs one or more application threads which communicate with threads on other processors via messages. When a message travels through the network, it incurs a network delay proportional to the number of links (hops) traversed, plus any additional delay caused by channel contention. We want to simulate the network accurately enough so as to reflect the additional network delay caused by network contention (hot spots). This entails simulating the progress of each packet through the interconnection network hop by hop.

2.2 Definitions

Our research deals with *parallel discrete event simulation* (PDES). This model assumes that the *entities* making up the simulated system change state only as a result of discrete, timestamped *events*. An event's timestamp corresponds to the time at which it

*E-mail: ulana@mit.edu, weihl@pa.dec.com. Prof. Weihl has moved to Digital's Systems Research Center and is no longer at MIT. Ulana Legedza was supported by a National Science Foundation Graduate Fellowship. This research was also supported by the Advanced Research Projects Agency under Contract N00014-94-1-0985, by grants from IBM and AT&T, and by an equipment grant from DEC.

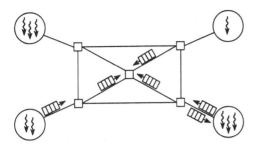

Figure 1: **Target Architecture.** Circles denote processor nodes running application threads. Squares are network switches.

occurs in the simulated system (*simulated time*). Each of a parallel simulator's *host processors* simulates one or more entities by processing relevant events in non-decreasing timestamp order.

A host processor is at simulated time t when it is about to process an event with timestamp t. Because of communication between components of the simulated system, host processors can generate events that need to be executed by other host processors. These events are transferred from one host processor to another via timestamped *event transfer messages*.

In Parallel Proteus, each target processor and network switch is an entity. Each host (CM-5) processor simulates one or more target processors or switches by maintaining a queue containing events of the following types: thread execution, message send/receive, and packet routing. When one target processor or switch sends a message to another, the host processor simulating the first processor or switch sends an event to the host processor simulating the second.

2.3 Synchronization

The chief difficulty in PDES is handling causality errors, which occur when event transfer messages arrive late. For example, one host processor can simulate a processor that sends a message at simulated time t to another target processor (simulated by a second host processor). If, in the simulated system, this message is scheduled to arrive at the destination target processor at time $t + q$, an event with timestamp $t + q$ is sent from the first host processor to the second. A causality error occurs if simulated time on the second host processor has exceeded $t + q$ when it receives this event.

Our work focuses on conservative PDES, in which synchronization is used to avoid causality errors. Proper synchronization ensures that when a host processor processes an event with timestamp t, it will never receive an event with timestamp smaller than t from another host processor.

How often synchronization is needed depends on the simulated system. If the minimum time for a message to travel between two simulated entities A and B is equal to q cycles, then the two host processors simulating them (X and Y, respectively), must synchronize at least every q cycles of simulated time. Thus, the simulated time on X will always stay within q cycles of simulated time on Y and no causality errors will occur. The minimum value of q for the entire system is called the *synchronization time quantum Q*. In the case of multiprocessor target architectures, the synchronization time quantum Q is equal to the minimum delay incurred by a message traveling between any two target processor nodes or network switches. (The term *quantum* also signifies the period of time

between synchronizations during which simulation work is done).

The simplest way to perform the necessary synchronization is to execute a global barrier every Q simulated cycles. We refer to this technique as **periodic global barriers**. Hardware support for global synchronization (such as on the CM-5 or Cray T3D) makes each global barrier relatively efficient and easy to implement. However, simulator performance suffers if the barriers must be performed very frequently, or if load imbalance causes long waiting times at synchronization points.

3 Performance Issues

While the primary goal of using parallelism in simulation is to improve performance, synchronization overhead can limit speedup. Synchronization overhead depends on four factors: frequency, duration, level of detail and number of simulated entities. The frequency of synchronizations is controlled by the synchronization time quantum Q. The duration of a synchronization depends on the time it takes to execute the synchronization operation and on the time spent waiting at the synchronization point. Clearly, the lengthier and/or more frequent the synchronizations, the larger the synchronization overhead. However, in very detailed simulations, simulation work outweighs synchronization overhead, even if the synchronizations are very frequent. The same happens in simulations of large target systems, where each host processor is responsible for a large number of entities. Because more work is done between synchronizations, the synchronization overhead is amortized over many target processors.

In simulators of parallel computers with fast networks, accurate network simulation usually requires the value of Q to be very small and, consequently, synchronization to be very frequent. Low overhead techniques for simulating the behavior of each target processor (direct execution as in Proteus and Tango [14] or threaded code [3]) cause synchronization overhead to outweigh the time spent doing simulation work. Large memory requirements (for simulator state or application data) for each target processor prevent the simulation of a large number of target processors by each host processor. Consequently, synchronization overhead dominates simulation time.

For the target architectures we consider, Q equals 2 cycles of simulated time. This is due to the 2-cycle minimum delay through each hop of the target network (1 cycle for wire delay, 1 cycle for switch delay). With such a small Q, we were not surprised to find that, in our experiments with Parallel Proteus (using periodic global barriers), synchronization overhead accounts for 70% to 90% of total simulation runtime and, therefore, severely limits speedup. In some simulations, the high synchronization overhead was also due to long waiting times at synchronization points. Some researchers have explored methods of reducing synchronization overhead by decreasing target network simulation accuracy. (This increases Q, decreasing synchronization frequency). Because decreasing accuracy is not always desirable, our work focuses on reducing synchronization overhead while maintaining a high degree of accuracy in network simulation. The local barrier and predictive barrier scheduling techniques described in the following two sections accomplish this goal.

4 Local Barriers

Long waiting times at barrier synchronizations are a chief component of the problematic synchronization overhead. They are caused by load imbalance during a quantum. The local barrier approach, like the local synchronization techniques commonly used in scientific computing and in other types of PDES, reduces waiting time by reducing the number of other processors for which each host processor must wait at each synchronization point. This section describes the local barrier technique and explains how it was implemented on the CM-5 for Parallel Proteus.

4.1 Technique

In most simulations, a host processor must keep within Q cycles of the simulated time of only several other processors - its *nearest neighbors*. The nearest neighbors of host processor X are those host processors that simulate entities that, in the simulated system, are directly connected to any of the entities simulated on processor X. In a local barrier, each host processor participates in a barrier synchronization with these nearest neighbors. Once a host processor and its nearest neighbors have reached the barrier, the host processor can move on to simulate the next quantum[1]. However, its nearest neighbors may still be left waiting for their own nearest neighbors to reach the synchronization point. Therefore, some host processors may be done with a local barrier while others are still waiting.

Loosely synchronizing the processors in this way (as opposed to keeping them tightly synchronized as in periodic global barriers) shortens barrier waiting times when the simulation work is not equally distributed among the host processors during a quantum. Only a few processors wait for each slow (heavily loaded) processor. Therefore, unless the same processor is heavily loaded during every quantum, the simulation is not forced to be as slow as the most heavily loaded processor in each quantum. Instead, some lightly loaded processors are allowed to go ahead to the next quantum while heavily loaded processors are still working on the previous quantum; the heavily loaded processors will catch up in a future quantum when they have less simulation work to do.

While this technique alleviates the problem of waiting, it introduces a new problem of software and communication overhead involved in performing local barriers in the absence of hardware support.

4.2 Implementation

In Parallel Proteus, the nearest neighbors of each host processor are determined at the beginning of each simulation. Each host processor, using information about the target network, determines which target processors and network switches are adjacent (one hop away on the simulated network) to the target processors and switches it is responsible for simulating. The host processors that are responsible for simulating these adjacent target processors and switches are the nearest neighbors.

As in the periodic global barrier technique, host processors synchronize every Q cycles. Between synchronizations, each host processor keeps track of how many event transfer messages it sends to (and how many it receives from) each of its nearest neighbors during the current quantum. Upon reaching a barrier, a host processor X sends to each of its nearest neighbors Y_i a count of the event messages that were sent from X to Y_i in the previous quantum. Processor X then waits until it receives similar information from each of its nearest neighbors. It polls the network until it receives and enqueues all of the incoming events it was told to expect, then goes on to simulate the next quantum.

In this approach, a processor may receive event transfer messages generated in the next quantum while still waiting on some from the

---

[1] A processor's nearest neighbors are not necessarily the processors closest to it on the host machine; they depend on the system being simulated and its layout on the host machine.

last quantum. In order to distinguish event messages from different quanta, successive quanta are labeled RED and BLACK and each event transfer message is sent with a quantum identifier (RED or BLACK). Since two nearest neighbors are never more than one quantum apart, only two distinct identifiers are needed.

5 Predictive Barrier Scheduling

In contrast to the local barrier technique, predictive barrier scheduling improves performance by reducing the frequency of synchronizations rather than by making each synchronization faster. Predictive barrier scheduling takes advantage of the fact that, during periods of the simulation when the simulated entities do not communicate, synchronization is not necessary. It is only necessary to synchronize when communication is taking place, to make sure it is simulated correctly. Therefore, performance may be improved by eliminating the unnecessary periodic synchronizations performed during computation phases. Predictive barrier scheduling accomplishes this by predicting when communication is going to occur in the target system and scheduling synchronizations only during communication phases.

In effect improving the lookahead [13] of simulations, this approach seems especially promising for applications with long local computation phases. The following sections overview the general structure of predictive barrier scheduling and describe in detail the compile-time and runtime prediction mechanisms it uses.

5.1 Overview

While synchronizations are scheduled statically in periodic global barriers (every Q simulated cycles), synchronizations in predictive barrier scheduling are scheduled dynamically, at runtime, based on the current communication behavior in the target system. Synchronizations are scheduled to occur frequently during communication phases, and infrequently during computation phases. The main simulator loop, executed by each host processor i, shows how this policy is implemented:

```
WHILE (NOT DONE)
    Synchronize; /* global barrier */
    s_i = local minimum time of next
        communication operation;
    S = GLOBAL_MIN(s_i);

    Simulate each target processor & network switch
        up to simulated time S;
END.
```

After each global synchronization (which ensures that all host processors are at the same simulated time and that all pending event transfer messages have been received), the host processors agree on a time at which to perform the next synchronization. Each host processor first determines the earliest time that any of its entities will next communicate. In order to calculate this s_i, each host processor examines the state of each of its entities, i.e. processing nodes and network switches. If a network switch has a packet in a buffer or on incoming or outgoing wires, then it will be communicating soon, otherwise not. Predicting when target processor nodes will communicate is more difficult, since the application threads they run may send messages at any time. Predictive barrier scheduling uses a combination of compile-time and runtime analysis to predict when application threads will communicate. These are described in the next two sections.

88

Once each host processor has determined s_i, computing S, the minimum time at which any target entity next issues a communication operation, is straightforward. Each host processor contributes its s_i to a global minimum reduction operation. Then, since all processors are certain that no event transfer messages will be generated until simulated time S, they go ahead to simulate each of their entities up to simulated time S. (The global synchronization and global minimum cannot be combined into a single global operation because all pending event transfer messages must be received before computing each s_i).

5.2 Runtime Analysis

The future behavior of an application thread can easily be determined by simply allowing the thread to execute further and observing its actions. Doing this without advancing the simulation time clock provides a very accurate mechanism for predicting how long threads will run before communicating. It can be used by host processors at runtime to determine when application threads will communicate and to schedule synchronizations accordingly. For example, if, at time t, all application threads are allowed to run ahead, and none communicate for 500 cycles, then the host processors know that synchronization is not needed until $t + 500$. With the help of the Proteus simulator quantum mechanism, predictive barrier scheduling runtime analysis predicts the future communication of threads in just this manner.

Like Proteus, Parallel Proteus simulates a thread executing on a simulated processor at time t by allowing the thread to execute up to 1000 *local* instructions[2] at once without interruption. This 1000 cycle limit is called the *simulator quantum*. While this technique allows target processors to drift apart in time by more than the value of the synchronization time quantum Q, it does not necessarily introduce any inaccuracy into the simulation.[3] The reason is that local instructions can be performed at any time and in any order as long as non-local operations are performed at the correct time and in the correct order. To ensure the correct timing and ordering of non-local operations, a thread is interrupted as soon as it encounters a non-local operation. Control then returns to the simulator and the non-local operation is delayed until the simulator has processed all earlier non-local events. This technique allows the simulator to achieve good performance without sacrificing accuracy (see appendix A in [17]).

Predictive barrier scheduling uses the 1000-cycle window into the future provided by the simulator quantum mechanism to determine the future communication behavior of application threads. If, at time t, all application threads simulated by host processor i have executed 1000 cycles into the future without hitting a non-local or communication operation (and the network switches it simulates have no pending messages), then $s_i = t + 1000$, because the host processor knows that none of its entities will communicate before $t + 1000$.

---

[2]Local instructions are those that affect only data local to the target processor on which they are executed. Non-local operations are those that potentially interact with other parts of the simulated system. Examples of non-local operations are message sends, checks for interrupts, and access to data shared by application threads and message handlers. Synchronization variables are an example of such shared data. Special routines simulate the functionality and concomitant cost of non-local operations.

[3]Actually, the 1000 cycle simulator quantum *does* produce inaccuracy in sequential Proteus, but this has been fixed in Parallel Proteus [17].

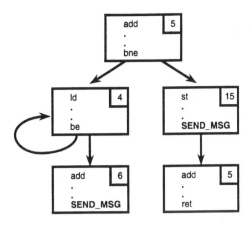

Figure 2: **Example basic block graph.**

5.3 Compile-time Analysis

Because the predictive barrier scheduling runtime analysis involves stopping at communication operations, those host processors simulating frequently-communicating threads will have less work to do at some synchronization points than those simulating threads that communicate infrequently. In order to keep the runtime analysis workload reasonably balanced among host processors, a limit is placed (1000 cycles) on the amount of time a thread is allowed to run ahead. Therefore, while runtime analysis is a powerful prediction mechanism, it cannot be used to look arbitrarily far into the future. For this reason, predictive barrier scheduling augments the prediction power of the runtime analysis with information generated at compile-time.

Dataflow analysis of the application code is done at compile-time to determine the minimum distance (in cycles) to a non-local or communication operation from each point in the application code. Then, the code is instrumented with instructions which make these minimum distances accessible to the simulator at runtime. When the application thread is executing, the code added in the instrumentation phase updates a variable which holds the value of the current minimum time (in simulated cycles) until the thread executes a non-local instruction. When computing s_i, each host processor i examines these variables (one for each thread) in order to increase the prediction values generated by the runtime analysis.

5.3.1 Dataflow Analysis

At compile-time, a basic block (control flow) graph of the application code to be simulated is constructed, and dataflow analysis is performed on it. Each basic block consists of a sequence of local, non-branching instructions followed by a branch instruction or a procedure call. Each basic block is labeled with its execution length in cycles, and has one or two pointers leaving it which indicate where control flows after leaving the block (see Figure 2). This graph is used to calculate a conservative estimate of the minimum distance (in cycles) to a non-local operation from the beginning of each basic block. (In Parallel Proteus, threads are never interrupted in the middle of basic blocks; therefore, estimates are only needed for the beginning of basic blocks). Because we did not implement inter-procedural analysis, every procedure call is assumed to lead to a non-local operation.

```
FOREACH basic block B in graph
    estimate(B) = sizeof(B)
ENDFOR
DO
    change = false
    FOREACH basic block B in graph
        old_estimate = estimate(B)
        IF (B ends in procedure call)
            THEN estimate(B) = sizeof(B)
        ELSE IF (B has 1 successor)
            THEN estimate(B) = sizeof(B) +
                                estimate(successor(B))
        ELSE estimate(B) = sizeof(B) +
                        MIN (estimate(left_succ(B)),
                                estimate(right_succ(B)))
        IF (estimate(B) != old_estimate)
            THEN change = TRUE
    ENDFOR
UNTIL change == false
```

Figure 3: **Iterative Dataflow Analysis.**

All communication operations are found at the end of basic blocks. Therefore, a first estimate of the minimum distance from the beginning of a basic block to a non-local operation is the size of the basic block. If the block ends with a procedure call (which is either a non-local operation or assumed to immediately lead to one), then the estimate is done. However, if the block ends with a branch statement (a *local* operation), the following is added to its current estimate: the estimate for the basic block following it or, if it ends in a conditional branch, the minimum of the two estimates for the two blocks following the first block. The minimum distances to non-local operations for all the basic blocks in the graph are computed iteratively using the algorithm of Figure 3 (based on algorithm 10.2 in [2]).

5.3.2 Code Instrumentation

After the minimum distance to non-local operation has been determined for each block, each block is instrumented with code that records this value. When a thread gets interrupted or makes a procedure call which causes control to go back to the simulator, the thread's minimum time until non-local operation can be accessed in the variable where it was stored immediately before the thread was suspended. This value is used by the host processor when calculating s_i.

5.4 Summary

In predictive barrier scheduling, compile-time analysis is used to instrument code with instructions which store information about each thread's future communication behavior. At runtime, this information is combined with runtime analysis to generate an estimate of how long each thread will run before next communicating. During each barrier synchronization, each host processor uses this estimate, along with information about the state of the network switches it is simulating, to determine the minimum time until any one of its entities next communicates. Each processor contributes its local minimum to a global minimum operation to determine a global lower bound on the time any entity will next communicate; the next barrier synchronization is scheduled for this time.

This technique adds some overhead to each synchronization operation. The hope is that it will eliminate so many of the synchronization operations that it will improve performance over periodic global barriers even with a higher overhead cost per synchronization. It will clearly be most beneficial for simulations of applications that have local computation phases of considerable length.

6 Experiments

We incorporated local barriers and predictive barrier scheduling into Parallel Proteus and compared their performance with that of periodic global barriers. This section describes the experiments performed, and presents and discusses performance results.

6.1 Target Architecture

We simulated two dimensional mesh architectures with 16 to 1024 processor nodes and switches. Packets are routed through the network using virtual cut-through routing with infinite buffers.

6.2 Applications

The applications considered in this study are *SOR* (successive over-relaxation) and parallel *radix* sort. *SOR* was chosen to represent parallel applications with very regular communication patterns and long computation phases. In contrast, *radix* represents applications in which communication is more frequent and irregular. By varying parameters of both applications, we were able to experiment with a wide range of computation-to-communication ratios.

6.2.1 SOR

SOR is a stencil computation that iteratively solves PDE's [4]. Each iteration of the algorithm performs a relaxation function on a grid of points. This function requires only the value of the point to be updated and the values of adjacent points. Subblocks of this grid are distributed among the processors of the parallel machine. During each iteration, each processor performs the relaxation function on the grid points assigned to it and communicates with a fixed set of grid neighbors to obtain border values.

We used grid sizes of 2^{11} to 2^{20} entries, and up to 625 target processors. This application alternates between communication phases and long computation phases.

6.2.2 Radix Sort

Parallel radix sort sorts d-digit radix r numbers in d passes of counting sort [5]. The numbers to be sorted are distributed evenly among the processors. Each pass consists of 3 phases: counting, scanning and routing. The counting phase involves local computation only. The scanning phase consists of r parallel prefix scans. In the routing phase, each processor sends its data points to new locations.

This application has a short local computation phase in the count phase, and much communication in the scanning and routing phases. We used 2-digit radix-64 numbers, requiring 2 passes and 64 scans per pass. 8192 numbers were assigned to each target processor and 64 to 1024 processors were simulated.

6.3 Experimental Methodology

We ran Parallel Proteus on a 32-node CM-5 partition. Each CM-5 node is a 33 MHz Sparc processor with 32 megabytes of RAM and no virtual memory. In order to get accurate timings and decrease variability, experiments were run in "dedicated" mode. This means that timesharing is turned off, and each application runs to completion without being interrupted to run other applications.

The only source of variability, therefore, is in the routing of messages through the host network. In practice, this variability was very small. The data presented are averages ($\overline{X}$) of three timings, with $\sigma/\overline{X} \leq 4\%$.

6.4 Predictive Barrier Scheduling

We evaluated predictive barrier scheduling against the baseline periodic global barrier approach by examining three criteria: overhead, percentage of barriers eliminated, and overall performance improvement.

As expected, experiments show that predictive barrier scheduling with both runtime and compile-time analysis always performs better than runtime analysis alone. However, the runtime analysis is in fact responsible for the overwhelming majority of the barriers eliminated. The compile-time analysis improves upon runtime analysis alone by eliminating an additional 4% to 26% of the barriers executed under the baseline periodic global barrier approach. We focus on the results for the complete predictive barrier scheduling approach.

6.4.1 Overhead

Predictive barrier scheduling adds overhead in four areas:

- compilation,
- application code execution,
- barrier scheduling, and
- barrier waiting time.

Some overhead is incurred at compile-time to perform dataflow analysis. This overhead is negligible in our implementation, because the necessary data structures are constructed and provided by the program that adds cycle-counting instructions to the application code.

During code instrumentation, predictive barrier scheduling adds 6 instructions to each basic block of the application, but only a small percent of total runtime is spent executing them. Their overhead is negligible compared to synchronization overhead, which accounts for 80% of simulation time.

During each barrier synchronization, host processors schedule the next barrier. This entails 5 to 50 cycles of additional work, and an additional global reduction operation (150 cycles, 4.5 microseconds).

As a result of less frequent synchronization, more simulation work is done between barriers, and load imbalance during quanta increases. This lengthens each barrier by increasing waiting times. In our experiments, each barrier (typically 20 to 600 microseconds long) becomes 20% to 1400% longer. The less frequent the synchronizations, the longer they are.

6.4.2 Barriers eliminated

The purpose of predictive barrier scheduling is to eliminate unnecessary barriers which occur during computation phases. Our experiments show that this method does, in fact, reduce the number of barriers executed by 12% to 95%. As expected, the number of barriers eliminated is greater in the simulation of applications with long periods of local computation between communication phases. To illustrate this feature, we graph the number of barriers executed versus *granularity*. Granularity is a measure of the length of local phases of computation relative to the length of communication phases. Applications with large granularity have long local computation phases. Those with small granularity are dominated by communication and short computation phases.

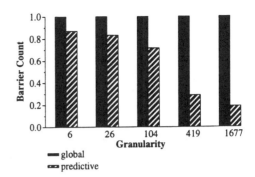

Figure 4: **Normalized barrier count for PBS and PGB**. *SOR*, 625 target processors, 32 host nodes, varying grid size.

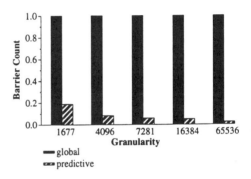

Figure 5: **Normalized barrier count for PBS and PGB**. *SOR*, 1024 x 1024 grid size, 32 host nodes, varying number of target processors.

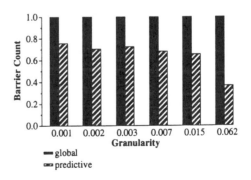

Figure 6: **Normalized barrier count for PBS and PGB**. *Radix*, 8192 numbers per target processor, 32 host nodes, varying number of target processors.

Granularity is computed differently for each application because the length of local computation phases depends on application-specific parameters. We define granularity for *SOR* to be equal to the number of data points assigned to each target processor. In *radix*, granularity is defined to be equal to the inverse of the number of target processors. Figures 4, 5, and 6 show that for both *SOR* and *radix*, the number of barriers eliminated increases with granularity. In general, *radix* has shorter computation phases than *SOR*, so fewer barriers are eliminated in *radix* than in *SOR*.

6.4.3 Performance Improvement

The performance improvement achieved by predictive barrier scheduling over the periodic global barrier approach ranges from −5% to +65%. Because predictive barrier scheduling lengthens each barrier, no improvement is seen when few barriers are eliminated. In general, about 30-40% of the barriers (otherwise executed under the periodic global barrier approach) have to be eliminated in order to improve performance. As we expected, performance improvement increases with granularity, just as demonstrated in the previous section. This is evident in the graphs of normalized simulator runtime for *SOR* and *radix*, figures 7, 8, and 9. Little improvement (only up to 10%) is seen in *radix* because its computation phases are short. *SOR* with large data sizes has large granularity and, therefore, achieves large performance improvements (up to 65%). Clearly, the predictive barrier scheduling method is only useful for applications with reasonably long local computation phases.

6.5 Local Barriers

The purpose of the local barrier approach is to improve the performance of simulators like Parallel Proteus by reducing the waiting time at synchronization points. Results show that this approach is most effective in simulations of applications with small granularity.

6.5.1 Overhead

The local barrier approach adds overhead to each synchronization because it requires each host processor to send, receive, and await the individual messages of each of its nearest neighbors. In contrast to hardware-supported global barriers, there is no hardware support on the CM-5 for the pairwise synchronizations required for local barriers. In the best case, when all processors are already synchronized, a global barrier (on the CM-5) takes 150 cycles (4.5 microseconds). Under the same conditions, a local barrier takes anywhere from 800 to 1300 cycles (24 to 39 microseconds), depending on the number of nearest neighbors each host processor has. Because of this high overhead, the local barrier method is expected to do better only when the periodic global barrier approach has long waiting times at each synchronization. In that case, local barriers improve performance by decreasing the waiting times.

6.5.2 Performance Improvement

As expected, experiments show that the local barrier approach improves performance by decreasing barrier waiting time in situations where the periodic global barrier approach suffers from long waiting times. This occurs in applications of small granularity, where communication is frequent and computation phases are short. In large granularity applications, on the other hand, Parallel Proteus (using periodic global barriers) executes the long computation phases 1000 cycles at a time (because of the simulator quantum approach, described in 5.2). This leads to the execution of many unnecessary barriers in a row, with no simulation work in between. The waiting time at most of the barriers, then, is very short.

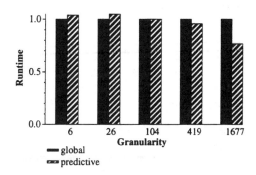

Figure 7: **Normalized simulator runtime for PBS and PGB.** *SOR*, 625 target processors, 32 host nodes, varying grid size.

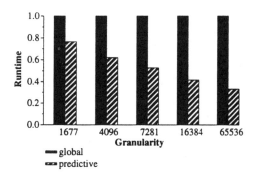

Figure 8: **Normalized simulator runtime for PBS and PGB.** *SOR*, 1024 x 1024 grid size, 32 host nodes, varying number of target processors.

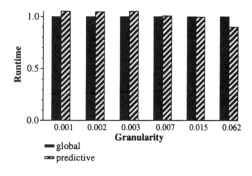

Figure 9: **Normalized simulator runtime for PBS and PGB.** *Radix*, 8192 numbers per target processors, 32 host nodes, varying number of target processors.

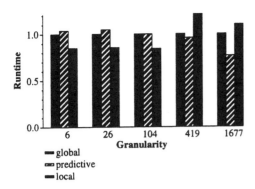

- global
- predictive
- local

Figure 10: **Normalized simulator runtime for LB, PBS and PGB.** *SOR*, 625 target processors, 32 host nodes, varying grid size.

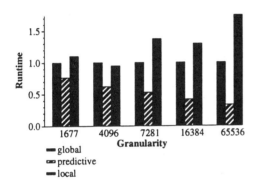

- global
- predictive
- local

Figure 11: **Normalized simulator runtime for LB, PBS and PGB.** *SOR*, 1024 x 1024 grid size, 32 host nodes, varying number of target processors.

Local barriers shorten synchronizations in small granularity applications by up to 25%. In large granularity applications where barriers are already short, the local barrier approach lengthens barrier time by up to 192%.

Graphs of normalized simulator runtime (figures 10, 11, and 12) show that the behavior of the local barrier approach complements that of predictive barrier scheduling. Predictive barrier scheduling improves performance for applications with large granularity, while local barriers improve performance for applications with small granularity. Local barriers improve performance most in *radix* (up to 24%) and in small granularity *SOR*.

6.6 Discussion

The complementary relationship between predictive barrier scheduling and the local barrier approach suggests that one might combine the two techniques to achieve more consistent performance improvement. One way to do this is to use each technique in the situation where it does better: the local barrier approach during communication phases and predictive barrier scheduling during computation phases. In this way, unnecessary barriers in the computation phases will be eliminated by predictive barrier scheduling. However, the extra overhead required will not be incurred in the communication phases. For its part, the local barrier approach will shorten the

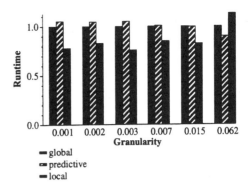

- global
- predictive
- local

Figure 12: **Normalized simulator runtime for LB, PBS and PGB.** *Radix*, 8192 numbers per target processor, 32 host nodes, varying number of target processors.

waiting times in communication phases.

The difficulty lies in determining when to switch from one technique to the other. One approach is to switch adaptively at runtime. Under predictive barrier scheduling, the simulator can monitor application communication by counting event transfer messages at runtime. If the simulator detects frequent communication, it will switch to the local barrier approach. However, switching from local barriers to predictive barrier scheduling is more complicated, because a global decision must be made to switch, but processors are doing *local* synchronization. To remedy this, each processor could continue to monitor event transfer traffic while synchronizing locally every Q cycles, but global synchronizations could be performed every $100 * Q$ cycles to facilitate a global decision. If there has been little communication traffic, signifying a computation phase, the simulator would switch back to predictive barrier scheduling. We have not experimented yet with this adaptive technique, but it is clearly worth doing so.

While our results are useful for observing the complementary behavior of predictive barrier scheduling and local barriers, the exact performance data is very specific to the particular host architecture (CM-5) we used in our experiments. Our experiments show that, in general, predictive barrier scheduling achieves greater performance improvements than the local barrier approach. However, the success of predictive barrier scheduling is due in part to the CM-5's fast global minimum operation; without it, this technique would be much slower. Local barriers do not perform as well because of high messaging overhead. On different host architectures, the relative performance of the two techniques will be different. Some multicomputers have support for fast fine-grain synchronization, but little or no support for global synchronization (e.g., Alewife [1]). Local barriers are likely to perform much better on such host machines, while predictive barrier scheduling will suffer from high overheads for its global operations. Therefore, the two techniques are also complementary with regard to the host architectures for which they are suited.

While the local barrier approach and predictive barrier scheduling have been evaluated in the context of a direct-execution simulator, they are certainly also applicable to simulators which simulate application code execution in a different way (e.g., threaded code [3]). First, local barriers do not depend on direct execution in any way.

Second, while our implementation of predictive barrier scheduling does rely on Parallel Proteus's support for direct execution, this is not essential to the technique. All that is needed to implement predictive barrier scheduling is a way of associating with each value of an application's program counter, an estimate of the time until the application will next communicate. The necessary analysis can be done at compile-time as in Parallel Proteus, but instead of instrumenting code, the information generated at compile-time can be stored in a table. As each instruction is simulated, information about future communication behavior can be looked up in the table. Therefore, the applicability of local barriers and predictive barrier scheduling extends to more simulators than just the one described here.

7   Related Work

The methods that other researchers have developed to reduce synchronization overhead in parallel simulators of parallel computers include reducing network simulation accuracy, balancing load, and improving lookahead. Several of these approaches will be described here as they relate to our work.

Some simulators of parallel computers are extremely detailed (e.g., cycle-by-cycle simulators such as NWO-P, a detailed parallel simulator of the MIT Alewife machine [15]), with large overheads for simulating each cycle that far outweigh synchronization overhead. In contrast, our work deals with the synchronization overhead that dominates when low overhead techniques are used to simulate processor behavior.

The Wisconsin Wind Tunnel and Parallel Tango Lite are two direct execution-based parallel simulators of shared memory multicomputers [21] [14]. They synchronize using periodic global barriers. They achieve good performance by decreasing network simulation accuracy, which allows them to synchronize infrequently. The WWT researchers have explored a range of network simulation models (from very accurate to not very accurate) [7]. All of these could easily be incorporated into Parallel Proteus, but would not solve the problem of reducing synchronization overhead while maintaining accurate network simulation. However, WWT and PTL cannot exploit lookahead in the same way as Parallel Proteus can, because they simulate shared memory architectures. Communication can potentially happen on every memory reference in shared memory systems, so it is difficult to identify ahead of time periods of computation during which it is certain that no communication will take place. Also, all accesses to shared data (whether requiring communication or not) potentially affect other target processors, so it is not correct to allow application threads to run ahead until a communication operation is encountered.

LAPSE is a conservative, direct execution-based parallel simulator of the message-passing Intel Paragon [10] [11] [12]. It achieves good performance by exploiting two sources of lookahead. First, like the runtime analysis in predictive barrier scheduling, LAPSE lets some application code execute in advance of the simulation of its timing. However, unlike Parallel Proteus, LAPSE does not augment this technique with compile-time analysis. Second, a large amount of lookahead results from the target and level of detail of LAPSE's network simulation. LAPSE simulates only store-and-forward networks, and only at the packet-switching level of detail. As a result, LAPSE's synchronization time quantum Q is fairly large (4750 cycles = packet-switching time) compared to that of Parallel Proteus (2 cycles = flit-switching time). Parallel Proteus's synchronization time quantum is so small because it simulates modern, high-speed interconnection networks that use cut-through routing; these require a very fine-grained clock for accurate (flit-level) simulation. Therefore, exploiting large amounts of lookahead in Parallel Proteus is much more difficult than it is in LAPSE.

SPaDES is a conservative parallel simulation approach used for simulating symmetric multiprocessors on shared memory multicomputer hosts [16]. It uses load balancing and split-phase (or fuzzy) barriers to avoid synchronization overhead. While effectively reducing waiting time for SPaDES simulations, balancing load in Parallel Proteus would involve too much overhead for transferring simulation state between host processors. In "aggressive" mode, SPaDES allows the host processors to be only loosely synchronized. This technique is similar in effect to local barriers (or nearest-neighbor synchronization).

8   Conclusions

Parallelism is necessary for fast, detailed simulation of large multicomputers. Synchronization overhead, however, often severely limits the performance of conservative parallel simulators. This occurs because low-latency communication in simulated networks requires frequent synchronization of simulator processes. One way to reduce synchronization overhead is to sacrifice accuracy in the simulation of the network. Focusing on local barriers and predictive barrier scheduling, our research demonstrates that for simulations of message-passing parallel computers, nearest neighbor synchronization and application-specific optimization can improve performance by reducing synchronization overhead *without* sacrificing accuracy in network simulation.

In our experiments, local barriers improved the performance (by up to 24%) of communication-bound simulations by reducing waiting time at synchronization points. Predictive barrier scheduling, on the other hand, improved the performance (by up to 65%) of computation-bound simulations by eliminating unnecessary synchronizations. Because of their complementary behavior, we advocate a hybrid adaptive approach that dynamically chooses between the two techniques.

Acknowledgements

We thank Andrew Myers and Eric Brewer for their help in developing some of the ideas which led to this research. Steve Keckler, Rob Bedichek, Andrew Myers, and Benjamin Hidalgo provided useful comments that improved the presentation of this paper.

References

[1] Anant Agarwal, Ricardo Bianchini, David Chaiken, Kirk L. Johnson, David Kranz, John Kubiatowicz, Beng-Hong Lim, Kenneth Mackenzie, and Donald Yeung. The MIT Alewife Machine: Architecture and performance. In *Proceedings of the 22nd Annual International Symposium on Computer Architecture*, June 1995.

[2] Alfred A. Aho, Ravi Sethi, and Jeffrey D. Ullman. *Compilers: Principles, Techniques, and Tools*. Addison-Wesley, 1986.

[3] Robert C. Bedichek. Talisman: Fast and accurate multicomputer simulation. In *Proceedings of SIGMETRICS '95*, 1995.

[4] Bertsekas and Tsitsiklis. *Parallel and Distributed Computing: Numerical Methods*. Prentice Hall, Englewood Cliffs, NJ, 1989.

[5] Guy E. Blelloch, Charles E. Leiserson, Bruce M. Maggs, C. Greg Plaxton, Stephen J. Smith, and Marco Zagha. A

comparison of sorting algorithms for the Connection Machine CM-2. In *Proceedings of the Symposium on Parallel Algorithms and Architectures*, July 1991.

[6] Eric A. Brewer, Chrysanthos N. Dellarocas, Adrian Colbrook, and William E. Weihl. Proteus: A high-performance parallel architecture simulator. Technical Report MIT/LCS 516, Massachusetts Institute of Technology, September 1991.

[7] Douglas C. Burger and David A. Wood. Accuracy vs. performance in parallel simulation of interconnection networks. In *Proceedings of the 9th International Parallel Processing Symposium*, April 1995.

[8] David R. Cheriton, Hendrik A. Goosen, Hugh Holbrook, and Philip Machanick. Restructuring a parallel simulation to improve behavior in a shared-memory multiprocessor: The value of distributed synchronization. In *Proceedings of the Seventh Workshop on Parallel and Distributed Simulation*, pages 159–162, May 1993.

[9] Thinking Machines Corporation. CM-5 technical summary, 1992.

[10] Philip M. Dickens. Personal communication. January 1996.

[11] Philip M. Dickens, Philip Heidelberger, and David M. Nicol. Parallelized direct execution simulation of message-passing parallel programs. Technical Report 94-50, ICASE, June 1994.

[12] Philip M. Dickens, Philip Heidelberger, and David M. Nicol. Parallelized network simulators for message-passing parallel programs. In *Proceedings of MASCOTS '95*, January 1995.

[13] Richard M Fujimoto. Parallel discrete event simulation. *Communiations of the ACM*, 33(10):30–53, October 1990.

[14] Stephen R. Goldschmidt. *Simulation of Multiprocessors: Accuracy and Performance*. PhD thesis, Stanford University, June 1993.

[15] Kirk Johnson, David Chaiken, and Alan Mainwaring. NWO-P: Parallel simulation of the Alewife machine. In *Proceedings of the 1993 MIT Student Workshop on Supercomputing Technologies*, August 1993.

[16] Pavlos Konas and Pen-Chung Yew. Improved parallel architectural simulations on shared-memory multiprocessors. In *Proceedings of The 8th Workshop on Parallel and Distributed Simulation (PADS94)*, July 1994.

[17] Ulana Legedza. Reducing synchronization overhead in parallel simulation. Technical Report MIT/LCS 655, Massachusetts Institute of Technology, June 1995.

[18] David Nicol and Richard Fujimoto. Parallel simulation today. Technical Report 92-62, ICASE, 1992.

[19] David M. Nicol. Performance bounds on parallel self-initiating discrete-event simulations. *ACM Transactions on Modeling and Computer Simulations*, 1(1):24–50, 1991.

[20] David M. Nicol. The cost of conservative synchronization in parallel discrete event simulations. *Journal of the ACM*, 40(2):304–333, April 1993.

[21] Steven K. Reinhardt, Mark D. Hill, James R. Larus, Alvin R. Lebeck, James C.Lewis, and David A. Wood. The Wisconsin Wind Tunnel: Virtual prototyping of parallel computers. In *Proceedings of the 1993 ACM SIGMETRICS Conference*, May 1993.

Session 6

Techniques III: Granularity and Partitioning in Parallel Simulation

Session Chair
Wayne M. Loucks, University of Waterloo, Canada

Concurrency Preserving Partitioning (CPP)
for Parallel Logic Simulation

Hong K. Kim and Jack Jean
{hkim,jjean}@cs.wright.edu
Department of Computer Science and Engineering
Wright State University
Dayton, Ohio 45435, USA

Abstract

Based on a linear ordering of vertices in a directed graph, a linear-time partitioning algorithm for parallel logic simulation is presented. Unlike most other partitioning algorithms, the proposed algorithm preserves circuit concurrency by assigning to processors circuit gates that can be evaluated at about the same time. As a result, the concurrency preserving partitioning (CPP) algorithm can provide better load balancing throughout the period of a parallel simulation. This is especially important when the algorithm is used together with a Time Warp simulation where a high degree of concurrency can lead to fewer rollbacks and better performance. The algorithm consists of three phases, and three conflicting goals can be separately considered in each phase so to reduce computational complexity. A parallel gate-level circuit simulator is implemented on an Intel Paragon machine to evaluate the performance of the CPP algorithm. The results are compared with two other partitioning algorithms to show that reasonable speedup may be achieved with the algorithm.

1 Introduction

Logic simulation is a primary tool for validation and analysis of digital circuits. To reduce the simulation time of large circuits, parallel logic simulation has attracted considerable interest in recent years [1]. As in many other parallel simulations, a good partitioning algorithm is a key to achieve good performance in parallel logic simulation, especially since the event granularity is relatively small compared to other types of simulations. Partitioning algorithms can usually be classified into two categories: static and dynamic. Static partitioning is performed prior to the execution of the simulation and the resulting partition is fixed during the simulation. A dynamic partitioning scheme attempts to keep system resources busy by migrating computation processes during the simulation. Since dynamic partitioning involves a lot of communication overhead [11], static partitioning is considered in this paper.

A good partitioning algorithm is expected to speed up parallel simulations. This may be achieved by focusing on three competing goals: to balance processor workload, to minimize interprocessor communication and synchronization, and to maximize concurrency. Among those goals, the maximization of concurrency is mostly overlooked by previous partitioning algorithms for logic simulation. Maximizing concurrency means partitioning a circuit such that at any time instance as many independent logic gates as possible are assigned to different processors. This can be achieved if workload is balanced among the processors all the time. However, most previous algorithms balance the accumulated amount of workload over the whole simulation period instead of the workload at any time instance.

The concurrency preserving partitioning (CPP) algorithm proposed in this paper for parallel logic simulation takes the above three goals into consideration. It is a linear-time and non-iterative algorithm that runs relatively fast. It achieves a good compromise with a high degree of concurrency, a balanced workload, and reasonable amount of interprocessor communication. The compromise leads to a significant speedup obtained with a Time Warp parallel logic simulator implemented on an Intel Paragon. In Section 2, previous partitioning works in parallel logic simulation are summarized. Section 3 describes the rationale and the three phases of the proposed algorithm. The performance of the algorithm is evaluated in Section 4. Section 5 concludes the paper.

2 Previous Works

A number of partitioning algorithms have been proposed for circuit simulations with slightly different emphasis. To compare several partitioning algorithms, we use four performance measures: load balance, interprocessor communication, run time used for the partitioning itself, and concurrency. Even though random partitioning and string partitioning [12] yield relatively good concurrency, they tend to generate a large amount of interprocessor communication [16]. The iterative min-cut algorithms are able to achieve a small amount of interprocessor communication between processors [6, 9], but it may lead to unbalanced workloads. To accommodate multiple competing goals, a simulated annealing method may be used for partitioning [3, 8]. However, the method is slow, especially when high quality solutions are to be achieved.

Partitioning algorithms based on clustering techniques such as the cone partitioning method or the Corolla method are used to improve the interprocessor communication overhead [14, 15, 16, 17]. These partitioning algorithms consist of two phases: a fine grained clustering phase and an assignment phase. In the first phase, clustering is performed to increase granularity. In the second phase, clusters are assigned to processors so to either reduce interprocessor communication or achieve load balancing.

A problem with most previous partitioning algorithms is that they do not produce a high degree of concurrency [4]. They usually try to balance the *accumulated* workload instead of trying to balance the *instantaneous* workload. This leads to performance degradation caused by rollbacks when a Time Warp parallel simulation is performed. The proposed CPP algorithm is designed to take concurrency into consideration and achieve a good compromise among the different competing goals.

3 Partitioning Algorithm

For partitioning purposes, a circuit may be represented as a directed graph, $G = (V, E)$, where V is the set of nodes, each denoting a logic gate or a flip-flop, and $E \in (V \times V)$ is the set of directed edges between nodes in V. Three special subsets of V are I, O, and D, representing the set of primary input nodes, the set of primary output nodes, and the set of flip-flop nodes, respectively. Several assumptions are made in this paper regarding a circuit graph.

1. For each node, the *in-degree* and the *out-degree* are bounded by a constant. This assumption corresponds to the finite amount of fan-ins and fan-outs of logic gates in a circuit.

2. Associated with each node v_i, there is an *activity level*, a_i, that denotes the estimated number of events to be simulated for the node.

3. Associated with each edge e_i, there is an *edge weight*, w_i, that denotes the estimated number of events to be sent over the edge.

Note that both activity levels and edge weights may be obtained through circuit modeling or through pre-simulation [5]. They are assumed to be unity when neither modeling nor pre-simulation are attempted. Another point to mention is that the graph may contain cycles due to the existence of flip-flops.

The partitioning algorithm proposed in this paper assigns nodes in a directed graph to processors of an asynchronous multiprocessor. It consists of three phases so that conflicting goals may be considered separately and computational complexity may be reduced. As a matter of fact, the computational complexity of each phase is a linear function of the total number of vertices. For a graph with $|V|$ nodes these three phases are as follows.

Phase 1: Divide a graph into a set of disjointed subgraphs so that (1) each subgraph contains a primary input node and a sizable amount of other nodes that can be reached from the primary input node and (2) the *weighted* number of edges interconnecting different subgraphs is minimized.

Phase 2: Assign distinct numbers from $[1, |V|]$ to graph nodes so that (1) nodes inside a subgraph are labeled with consecutive numbers and (2) for most heavy-weighted edges, the numbers assigned to their two end-nodes are either consecutive numbers or with only a small difference.

Phase 3: Assign nodes to processors so that (1) only nodes with consecutive numbers are assigned to a processor and (2) the workload of processors are roughly balanced. Node activity levels are used in this phase when processor workload is computed.

In the first phase, primary input gates which are the starting points of the parallel simulation are assigned to different subgraphs so as to increase simulation concurrency. At the same time, the goal of minimizing interprocessor communication is considered. In the second phase, minimizing interprocessor communication is still the goal. In addition, the linear numbering of graph nodes allows a simple procedure in the last phase to achieve load balancing without compromising much of the concurrency and the interprocessor communication.

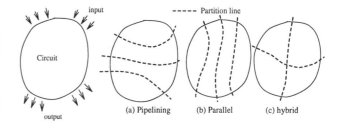

Figure 1: Partitions: (a) Pipelining, (b) Parallel, and (c) hybrid

3.1 Phase 1: Subgraph Division

Primary Inputs and Concurrency: In Figure 1, primary inputs and outputs are indicated for a graph where the majority of edges are assumed to go vertically from primary inputs to primary outputs. Also shown in the figure are three potential partitioning solutions: pipelining, parallel, and hybrid. With the pipelining scheme, the processors work in a pipelined fashion where a processor cannot start until its predecessor (the one above it) has finished some tasks and sent an event over. In a Time Warp parallel simulation this may cause erroneous computations and introduce a lot of rollbacks. The problem becomes even worse when the circuit size is increased. On the contrary, the parallel scheme produces maximum concurrency at the beginning of execution. It reduces the differences between local virtual times (LVT's) and distances of rollbacks in optimistic simulations. This scheme is adopted in this phase in a way that preserves concurrency and minimizes interprocessor communication.

The first phase divides a graph into a set of disjointed subgraphs, each subgraph containing a primary input node and a sizable amount of other nodes that can be reached from the primary input node. It is also desirable that the *weighted* number of edges interconnecting different subgraphs is minimized. A greedy algorithm is used to achieve these two objectives. Basically, a node is assigned to a subgraph only after all its parent nodes have been assigned. Furthermore, only those subgraphs to which its parent nodes belong are considered in the node assignment. Since this simple algorithm works only on an acyclic graph, flip-flops are processed before the application of the algorithm so to automatically remove cycles in a graph for sequential circuits.

A description of the detailed algorithm is shown in Figure 2 where an array Visited[·] is used to keep track of the sum of the number of parent nodes that have been assigned and the number of parent nodes that are driven by flip-flop outputs. Therefore a node can be assigned only after its Visited[·] value is the same as its in-degree. At that time, the node is assigned in a greedy way to minimize potential interprocessor communication. To assign a node to one of those subgraphs that its parent nodes belong to, the criterion used is to select the one with the *largest sum of edge weights* between the node and the subgraph. When there is a tie, the node is assigned to the subgraph that contains the parent node with the smallest rank. Here the rank of a node is the length of the shortest path from the root of the subgraph to which it belongs to the node. The tie-breaker is used so to somehow balance the sizes of subgraphs.

The algorithm used to traverse the graph and assign all the nodes is pretty efficient. Since each edge is visited only once and the number of edges per node is assumed to be bounded by a constant, the time complexity of this phase is of $O(|V|)$ where $|V|$ is the number of gates in a circuit. Note that the division into subgraphs is independent of the ordering of primary inputs. A simple proof based on induction on node ranks can be used to show that all the nodes will even-

Phase1_Procedure(G, D, I)
/* G is an input graph, D is the set of flip-flop gates, and I is the set of primary input gates. Initially there are $|D| + |I|$ subgraphs, each one containing either one flip-flop gate or one primary input node. At the end, there are only $|I|$ subgraphs. */
/* The global variables Visited[·] are initially set to zero */
for(each vertex w in D)
  for(each child vertex v of w)
    Increase Visited[v] by 1
    if (Visited[v] is equal to in_degree[v])
        /* all parents have been assigned */
      then assign_child_to_subgraphs_recursively(v)
  endfor
endfor
for(each v in I)
  assign_children_to_subgraphs_recursively(v)

procedure assign_child_to_subgraphs_recursively(v)
  If (v is not a primary input gate),
    then assign_to_subgraph (v);
  for(each child vertex w of v)
    Increase Visited[w] by 1
    if(Visited[w] is equal to in_degree[w])
        /* all parents have been assigned */
      then assign_child_to_subgraphs_recursively(w);
  endfor

procedure assign_to_subgraph (v)
  For each subgraph that the parent nodes of v belong to, compute the sum of edge weights between v and the subgraph.
  If (v is a flip-flop)
    then Assign the subgraph that includes v to the (parent) subgraph that has the largest sum of edge weights.
    else Assign v to the subgraph that has the largest sum of edge weights. If there is a tie, assign to the one that leads to smaller rank for v.
    /* The rank of v is the length of the shortest path from the root of the subgraph to v. */
  endif
  Calculate the rank to v from parents in the assigned subgraph.
  Update the connectivity matrix that shows the sum of edge weights between different subgraphs.
  /* The connectivity matrix is used in the second phase of the algorithm. */

Figure 2: Phase 1: Divide a graph into disjointed subgraphs

tually be assigned with the algorithm.

Several interesting differences between this phase and other algorithms are noted here. (1) Since redundant computations as used in cone partitioning [14, 15] are not allowed, a circuit is partitioned into disjointed subcircuits without overlapping. (2) The assignment of each node is based on parent nodes. This is different from other schemes that are based on children nodes [13, 16]. The advantage is in the higher concurrency that can be preserved in this scheme. (3) A node is assigned only after all its parent nodes are assigned and the *greedy* assignment is adopted. In some previous works, a node is assigned right after its first parent(child) is assigned and the node is assigned to the parent(child) without considering other parent(child) nodes [12, 13, 14, 15]. Such methods may lead to unbalanced global structures, namely, the first subgraph is significantly larger than the others.

In [16], primary input gates are evenly assigned to processors. Since subgraphs may be of very different sizes, such a scheme may produce an unbalanced assignment. With the second and third phases, our algorithm resolves the problem by allowing a subgraph to be assigned to multiple processors without compromising much about the concurrency and the interprocessor communication issues.

3.2 Phase 2: Vertex Numbering

For a graph with $|V|$ nodes, this phase assigns distinct numbers from $[1, |V|]$ to nodes so that nodes inside a subgraph are labeled with consecutive numbers and, for most heavy-weighted edges, the numbers assigned to their two end-nodes are either consecutive numbers or with only a small difference. There are basically two parts of the numbering. One is about the ordering of the subgraphs and the other is about the ordering of nodes inside each subgraph.

For the ordering of the subgraphs, a connectivity matrix obtained in the first phase is used. A connectivity matrix is a $p \times p$ matrix, where p is the number of disjointed subgraphs, and the matrix element at location (i, j), C_{ij}, denotes the sum of edge weights between subgraphs i and j. Consider an undirected graph with p nodes and p^2 edges with C_{ij} as the edge weight on the edge connecting nodes i and j. The ordering problem can be formulated into a graph problem where the objective is to find a path that reaches all the nodes and has the maximal sum of edge weights. The problem is similar to the NP-complete traveling salesman problem. Here a greedy algorithm of complexity of $O(p^2)$ is used to find such a path. The path is built up node by node so that out of each node the edge with the largest weight is added to the path.

As to the ordering of nodes inside each subgraph, a linear-time depth-first-search (DFS) scheme is used to traverse the subgraph. The advantage of using the DFS approach is that many topologically adjacent nodes are labeled with numbers of similar values.

Table 1: ISCAS Benchmark Circuits

Circuit	No. of gates	No. of input gates	No. of output gates	No. of flip-flops
s15850.1	10383	77	150	534
s38417	23843	28	106	1636
s38584.1	20717	38	304	1426

The node numbering in this phase basically places a total ordering among the nodes so as to enable a simple procedure in the last phase to achieve load balancing. In the meantime, it puts nodes with heavy-weighted edges close to each other so that, after processor assignment, both edge-cut ratio and message latency delay can be reduced. Because normally $p^2 < |V|$, the execution time complexity of phase 2 is of $O(|V|)$.

3.3 Phase 3: Processor Assignment

In this phase nodes are assigned to processors so that only nodes with consecutive numbers are assigned to a processor and the workload of processors are roughly balanced. Node activity levels are used in this phase when processor workload is computed. All the node activity levels are first summed up to get the total activity, and the average workload per processor is computed as the total activity divided by the number of processors. A linear-time algorithm is then used to assign to processors, one by one, nodes with consecutive numbers so that the workload of each processor is close to the average workload.

Even though this last phase considers only load balancing, the overall algorithm is expected to show good performance in concurrency and interprocessor communication. This is because, after the first two phases, the nodes are arranged in a way that the concurrency and interprocessor communication factors are insensitive to a slight change in processor assignment boundaries in Phase 3.

4 Simulation Results and Comparison
4.1 Simulation Model and Environment

In this paper, the effects of the CPP algorithm on the Time Warp algorithm are studied. In the Time Warp algorithm [7], a processor executes events in timestamp order and the local simulation time of a processor is called a local virtual time (LVT). Whenever a processor receives an event with a timestamp less than the LVT, it rolls back immediately to the state just before the timestamp of that event. Even though the Time Warp algorithm has a high degree of parallelism, the number of rollbacks must be reduced to get better performance.

The experiments were performed on an Intel Paragon XP/S machine. The machine is a massively parallel processor that has a large number of computing nodes interconnected by a high-speed mesh network. Each node has two identical 50 MHz Intel i-860XP processors and 32 Mbytes of memory. One processor executes user and operating system codes while the other is dedicated to message passing. Each node runs the XP/S operation system under Paragon NX environment. Several of the largest sequential ISCAS benchmark circuits [2] were used as test cases. Their characteristics are summarized in Table 1. One hundred random input vectors were used for the simulation of each circuit and the first ten of them were used in the pre-simulation to get estimates of node activity levels and edge weights. The gate-level unit delay model was adopted. For each of those ISCAS circuits, the CPP algorithm finished the partitioning part of simulation within 5 seconds on a DEC alpha 3000/400 workstation.

4.2 Performance Comparison

To facilitate comparison, two other partitioning algorithms were implemented. They are the *random* partitioning and the *depth first search* (DFS) partitioning. The random partitioning scheme randomly assigns circuit gates into processors with the constraint that each processor is allocated roughly the same number of circuit gates. Even though the random partitioning scheme introduces a lot of communication overhead, it is expected to provide pretty good load balancing [11, 16]. The DFS partitioning scheme uses a basic depth first search to traverse a circuit graph starting from a pseudo root that has one directed edge to each primary input gate. The traversing is therefore guaranteed to visit each gate once. The sequence of gates is then assigned to the processors, with each processor getting roughly equal number of gates [8, 10]. This scheme generates partitions with relatively low interprocessor communication and achieves balanced processor workloads. However, the DFS scheme does not consider concurrency issue, unlike the CPP algorithm. Note that both node activity levels and edge weights were not considered in either random or DFS scheme.

These three partition algorithms were evaluated by comparing the following performance measures: the ratio of edge cut, the ratio of external events, the ratio of erroneous events, the execution time, and the speedup. Here the ratio of edge cut is defined as the number of cut-edges (i.e., edges between nodes on different processors) divided by the total number of edges in a circuit and the ratio of external events is defined as the number of external events divided by the total number of external and internal events. These two performance measures are related to interprocessor communication. Note that a cut-edge does not necessarily produce an external event while an external event does imply the existence of a cut-edge.

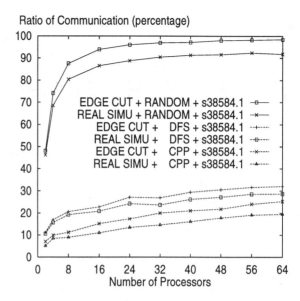

Figure 3: Inter-processor communication

Interprocessor Communication In Figure 3, partitioning results of the s38584.1 circuit are summarized in terms of the ratio of edge cut (indicated in the figure as EDGE CUT) and the ratio of external events in real simulation (indicated in the figure as REAL SIMU). As can be seen from the diagram, these two performance measures are pretty consistent in that each pair of curves for one partitioning algorithm exhibit the same trend as the number of processors increases. Another observation of the diagram is that the CPP algorithm consistently produces lower ratio of external events than those of the other two algorithms. As a matter of fact, when bipartitioning (two-processor partitioning) is performed, the ratio of external events for the CPP algorithm is 5%. This compares favorably with several other partitioning algorithms such as Flip-flop-Clustering (10%), Min-Cut (15%), and Levelizing (20%). These results were reported in [17]. Even though the Corolla-clustering algorithm [17] with its ratio of external events as 0.6% for bipartitioning definitely outperforms the CPP algorithm in this regard, it is relatively slow and does not take concurrency into consideration.

With the CPP algorithm, it appears that the number of external events would not be a severe limiting factor for the performance of the Time Warp parallel simulation. This can be seen from the diagram that, even when 64 processors are used, the ratio of external events is still less than 20 percent. And it is expected that the ratio of external events drops as the size of a circuit increases. It is therefore interesting to check out the other limiting factor in Time Warp simulation, the rollback overhead.

Ratio of Erroneous Events (percentage)

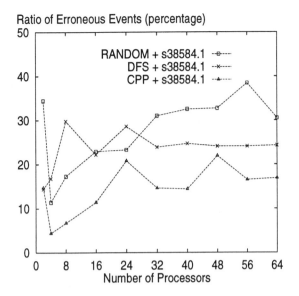

Figure 4: Ratio of erroneous events

Event Rollback The ratios of erroneous events versus the number of processors are summarized in Figure 4 for the three partitioning schemes. To read the diagram, see for example, less than 18 percent of events were canceled for the s38584.1 circuit with 20717 gates when the CPP algorithm was used for 64 processors. Apparently the CPP algorithm introduces lower ratios of erroneous events than those of the DFS and the RANDOM schemes.

Execution Time (in seconds)

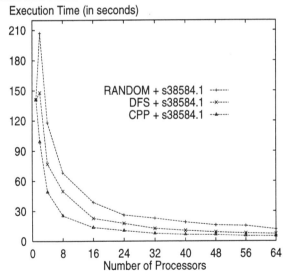

Figure 5: Execution time

Simulation Execution Time Figure 5 shows the execution times for simulating the s38584.1 circuit with different algorithms. Here the execution time excludes the time for partitioning, reading input vectors, and printing output vectors. Note that, when the number of processors is fixed, experiments show that the execution time increases linearly with the number of randomly generated input vectors. For real circuit simulations, the circuit is expected to be larger and much higher number of input vectors are required. It therefore makes sense to exclude the time to perform partitioning.

Table 2 lists the values used in Figure 5 as well as the execution times for simulating two other circuits. It shows that the parallel simulation of s38584.1 can be executed in 5 seconds using 64 processors while the sequential simulation takes 140 seconds. It also shows that, when same number of processors is used, the parallel simulation with the CPP algorithm is usually faster than with the other two algorithms for the s38584.1 circuit. In particular, when two processors are used, the RANDOM and DFS algorithms do not get any speedup because the RANDOM algorithm suffers from a lot of interprocessor communication while the DFS algorithm does not provide a high degree of load balancing over time, i.e., it does not provide enough concurrency and therefore causes a lot of rollbacks.

Processor Workload (No. of events evaluated)

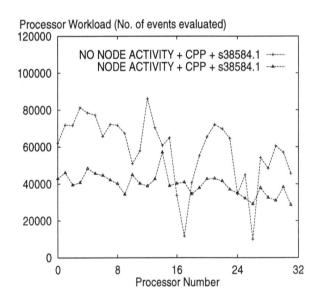

Figure 6: Processor workload

Load Balancing Figure 6 shows the processor workloads obtained with parallel simulations when the CPP algorithm is used with or without the node activity levels. The activity levels were obtained through presimulation. Each point in the figure denotes the total number of events evaluated for a specific processor. Apparently better load balancing is achieved when the node activity levels are available in Phase 3 of the CPP algorithm. Note that unbalanced workload increases the number of erroneous events, increases the amount of rollbacks, and prolongs a parallel simulation.

103

Table 2: The execution time (in seconds); $CPP1$ (=CPP without node activity), CPP (=CPP with node activity).

Experiment		No. of Processors										
Circuit	Partitioning	1	2	4	8	16	24	32	40	48	56	64
s38584.1	RANDOM	141.0	209.9	118.0	68.2	38.8	26.1	22.9	19.1	16.1	15.4	12.0
	DFS	141.0	148.4	77.0	49.8	22.9	17.9	12.8	10.8	9.2	8.1	7.5
	CPP1	141.0	117.9	55.9	27.6	14.5	10.7	9.4	10.9	9.5	7.6	6.6
	CPP	141.0	99.2	49.1	25.5	13.8	9.7	7.9	6.8	6.4	5.3	5.0
s38417	CPP	103.0	67.9	32.4	15.2	8.2	6.3	4.8	4.7	4.2	3.2	3.3
s15850.1	CPP	42.5	28.4	14.1	8.3	5.8	5.0	4.3	4.0	3.9	3.2	3.4

Speedup *Speedup* is defined as the ratio of the execution time of the best sequential simulator to that of the parallel simulator. For most circuits, reasonable speedups may be obtained when the number of processors is small and there are enough events to be executed concurrently. In Figure 7, speedups obtained with different algorithms are shown. The figure shows that the performance of a Time Warp simulation is very sensitive to partitioning when large number of processors are employed and the CPP algorithm achieves better speedup than those of the RANDOM and the DFS partitioning algorithms. Note that when the number of processors is near 40, the CPP algorithm without node activity consideration degrades and performs roughly the same as DFS does. One explanation is that there are only 38 primary input gates in the s38584.1 circuit. Since the main difference between CPP and DFS is the concurrency issue and Phase 1 of CPP takes care of concurrency by getting disjointed subgraphs, one for each primary input gate, the CPP without node activity is expected to degrade when the number of processors is close to the number of primary input gates.

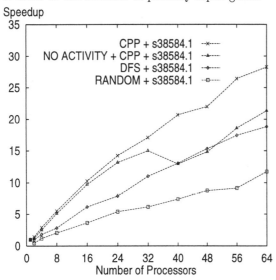

Figure 7: Speedups of ISCAS s38584.1

Another observation from the figure is that, when the number of processors is below 32, the performance of the CPP algorithm is almost not influenced by the decision to consider node activity levels and edge weights. However, when more processors are added, the advantage of having extra knowledge from the presimulation becomes critical. In Figure 8, the speedups of three large ISCAS89 circuits are displayed. A significant speedup of 31 with 64 processors was obtained for the s38417 circuit.

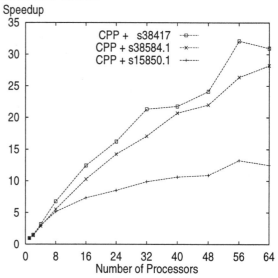

Figure 8: Speedups for CPP with Node Activity

5 Conclusions

A 3-phase partitioning algorithm was developed for parallel logic simulation, in which three different goals were separately considered so to achieve a good compromise. The concurrency preserving partitioning (CPP) algorithm has the following characteristics. First, unlike most other partitioning algorithms, the CPP algorithm takes concurrency between processors into consideration. It preserves the concurrency of a circuit by dividing the entire circuit into subcircuits to capture global circuit structure. That consideration reduces the gap between LVTs and it in turn reduces the number of erroneous events. Second, load balancing in Phase 3 is achieved in a way without the need to consider other goals such as concurrency and interprocessor communication cost. Finally, even though most partitioning algorithms are iterative, the CPP algorithm is non-iterative and is of linear time complexity. It is therefore more practical for extremely large circuits to use the CPP algorithm instead of other partitioning algorithms that have higher time complexity.

The optimistic parallel simulation algorithm combined with the CPP algorithm enables a powerful parallel gate-level circuit simulator. A significant speedup of 31 with 64 processors was obtained on an Intel Paragon machine. The results are encouraging, especially because of the extremely low granularity of the application. Note that the CPP algorithm can also be applied to other problems, such as the partitioning of directed task graphs onto a finite number of processors.

We are currently investigating a model to estimate the node activity levels and the edge weights without the need to perform pre-simulation. That model may be useful for both static partitioning and load balancing. Another research topic is to examine the feasibility of the CPP algorithm on a network of homogeneous/heterogeneous workstations.

Acknowledgments

The authors would like to thank Peter Raeth of the Flight Dynamics Directorate of Wright Laboratory and the ASC Major Shared Resource Center of the US Air Force for providing Paragon access and support.

References

[1] M. L. Bailey, J. V. Briner, Jr., and R. D. Chamberlain, "Parallel Logic Simulation of VLSI Systems," ACM Computing Surveys, Vol. 26, No. 3, pp. 255-294, September 1994.

[2] F. Brglez, D. Bryan, and K. Kozminski, "Combinational Profiles of Sequential Benchmark Circuits," Proc. of the IEEE International Symp. on Circuits and Systems, pp. 1929-1934, 1989.

[3] Azzedine Boukerche and Carl Tropper, "A Static Partitioning and Mapping Algorithm for Conservative Parallel Simulations," Proc. of 8th Workshop on Parallel and Distributed Simulation, pp.164-172, 1994.

[4] J. V. Briner Jr., "Parallel Mixed-Level Simulation of Digital Circuits Using Virtual Time," Ph.D. Dissertation, Duke University, 1990.

[5] Roger D. Chamberlain and Cheryl D. Henderson, "Evaluating the Use of Pre-Simulation in VLSI Circuit Partitioning," Proc. of 8th Workshop on Parallel and Distributed Simulation, pp.139-146, 1994.

[6] C. M. Fiduccia and R. M. Mattheyses, "A Linear-Time Heuristic for Improving Network Partitions," Proc. of the Design Automation Conference, pp. 175-181, 1982.

[7] D. R. Jefferson, "Virtual Time," ACM Trans. on Programming Languages and Systems, Vol. 7, No. 3, pp. 404-425, July 1985.

[8] K. L. Kapp, T. C. Hartrum, and T. S. Wailes, "An Improved Cost Function for Static Partitioning of Parallel Circuit Simulations Using a Conservative Synchronization Protocol," Proc. of 9th Workshop on Parallel and Distributed Simulation, pp. 78-85, 1995.

[9] B. W. Kernighan and S. Lin, "An Efficient Heuristic Procedure for Partitioning Graphs," Bell System Technical Journal, Vol. 49, pp. 291-307, Feb. 1970.

[10] Pavlos Konas and Pen-Chung Yew, "Parallel Discrete Event Simulation on Shared-Memory Multiprocessors," The 24th Annual Simulation Symposium, pp. 134-148, April 1991.

[11] S. A. Kravitz and B. D. Ackland, "Static vs Dynamic Partitioning of Circuits for a MOS Timing Simulator on A Message-Based Multiprocessor," Proc. of the SCS Multiconference on Distributed Simulation, pp. 136-140, 1988.

[12] Y. H. Levendel, P. R. Menon, and S. H. Patel, "Special Purpose Computer for Logic Simulation Using Distributed Processing," Bell System Technical Journal, Vol. 61, No. 10, pp. 2873-2909, Dec. 1982.

[13] B. A. Malloy, E. L. Lloyd, and M. L. Soffa, "Scheduling DAG's for Asynchronous Multiprocessor Execution," IEEE Transactions on Parallel and Distributed Systems, Vol. 5, No. 5, pp.495-508, May 1994.

[14] N. Manjikian and W. M. Loucks, "High Performance Parallel Logic Simulation On A Network of Workstations," Proc. of 7th Workshop on Parallel and Distributed Simulation, pp.76-84, 1993.

[15] R. B. Mueller-Thuns, D. G. Saab, R. F. Damiano, and J. A. Abraham, "VLSI Logic and Fault Simulation on General-Purpose Parallel Computers," IEEE Trans. on Computer-Aided Design, Vol. 12, No. 3, pp. 446-460, March 1993.

[16] S. P. Smith, B. Underwood, M. R. Mercer, "An Analysis of Several Approaches to Circuit Partitioning for Parallel Logic Simulation," IEEE International Conference on Computer Design, pp. 664-667, 1987.

[17] C. Sporrer and H. Bauer, "Corolla Partitioning for Distributed Logic Simulation of VLSI-Circuits," Proc. of 7th Workshop on Parallel and Distributed Simulation, pp.85-92, 1993.

Hierarchical Strategy of Model Partitioning for VLSI–Design Using an Improved Mixture of Experts Approach

K. Hering & R. Haupt
Universität Leipzig, Inst. für Informatik
Augustusplatz 10/11
04109 Leipzig, Germany

Th. Villmann
Inst. für Techno- und Wirtschaftsmathematik
E.-Schrödinger-Str., Geb. 48/575
67663 Kaiserslautern , Germany

Abstract

The partitioning of complex processor models on the gate and register-transfer level for parallel functional simulation based on the clock-cycle algorithm is considered. We introduce a hierarchical partitioning scheme combining various partitioning algorithms in the frame of a competing strategy. Melting together different partitioning results within one level using superpositions we crossover to a mixture of experts one. This approach is improved applying genetic algorithms. In addition we present two new partitioning algorithms both of them taking cones as fundamental units for building partitions.

1 Introduction

Logic design for whole microprocessor structures is accompanied with time-extensive simulation processes. Within the design strategy outlined in [14] the verification of functional (logical) behavior is strictly separated from the analysis of timing aspects. In this context the background of the present paper is given by simulation processes for functional design verification on gate and register-transfer level (logic simulation) where sequences of machine instructions or microcode are taken as test cases and underlying models comprise complex parts of processor structures. Under these assumptions the usage of cycle-based simulators is to be preferred. *TEXSIM*[1] is a high performance simulator for logic simulation of synchronous designs using the *clock-cycle algorithm*. To achieve a significant reduction of running time for simulations the task is to parallelize them. Thereby a parallel *TEXSIM* simulation consists of several co-operating *TEXSIM* instances running on loosely coupled RS/6000 processors (system *SP2* of IBM) over parts of the whole

---

[1]copyright by IBM

model. As a basic assumption, the process of the evaluation of combinational logic during the parallel simulation of a cycle has to be left unchanged. Therefore special *fan-in cones* are chosen as building blocks for model partitioning. A partition is directly related to certain workloads of the processors involved in later parallel simulation and communication overhead between co-operating *TEXSIM* instances and, hence, to the speed-up possible due to parallelization. The amount of time acceptable for partitioning depends on the expected total duration of all simulation runs to be performed regarding to a corresponding model. Simulation processes we are dealing with are characterized by a large number of time-extensive runs concerning a given model.

2 Definitions

First, we define a structural model for the logic design on gate and register-transfer level. The underlying hardware is supposed to be synchronous. Basic components are given by the sets M_I, M_O, M_E, M_L, M_S (global inputs, global outputs, logical elements, storing elements, signals). M_E includes all elements which represent combinational logic within the hardware to be simulated. Signals of M_S are interpreted as wires. The elements of the set M_L possess storing function and are cycle limiting in the sense of the *clock-cycle* algorithm. We concentrate the elements of all pairwise disjoint sets M_I, M_O, M_E and M_L to the set of boxes $M_B = M_I \cup M_O \cup M_E \cup M_L$. On the basis of these sets the hardware model can be considered as a directed bipartite graph. Therefore, we introduce the relation $M_\mathcal{R} \subseteq (M_B \times M_S) \cup (M_S \times M_B)$ describing the connections between boxes and signals. Using the sets of successors $\mathcal{N}_G^+(x) = \{y|(x,y) \in \mathcal{R}\}$ and predecessors $\mathcal{N}_G^-(x) = \{y|(y,x) \in \mathcal{R}\}$ for any directed graph $G = (X, \mathcal{R})$ and $x \in X$ we define:

Definition 2.1 *Let M_I, M_O, M_E, M_L, and M_S be pairwise disjoint and nonempty sets. M_B and $M_\mathcal{R}$ are*

106

defined as above. $M = (M_I, M_O, M_E, M_L, M_S, M_R)$ is called **hardware model** if the corresponding directed bipartite graph $G(M) = (M_B, M_S, M_R)$ [5, 13] satisfies the following conditions:

1. $\left\{ x \mid x \in M_B \cup M_S \land \mathcal{N}_{G(M)}^{-}(x) = \emptyset \right\} = M_I$,

2. $\left\{ x \mid x \in M_B \cup M_S \land \mathcal{N}_{G(M)}^{+}(x) = \emptyset \right\} = M_O$,

3. any directed cycle in $G(M)$ includes at least one element of M_L.

M_I and M_O are the sets of all sources and sinks of $G(M)$, respectively. Condition 3 ensures the absence of directed cycles only including elements of $M_E \cup M_S$. This corresponds to the exclusion of asynchronous combinational feedbacks.

Due to our parallelization approach, cutting signals of M_S during a partitioning of M is only permitted at cycle-boundaries related to the clock-cycle algorithm. Therefore, we are forced to define basic units for partitioning which are known as *cones* [12, 6, 7] with respect to an arbitrarily chosen hardware model M:

Definition 2.2 The **fan-in cone** $co_I(x)$ of an element $x \in M_O \cup M_E \cup M_L$ is recursively defined by:

1. $x \in co_I(x)$,

2. $y \in M_E \land \mathcal{N}_{G(M)}^{+}(\mathcal{N}_{G(M)}^{+}(y)) \cap co_I(x) \neq \emptyset \rightarrow y \in co_I(x)$.

The **fan-out cone** $co_O(x)$ of $x \in M_I \cup M_E \cup M_L$ is analogously defined using the sets of predecessors.

Let us take a cone $co(x)$ as a special fan-in cone the head element x of which satisfies $x \in M_O \cup M_L$. All the cones form the set $Co(M)$ as the set of basic units for the partitioning of M. An example illustrating the introduced sets M_I, M_O, M_E, M_L and cones for a simple hardware model is depicted in Fig. 1. The number of cones belonging to $Co(M)$ is $m_c = |Co(M)| = |M_L| + |M_O|$. A box $b \in M_E$ (logical element), from which directed paths (with all intermediate boxes being elements of M_E) to the heads of different cones $\hat{c}_i \in Co(M)$, $i = 1, \ldots, m$ exist, belongs to all of the m different cones $\hat{c}_i$: $b \in \cap_{i=1}^{m} \hat{c}_i$. These cones $\hat{c}_i$ are called to be *overlapping*. Considering all cones c_i of the model we get:

$$\sum_{i=1}^{m_c} |c_i| \geq \left| \bigcup_{i=1}^{m_c} c_i \right| = |Co(M)| + |M_E| \ . \quad (2.1)$$

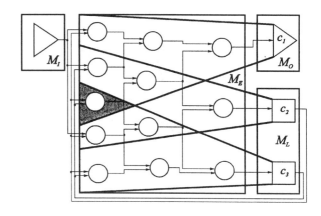

Figure 1 – hardware model with cones (shaded)

If overlapping cones are distributed to different processors one has to take into account the multiple evaluation of boxes in parallel simulations.[2] In the following, $\mathcal{C}$ always denotes nonempty subsets of $Co(M)$.

Definition 2.3 *1.)* The **box-related cone overlap degree** $u : M_E \rightarrow \mathbb{N}$ is defined by $u(b) = |\{c \mid c \in Co(M) \land b \in c\}|$, giving the number of cones which contain the box $b \in M_E$.
2.) The **overlap region** $ovr(\mathcal{C})$ of a set of cones $\mathcal{C}$ is the set of boxes belonging to these and only these cones $c \in \mathcal{C}$:

$$ovr(\mathcal{C}) = \left(\bigcap_{c \in \mathcal{C}} c \right) \setminus \left(\bigcup_{c' \in Co(M) \setminus \mathcal{C}} c' \right) \ . \quad (2.2)$$

All elements of the set $M_E \cup M_L \cup M_O$ are uniquely distributable into overlap regions $ovr(\mathcal{C})$. Using $P^* = 2^{Co(M)} \setminus \{\emptyset\}$ we get:

$$\sum_{\mathcal{C} \in P^*} |ovr(\mathcal{C})| = |Co(M)| + |M_E| \ . \quad (2.3)$$

In general, most of the overlap regions $ovr(\mathcal{C})$ are empty sets. The set of boxes of a cone c is uniquely decomposable into overlap regions $ovr(\mathcal{C})$ with $c = \bigcup_{(\mathcal{C} \in P^* \land c \in \mathcal{C})} ovr(\mathcal{C})$ and $|c| = \sum_{(\mathcal{C} \in P^* \land c \in \mathcal{C})} |ovr(\mathcal{C})|$. The set of all overlap regions $ovr(\mathcal{C})$ allows the construction of an equivalent weighted overlap hypergraph GU identifying the nodes with cones and the hyperedges with cone sets $\mathcal{C}$ corresponding to nonempty overlap regions $ovr(\mathcal{C})$ with $|\mathcal{C}| > 1$ [6].

---

[2]On the other hand, communication between the processors is reduced to communication at the clock-cycle boundaries. Of course, replication in the evaluation of boxes is an additional restricting factor and has to be minimized.

Next, we introduce the terms partitioning and partition by means of two nonempty sets U and V.

Definition 2.4 *1.) A **partitioning** of U with respect to V is a unique map $\Phi : U \to V$ assigning each element $u \in U$ to an element $v \in V$.*
*2.) A **partition** Ψ_Φ of U related to the partitioning $\Phi : U \to V$ is given by $\Psi_\Phi = \{\Phi^{-1}(v) \mid v \in \mathrm{cod}\ \Phi\}$, where $\mathrm{cod}\ \Phi$ is the range of Φ.*

An element $v \in \mathrm{cod}\ \Phi$ represents the partition component $\Phi^{-1}(v)$ containing all elements $u \in U$ which are mapped onto v. Here, we identify U with the set of cones $Co(M)$ and V with the set $\mathcal{B}$ of m_b blocks representing processors. If not specified otherwise we consider surjective partitionings.

The task is to find a partitioning $\Phi_{opt} : Co(M) \to \mathcal{B}$ for the given sets $Co(M)$ and $\mathcal{B}$, which leads to a significant lower running time T_{par} for parallel simulation of a clock-cycle in comparison with T_{seq} in the sequential case. To achieve this goal we consider quality functions taking into account several aspects such as interprocessor communication, workload balance and replication rate influencing T_{par}. Then, for a certain quality function Ω one has to determine a partitioning Φ_{opt}^Ω which optimizes Ω. Currently we consider

$$\Omega = \max_{B \in \mathcal{B}} (W(B)) \qquad (2.4)$$

as to be minimized where

$$W(B) = \left| \bigcup_{c \in \Phi^{-1}(B)} c \right| . \qquad (2.5)$$

$W(B)$ can be interpreted as *workload* of block B under the assumption of an unique time unit $\tau = 1$ for the evaluation of each box. $W(B)$ can be also expressed in terms of overlap regions: $W(B) = \sum_{(C \in P^* \wedge C \cap \Phi^{-1}(B) \neq \emptyset)} |ovr(C)|$. For sequential simulation we have with (2.3) the sequential workload as

$$W_{seq} = |Co(M)| + |M_E| \qquad (2.6)$$

which is equal to the sum of boxes to be evaluated.

3 Hierarchical Partitioning
3.1 Hierarchical Strategy and the Mixture of Experts Approach

In the applications considered here the ratio between m_c as the number of cones and m_b as the number of blocks may be up to the range of $10^5 - 10^6$. Therefore, we focus onto a hierarchical strategy [1] which has been successfully applied to data extensive problems as, for instance, non-linear principle component

analysis (PCA) and robotics [10]. To gradually reduce the range of the problem we introduce a general q-level partitioning scheme according to Def. 2.4:

Definition 3.1 *A **q-level partitioning** of U with respect to V is defined by $\Phi_H : U \to V$ with $\Phi_H = \Phi_q \circ \Phi_{q-1} \circ \ldots \circ \Phi_1$ where $\Phi_j : V_j \to V_{j+1}$ and $V_1 = U$, $V_{q+1} = V$ and furthermore $|V_1| \geq |V_2| \geq \ldots \geq |V_{q+1}|$.*

Clearly, in general Φ_H is only an approximation of Φ_{opt}. In our application we use a 2-level scheme $\Phi_H = g \circ f$, i.e. $V_1 = U = Co(M)$, $V_2 = \mathcal{S}$ and $V_3 = V = \mathcal{B}$:

$$\Phi_H : Co(M) \xrightarrow{f} \mathcal{S} \xrightarrow{g} \mathcal{B} . \qquad (3.1)$$

Thereby, $\mathcal{S}$ is a set of elements S_l, the pre-images $s_l = f^{-1}(S_l)$ of which are called *super-cones*. We remark that super-cones are collections of usual cones.[3] In contrast to the determination of the cones the realizations of g and f are free. This allows an optimal adaptation. However, often an *a priori* optimal choice is not possible [5]. To overcome this difficulty we prefer in each level of the hierarchical scheme a strategy introduced in neurodynamics by Jordan et al. [2] which is called *mixture of experts*.

For a q-level scheme we consider several partitioning algorithms A_i^j, $i = 1 \ldots m_j$ corresponding to maps Φ_i^j and working in a parallel way in one hierarchical step j representing various partitioning heuristics. The resulting partitions $\Psi_{A_i^j}$ are compared with respect to a quality measure and the β_j best of them will form the basis for the algorithms A_l^{j+1} of the next level which generate partitions $\Psi_{A_i^j, A_l^{j+1}}$. Thereby, the images of the super-cones of a partition $\Psi_{A_i^j}$ given by Φ_i^j are taken as the new basic units. The final result of a q-level scheme is a partition $\Psi_{A_{i_1}^1, A_{i_2}^2, \ldots, A_{i_q}^q}$ the quality measure of which is the best in the last level. However, as yet this describes only a simple strategy of competing experts.

By introducing superpositions $\tilde{\Psi}$ of a set $\Pi = \{\Psi_1, \ldots, \Psi_k\}$ of partitions within a certain level we next extend the competing approach to a mixture one. In this context $\tilde{\Psi}$ plays the role of a generating system, i.e. each super-cone of a partition $\Psi_i \in \Pi$ is expressible in terms of super-cones $\tilde{s}_l \in \tilde{\Psi}$:

---

[3]On the other hand, the cones themselves are sets of boxes which are elements of $\mathcal{M} = M_E \cup M_L \cup M_O$. Therefore, we can regard the concentration of these as an initial 'partitioning' $\Phi_0 : \mathcal{M} \to Co(M)$. In this way we obtain $\Phi_H^* = g \circ f \circ \Phi_0$ as an extended 2-level scheme. The definition of the cones uniquely determines the map Φ_0. Yet, Φ_0 is not a partitioning in the sense of Def. 2.4.

Definition 3.2 *Let $\Pi = \{\Psi_1, \ldots, \Psi_k\}$ be a system of partitions of the set U. The elements of Ψ_i are denoted by s_i^j, $j = 1 \ldots n_i$. $\tilde{\Psi} = \{\tilde{s}_1, \ldots, \tilde{s}_m\}$ is called a **superposition** of Π if and only if:*

1. *$\tilde{\Psi}$ is a partition of U*

2. *$\tilde{\Psi}$ is a generating system for each $\Psi_i \in \Pi$, i.e., for each $s_i^j \in \Psi_i$ $(i = 1 \ldots k$, $j = 1 \ldots n_i)$ exist $\tilde{s}_{l_1}, \ldots, \tilde{s}_{l_r} \in \tilde{\Psi}$ such that $s_i^j = \tilde{s}_{l_1} \cup \ldots \cup \tilde{s}_{l_r}$.*

Def. 2.4 yields $\emptyset \notin \tilde{\Psi}$. The elements of U taken as single sets form a superposition $\hat{U}$ of Π. However, we want to have a superposition the granularity of which is rougher than the granularity of $\hat{U}$, i.e., $|\hat{U}| > |\tilde{\Psi}|$. Therefore we consider a special construction of superpositions:

Theorem 3.3 *Let $\Pi = \{\Psi_1, \ldots, \Psi_k\}$ be a system of partitions of the set U. The elements of Ψ_i are denoted by s_i^j, $j = 1 \ldots n_i$. Furthermore, let Ψ^* be given as*

$$\Psi^* = \left\{ s_{j_1 \ldots j_k}^* \mid s_{j_1 \ldots j_k}^* = \bigcap_{i=1 \ldots k} s_i^{j_i} \right\} \setminus \{\emptyset\} \quad (3.2)$$

with $j_i = 1 \ldots n_i$. Then Ψ^* is a superposition of Π. Furthermore, for all superpositions $\hat{\Psi}$ of Π with $\hat{\Psi} \neq \Psi^*$ the relation $|\hat{\Psi}| > |\Psi^*|$ is valid, i.e. Ψ^* has the maximum granularity.

Proof: The proof of the theorem is shown in the Appendix.

Following the theorem we are able to determine a superposition Ψ^* of maximum granularity by k–times intersections according to (3.2). Yet, in general we only have $|\hat{U}| \geq |\Psi^*|$. The structure of Ψ^* depends on the properties of the partitions $\Psi_i \in \Pi$ which represent the different partitioning heuristics (realized by the corresponding algorithms). Hence, all used strategies influence the superposition, i.e., the expert knowledge of the algorithms is mixed in Ψ^*. We add a superposition according to Theorem 3.3 as a special partition to the β_j best of one hierarchical level j so that it may be used in the next level, too.

Returning to our 2–level scheme, the use of a superposition is suitable after the first partitioning level. If we assume that we have various algorithms A_i^1 realizing the maps $f_i : Co(M) \to S_i$ we obtain $\Psi_i = f_i^{-1}(S_i)$ according to Def. 2.4. S_i are sets of the mappings of the super–cones determined by the partitions Ψ_i, respectively. In analogy, we introduce the abstract map $f^* : Co(M) \to S^*$ where S^* is representing the set of super–cones $s_l^* \in \Psi^*$ and $\Psi^* = (f^*)^{-1}(S^*)$. Then each element of the set system $\Sigma_f = \{S_1, \ldots, S_{\beta_1}, S^*\}$

can be taken as a new system of basic units for partitioning in the second level.

However, the above mixture strategy is a very simple one. In the next section we will improve this strategy using genetic algorithms. Thereby, condition 2 of Def. 3.2 becomes important.

3.2 Improved Mixture of Experts Approach Using Genetic Algorithms

In this part we extend the mixture approach introduced in section 3.1 using *genetic algorithms* (GAs) [1]. In GAs, populations of individuals (parents) produce new individuals (children) in a manner which is inspired by biological evolution and reproduction. The individuals are strings describing a set of parameters which are to be optimized.[4] For applying GAs to graph partitioning let us consider a partitioning map $\Phi : U \to V$. Furthermore, one has to optimize Φ regarding to a certain quality function Ω (fitness function). In this context an individual j represents a certain partition, determined by a map Φ_j. The i-th component of the string is associated with the i–th element of U containing the mapping goal which is an element of V. Several authors have applied GAs to graph partitioning, for instance [8].

However, we will involve this approach into the above described hierarchical strategy. Here we focus onto the 2–level scheme (3.1). In general, GAs may be used in each hierarchical level. Yet, because of the large number of cones in $Co(M)$ the string of an individual representing a partition of $Co(M)$ is often too long for mastering. On the other hand, if applying GAs in the second level of the hierarchical scheme, they require a uniform set of basic elements. To serve this assumption the use of the superposition Ψ^* specified in (3.2) of Theorem 3.3 is appropriate because of its property as a *generating system*. In this context the initial population for the GA is based on the set of all partitions determined in the first level which now are described in terms of the elements of S^*. We emphasize again that the several algorithms represent various partitioning strategies the best of which *a priori* is unknown. Still more, in general a merging strategy will improve the result significantly. We can realize such a strategy using the recombination by *crossing over* in GAs to join different properties of two individuals (partitions) into new ones. The crossing over scheme may be interpreted as a more general exchanging than the simpler one in the algorithm of KERNIGHAN AND LIN [3]. However, we have to take into account a second argument, how much of the old individuals get the chance to be allowed for the competing step (se-

---

[4]For a more detailed introduction see for instance [4].

lection) to build the new population. Let us suppose that μ parent individuals produce λ children. Two contrary methods are well known: 1) the μ best of the λ children only form the new population with $\mu < \lambda$; 2) all $\mu + \lambda$ individuals are allowed for the selection process.[5] In the second case the best solution is preserved. Yet, it tends to a stagnation into a local minimum. In the first scheme this property is weakened. On the other hand, good solutions may get lost here. Therefore, we introduce a new so–called $[\mu * \lambda]$–scheme which balances both strategies: at a time t now $\mu_t + \lambda$ individuals have to be taken into consideration with $\mu_t = \text{int}\,[(\mu - \mu_\alpha) \cdot \sigma(t)] + \mu_\alpha$. Thereby, $\text{int}\,[x]$ stands for the integer value of x. The function $\sigma(t)$ is of decreasing sigmoid type with $0 \le \sigma(t) \le 1$. μ_α describes the final survival probability for the parent individuals. We have $\mu_0 = \mu$ and $\lim_{t\to\infty} \mu_t = \mu_\alpha$.

The whole procedure, which includes the generation of a superposition and following GA, finally leads to the complete scheme of the improved hierarchical mixture strategy depicted in Tab. 3.2.

3.3 Special Experts

Our mixture of experts approach is a framework for applying several partitioning algorithms as experts. A survey of algorithms suitable for parallel logic simulation is given in [13]. We distinguish *direct* and *iterative* partitioning algorithms which construct a single partition resulting from basic units without building intermediate partitions or require an initial partition which is gradually improved according to a quality function, respectively.

We have developed two new direct algorithms on the basis of cones aiming at balanced workload and minimum replication, the *Backward-Cone-Concentration* algorithm (n-BCC) and the *Minimum-Overlap Cone-Cluster* algorithm ($MOCC$).

The basic idea of n-BCC consists in iteratively assigning sets of cones to blocks with preferred choice of n cones overlapping each other using the box-related cone overlap degree u of Def. 2.3:

1. Fix a value n^* with smallest distance to n in the range of u; all boxes in M_F are assumed to be unmarked.

2. Choose a box e within all unmarked boxes out of $u^{-1}(n^*)$ and search its *fan-out cone* $co_O(e)$ (see Def. 2.2) to find the head elements of the n^* cones covering e. These n^* cones are assigned to a block possessing the lowest number of cones

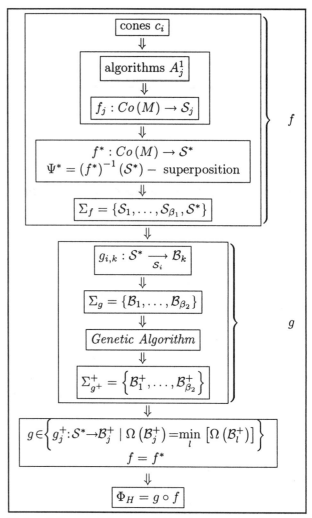

Tab. 3.2. : Scheme of the improved mixture of experts strategy using genetic algorithms

for the moment and all boxes of the selected cones become marked. If there is a remaining unmarked box $e \in u^{-1}(n^*)$, then step 2 is repeated.

3. If there exists $n' \in \text{cod}\,u$ with $u^{-1}(n')$ containing an unmarked box, then such a n' is taken as the new n^* and one has to continue with step 2. Otherwise, the algorithm terminates.

Contrary to $MOCC$ explained below, n-BCC does not explicitly use knowledge concerning the number of boxes in overlap regions or cones. First of all, n-BCC has been designed for application at the first level of our hierarchical strategy.

$MOCC$ successively constructs a partition using the specifics of the weighted overlap hypergraph GU corresponding to the hardware model M. With this algorithm the objective is to achieve partitions with

---
[5]These correspond to the $[\mu, \lambda]$– and $[\mu + \lambda]$–scheme in the notions of RECHENBERG and SCHWEFEL, respectively [9, 11].

blocks containing hypergraph nodes (cones) connected among one another with high-weighted hyperedges:

1. Initially, m_b cones of $Co(M)$ are assigned to the m_b blocks.

2. Taking block $B_i \in \mathcal{B}$ with the lowest number of boxes, we are looking for that overlap region $ovr(\mathcal{C}^*)$ of B_i with $\mathcal{C}^* \cap \Phi^{-1}(B_i) \neq \emptyset$ which maximizes the product $|ovr(\mathcal{C}^*)| \cdot \left| \mathcal{C}^* \setminus \bigcup_{j=1...m_b} \Phi^{-1}(B_j) \right|$.

3. Assign the set of these up to now not considered cones $\mathcal{C}^* \setminus \bigcup_{j=1...m_b} \Phi^{-1}(B_j)$ concerning the selected overlap region $ovr(\mathcal{C}^*)$ to the block B_i.

4. If free cones exist yet, proceed with step 2. Otherwise the partition is complete and the algorithm stops.

MOCC aims at a minimum of multiple evaluation of boxes on different processors keeping a balanced workload corresponding to the resulting partition. If two-stage partitioning is necessary the complex structure of GU implies preferably applying *MOCC* to the second level of the hierarchical partitioning scheme.

4 Experimental Results – Conclusions

Finally, we present a special application of the improved mixture of experts strategy (Tab. 3.2) for a specific hardware model M representing a processor structure with $|M_E| = 16\,398$ boxes.[6]

For the initial hierarchical level we use a set of n-BCC algorithms A_k^1 with varying parameters n and numbers of super-cones m_s. The crossing to the second level requires the production of an initial population Σ_g for the genetic algorithm to be applied. Generally, each S_i resulting from the first level allows the production of many individuals $\mathcal{B}_k$ in the second level $g_{i.k} : S^* \xrightarrow[S_i]{} \mathcal{B}_k$, using the elements of S^* as new basic units and keeping such units together in one block of $\mathcal{B}_k$ which correspond to one and the same super-cone belonging to S_i. Here, we restrict the number of created initial individuals $\mathcal{B}_k$ to one for each S_i. For the evaluation of individuals within the genetic algorithm and for choosing the final partition described by Φ_H, the quality function $\Omega \underset{(2.4)}{=} \max_{B \in \mathcal{B}} (W(B))$ (maximum workload) is taken.

In Fig. 2 the quality function Ω, applied to the partitioning results of the first hierarchical level of n-BCC for various $m_s = 2 \ldots 50$ with the parameters $n = 1 \ldots 100$, is shown.

---

[6]provided by *IBM*

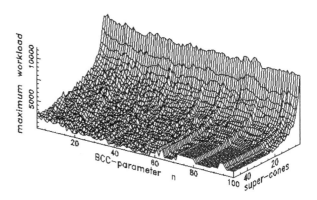

Figure 2 – Quality function Ω (maximum workload) for partitions resulting from the n-BCC for various numbers of super–cones and values of parameters n.

In our exemplary application of the hierarchical scheme we investigate 3 cases for application of GAs differing in the initial population which is randomly chosen out of corresponding partitioning results of the first hierarchical level. In all tests the maximum number of blocks is limited to $m_b = 32$.

First, we build the initial population only from partitions consisting of 32 super–cones, i.e. $m_s = 32$. The evaluation in time (number of generations) of the fitness according to the best individual (partition) of the population is shown in Fig. 3 (short dashed line). The Ω–value of the fittest individual decreases from 2250 to 1899 with $m_b = 32$. In the second example all initial partitions are formed over $m_s = 16$ super–cones. Starting with a best individual of $\Omega_{\text{start}} = 2896$ the final solution gives a partition with $\Omega_{\text{end}} = 1985$ and $m_b = 32$ (straight line in Fig. 3). Yet, this is better than the start value in the first case but its final value is not reached. Nevertheless, the difference between Ω_{start} and Ω_{end} in the second example is more than 900 because there is a high variability in crossing from 16 super–cones up to 32 blocks in a partition. Therefore, in the last experiment we merge individuals of varying parameter n of the n–BCC algorithm on the one hand side and individuals with different numbers m_s on the other hand in the initial population. In fact, this leads to a better performance, i.e. the final value of the fittest individual now is $\Omega_{\text{end}} = 1803$ with $m_b = 32$ again (long dashed line in Fig. 3).

These first results show that a mixture of the *a priori* chosen strategies represented by the various n–BCC instances leads to improved partitions. The successful application of the GAs to the mixture strategy of partitioning algorithms was demonstrated using the idea

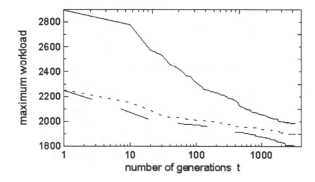

Figure 3 – Maximum workload of the best partition generated by a GA for $m_{s_1} = 16$ (short dashed), $m_{s_2} = 32$ (straight line) and for a mixed initial population (long dashed line) with respect to time (number of generations), see text.

of superposition of partitions.

Acknowledgement

This work was supported by DEUTSCHE FORSCHUNGSGEMEINSCHAFT (DFG) under the grant **SP 487/1–2**.

5 Appendix

Proof of Theorem 3.3:

(I) Ψ^* is a generating system:
Let $s_i^j \in \Psi_i$ be arbitrarily chosen. We construct the sets S_l with $l \neq i$ according to the following rule: if $s_i^j \cap s_l^{j'} = \tilde{s}_l^{j'}$ with $s_l^{j'} \in \Psi_l$ and $\tilde{s}_l^{j'} \neq \emptyset$ holds then $\tilde{s}_l^{j'} \in S_l$. Then for each l the relation $\bigcup_{j'} \tilde{s}_l^{j'} = s_i^j$ is valid. We consider the set $\Xi^* =$

$$\left\{ s_{j_1' \ldots j_k'}^* \mid s_{j_1' \ldots j_k'}^* = \bigcap_{\substack{l=1\ldots k \\ l \neq i}} \tilde{s}_l^{j_l} \; ; \; \tilde{s}_l^{j_l} \in S_l \right\} \setminus \{\emptyset\}.$$

Because of the definition of the $\tilde{s}_l^{j_l}$ as intersections with $s_i^j \in \Psi_i$ we have $s_{j_1' \ldots j_k'}^* \in \Psi^*$ for $s_{j_1' \ldots j_k'}^* \neq \emptyset$ and, furthermore, $\bigcup_{s_{j_1' \ldots j_k'}^* \in \Xi^*} s_{j_1' \ldots j_k'}^* \subseteq s_i^j$. It still remains to show $\bigcup_{s_{j_1' \ldots j_k'}^* \in \Xi^*} s_{j_1' \ldots j_k'}^* \supseteq s_i^j$: We take an arbitrary but fixed $u \in s_i^j$. For each set S_l one and only one $\tilde{s}_l^{j_l^*}$ exists such that $u \in \tilde{s}_l^{j_l^*}$, i.e., $u \in \bigcap_{\substack{l=1\ldots k \\ l \neq i}} \tilde{s}_l^{j_l^*}$ with $\bigcap_{\substack{l=1\ldots k \\ l \neq i}} \tilde{s}_l^{j_l^*} \in \Xi^*$.

(II) Ψ^* is a partition of U:

Lemma 5.1 *For $s_i^* \in \Psi^*$ and $s_j^* \in \Psi^*$ with $i \neq j$ holds: $s_i^* \cap s_j^* = \emptyset$, i.e. the elements of Ψ^* are pairwise disjoint.*

According to (I) Ψ^* is a generating system for the $s_i^j \in \Psi_i$. Furthermore, it is assumed, that all Ψ_i are partitions of U themselves. Then one can find for each element $u \in U$ a super–cone $s_{j^*}^* \in \Psi^*$ such that $u \in s_{j^*}^*$. Lemma 5.1, the proof of which is shown below, ensures that the elements of Ψ^* are pairwise disjoint.

(III) Ψ^* has the maximum granularity:

Lemma 5.2 *Let Π, $\hat{\Psi}$ and Ψ^* be defined as in Theorem 3.3. Then, for each super–cone $\hat{s} \in \hat{\Psi}$ a super–cone $s^* \in \Psi^*$ exists such that $\hat{s} \subseteq s^*$ is valid.*

For arbitrary elements $u \in U$ and partitions Ψ of U let u^Ψ denote the uniquely determined super–cone $s \in \Psi$ for which $u \in s$ is satisfied. We choose a set $\mathcal{R}$ of elements $u_1, u_2, \ldots, u_{|\Psi^*|}$ with $u_j \in U$, $j = 1 \ldots |\Psi^*|$ in such a way that for the set $\mathcal{R}^* = \{ u_j^{\Psi^*} \mid j = 1 \ldots |\Psi^*| \}$ the relation $\mathcal{R}^* = \Psi^*$ holds. Using this construction and Lemma 5.2 we have for each of the considered u_j the relation $u_j^{\hat{\Psi}} \subseteq u_j^{\Psi^*}$ with $u_j^{\hat{\Psi}} \in \hat{\Psi}$ and $u_j^{\Psi^*} \in \Psi^*$. The sets $u_j^{\hat{\Psi}}$ form the set $\hat{\mathcal{R}} = \{ u_j^{\hat{\Psi}} \mid j = 1 \ldots |\Psi^*| \}$. Since Ψ^* is a partition it follows that $u_i^{\Psi^*} \cap u_j^{\Psi^*} = \emptyset$ for $i \neq j$ and therefore we get $u_i^{\hat{\Psi}} \cap u_j^{\hat{\Psi}} = \emptyset$. This leads to the inequality $\left| \hat{\Psi} \right| \geq \left| \hat{\mathcal{R}} \right| = |\mathcal{R}^*|$.

Next we derive the corresponding strong inequality. Because of the assumption $\Psi^* \neq \hat{\Psi}$ at least one index j' exists with $u_{j'}^{\hat{\Psi}} \subset u_{j'}^{\Psi^*}$. Consider an element $\hat{u} \in u_{j'}^{\Psi^*} \setminus u_{j'}^{\hat{\Psi}}$. Using Lemma 5.2 and $\hat{u} \in u_{j'}^{\Psi^*}$ we get $\hat{u}^{\hat{\Psi}} \subseteq u_{j'}^{\Psi^*}$.[7] Hence, for each $i = 1 \ldots |\Psi^*|$ one has $u_i^{\hat{\Psi}} \cap \hat{u}^{\hat{\Psi}} = \emptyset$. This leads to the inequality

$$\left| \hat{\Psi} \right| \geq \left| \hat{\mathcal{R}} \cup \{ \hat{u}^{\hat{\Psi}} \} \right| = \left| \hat{\mathcal{R}} \right| + 1 > |\Psi^*| \qquad (5.1)$$

which completes the proof of Theorem 3.3. □

It remains to show that the Lemmata 5.1 and 5.2 hold:

Proof of Lemma 5.1:

Let $s_{i_1 \ldots i_k}^* \in \Psi^*$ and $s_{j_1 \ldots j_k}^* \in \Psi^*$ be given with $(i_1, \ldots, i_k) \neq (j_1, \ldots, j_k)$. Then an index l exists such that $i_l \neq j_l$. Further we have $s_{i_1 \ldots i_k}^* = s_1^{i_1} \cap \ldots \cap s_l^{i_l} \cap \ldots \cap s_k^{i_k}$ and $s_{j_1 \ldots j_k}^* = s_1^{j_1} \cap \ldots \cap s_l^{j_l} \cap \ldots \cap s_k^{j_k}$. Then we obtain for the intersection $s_{i_1 \ldots i_k}^* \cap s_{j_1 \ldots j_k}^*$ the relation

---

[7] Moreover, we remark that $u_{j'}^{\hat{\Psi}} \neq \emptyset$ yields because $\hat{\Psi}$ being a partition and, hence, $\hat{u}^{\hat{\Psi}} \subset u_{j'}^{\Psi^*}$ is valid.

$$s^*_{i_1...i_k} \cap s^*_{j_1...j_k} = s^{i_1}_1 \cap s^{j_1}_1 \cap ... \cap s^{i_l}_l \cap s^{j_l}_l \cap ... \cap s^{i_k}_k \cap s^{j_k}_k .$$

The definition of Ψ^* in (3.2) yields $s^{i_l}_l \in \Psi_l$ and $s^{j_l}_l \in \Psi_l$. Because Ψ_l is a partition of U, $s^{i_l}_l \cap s^{j_l}_l = \emptyset$ is valid. $\square$

Proof of Lemma 5.2:

For the proof of the lemma we show that the following assumption leads to a contradiction:

assumption: There exists a super–cone $\hat{s} \in \hat{\Psi}$ such that it could not be found a super–cone $s^* \in \Psi^*$ with $\hat{s} \subseteq s^*$.

Consider a super–cone $\hat{s} \in \hat{\Psi}$ satisfying the above assumption. Because Ψ^* is a partition $|\hat{s}| \geq 2$ follows. In particular, there exist 2 elements u_1, $u_2 \in \hat{s}$ with 1) $u_1 \in s^*_1$ and $s^*_1 \in \Psi^*$ and 2) $u_2 \in s^*_2$ and $s^*_2 \in \Psi^*$ such that $s^*_1 \neq s^*_2$ is valid. Let these be given as $s^*_1 = \bigcap_{i=1...k} s^{j_i}_i = s^*_{j_1...j_k}$ and $s^*_2 = \bigcap_{i=1...k} s^{h_i}_i = s^*_{h_1...h_k}$. Since $s^*_1 \neq s^*_2$ one can find an index $l \in \{1,...,k\}$ for which $j_l \neq h_l$ holds. For the corresponding super–cones $s^{j_l}_l$ and $s^{h_l}_l$ we have: $s^{j_l}_l, s^{h_l}_l \in \Psi_l$ and, hence, we get

$$s^{j_l}_l \cap s^{h_l}_l = \emptyset . \tag{5.2}$$

Furthermore, $\hat{\Psi}$ is a superposition of Π, i.e., one can describe the super–cone $s^{j_l}_l$ in terms of the elements of $\hat{\Psi}$. First, we remark that the relations $u_1 \in \hat{s} \cap s^*_1$, $u_2 \in \hat{s} \cap s^*_2$, $s^*_1 \subseteq s^{j_l}_l$ and $s^*_2 \subseteq s^{h_l}_l$ lead to

$$\hat{s} \cap s^{j_l}_l \neq \emptyset \quad \text{and} \quad \hat{s} \cap s^{h_l}_l \neq \emptyset . \tag{5.3}$$

Hence, there exists a decomposition of the super–cone $s^{j_l}_l$ into super–cones $\hat{s}_r \in \hat{\Psi}$:

$$s^{j_l}_l = \bigcup_{r=1...t} \hat{s}_r \tag{5.4}$$

and we get $\hat{s} \cap s^{j_l}_l \underset{\text{Eq.(5.4)}}{=} \hat{s} \cap \left(\bigcup_{r=1...t} \hat{s}_r \right) = \bigcup_{r=1...t} (\hat{s} \cap \hat{s}_r) \underset{\text{Eq.(5.3)}}{\neq} \emptyset$. Then an index r^* exists with $\hat{s} = \hat{s}_{r^*}$, i.e.

$$s^{j_l}_l = \hat{s}_1 \cup ... \cup \hat{s} \cup ... \cup \hat{s}_t . \tag{5.5}$$

On the other hand, from (5.3) it follows that one can find an element $\tilde{u} \in \hat{s} \cap s^{h_l}_l$ which implies $\tilde{u} \in \hat{s}$ and therefore with (5.5) $\tilde{u} \in s^{j_l}_l$. Yet, this is a contradiction to (5.2) and the lemma is shown. $\square$

References

[1] K. Hering, R. Haupt, and T. Villmann. An Improved Mixture of Experts Approach for Model Partitioning in VLSI–Design Using Genetic Algorithms. Technical Report 14, University of Leipzig / Inst. of Informatics, Germany, 1995.

[2] M. I. Jordan and R. A. Jacobs. Hierarchical Mixture of Experts and the EM Algorithm. In P. Morasso, editor, *Proc. ICANN'94*, pages 479–486. Springer, 1994.

[3] B. W. Kernighan and S. Lin. An efficient heuristic procedure for partitioning graphs. *Bell Systems Technical Journal*, 49(2):291–307, 1970.

[4] J. R. Koza. *Genetic Programming*. MIT Press, 1992.

[5] T. Lengauer. *Combinatorial Algorithms for Integrated Circuit Layout*. Teubner-Verlag Stuttgart and JOHN WILEY & SONS, 1990.

[6] N. Manjikian. High performance parallel logic simulation on a network of workstations. TechReport T-220, CCNG, University of Waterloo, 1992.

[7] R. B. Mueller-Thuns, D. G. Saab, R. F. Damiano, and J. A. Abraham. VLSI Logic and Fault Simulation on General Purpose Parallel Computers. *IEEE Trans. on Computer-Aided Design of Integrated Circuits and Systems*, 12:446–460, 1993.

[8] H. Mühlenbein, M. Gorges-Schleuter, and O. Krämer. Evolution Algorithm in Combinatorial Optimization. *Parallel Computing*, (7):65–88, 1988.

[9] I. Rechenberg. *Evolutionsstrategie - Optimierung technischer Systeme nach Prinzipien der biologischen Information*. Fromman Verlag Freiburg (Germany), 1973.

[10] H. Ritter, T. Martinetz, and K. Schulten. *Neural Computation and Self-Organizing Maps: An Introduction*. Addison-Wesley, Reading, MA, 1992.

[11] H.-P. Schwefel. *Numerical Optimization of Computer Models*. Wiley and Sons, 1981.

[12] S. P. Smith, B. Underwood, and M. R. Mercer. An analysis of several approaches to circuit partitioning for parallel logic simulation. In *Proceedings IEEE International Conference on Computer Design (ICCD)*, pages 664–667, 1987.

[13] C. Sporrer. *Verfahren zur Schaltungspartitionierung für die parallele Logiksimulation*. Verlag Shaker Aachen, 1995.

[14] W. G. Spruth. *The Design of a Microprocessor*. Springer Berlin, Heidelberg, 1989.

The *APOSTLE* simulation language: granularity control and performance data

Paul Wonnacott and David Bruce,
Defence Research Agency, Malvern,
Worcestershire WR14 3PS, United Kingdom.
E-mail: {pwonnacott, dib}@dra.hmg.gb

Abstract

A simulation-oriented language can significantly enhance the usability of Parallel Discrete Event Simulation (PDES) by hiding the complexities of the synchronization protocol used to ensure that events are processed in the correct order. The higher-level interface presented to the user by such a language also allows optimizations to be performed that are difficult and cumbersome with current parallel simulators, such as granularity control. APOSTLE is a new high-level simulation-oriented language for PDES, and in this paper we report that the APOSTLE granularity control mechanism reduced simulation run-times by as much as 80%. We also report that APOSTLE achieved a parallel speed-up of around 9 on 16 processors relative to its optimized sequential implementation and a parallel speed-up of around 6 on 16 processors relative to MODSIM II. Overall, we believe that the widespread success of PDES can only be achieved using a simulation-oriented language, and that APOSTLE has made a significant contribution towards this goal.

1 Introduction

To date most research into Parallel Discrete Event Simulation (PDES) has focused on the fundamental synchronization protocols used to ensure that events are processed in the correct order. Those researchers adopting a quantitative research methodology have typically built their parallel simulators using existing sequential languages enhanced with library support to exploit the underlying parallel or distributed architecture. Although PDES has been shown to achieve good speed-up for a variety of simulations (Fujimoto 93), the simulations used have generally been either small and synthetic, or consist of large numbers of simple entities. Generally, the complexities of PDES and the poor modelling support provided by current simulators make it difficult to implement large simulations consisting of entities with complex states.

Most parallel simulators require detailed knowledge of the synchronization protocol used to achieve both a correctly working parallel simulation and good performance (Fujimoto 93). For example, with conservative simulators the user must be familiar with the issues of lookahead and known Logical Process (LP) connectivity, and with optimistic simulators they must be familiar with the issues of state saving and rollback (although our recent work on state saving has made some progress in this area (Bruce 95)). Also, it is almost impossible to construct a fully robust parallel simulator based on an existing sequential language, as the users of such a simulator are trusted to obey the conventions laid down by the originators of the simulator. These conventions cannot be enforced, and any mistakes made can lead to an incorrect parallel simulation that is difficult to debug. Our experience with an optimistic simulator at DRA Malvern for a British Army logistics simulation has reported these difficulties (Hoare et al. 95). (Buhr 95) also argues that concurrency libraries for sequential programming languages can be unsafe, and that language-based extensions are required for correct concurrent semantics.

Historically, the first discrete event simulation packages were based on libraries for early sequential programming languages. However, it was soon realised that a dedicated language for simulation could provide better modelling support (Nance 93). These arguments could also be applied to PDES. For example, consider the choice of *world-view* (also known as a conceptual framework or strategy) (Evans 88). A world-view imposes a particular way of expressing behaviour in a simulation. Most PDES research has been based on the notion of a Physical Process (PP) – an entity from the model to be simulated on a parallel computer – and an LP – the implementation of a PP in a parallel simulation. LPs communicate with each other via time-stamped *messages* or *events*. Upon receipt of a message at time T, an LP may change its state at time T and send zero or more messages to other LPs for a time greater than T. These notions provide a conceptual framework similar to the *event-scheduling* world-view, which is considered to be the least expressive and hardest to use of the three main world-views[†]. Modern simulation languages tend to favour the *process-interaction* world-view, in which behaviour can be expressed as a natural sequence of state changes. This approach also enhances modularity when compared with the event-scheduling world-view.

A simulation-oriented language can significantly enhance the usability of PDES by hiding the complexities of the synchronization protocol used to ensure that events are processed in the correct order. The higher-level interface presented to the user by such a language can also allow optimizations to be performed that are difficult and cumbersome at the lower-level interface of current parallel simulators. A good example of this is *granularity control* (Baezner et al. 90; Rich and Michelsen 91). A granularity control mechanism transforms multiple fine grained events into a single coarser grained event, so that the per event overheads are spread over many changes of state.

[†] The three main world-views are event-scheduling, activity-scanning and process-interaction, although activity-scanning's popularity is somewhat limited to the U.K.

114

APOSTLE is a new high-level simulation-oriented language for PDES, and in this paper we present performance figures for the Meiko CS-2, a SPARC-based distributed memory multiprocessor. We begin in section 2 by comparing APOSTLE with other related PDES languages, although further details on the APOSTLE language and a rationale for its design can be found in (Wonnacott and Bruce 1995a). Section 3 further motivates the need for granularity control and briefly describes APOSTLE's granularity control mechanism ((Wonnacott and Bruce 95b) contains more details, as APOSTLE's support for granularity control is a fundamental part of its overall implementation). In section 4 we describe the three benchmark simulations used in this paper: super-ping, a generalization of the ping-pong simulation; a queuing network simulation intended to mimic the Colombian health care simulation (Baezner et al. 90); and a logic gate simulation of a 32-bit adder. These simulations were used to explore the effect of APOSTLE's granularity control mechanism, which reduced simulation runtimes by as much as 80%. We also present the parallel speed-up figures for the three benchmark simulations. APOSTLE achieved a parallel speed-up of around 9 on 16 processors relative to its optimized sequential implementation. To put APOSTLE's performance into context, we also compare its sequential performance against MODSIM II (CACI 91), which was developed from the US Army's version of ModSim (Rich and Michelsen 91). MODSIM was between 1.5 and 2.5 times faster than sequential APOSTLE, but APOSTLE was still able to achieve a parallel speed-up of around 6 on 16 processors relative to MODSIM. Our performance data is presented in section 5. Finally, section 6 gives our conclusions and suggestions for future work.

2 Related work

In this section we briefly compare APOSTLE with ModSim (Rich and Michelsen 89, 91), MOOSE[†] (Waldorf and Bagrodia 94), MOSS (Blanchard and Lake 95) and Sim++ (Baezner et al. 90).

APOSTLE has much in common with these languages, which are based on the object-oriented paradigm and the process-interaction world-view. APOSTLE supports *delegation-based* inheritance (Lieberman 86) rather than class-based inheritance due to its power and flexibility. APOSTLE and MOSS also have support for *part-of* object relationships (Blake and Cook 87).

Sim++ allows the behaviour of each LP to be expressed as a single process (from the process-interaction world-view) – these processes communicate via an asynchronous message passing mechanism. The other languages allow each method that an object implements to be a process. The behaviour of APOSTLE and ModSim objects can be implemented by a set of concurrent methods; i.e., APOSTLE and ModSim objects support intra-object concurrency. All of the languages provide some support for concurrency control. For example, APOSTLE has *predicate path expressions* (Andler 79), and MOOSE methods have a guard associated with them which must be true before a method can begin execution. APOSTLE also has *ordering rules* to prioritize methods blocked due to concurrency control.

An APOSTLE method can wait for a period of simulation time to elapse or until a Boolean expression becomes true using the wait until expression (Vaucher 73). The wait until expression can emulate the interruptible wait statements provided by most of the other languages.

APOSTLE's method invocation mechanism is asynchronous and uses *promises* (Liskov and Shira 88). The promise returned by an invocation of a method can be used to synchronize with the completion of the method, and thus recover any return value. Promises are useful for ensuring that simulation start-up is performed in parallel. In ModSim and MOSS synchronous methods can only return values, asynchronous methods cannot.

APOSTLE allows objects to communicate via *ports*, which must be connected before a method can be invoked (i.e., APOSTLE is both *weakly* and *strongly* distributed (Wegner 91)). Ports enhance modularity and code reuse – they allow objects to be used in a "plug-and-play" manner. APOSTLE also supports *garbage collection* and an *object-centred* representation (where *all* values in the language should be considered to be objects, even primitive values such as integers, reals, etc.). None of the other languages support these features.

The prototype implementation of APOSTLE follows that of ModSim and Sim++; i.e., APOSTLE runs on top of an existing optimistic simulator written in C++. The optimistic simulator currently being used is based on the Breathing Time Buckets (BTB) synchronization protocol (Steinman 92), and was developed at DRA Malvern (Booth 93, Damitio et al. 94, Hoare et al. 95). State saving is handled using *persistent data structures* (Bruce 95), which have the property that any modified state is automatically incrementally saved. State saving costs remain constant with respect to the state size of an LP, and rollback and fossil collection costs are proportional to the amount of state saved. The optimistic simulator does not support pre-emption. Further details on the implementation of APOSTLE can be found in (Wonnacott and Bruce 95b). The implementation of MOOSE is based on the space-time synchronization protocol (Bagrodia et al. 91), which allows the expression of both conservative and optimistic synchronization protocols in the same framework. MOSS has an interpretive implementation based on conservative protocols. Lookahead is calculated automatically and the connectivity of LPs can be changed dynamically. (Blanchard and Lake 95) also discuss their use of collocating references to provide support for LP migration.

3 Granularity control

In PDES it is often the case that the granularity of an event is small when compared with the per event overheads. For example, in gate-level VLSI simulation (Bailey et al. 94) an event could only amount to a few instructions. Greater efficiency could therefore be obtained if the execution of multiple events could be coalesced so that the overheads of a single event could be spread over many changes of state. Generally, this also implies that LPs should be coalesced, therefore granularity control is performed at the expense of a reduction in the amount of available parallelism. Reducing the number of LPs required can also be beneficial. For example, with fewer LPs, determining the processor identi-

---

† MOOSE is an object-oriented extension of Maisie (Bagrodia and Liao 94).

fier and address for an LP from its user identifier is generally more efficient. However, with larger state sizes it is essential that incremental state saving is used, as saving the entire state of an LP containing many objects when only one object is modified is clearly inefficient. With events of larger granularity, pre-emption becomes increasingly important to stop the execution of large grained straggler events.

Our experience with an optimistic simulator based on C++ for a British Army logistics simulation showed that changing the granularity of a parallel simulation involves a significant amount of recoding (Hoare et al. 95). This was because the simulator has two object models with two separate modes of communication: LPs, which are the units of parallelism and communicate by scheduling events; and C++ objects, which can only exist inside an LP and communicate by member function invocation. (Rich and Michelsen 89) also report that changing the granularity of a parallel simulation in ModSim had to be done contrary to a pure object-oriented design methodology, as an object's state and behaviour must be artificially inflated with that of other objects. With a single object model, which can be provided by a simulation-oriented language such as *APOSTLE*, changing the granularity of a parallel simulation requires minimal recoding. In fact, all that is required in *APOSTLE* is to change the identifier of the LP that the object is to be created on.

Our prototype *APOSTLE* implementation consists of a compiler written in C++ using lex++ and yacc++ and a run-time system, also written in C++, built on top of the BTB simulator (Wonnacott and Bruce 1995b). *APOSTLE* objects are referenced or identified using GlobalMachineIDs, which consist of a C++ pointer and the identifier given to the LP by the underlying simulator. Each LP records the pointers of all the *APOSTLE* objects it is responsible for, so that the creation of objects can be undone on rollback. Objects that share the same LP can then communicate via shared-memory, as they are guaranteed to be in the same process on a single processor, instead of using the event scheduling mechanism[†]. This means that incrementing reference counts (Wonnacott and Bruce 95b), collecting values from promises, starting methods for the current simulation time, etc., can now be done locally without scheduling an event. Events are only scheduled for inter-LP communication, to perform a wait for, or to invoke a method for some future time. If a method is invoked on a local object for a future time, the method, together with its start time, is queued locally. When the method processing for the current simulation time has finished, the pending method queue is examined and a WakeUp event is scheduled for the start time of the earliest method.

Of the languages mentioned in section 2, only Sim++ has support for granularity control – indeed (Rich and Michelsen 91) report that this is an important deficiency of ModSim. Sim++'s granularity control mechanism is based on *clusters* (Baezner et al. 90). Clusters may contain more than one Sim++ object and each cluster is mapped to an LP. Objects mapped to the same cluster can communicate via member function calls, whereas objects mapped to different clusters must communicate via the event scheduling mechanism. Note that if a change of mapping of objects to clusters is required, the communication mechanism between objects may need to be changed. This is not the case for *APOSTLE*, as we have a single mechanism that works for both intra-LP or inter-LP object communication.

4   Benchmark simulations

In this section we briefly describe the three benchmark simulations used in this paper. *APOSTLE* objects were mapped to LPs, and LPs were mapped to processors, so that the majority of the inter-object communication used the cheapest mechanism available. These mechanisms are (in increasing order of cost) shared memory communication in a single LP, event scheduling between LPs on the same processor, and event scheduling between LPs on different processors. The mapping of LPs to processors was done in such a way as to ensure that regardless of the number of LPs used the "mapping" of objects to processors always remained the same. This ensured that any improvements in run-time were due to granularity control and not a change of static load balance.

4.1   Super-ping

The super-ping simulation is a generalization of the ping-pong simulation and consists of 512 ping-pong objects connected in a ring. Each ping-pong object implements the method ping, which simply invokes the ping method on its neighbour. Super-ping was also described in (Wonnacott and Bruce 95b).

In this paper we explore the effect of mapping super-ping objects to LPs in a 1-to-1 fashion (512 LPs), 2-to-1 fashion (256 LPs), 4-to-1 fashion (128 LPs), up to a 32-to-1 fashion (16 LPs).

4.2   Colombian health care

The Colombian health care simulation (Baezner et al. 90) is essentially a hierarchically structured queuing network. Each node consists of a village and local health centre. Patients visit their local health centre for treatment, but may be referred to a more specialized health centre at the next layer up in the hierarchy. The topmost health centre is assumed to be able to treat all illnesses.

In figure 1 we present an illustration of the implementation of each node in the tree, an object of type VandHC, which is implemented as having parts of type Village and HealthCentre. The graphical representation of *APOSTLE* objects was described in (Wonnacott and Bruce 95a). Patients arrive from their local village, or from the health centre in the next level down, via an invocation of the jobIn method for the object of type HealthCentre. Patients leave the health centre for further treatment via an invocation of the jobOut method. In this paper, we have used a version of the Colombian health care simulation in which patients do not return to their home village after treatment (i.e., the queuing network is *open*). The simulation consists of 31 objects of type VandHC connected into a binary tree, plus an additional VandHC object *V* connected to the root of the tree. The root of the tree forwards patients to *V*, and *V* forwards patients to

---

† LPs are in some sense multithreaded, although the concurrency is implemented in a coroutine style. Such concurrency is in some sense "already there", as *APOSTLE* allows the behaviour of an object to be expressed using multiple concurrent methods.

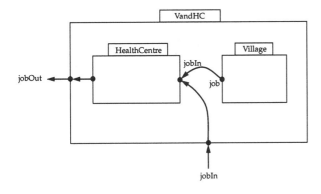

Figure 1: An implementation of an object of type VandHC in the Colombian health care simulation.

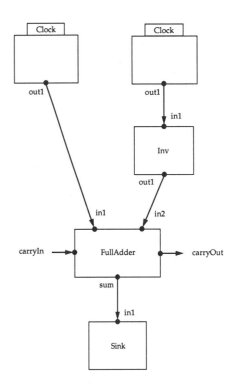

Figure 2: A single bit slice from the logic gates simulation.

itself. The additional object of type VandHC simply evens out the number of VandHC objects to 32. In this paper we have used two different onward referral rates for patients by a health centre – 10% and 90% – as (Baezner et al. 90) suggested that the effect of granularity control is related to the onward referral rate for patients. The implementations of the objects of type Health-Centre and Village is based on a generic set of objects for queuing network simulations.

In this paper we explore the issue as to whether objects of type Village should be mapped to their own unique LP, or with same LP that the corresponding object of type HealthCentre is mapped to (as for (Baezner et al. 90)). This gives simulations of 64 and 32 LPs respectively. The mapping of LPs to processors was based on a depth-first traversal of the hierarchical health care system.

4.3 Logic gates

The logic gates simulation is a simulation of a 32-bit adder. The implementation of objects of type FullAdder is based on two objects of type HalfAdder and a single object of type Or. Objects of type HalfAdder are in turn implemented by an object of type And and an object of type Xor. Each adder receives its inputs from two objects of type Clock, which may be fed through an object of type Inv, and the outputs from the adders are sent to objects of type Sink. The adder's carries are connected in the obvious way. Figure 2 presents an illustration of a single bit slice from this simulation.

In this paper we explore the effect of four different mappings of the logic gates simulation using 32, 128, 224 and 480 LPs. With 32 LPs each bit slice N is mapped to LP N. If the objects of type Clock and Sink are also mapped to their own LP we get a simulation of 128 LPs. By mapping the constituent parts of an object of type FullAdder to unique LPs we get a simulation of 224 LPs. Similarly, by mapping the constituent parts of an object of type HalfAdder to unique LPs we get a simulation of 480 LPs.

5 Performance

In this section we present performance figures illustrating the effect of the *APOSTLE* granularity control mechanism. We also present *APOSTLE*'s parallel speed-up figures and compare its performance against MODSIM II. Performance figures are presented for a Meiko CS-2 distributed memory multiprocessor with 22 50MHz SuperSPARC+ processors. Each processor has a 1Mbyte external cache and 32Mbytes of memory. Two of the processors are dedicated I/O nodes, giving 20 usable processors. The processors are connected using a dedicated communications network, giving a peak bandwidth of 50Mbytes/s/processor in each direction. The CS-2 also has hardware support for processor synchronization and an inter-processor DMA capability; these facilities were used to great effect by the underlying simulator.

The C++ code output by the *APOSTLE* compiler was hand optimized to make use of an efficient representation of primitive values (Wonnacott and Bruce 95b). The C++ code was then further optimized for purely asynchronous method invocations (i.e., when the promise returned from a method invocation is immediately discarded, as the invoked method will never be synchronised with). This optimization uses a specialised purely asynchronous method invocation mechanism that does not create a promise. Work is in progress to perform these optimizations automatically by the compiler.

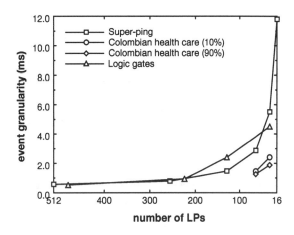

Figure 3: A graph of the event granularity against the number of LPs for the benchmark simulations.

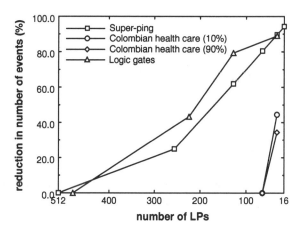

Figure 4: A graph of the percentage reduction in the number of events processed against the number of LPs for the benchmark simulations.

The sequential implementation of *APOSTLE* did not perform any state saving and used an optimized sequential simulator. All performance figures presented in this paper *exclude* start-up costs – this gives a more representative comparison.

5.1 Granularity control

The performance figures presented in sections 5.1.1 to 5.1.3 include breakdowns of the contributions made to the overall run-time from four categories: `wait` records the amount of time spent synchronizing with other processors (i.e., the time spent waiting for other processors to cross their Local Event Horizon (LEH) at the end of a cycle (Steinman 92)); `commit` records the time spent committing an event, which includes the time spent performing fossil collection; `event` records the time spent queuing events, transmitting events to other processors. etc.; and `process` records the time spent processing events (i.e., the time spent in the *APOSTLE* run-time system and in user code). The BTB simulator was configured so that as soon as a processor crossed its LEH, event processing ceased for that processor; i.e., no events were processed optimistically after the LEH had been crossed. This configuration consistently gave the best run-times, as in all cases the number of rollbacks was insignificant.

We begin by showing the primary effects of the *APOSTLE* granularity control mechanism from the perspective of the underlying simulator; i.e., the increase in the average event granularity as the number of LPs decreased (figure 3), and the percentage reduction[†] in the number of events processed as the number of LPs increased (figure 4). These measurements were taken from parallel *APOSTLE*. Super-ping exhibited the widest range of event granularities, from around 0.6ms for 512 LPs to around 12ms for 16 LPs. The event granularities for logic gates began at around 0.5ms for 480 LPs and rose to only around 4.5ms for 32 LPs. For

Colombian health care, the 10% onward referral rate gave event granularities of around 1.5ms for 64 LPs and around 2.5ms for 32 LPs; the 90% onward referral rate gave event granularities of around 1.25ms for 64 LPs and around 1.75ms for 32 LPs.

For super-ping and logic gates, the percentage reduction in the number of events processed as the number of LPs is decreased showed similar characteristics; i.e., both rose to around 90% for 32 LPs. The reductions for Colombian health care were smaller: around 45% for the 10% onward referral rate and around 35% for the 90% onward referral rate. The latter was less than the former because for the 90% onward referral rate a greater proportion of the communication was between health centres for which the granularity control had no effect.

5.1.1 Super-ping

In figure 5 we present a graph of the run-time breakdown against the number of objects per LP on eight processors. The graph for eight processors was typical for this simulation. This graph shows how the overall run-time fell as the number of LPs decreased, and that these reductions were largely due to the reduction in the `event` costs. The `event` costs fell because a primary effect of the *APOSTLE* granularity control mechanism was to decrease the number of events processed. Note how the run-time actually increased as the number of objects per LP increased from 16 to 32. This was caused by the `event` curve, which initially fell as the number of objects per LP increased, reached a minimum but then rose again. The shape of the `event` curve was determined by two factors. As the number of objects per LP increased, there were fewer events scheduled and thus less data had to be packed and unpacked into events. This lead to a reduction in the `event` costs. However, as the number of objects per LP increased, the LPs' method queues grew in size, and thus method queuing operations became increasingly expensive. For small numbers of objects per LP the reduction in the event scheduling costs outweighed the increase in the method queuing costs,

---

† The percentage reductions in this paper were calculated using the formula
$100 \times$ actual reduction ÷ original value.

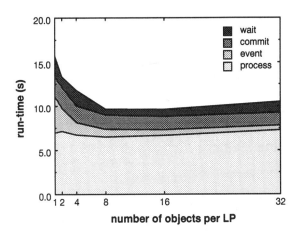

Figure 5: A graph of the run-time breakdown against the number of objects per LP for super-ping on eight processors.

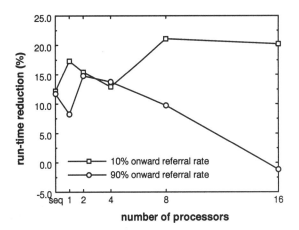

Figure 7: A graph of the percentage reduction in run-time against the number of processors for two different mappings of objects to LPs for Colombian health care.

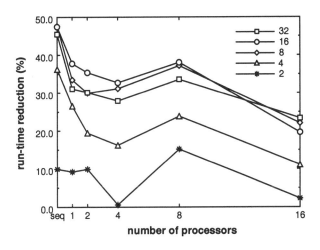

Figure 6: A graph of the percentage reduction in run-time against the number of processors for various mappings of objects to LPs for super-ping.

however for large numbers of objects per LP the latter outweighed the former.

In figure 6 we present a graph of the percentage reduction in run-time against the number of processors for different numbers of objects per LP. For a given number of processors, this reduction is calculated relative to the one object per LP version. The largest run-time reduction approached 50% for sequential *APOSTLE* using 16 objects per LP; parallel *APOSTLE* gave a maximum run-time reduction of about 40% on eight processors for 16 objects per LP. The percentage reduction in run-time generally decreased as the number of processors is increased, although there was a maximum point for all curves at eight processors

(but this is not the maximum percentage reduction in run-time). This reduction was because the *APOSTLE* granularity control mechanism cannot reduce the per cycle overheads (for example, sending the value of the LEH to the other processors and performing a barrier synchronisation after the events have been sent to their respective processors). The per cycle overheads were therefore proportionally larger as the number of processors was increased because there were fewer events to be processed per processor per cycle. In fact, the situation was worse than this as the per cycle overheads also increased with the number of processors.

5.1.2 Colombian health care

For Colombian health care, it is clear that mapping villages and health centres to the same LP was the better strategy (figure 7[†]) as, apart from the 90% onward referral rate on 16 processors, this gave a reduction in the overall run-time. However, these reductions were generally small when compared with super-ping, as figure 4 shows that mapping villages and health centres to the same LP only reduced the number of events processed by 45% at best (cf. 90% for super-ping).

On the whole, the 10% onward referral rate gave the best run-time reductions when villages were mapped to their own LP, as there was a larger reduction in the number of events processed (see figure 4) when compared with the 90% onward referral rate. In the case of the 90% onward referral rate, a larger proportion of the communication was between health centres than for the 10% onward referral rate, and mapping villages to the same LP had no effect upon this communication.

---

† A negative percentage reduction in run-time indicates that the run-time actually increased.

5.1.3 Logic gates

In figure 8 we present a graph of the run-time breakdown against the number of LPs on eight processors. The graph for eight processors was again typical for this simulation. Figure 8 shows that the run-time fell dramatically as the number of LPs decreased, and that this time the reductions were largely due to the reduction in the `wait` costs. This can be explained by the observation that for large numbers of LPs, more BTB cycles were required to achieve the same simulation end time than for small numbers of LPs. In fact, five times as many cycles were required for 480 LPs than for 32 LPs.

APOSTLE's part-of relationships are implemented by objects forwarding methods to other objects, in much the same way as (Blake and Cook 87). If a method must be forwarded to an object in another LP, an event must be scheduled for the current simulation time with the first sequence field[†] incremented by one (Wonnacott and Bruce 95b). Such events lead to early LEHs. If a method is to be forwarded to another object in the same LP, no event need be scheduled and therefore no LEH will be crossed. Thus fewer cycles were needed to achieve the same simulation end time in this case. In principle, the forwarding of methods can be optimized away if it can be shown that an object does not dynamically change its object parts. In this case the number of cycles required to achieve the same end simulation time would be the same regardless of the number of LPs used. This problem is symptomatic of the simulator's difficulty in dealing with events that happen "just after now". Changing the state "just after now" inside an LP is trivial – the appropriate C++ function is simply called. Changing the state "just after now" in another LP requires an event to be scheduled and an increase in simulation time. It is worth noting that changing the mapping of objects to LPs can subtly change the time at which methods start, although the `double` part of the simulation time will always be the same; the importance of this is for future investigation.

Figure 8 also shows that the `commit` and `event` costs both fell as the number of LPs decreased. The reduction in the `commit` costs was largely caused by a reduction in the total amount of mutable state as the number of LPs decreased. Each LP has a fixed amount of mutable state (for example, to implement data structures to ensure that object creation is undone on rollback). Thus, as the number of LPs fell the total amount of mutable state in the simulation fell, and hence the `commit` costs fell. Also, in *APOSTLE*, committal not only performs fossil collection, but also tests for run-time errors and output, which can only be acted upon when the event that caused them cannot be rolled back. With fewer events being processed, there were fewer instances of these fixed per event costs, and hence a reduction in the total time spent committing events. The reductions in the `event` costs were more dramatic than for super-ping because fewer cycles led to fewer contributions from the fixed per cycle overheads.

In figure 9 we present a graph of the percentage reduction in run-time against the number of processors for different numbers of LPs. The largest run-time reduction approached 80% on 8 and 16 processors for the 32 LP version. Up to two processors, figure 9 is

---

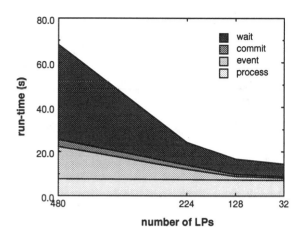

Figure 8: A graph of the run-time breakdown against the number of LPs for logic gates on eight processors.

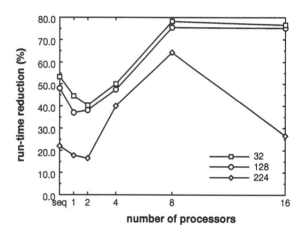

Figure 9: A graph of the percentage reduction in run-time against the number of processors for different numbers of LPs for logic gates.

somewhat reminiscent of super-ping, however after this point the percentage reduction in run-time climbs sharply up to eight processors. This is because above two processors the `wait` costs began to grow significantly (this is somewhat to be expected for BTB), and thus any reductions in the number of cycles needed gave large run-time reductions.

5.1.4 Discussion

APOSTLE's granularity control mechanism will only give run-time reductions when, as a result of mapping multiple objects to the same LP, there are a reasonable number of simultaneous events for the LP itself. For example, consider the idealised case of super-ping. With a 32-to-1 mapping of ping-pong objects to

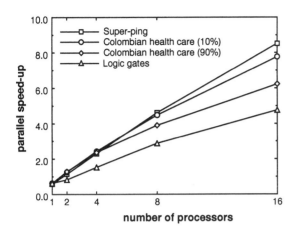

Figure 10: A graph of parallel speed-up against the number of processors for the benchmark simulations.

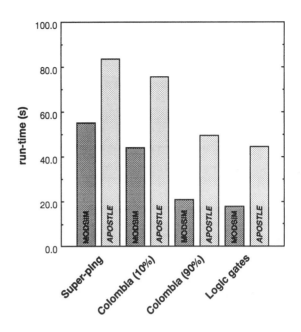

Figure 11: A bar chart illustrating the sequential performance of *APOSTLE* relative to MODSIM II.

LPs, and the fact that each `ping` method invokes the `ping` method on its neighbour ten units of simulation time into the future, we get 31 method invocations for objects in the same LP at the same future simulation time. *APOSTLE*'s granularity control mechanism transforms these into a single `Wakeup` event. With a 1-to-1 mapping there would, of course, need to be 31 `Invok-eReq` events (Wonnacott and Bruce 95b). In principle, it would be possible for an LP to internally advance its state to a time greater than the time of the event being processed, if the LP was able to calculate some lookahead.

The locality of an *APOSTLE* object is discovered dynamically at run-time. When a method informs the *APOSTLE* run-time system that it wishes to invoke a method on another object, a test is done to see if the object's `GlobalMachineID` indicates that it is mapped the same LP. If so, then granularity control can be applied. For those objects that are guaranteed to be mapped to the same LP, it would be more efficient if they could refer to each other using their C++ pointers, as in Sim++ (Baezner et al. 90), so that the dynamic test could be eliminated. Conceptually this should present no problems for the *APOSTLE* run-time system, although such a facility has not been implemented yet. It may also be beneficial to change or swizzle (Moss 92) the `GlobalMa-chineIDs` passed to an object (as the result of a method invocation) to just their C++ pointers if the objects are mapped to the same LP.

In this paper we have shown that granularity control can give large run-time reductions for *APOSTLE*, and provided some analysis as to where these reductions come from. However, it is clear that a simple analytical or cost model for granularity control is required to validate our analysis; to allow users to make rational decisions as to what mappings of *APOSTLE* objects to LPs to use; and to eventually allow the compiler to automatically place *APOSTLE* objects on LPs without user intervention.

5.2 Parallel speed-up

In figure 10 we present a graph of the parallel speed-up against the number of processors for the three benchmark *APOSTLE* simulations. The parallel speed-ups were measured relative to sequential *APOSTLE*, and were generated using the mapping of objects to LPs that gave the best run-time. As figure 10 shows, *APOSTLE* achieved a parallel speed-up of around 9 on 16 processors for super-ping. The logic gates simulation gave the worst parallel speed-up on 16 processors because as the adder's outputs became stable, there was less parallelism to extract.

Note that *APOSTLE*'s granularity control mechanism affected *APOSTLE*'s parallel speed-up relative to itself, although since granularity control reduced the overall simulation run-time, it would improve *APOSTLE*'s parallel speed-up relative to any other sequential discrete event simulation language. For super-ping, note how the sequential simulator gave the best run-time reductions using granularity control. This effectively reduced the parallel speed-up. However for logic gates, the situation was reversed.

5.3 Comparison with MODSIM II

To put *APOSTLE*'s performance in context, figure 11 presents a bar-chart summarising *APOSTLE*'s sequential performance compared with the equivalent MODSIM II (CACI 91) simulations. MODSIM is a commercial, sequential, object-oriented simulation language developed from the US Army's version of ModSim (Rich and Michelsen 91). We can report that MODSIM is between

1.5 and 2.5 times faster than sequential *APOSTLE*. We regard these figures as highly encouraging for our prototype implementation (especially given the sophistication of the *APOSTLE* language), as for super-ping *APOSTLE* therefore achieved a parallel speed-up of around 6 on 16 processors relative to MODSIM[†]. It is clear that any language for PDES must approach sequential simulation language efficiency when optimized for a single processor, so that any parallel speed-ups gained are real ones compared with the best uniprocessor simulation technology. *APOSTLE* has taken the first steps to achieve this important objective.

6 Conclusions and future work

APOSTLE is a new high-level simulation-oriented language for PDES, and in this paper we have presented performance figures for three benchmark simulations. We discussed the performance of the *APOSTLE* granularity control mechanism, which reduced simulation run-times by as much as 80%. Changing the granularity of an *APOSTLE* simulation required minimal recoding, as *APOSTLE* has a single object model. We also presented *APOSTLE*'s parallel speed-up performance – *APOSTLE* achieved a parallel speed-up of around 9 on 16 processors. To put the performance of our prototype implementation into context, the performance of sequential *APOSTLE* was compared with that of MODSIM II. Although MODSIM was between 1.5 and 2.5 times faster than sequential *APOSTLE*, *APOSTLE* still achieved a parallel speed-up of around 6 on 16 processors relative to MODSIM.

Clearly there is much work that still remains to be done to further reduce overheads and improve performance. Our future work will be concerned with developing compiler optimization techniques to reduce the amount of state saving required. Currently, the compiler and run-time system introduces extra unnecessary mutable state into a simulation – this is exemplified by the super-ping simulation which is stateless. We need to develop techniques to compile simple uses of *APOSTLE*'s generalized mechanisms into efficient representations. For example, if a method does not elapse simulation time then its implementation can be based on a procedure rather than a coroutine, and if a purely asynchronous method invocation, or a synchronous method invocation is performed, the creation of a promise is unnecessary. We also intend to build a dedicated run-time system for *APOSTLE* to overcome the "mismatch" (Rich and Michelsen 91) between the services required by *APOSTLE* code and those provided by the underlying simulator. For example, this will allow us to integrate fossil collection and *APOSTLE*'s garbage collection into a single unified garbage collection model.

Overall, we believe that the widespread success of PDES can only be achieved using a simulation-oriented language. The use of parallel simulators based on existing sequential languages is difficult and error prone. It is therefore essential that the complexities of PDES are hidden from the user if PDES is to be adopted by sequential discrete event simulation users. We believe that *APOSTLE* has made a significant contribution towards this goal.

---

† The MODSIM II comparison was performed on another SPARC-based machine, and this speed-up figure therefore assumes that we would see similar results if MODSIM were run on one node of the CS-2.

Acknowledgements

We would like to thank Brian Roberts for his vision in starting the *APOSTLE* work and his continual support; Chris Booth, Mike Kirton and Roy Milner for their efforts in developing and maintaining the BTB simulator and their comments on this paper; Tom Lake of GLOSSA for many stimulating discussions on PDES; Steve Turner of Exeter University for his guidance and input; and finally the anonymous referees for their helpful comments and suggestions.

This work was supported by the U.K. Ministry of Defence under Strategic Research projects AS02BN11 and AS05BN23.

References

Andler, S. "Predicate Path Expressions". In *Proc. 6th ACM Symp. on the Principles of Programming Languages* (San Antonio, Texas, 29-31 January 1979). 226-236.

Baezner, D.; et al. "Sim++™: The Transition to Distributed Simulation". In *Proc. SCS Multiconf. on Distributed Simulation* (San Diego, California, 17-19 January 1990). 211-218.

Bagrodia, R. L.; et al. 1991. "A Unifying Framework for Distributed Simulation". *ACM Transactions on Modelling and Computer Simulation*, vol. 1, no. 4 (October), 348-385.

Bagrodia, R. L. and W.-T. Liao. 1994. "Maisie: A Language for the Design of Efficient Discrete-Event Simulations". *IEEE Trans. on Software Engineering*, vol. 20, no. 4 (April), 225-238.

Bailey, M. L.; et al. 1994. "Parallel Logic Simulation of VLSI Systems". *ACM Computing Surveys*, vol. 26, no. 3 (September), 255-294.

Blake, E. and S. Cook. "On Including Part Hierarchies in Object-Oriented Languages, with an Implementation in Smalltalk". In *Proc. of the European Conf. on Object-Oriented Programming* (Paris, France, 15-17 June 1987). 45-54.

Blanchard, T. D. and T. W. Lake. "Distributed Simulation with Locality". In *Proc. 9th Workshop on Parallel and Distributed Simulation* (Lake Placid, New York, 14-16 June 1995). 195-198.

Booth, C. J. M.; et al. "Experiences in Implementing the Breathing Time Buckets Algorithm on a Transputer Array". In *Proc. IASTED International Conference on Modelling and Simulation*, (Pittsburgh, Pennsylvania, 10-12 May 1993). 274-277.

Bruce, D. I. "The treatment of state in optimistic systems". In *Proc. 9th Workshop on Parallel and Distributed Simulation*, (Lake Placid, New York, 14-16 June 1995). 40-49.

Buhr, P. A. 1995. "Are Safe Concurrency Libraries Possible?". *Communications of the ACM*, vol. 38, no. 2, 117-120.

CACI. 1991. "MODSIM II™ Reference Manual", CACI Products Company, La Jolla, California.

Damitio, M.; et al. "Comparing the Breathing Time Buckets Algorithm and the Time Warp Operating System on a Transputer

Architecture". In *Proc. of the European Simulation MultiConf.* (Barcelona, Spain, 1-3 June 1994). 141-145.

Evans, J. B. 1988. *Structures of discrete event simulation: an introduction to the engagement strategy.* Ellis Horwood Ltd.

Fujimoto, R. M. 1993. "Parallel Discrete Event Simulation: Will the Field Survive?". *ORSA Journal on Computing*, vol. 5, no. 3 (Summer), 213-230.

Hoare, P.; et al. "The Application of High Performance Parallel Computing to Military Simulation". In *Proc. 1995 Simulation Multiconf. (Military, Government and Aerospace Simulation)* (Phoenix, Arizona, 9-13 April 1995). 115-119.

Lieberman, H. "Using Prototypical Objects to Implement Shared Behaviour in Object Oriented Systems". In *Proc. of the Conf. on Object-Oriented Programming, Systems, Languages and Applications* (Portland, Oregon, 29 September-2 October 1986). 214-223.

Liskov, B. and L. Shrira. "Promises: Linguistic Support for Efficient Asynchronous Procedure Calls in Distributed Systems". In *Proc. ACM SIGPLAN Conf. on Programming Language Design and Implementation* (Atlanta, Georgia, 22-24 June 1988). 260-267.

Moss, J. E. B. 1992. "Working with Persistent Objects: To Swizzle or Not to Swizzle". *IEEE Trans. on Software Engineering*, vol. 18, no. 8 (August), 657-678.

Nance, R. E. "A history of discrete event simulation programming languages", *Proc. History of Programming Languages Conf.* (Cambridge, Massachusetts, 20-23 April 1993). Published as ACM SIGPLAN Notices, vol. 28, no. 3 (March), 149-175.

Rich, D. O. and R. E. Michelsen. 1989. *Writing Parallel Discrete-Event Simulations in ModSim: Insight and Experience.* Technical Report LA-UR-89-3104, Los Alamos National Laboratory, Los Alamos, New Mexico 87545.

Rich, D. O. and R. E. Michelsen. "An assessment of the MODSIM/TWOS parallel simulation environment". In *Proc. of the 1991 Winter Simulation Conf.* (Pheonix, Arizona, 8-11 December 1991). 509-518.

Steinman, J. S. 1992. "SPEEDES: A Multiple-Synchronization Environment for Parallel Discrete-Event Simulation". *International Journal of Computer Simulation*, vol. 2, no. 3, 251-286.

Vaucher, J. G. "A 'WAIT UNTIL' Algorithm for General Purpose Simulation Languages". In *Proc. of the 1973 Winter Simulation Conf.* (San Francisco, California, January 1973). 77-88.

Waldorf, J. and R. Bagrodia. 1994. "MOOSE: A Concurrent Object-Oriented Language for Simulation". *International Journal in Computer simulation*, vol. 4, no. 2, 235-257.

Wegner, P. "Design Issues for Object-Based Concurrency". In *Proc. Workshop on Object-Based Concurrent Computing at the European Conf. on Object-Oriented Programming* (Geneva, Switzerland, 15-16 July 1991). 245-256.

Wonnacott, P. and D. Bruce. "The design of *APOSTLE* — a high-level, object-oriented language for parallel and distributed discrete event simulation". In *Proc. 1995 Western Multiconf. on Computer Simulation (Object Oriented Simulation)* (Las Vegas, Nevada, 16-18 January 1995). 101-106.

Wonnacott, P. and D. Bruce. "A prototype implementation of *APOSTLE*, and its performance". In *Proc. 1995 Summer Computer Simulation Conf.* (Ottawa, Canada, 24-26 July 1995). 197-205.

Session 7

Applications II: Logic and Circuit Simulation

Session Chair
Rassul Ayani, Royal Institute of Technology, Sweden

Conservative Circuit Simulation on Shared–Memory Multiprocessors*

Jörg Keller[†]   Thomas Rauber   Bernd Rederlechner

Universität des Saarlandes, FB 14 Informatik

Postfach 151150, 66041 Saarbrücken, Germany

Email: {jkeller|rauber|brd}@cs.uni–sb.de

Abstract

We investigate conservative parallel discrete event simulations for logical circuits on shared-memory multiprocessors. For a first estimation of the possible speedup, we extend the critical path analysis technique by partitioning strategies. To incorporate overhead due to the management of data structures, we use a simulation on an ideal parallel machine (PRAM). This simulation can be directly executed on the SB-PRAM prototype, yielding both an implementation and a basis for data structure optimizations. One of the major tools to achieve these is the SB-PRAM's hardware support for parallel prefix operations. Our reimplementation of the PTHOR program on the SB-PRAM yields substantially higher speedups than before.

1 Introduction

Large–scale shared-memory multiprocessors are likely to play an important role in parallel computing in the future, because they offer a much simpler programming model than traditional distributed-memory machines. Most of today's shared-memory machines are cache-based machines, i.e., they still use a physically distributed memory but each processor is equipped with a one-level cache or a two-level cache-hierarchy. The cache coherence is provided by the hardware. The memory access time of these machines is not uniform but depends on the physical location of the data being accessed. For this reason, they are called nonuniform memory access time (NUMA) machines. These machines rely on the locality of most applications and try to hide the memory latency by caching. Examples of NUMA machines are the KSR1/2 [2] from Kendall Square Research, the Stanford Dash [16], and the SPP1000 from Convex.

Although cache-based machines show a good performance for most regular applications with an appropriate locality, they fail to get good speedups for irregular applications with a lot of non-local memory accesses. Typical examples of such applications are particle–based simulations like MP3D [20], routing algorithms like LocusRoute [20], and discrete–event simulations like PTHOR [22].

Besides cache-based shared-memory machines, uniform memory access time (UMA) machines have been developed for which the memory access time is independent from the physical location of the data. Examples of such machines are bus-based shared-memory machines like the Multimax [2] from Encore Computer Corp., the C90, J90, and T90 series from Cray Research [2], and the SGI Challenge from Silicon Graphics. The disadvantage of bus-based systems is that they usually can only provide a small number of processors.

The SB-PRAM which is currently under construction at the University of Saarbrücken is an UMA machine that provides a shared address space with a fast memory access time [1]. The latency of the network between the processors and the memory modules is hidden by pipelining of processors, i.e., each physical processor simulates a number of virtual processors. Thus, a write operation to the global memory by a virtual processor takes the same time as an arithmetic operation, independently of the memory location that is addressed. A read operation is as fast as an arithmetic operation as well, but the result is available in the next but one instruction. Concurrent accesses to a single memory cell are allowed and combined, making the SB-PRAM behave like the CRCW[1] PRAM model known from theoretical computer science.

Besides the usual load and store operations to access memory cells, the SB-PRAM also offers *multiprefix* instructions which enable several processors to perform prefix operations on a memory cell in parallel. As an example, we sketch the execution of a multiprefix addition MPADD. Let $p_1, \ldots, p_n$ be the executing processors where each processor p_i contributes a local value o_i. Let s be a shared memory cell with value o. If $p_1, \ldots, p_n$ execute the MPADD operation synchronously, i.e., each processor p_i executes MPADD s, o_i, then after the operation, processor

---

*This work was supported by the German Science Foundation (DFG) under SFB 124 TP D4.

[†]Supported by a DFG Habilitation Fellowship.

---

[1]CRCW=concurrent read, concurrent write.

p_j holds the jth prefix sum

$$o + \sum_{i=1}^{j-1} o_i ,$$

s contains the sum

$$o + \sum_{i=1}^{n} o_i .$$

The multiprefix operations MPMAX, MPOR, and MPAND work similar.

A multiprefix operation is as fast as a read operation, independently of the number of participating processors. It is even possible that different groups of processors perform separate multiprefix operations in parallel. The multiprefix operations can be used for an efficient implementation of synchronization mechanisms (such as barriers without serialization [10]) and for the implementation of various parallel data structures for task management like priority queues or FIFO queues [19].

Because of its memory structure, the SB-PRAM is an ideal machine for the execution of irregular applications. In addition to running an application on the SB-PRAM, the machine can also be used to study the properties of a parallel program under ideal conditions, yielding a prediction of the maximum speedup that can be attained on other machines. We do this here for an algorithm from the area of parallel discrete event simulation (PDES) for the simulation of logical circuits.

A model for discrete event simulation assumes that the system being simulated only changes state at discrete points in time. For the simulation, the system is modeled as a collection of *logical processes* (LPs) that communicate via timestamped messages. For circuit simulations, typical LPs at varying levels of abstraction are transistors, NAND gates, flipflops, multipliers, etc., and their interconnections [3]. The state of the simulated model changes upon the occurrence of *events*, such as the change in output value of an individual gate. An event e may be *scheduled* by a certain number of other events, if these determine the occurrence of e.

The approaches to PDES can be distinguished into conservative and optimistic approaches. The approaches differ in the way they deal with causality errors caused by the distributed simulation, see [9] for a good overview. The conservative method [6, 8] forces an LP to block until it is safe to simulate an event, i.e., the events are simulated in strict timestamp order. This may lead to deadlocks that have to be recognized and resolved. In the optimistic approaches [12], there is no such restriction, i.e., an LP can execute events in the order in which they arrive. If this leads to a simulation that is not in timestamp order, a roll back to a safe state has to be performed and the effect of messages

which should not have been send must be eliminated by appropriate anti-messages.

We consider the PTHOR algorithm for the simulation of logical circuits, which uses a conservative approach. The PTHOR simulator is based on the sequential THOR simulator and has first been considered for a parallel implementation on the Stanford Dash by Soulé [22]. Soulé investigates the performance of the PTHOR simulator for three platforms: an ideal multiprocessor simulator called Tango [20], an Encore Multimax with 16 processors, and the Stanford Dash with 16 processors.

For a systematic analysis of the attainable speedup, we start with a critical path analysis of PTHOR on the benchmark circuits, which also takes into consideration the partitioning of the LPs among the processors. We extend the partitioning strategies investigated by Lin in [17] from static partitioning strategies to dynamic strategies and stealing strategies. Although this technique yields an upper bound on the speedup for the different benchmark circuits, it does not take into account the overhead for data structures. This can be done by running PTHOR on the SB-PRAM. As the SB-PRAM is under construction, we use a simulator that performs a cycle–by–cycle simulation of the actual machine. Thus, the simulator delivers the exact runtime of the real hardware.

We start with the existing PTHOR implementation from the SPLASH1 benchmark suite [20] and show how the maximum attainable speedup can be increased by several changes in the data structures, including the data structures for the LPs and the memory management. We compare the dynamic partitioning scheme using a centralized FIFO queue with the stealing scheme that uses a local queue for each processor. We also show that the use of NULL messages can result in a large increase of the speedup, depending on the benchmark circuit.

The rest of the paper is organized as follows. Section 2 presents the critical path analysis. Section 3 investigates the performance characteristics of the original PTHOR simulator. Section 4 presents the improvements that we added and discusses their effects.

2 Critical Path Analysis

Not all events occurring while simulating a circuit can be executed in parallel. The result of an event e can only be computed correctly if

1. all events preceding e on the same LP are executed,

2. the results of all events scheduling e are known to e.

2.1 Event Precedence Graphs

Consider the set of the events that occur during the simulation of a fixed experiment on a fixed model. From the above constraints, we can derive a partial order on this set, called "causality". The representation of this order as a directed graph $G = (V, E)$ is called "event precedence graph" (EPG), introduced independently by Berry and Jefferson [4] and Livny [18]. V is the set of events, (e_1, e_2) is an edge iff. e_1 schedules e_2 or e_1 is the last event before e_2 on the same LP. The weight function $\tau : V \to \mathbf{R}_0^+$ assigns to each event the runtime to execute it[2]. We call an event e_2 *dependent* on e_1 iff. there exists a path in G from e_1 to e_2.

Only events that are independent from each other can be executed in parallel. Hence, the EPG serves to compute a lower bound on the simulation's runtime. We assume that every LP is simulated on its own processor. Then, because of constraint 1, it can never happen that more than one event e is ready for execution on one processor. This unique event e can be executed as soon as constraint 2 is satisfied. Obviously, events e with indegree 0 can be executed immediately after the simulation starts.

If $START(e)$ and $END(e)$ denote the times when the execution of event e ideally starts and finishes, then

$$
\begin{aligned}
END(e) &= START(e) + \tau(e)\,, \\
START(e) &= \begin{cases} \max_{(e',e) \in E} END(e') & indeg(e) \geq 1 \\ 0 & \text{otherwise.} \end{cases}
\end{aligned}
$$

This recurrence equation is well defined because EPGs are acyclic. To compute END, one sorts the vertices topologically and evaluates them in this order. The time

$$
T_{crit} = \max_{e \in V} END(e)\,. \tag{1}
$$

is the runtime of an ideal simulation on a parallel machine with an arbitrary number of processors. T_{crit} is a lower bound on the parallel runtime of every conservative simulation strategy [13]. It is even a lower bound on optimistic strategies with aggressive cancellation [11].

The path defining the maximum in (1) is called *critical path*. Note that there may be several critical paths in an EPG.

The EPG also serves to compute a lower bound on the sequential runtime by

$$
T_{seq} = \sum_{e \in V} \tau(e)\,.
$$

So far, the computed runtimes ignore any computational overhead in addition to causality. If we assume that the overhead in a parallel simulation is greater than in a sequential simulation, then the quotient $S_{crit} = T_{seq}/T_{crit}$ defines an upper bound on the possible speedup for a particular experiment.

---

[2]This definition can be made independent of the underlying machine by defining $\tau(e)$ as a function on the indegree of e.

This overhead assumption is supported by the observation that normally all data structures from the sequential program are needed in the parallel version as well. The parallel program might need additional data structures to support information exchange between LPs.

2.2 Partitioning Strategies

For large circuits, real parallel machines do not have enough processors to assign each LP to a different processor. Hence, the LPs must be partitioned between the available processors.

On distributed memory multicomputers, a commonly used partitioning scheme is *static partitioning*. Every processor is assigned a fixed set of LPs, the sets are disjoint. Examples for static partitioning are cyclic distribution (LP_i is executed on processor $i \bmod p$), blockwise distribution (processor i executes $LP_{in/p+1}$ to $LP_{(i+1)n/p}$), and random distribution (each processor is assigned n/p LPs in a random fashion). If the numbering of LPs in the input data file is arbitrary, then any distribution resembles random partitioning.

There are a number of heuristic approaches to find better static partitionings [5, 14, 15, 23]. However, we did not consider those approaches. They mostly try to optimize communication costs which is not necessary as we use shared-memory machines.

On a shared memory multiprocessor, all processors have access to the data of every LP. Hence, an obvious strategy would be to have a central FIFO queue for LPs that are ready for execution. An idle processor simply picks the first queue element. We call this strategy *dynamic*. The standard method to find out when an LP becomes ready for execution is presented in Subsect. 3.1. The disadvantage of a central FIFO queue is the possible serialization overhead due to concurrent access of multiple processors. This overhead can be eliminated by a serialization-free parallel data structure on the SB-PRAM (see Subsect. 4.3).

Often however, shared memory multiprocessors need some locality in data referencing to exploit their caches and hence to obtain appropriate memory bandwidth. To achieve locality, the PTHOR program of the SPLASH1 benchmark suite [20] uses a so called *stealing strategy*: basically, this is a static strategy with local *task queues* for LPs that are ready for execution. In cases where the load is not balanced, an idle processor can "steal" an LP that is ready for execution but is assigned to another processor. The stealing strategy exploits locality as long as processors are busy and requires remote access only for load balancing when the processor is idle anyway.

In all these strategies, it may happen that a processor must choose between several LPs that are ready for execution. This can happen because either more than one LP assigned to a processor is ready, or because more than p

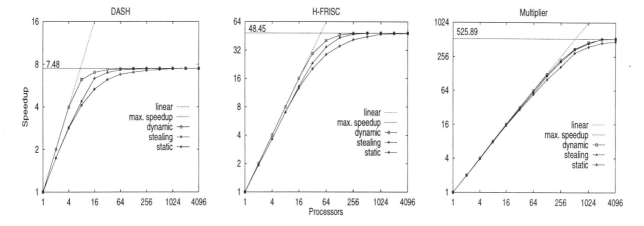

Figure 1: Speedup bounds for different partitioning strategies

LPs are ready in the central FIFO queue. In PTHOR, the processor chooses the LP that has been ready for execution for the longest time. This is easy to implement. Another popular method is to choose the LP with the smallest timestamp. This method leads to overhead. It requires that LPs which are ready to run are kept sorted according to their timestamps.

To get realistic runtime predictions $T_{crit}(p)$ depending on the number of processors p, it is necessary to model the partitioning strategy used in the critical path analysis. Note that these runtimes cannot be shorter than T_{crit}. All delays due to causality apply for both T_{crit} and $T_{crit}(p)$, and partitioning could introduce additional delays.

The inclusion of partitioning strategies in critical path analysis was first mentioned by Lin [17], but he only uses a static strategy.

To include one of the above partitioning strategies in critical path analysis, we assume that the number of available processors p is fixed. We maintain a timer $c(i)$ for each processor i, which specifies the computation time performed by i. If this processor executes an event e, the timer is increased by $\tau(e)$. As before, we evaluate the function END on the nodes of the EPG in topological order. For an event e executed on processor i, let $c_{old}(i)$ denote the value of $c(i)$ before the execution of e. Then

$$
\begin{aligned}
END(e) &= START'(e) + \tau(e), \\
START'(e) &= \max\left(c_{old}(i), START(e)\right).
\end{aligned}
$$

$START(e)$ is defined as above. The execution time consumed by simulating e is taken into account by updating $c(i)$ to

$$c(i) = END(e).$$

The different partitioning strategies lead to different assignments of LPs (and their events) to processors and hence to different results for $T_{crit}(p)$.

Note that the topological sort does not give a unique total order on the vertices, e.g. all vertices with indegree 0 could serve as the first node. Therefore we maintain a priority queue of all events that are ready for execution. The priority is the time when the events became ready. Removing the event with the smallest ready time ensures correct modeling.

2.3 Experiments

We computed the EPG's for three circuits delivered with the PTHOR simulator from the SPLASH1 benchmark suite [20].

- DASH models the cache coherency controller of the DASH multiprocessor [16] and represents 74,000 gate equivalents organized in 24,000 LPs.

- H-FRISC is a small RISC processor generated by a synthesis tool. It represents 7,000 gate equivalents organized in 5,000 LPs.

- Multiplier implements a multiplier of two 16-bit numbers. It also represents 7,000 gate equivalents organized in 5,000 LPs.

We use the input vectors that are delivered with the PTHOR program. We use the unit delay model, i.e. each gate and each register has a delay of 1. We simulate 5000 time units. We computed the speedup bound S_{crit} and bounds

$$S_{crit}(p) = \frac{T_{seq}}{T_{crit}(p)},$$

where $p = 2^i$, $i = 0, \ldots, 12$, for the three partitioning strategies. For the static and stealing strategies, we use a cyclic distribution. The curves are shown in Fig. 1.

The speedup bounds $S_{crit}(p)$ with partitioning reach the maximum speedup S_{crit} already for small numbers of processors. The dynamic partitioning strategy outperforms the other two in theory. For small processor numbers ($p \leq 16$), the stealing strategy behaves like the static strategy, for larger processor numbers it approaches the dynamic strategy. As the static strategy performs worst, we do not consider it in the sequel.

Second, note that causality restricts the available parallelism severely. The DASH circuit, also the largest one, obtains the worst speedup bound with 7.48. This contradicts statements in [22].

The strong influence of causality might result from the form of the LPs. The DASH circuit has LPs with up to 94 inputs. In contrast, the H-FRISC and the Multiplier circuits have LPs with up to 17 and 5 inputs, respectively. The more inputs an LP has, the more it can depend on events on other LPs. The events that schedule an event on an LP with many inputs might finish at vastly different computation times. As a conservative simulation must wait for the last of these events to finish, the delays due to causality can be large.

Soulé [22] proposes to combine LPs to larger units called "super LPs" to increase the speedup. As this increases the number of inputs per super LP, our results strongly discourage this proposal. In contrast, it might be wise to split large LPs into smaller units with fewer inputs.

We also investigated the granularity of the LP execution times as a possible source of speedup degradation. On the SB-PRAM, the evaluation of an LP needs at most 100 instructions. The majority of LPs take more than 50 instructions. Hence, the difference in execution time is small and could not explain such a large speedup degradation.

3 PTHOR

A widely used algorithm for circuit simulations on parallel machines is the Chandy–Misra–Bryant algorithm (CMB) [6, 8]. This algorithm is a conservative approach. We will first review the PTHOR program [22], which is an implementation of CMB on the Stanford Dash machine.

3.1 Description

PTHOR partitions the LPs of the simulated circuit with the stealing strategy sketched in Subsect. 2.2. It uses a cyclic distribution of LPs to processors.

There is a message channel between LP i and LP j if an input of component j in the simulated circuit is connected to an output of component i. If LP i computes a change of the output signal that occurs at *simulated* time t, then this output is put into a message with timestamp t. All LPs connected with LP i get a copy of this message in their appropriate input buffers.

Each processor maintains an *activation list* that contains all of its LPs for which new messages have arrived. If LP i sends a message to another LP j, it generates an entry for LP j in the activation list of the processor to which LP j is assigned.

An event e can only be simulated if all necessary inputs are present in the input buffers. An idle processor j tries to get an LP from its activation list. If its own list is empty, then it tries to steal an LP from another activation list. If the chosen LP has all necessary inputs, j can simulate one or several events from that LP correctly. In either case, this LP is removed from the activation list. It will be entered again if some new input message arrives.

It can thus happen that all activation lists become empty although some events could be simulated. Such a situation is called *deadlock*. The CMB algorithm tolerates deadlocks, because it is able to detect and to resolve all of them.

Deadlock detection can be implemented on a shared memory multiprocessor by maintaining a shared counter which is initially set to zero. A processor whose activation list becomes empty (and does not succeed in stealing) increases the counter. It decrements the counter again if it finds a new event to simulate. A deadlock has occurred if the counter equals the number of available processors.

To resolve the deadlock, one has to find at least one event that can be simulated. To do this, we search for a message m with the minimum timestamp $\tilde{t}$. Chandy and Misra prove that all events that occur at time $\tilde{t}$ (and hence have m as input) can be simulated [8].

3.2 Performance

Figure 2 shows the speedups for the benchmark circuits on three machines, with processor numbers ranging from 2 to 128. Only on the SB-PRAM we obtain a speedup larger than 1. The diagrams show absolute speedups: the sequential runtime is not the runtime of the parallel program with one processor. Instead, it is the runtime of the fastest sequential implementation we were able to find. For the SB-PRAM, we implemented a sequential event simulator using splay–trees [21] as priority queues. For Dash and Multimax, we used relative speedups and slowdown factors from [22].

Benchmark	DASH	H-FRISC	Multiplier
SB-PRAM (PTHOR)	10.4	7.4	5.4
Dash (PTHOR)	13.0	9.6	7.5
SB-PRAM (Reimpl.)	3.0	2.1	1.7

Table 1: Slowdown factors

Note that the parallel program on one processor is much slower than the sequential program on one processor of the same machine. The quotient between these two runtimes is called *slowdown factor*. Table 1 shows the slowdown

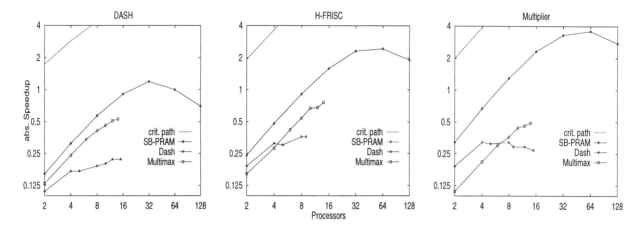

Figure 2: Absolute speedups of PTHOR on the Dash–, Multimax– and SB-PRAM–Multiprocessor.

factors for the three benchmark circuits on the SB-PRAM and the Dash machine. The latter are taken from [22].

The performance of PTHOR suffers from serialization. Serialization occurs during concurrent access to the shared counter for deadlock detection.

Benchmark	DASH	H-FRISC	Multiplier
Total no.	1,348,440	960,498	1,283,380
Contention	82.25%	94.6%	97.70%

Table 2: Lock contention on SB-PRAM with $p = 128$

The access to the counter is protected by a lock. Table 2 shows the total number of accesses to the shared counter and the fraction of accesses that were not directly granted. The time to access a lock is one instruction in both the Dash and the SB-PRAM, as both machines provide hardware support for read-modify-write operations.

Serialization is also caused by the computation of the minimum timestamp during deadlock resolution. This computation needs a loop over all processors and barrier synchronizations before and after the loop. The barriers are also implemented by locks. The first row of Table 3 shows the average number of instructions needed to resolve a deadlock in PTHOR on the SB-PRAM. The second row shows the corresponding numbers for the reimplementation (see next Section).

4 Reimplementation

Our reimplementation avoids the serializations mentioned above. We also improved the memory management and the realization of channels between LPs.

As mentioned in Sect. 1, the multiprefix operation

	DASH	H-FRISC	Multiplier
PTHOR	21,825	20,400	20,700
Reimpl.	525	450	700

Table 3: Duration of deadlock resolution on SB-PRAM with $p = 128$

serves to compute global sums and global minima in a small constant number of instructions. The last row of Table 3 shows the average number of instructions needed for deadlock resolution on the SB-PRAM using multiprefix.

4.1 Memory Management

During the simulation, one has to manage ten thousands of small list elements for message queues, activation lists etc. PTHOR never recycles elements, it even keeps those elements that are not in use anymore. This is a waste of memory resources and leads to unnecessary shared memory allocations. Furthermore, extracting list elements from the allocated memory leads to serialization because locks are used.

In the reimplementation, each processor maintains a so called *freelist*. After a processor has executed an event, some of the involved list elements might not be needed anymore. Then, the processor adds these to its own freelist. If a processor wants to allocate a list element, it first tries to obtain one from its freelist. If its freelist is empty, then it obtains a list element from an allocated shared memory block.

If a block containing l list elements is allocated, a shared counter c is initialized to l. A so called *R–pointer* is set to the beginning of the memory block. To obtain a list element from that block, a processor decreases the counter c with the help of multiprefix. This allows for concurrent

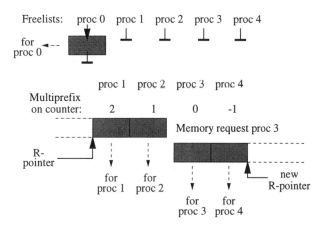

Figure 3: Memory management of list elements

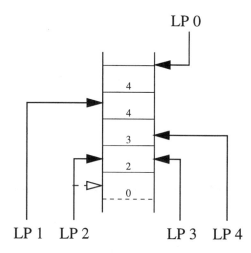

Figure 4: Single-In Multiple-Out queue

access of multiple processors without serialization. The result r of the prefix operation gives the number of remaining list elements. If $r \leq 0$ the memory block is exhausted. The processor that obtains value 0 then allocates a new memory block, all processors that received values less or equal to zero then repeat the allocation with the new block.

If a processor receives $r \geq 1$, it can cut off a list element from the memory block. To do this, it increases the R–pointer of this block by the size of a list element with the help of multiprefix. The value the processor obtains then determines the position of the list element. Figure 3 shows five processors that try to allocate a list element. Processor 0 finds an element in its freelist, the other four processors must allocate from a shared memory block with $c = 2$. After the multiprefix operation, $c = -2$, and processor i receives value $3 - i$. Thus, processors 1 and 2 get list elements from the current memory block. Processor 3 receives the value 0 and allocates a new block, from which processors 3 and 4 allocate their list elements.

4.2 Channel Queues

The realization of a channel is performed with a FIFO queue where one LP writes a message and all LPs connected to this channel read the message. As it is not clear when all LPs have read a message, PTHOR keeps all messages in these queues. We attach a shared counter to each message in the queue. The counter is initialized to the number of LPs connected to this channel. Each LP reading a message decreases its counter with the help of multiprefix. If the counter has reached zero, the processor accessing the message removes it from the queue and puts it into its freelist. We call this queue organization *single-in multiple-out queue (SIMO)*. It needs no locks. Figure 4 shows a SIMO queue where LP 0 writes and LPs 1 to 4 read. The uppermost two messages have not yet been read by any LP and hence have counters with values 4. The next two messages

have been read by LP 1 and LPs 1 and 4, respectively, and thus have counters with values 3 and 2. LP 2 has just read the lowermost message and thus decreased the message's counter to zero. The message now is removed from the queue.

Figure 5 shows the absolute speedups of PTHOR and the reimplementation on the SB-PRAM. The speedups of the reimplementation are much better than the PTHOR speedups. For the DASH benchmark, the speedup reaches the critical path bound. For H-FRISC and Multiplier there is still a gap between the bound from critical path analysis and the actual speedup. We try to tighten this gap by two means.

4.3 NULL-Messages and Dynamic Partitioning

First, we incorporate the concept of *NULL-messages*. In PTHOR, a message m is only sent when an LP i changes one of its outputs. In conservative simulation, m can be consumed when no messages with smaller timestamps arrive over this channel. The channel clock shows the timestamp of the last message sent over this channel. Deadlocks occur due to clocks not incremented far enough because of messages not sent. To prevent this, so called NULL-messages containing only a timestamp help to give better guarantees. Chandy and Misra show that deadlocks can be avoided completely if all events send all possible NULL-messages [7].

On distributed memory machines, the flood of NULL-messages can cause more overhead than the deadlock avoidance method. Therefore, one only sends part of the NULL-messages to avoid part of the deadlocks [9]. On shared memory machines, messages need not be sent explicitly. Every event can access each channel data structure in global memory. Therefore, instead of sending a message, one can update every channel clock directly. This re-

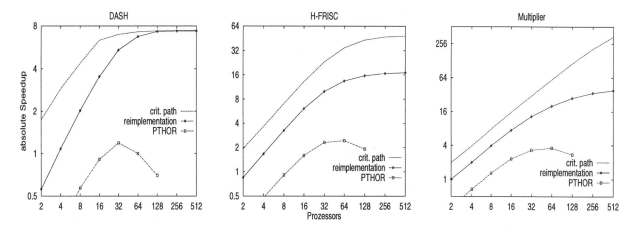

Figure 5: Absolute speedups before and after reimplementation on the SB-PRAM

moves most of the overhead of message passing (queue organization etc.) and makes NULL-messages a useful tool. To avoid deadlocks completely, every update of a channel clock must be followed by the activation of all LPs connected to this channel.

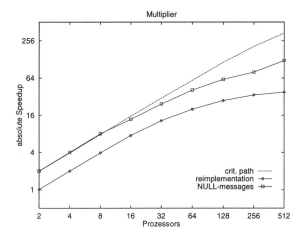

Figure 6: Use of NULL-messages

Figure 6 shows the speedup curves with and without NULL-messages for the Multiplier circuit. The use of NULL-messages almost doubles the speedup.

The situation is different for the H-FRISC circuit. Here, the use of NULL-messages results in an increase of activations by a factor of 6. The speedup drops by a factor of 5 to 6, depending on the number of processors. The reason lies in the different structures of the circuits. While Multiplier is purely combinatorial, H-FRISC contains cycles between registers. In these cycles, often several NULL-messages are sent (and hence activations happen) before an event can be simulated.

Second, we tried to use the dynamic partitioning strategy as an alternative to stealing. To do this, one needs a

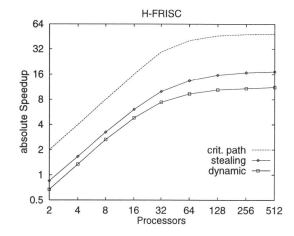

Figure 7: Absolute speedups for dynamic and stealing partitioning

shared FIFO queue as a global activation list. This list is accessed by all processors and hence need not lead to serialization. With the help of multiprefix, one can implement a FIFO queue that processes inserts or deletions of an arbitrary number of processors in a small constant number of instructions [19].

Figure 7 shows the speedups on H-FRISC for both strategies. The curves for the Multiplier circuit look similar. In contrast to theory, the dynamic strategy is not superior to stealing. A reason for this is that more than 90 % of all activations are satisfied from the processors' local activation lists, even for large processor numbers. However, the dynamic strategy leads to a simpler program code. Note that the difference between the two curves is even increasing. This results from a constant runtime overhead while accessing the central FIFO queue.

5 Conclusions

Our results show that critical path analysis permits good speedup predictions if partitioning strategies are included. For the benchmark circuits, the SB-PRAM comes close to the maximum speedup, allowing more accurate predictions. As a consequence of using a single framework, the tool for critical path analysis also yields an efficient implementation.

For the prediction, we consider absolute speedup values. This is important to evaluate the use of parallel machines in practice as relative speedups are up to 10 times higher than the absolute ones. To make parallel simulators competitive, it might be worth investigating whether the slowdown factors from sequential to parallel can be made smaller.

Experiments with the benchmark circuits reveal that the maximum speedup is strongly dependent on the circuit's structure. Of particular importance are the length of the cycles and the number of inputs per LP.

We presented several new serialization–free parallel data structures which seem to have a large impact on the programs performance. The efficiency of these data structures is based upon the use of parallel prefix operations.

The Dash machine supports so called fetch&op operations which are parallel increment/decrement. Hence, SIMO queues and improved deadlock detection could be implemented on the Dash as well. However, the Dash's fetch&op still leads to serialization. Memory management and improved deadlock resolution require parallel prefix sum and maximum with integers, respectively, and thus cannot be used on the Dash.

References

[1] F. Abolhassan, J. Keller, and W.J. Paul. On the Cost–Effectiveness of PRAMs. In *Proc. 3rd IEEE Symp. on Parallel and Distributed Processing*, pages 2–9, 1991.

[2] George Almasi and Allan Gottlieb. *Highly Parallel Computing*. Benjamin/Cummings, 2nd edition, 1994.

[3] M.L. Bailey, Jr. J.V. Briner, and R.D. Chamberlain. Parallel Logic Simulation of VLSI Systems. *ACM Computing Reviews*, 26(3):255–294, 1994.

[4] O. Berry and D. Jefferson. Critical path analysis of distributed simulation. In *Proceedings 1985 SCS Multiconference on Distributed Simulation*, pages 57–60, January 1985.

[5] Azzedine Boukerche and Carl Tropper. A Static Partitioning and Mapping Algorithm for Conservative Parallel Simulations. In *Proceedings of the 8th Workshop on Parallel and Distributed Simulation*, pages 164–172, July 1994.

[6] R. E. Bryant. Simulation of packet communications architecture computer systems. Technical Report MIT-LCS-TR-188, Massachusetts Institute of Technology, 1977.

[7] K. M. Chandy and J. Misra. Deadlock absence proofs for networks of communicating processes. *Information Processing Letters*, 94:185–189, November 1979.

[8] K. M. Chandy and J. Misra. Asynchronous distributed simulation via a sequence of parallel computations. *Communications of the ACM*, 24(11):198–206, April 1981.

[9] R. M. Fujimoto. Parallel discrete event simulation. *Communications of the ACM*, 33(10):30–53, October 1990.

[10] Thomas Grün, Thomas Rauber, and Jochen Röhrig. The programming environment of the SB-PRAM. In *Proc. 7th IASTED/ISMM Int.l Conf. on Parallel and Distributed Computing and Systems, Washington DC*, October 1995.

[11] Michial A. Gunter. Understanding supercritical speedup. In *Proceedings of the 1993 Winter Simulation Conference*, pages 81–87, December 1993.

[12] D. R. Jefferson. Virtual time. *ACM Transactions on Programming Languages and Systems*, 7(3):404–425, 1985.

[13] David Jefferson and Peter Reiher. Supercritical speedup. In *Proceedings of the 24th Annual Simulation Symposium*, pages 159–168, April 1991.

[14] Kevin L. Kapp, Thomas C. Hartrum, and Tom S. Wailes. An improved cost function for static partitioning of parallel circuit simulations using a conservative synchronization protocol. In *Proc. 9th Workshop on Parallel and Distributed Simulation*, pages 78–85, 1995.

[15] Pavlos Konas and Pen-Chung Yew. Partitioning for synchronous parallel simulation. In *Proc. 9th Workshop on Parallel and Distributed Simulation*, pages 181–184, 1995.

[16] Daniel Lenoski, James Laudon, Kourosh Gharachorloo, Wolf-Dietrich Weber, Anoop Gupta, John Hennessy, Mark Horowitz, and Monica S. Lam. The Stanford DASH multiprocessor. *IEEE Computer*, 25(3):63–79, March 1992.

[17] Yi-Bing Lin. Parallelism analyzers for parallel discrete event simulation. *ACM Transactions on Modeling and Computer Simulation*, 2(3):239–264, July 1992.

[18] M. Livny. A study of parallelism in distributed simulation. In *Proceedings 1985 SCS Multiconference on Distributed Simulation*, pages 94–98, San Diego, CA, January 1985.

[19] Jochen Röhrig. Implementierung der P4-Laufzeitbibliothek auf der SB-PRAM. Master's Thesis, Universität des Saarlandes, 1996.

[20] Jaswinder Pal Singh, Wolf-Dietrich Weber, and Anoop Gupta. SPLASH: Stanford Parallel Applications for Shared-Memory. *Computer Architecture News*, 20(1):5–44, 1992.

[21] D. D. Sleator and R. E. Tarjan. Self-adjusting binary search trees. *Journal of the ACM*, 32(3):652–686, 1985.

[22] Larry Soulé. *Parallel Logic Simulation: An Evaluation of Centralized-Time and Distributed-Time Algorithms*. PhD thesis, Stanford University, June 1992.

[23] Christian Sporrer and Herbert Bauer. Corolla partitioning for distributed logic simulation of VLSI-circuits. In *Proc. 7th Workshop on Parallel and Distributed Simulation*, pages 85–92, 1993.

Actor Based Parallel VHDL Simulation Using Time Warp

Venkatram Krishnaswamy   **Prithviraj Banerjee**

Center for Reliable and High-Performance Computing

University of Illinois

Urbana, Illinois 61801

{venkat,banerjee}@crhc.uiuc.edu

Abstract

One of the methods used to reduce the time spent simulating VHDL designs is by parallelizing the simulation. In this paper, we describe the implementation of an object-oriented Time Warp simulator for VHDL on an actor based environment. The actor model of computation allows the exploitation of fine grained parallelism in a truly asynchronous manner and allows for the overlap of computation with communication. Some preliminary results obtained by simulating a set of multipliers and some ISCAS benchmark circuits are provided. In addition, the importance of placing processes based on circuit partitioning techniques for improving runtimes and scalability is demonstrated. Results are reported on a Sun SPARCServer 1000 and an Intel Paragon.

1 Introduction

The design of a digital VLSI system commonly begins with a description of the system being written in a Hardware Description Language, an example of which is VHDL [1]. Subsequent to verifying the functionality of the description, it is given to a system to perform synthesis at varying levels of abstraction, beginning with architectural synthesis and ending with layout synthesis.

Verification of the functionality of the description can either be done by formal techniques, or by simulation. The latter method is more widely in use. Large amounts of time are spent simulating modern HDL descriptions and parallel processing is an attractive approach to reduce the runtimes. Parallel simulation of digital systems is appropriate due to the increased parallelism available in modern pipelined designs.

VHDL has been designed for documentation and simulation of digital systems. Digital systems may either be described behaviorally or structurally in terms of components and their connectivity. Hierarchical descriptions may be flattened out to a set of equivalent `processes` which may execute in parallel. Execution within a process is serial.

In this paper, we describe the design and implementation of a Time Warp based [2] parallel simulator for VHDL descriptions, which we call `ProperVHDL` . The simulator has been implemented on top of the ProperCAD II libraries [3] for providing an actor based [4] model for concurrent object oriented programming. The actor model of computation allows the exploitation of fine grained parallelism in a truly asynchronous manner and allows for the overlap of computation with communication. It is appropriate to implement a VHDL simulator in the context of an environment which provides support for fine grained parallelism because the amount of computation typically carried out in a VHDL process is typically small. We have simulated actual VHDL models, and the results indicate that this approach is sound.

The remainder of the paper is organized as follows. Section 2 describes some related work. In Section 3, we provide a brief overview of VHDL. Section 4 is an overview of the ProperCAD II environment. Section 5 contains a description of `ProperVHDL` and its implementation within ProperCAD II . Preliminary results from our first set of experiments are reported in Section 5.

2 Related Work

In this section, we mention some work in the area of parallel VHDL simulation, and environments for parallel simulation. Jade Simulations International Corporation [5] have described a Time Warp based VHDL simulator. It is implemented on top of the *Sim++* simulation system that is a C++ runtime environment for distributed simulation using Time Warp. However, no experimental results have been reported. Wilsey and McBrayer use the QUEST VHDL simulator based on Time Warp to investigate com-

This research was supported in part by the National Science Foundation under grant MIP-9320854, the Semiconductor Research Corporation under grant SRC 95-DP-109, and the Advanced Research Projects Agency under contract DAA-H04-94-G-0273 administered by the Army Research Office. We would also like to thank Intel Corporation for the donation of an Intel Paragon to the University of Illinois.

```
h_adder : process ( a_0, b_0 )

begin

  s_out <= a_0 xor b_0 after tpd ns;

  c_out <= a_0 and b_0 after tpd ns;

end process    ;
```

Figure 1: A VHDL process describing a half adder

bination of processes to increase the computation grainsize [6]. Willis and Siewiorek mention the Auriga system in [7], which is mostly concerned with techniques for optimizing VHDL compilation for parallel simulation. While they report numbers reflecting their compilation techniques, actual simulation runtimes are not provided. Kapp *et. al.* [8] have built a conservatively synchonized VHDL simulator based on the Chandy-Misra [9] algorithm. Vellandi and Lightner [10] describe a SIMD algorithm for parallel VHDL simulation and use compilation techniques for extracting parallelism from the source VHDL description. Wen and Yelick [11] use a library based runtime system to construct a parallel circuit simulator. Bagrodia *et. al.* have written the Maisie language for describing parallel simulations [12] and this has been used to implement a gate level logic simulator described by Cong *et. al.* in [13]. There has been a great deal of related work in parallel logic simulation, which has been surveyed by Bailey, Briner and Chamberlain in [14]. Much of the preliminary work in parallel logic simulation and its parallelization using asynchronous algorithms was first reported by Soule [15].

3   VHDL

The VHSIC Hardware Description Language (VHDL) was introduced as a standard by the IEEE [1] in 1987. It is a language intended for documentation and simulation of digital systems. It provides support for both behavioral and structural modeling of digital hardware. Hardware may be modeled in a hierarchical manner. When the hierarchy is flattened out, a VHDL description can be thought of as set of concurrent *processes* exchanging information through timestamped messages sent over a netlist of *signals*. While the processes execute in parallel, execution within them is serial. An example of a process statement is shown in Figure 1. The semantics of process execution is identical to that of discrete event systems, with processes looking up event queues, executing the events if any, and scheduling further events for the future.

4   ProperCAD II System Overview

Much of the work in parallel CAD reported to date suffers from a major limitation in that these proposed parallel algorithms are designed with a specific underlying architecture in mind. As a result, these applications perform poorly on architectures other than the one for which they were designed. Just as importantly, incompatibilities in programming environments make it difficult to port these programs across different parallel architectures. This limitation has serious consequences, since a parallel algorithm needs to be developed afresh for every target MIMD architecture.

One of the primary concerns of the ProperCAD project [16] is to address this portability problem by designing algorithms to run on a range of parallel machines including shared memory multiprocessors, distributed memory multicomputers, and networks of workstations. ProperCAD II is a C++ library which provides an object–oriented parallel interface based on the actor model of concurrent object–oriented computing [3].

The fundamental object in the actor model is the actor, an object which communicates with other actors via messages. All actions an actor takes are in response to messages. The actor model lacks explicit sequencing primitives. Synchronization is implicit and derives from the single threaded nature of individual actors. Since an actor cannot suspend execution implicitly in the middle of a computation, continuation passing style (CPS) [17] is used to express control and data dependences.

The Actor/CPS model extends the RPC model to support object-oriented programming and parallelism. Functions are invoked with respect to an actor. The call of an actor method is non-blocking and consequently actor methods do not return values. In Figure 2, the f member of actor a calls the g member of b but does not wait. Instead, a *continuation* is passed as an argument to g. The continuation that f passes, a.f', specifies that the object a and the method f' will process the value returned by g. In this case, f' will be that code in the RPC f which is dependent on the return value of g. g treats the continuation c as a function pointer; once the return value x is computed, g calls c with that value. Continuation variables are the parallel, object-oriented extrapolation of serial, procedural function pointers.

By mapping multiple actors onto a physical processor, the runtime system on each processor is able to schedule the ready-to-use actors on the processor and obtain high utilization by overlapping computation with communication.

As part of ProperCAD, a suite of parallel applications have been developed, as shown in Figure 3, that address the most significant tasks in VLSI design automation including circuit extraction [18], test generation [19], fault simulation [20], cell placement [21], and logic synthesis [22].

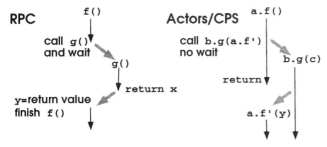

Figure 2: RPC and Actors/CPS.

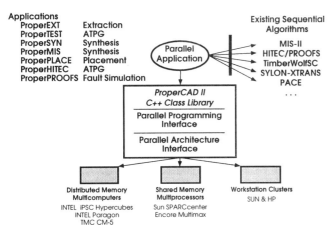

Figure 3: An overview of the ProperCAD project.

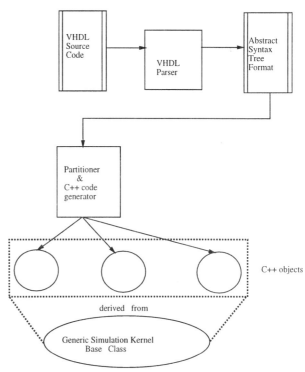

Figure 4: Overview of ProperVHDL.

5 ProperVHDL overview

The entire ProperVHDL system comprises a VHDL front end analyzer which parses the user's source VHDL into an abstract syntax tree form. This is used as an input to a code generator which produces a translation of the VHDL into C++. Each process is translated into a separate class, for which both .H and .C files are generated. The constructor of each such process contains data structures defining the signals and variables visible to the process statement. The translation of the process statement part is found in the executeProcess method of each of the generated classes. Wait statements, signal assignments and variable assignments are performed by making calls to methods in the VHDLActor class which is the base class for each of the generated classes. The derivation structure will be defined in greater detail in the forthcoming section. See Figure 4 for a pictorial depiction of the simulator.

5.1 Simulation Kernel

The simulation kernel provides the means for the execution of the simulation cycle as defined by the VHDL Language Reference Manual (LRM)[1]. Hence, the methods for extraction of events from the event queue, advancement of simulation time, insertion of events in the queue, and maintenance of the sensitivity lists are members of the ker-

nel. In addition, data structures and methods for performing Time Warp activities, such as state saving, rollback and GVT computation are also members of the kernel.

5.1.1 Mapping Logical Processes onto Actors

Each process in the source VHDL is translated into a C++ class. Each such class is derived from the VHDLActor class. The VHDLActor actor class is, in turn derived from the Actor class. The Actor class is a base class for all actors, provided by the ProperCAD II library. In other words, each process in the source VHDL is represented by an actor. The kernel methods and data structures referred to above are provided within the VHDLActor class.

The source VHDL is first flattened out into a set of process statements. The next step is translating each of the processes into a C++ class. To achieve this, we have written a code generator, which is described in the next section. For each process, a header file containing the declarations for data structures required by the process is generated. There is also a file containing methods for the class, namely the constructor, the destructor and the methods for executing the behavior embodied in the process statement.

The VHDLActor class has a virtual method called executeProcess. The executeProcess method in each of the derived classes is a translation of the actions comprising the corresponding process. The invocation of executeProcess is dependent upon whether or not a

137

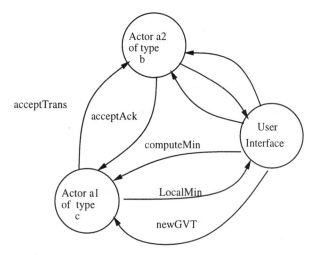

Figure 5: LP a1 invokes the `acceptTransaction` continuation on LP a2, which responds by invoking the `acceptAckMsg` continuation on a1. The UserInterface is shown sending and receiving GVT request continuations.

change has occurred in the *sensitivity list* of the `process`.

5.1.2 Communication between Logical Processes

Logical Processes (LP) in Time Warp communicate by means of exchanging messages. The pure actor model does not support the simple transfer of messages between communicating LP's. It is therefore necessary to communicate by calling *continuations* on the destination LP's. A continuation may be looked upon as a function pointer. Communication between the actors, which are the LP's, is performed by calling continuations upon one another. Continuations are called with arguments, and messages are exchanged between actors in this way.

The sending of an event from one LP to another is accomplished by invoking the `ActorMethod` on the receiver with appropriate parameters. In `ProperVHDL` the `ActorMethod` responsible for receiving events is called `acceptTransaction`. Similarly, `ActorMethods` exist for handling receipt of anti messages, requests for participation in GVT computation, and broadcasts of newly computed GVT. Sometimes, it may be necessary for the receiver to respond to a message by invoking an `ActorMethod` on the sender. In this case the continuation is included in the original message. The receiver has to merely execute it. An example of this situation occurs when using Samadi's algorithm for GVT [23] computation, in which the receipt of every event must be acknowledged by the receiver. Figure 5 shows some of the interactions which occur between LPs in terms of the continuations invoked upon one another.

5.1.3 Continuation Table

Since continuations are similar to function pointers in a global namespace, it is necessary to know the names of the actors in order to ensure that the continuation is called on the correct actor. The code which involves sending of messages is in the methods of `VHDLActor` which is the base class for all the actors. The actual actors which are started up are the classes generated by the VHDL front end. It is therefore impossible for the `VHDLActor` class to know the names of all the actors to which continuations are sent. This problem is tackled by generating a file which is essentially a table of all continuations, which can be indexed by a unique integer identifier given to each actor upon start up. Furthermore, this table is visible to each actor, and appropriate continuations are called by looking up the table. The table has been implemented as an `Aggregate`. This is a distributed data structure. There is a copy of the table on each processor, and each actor looks up the copy on its local node. There is therefore no extra overhead incurred in looking up the continuation table.

5.1.4 GVT Computation

For any realistic application of the Time Warp algorithm, it is necessary to pay attention to computing the *Global Virtual Time* or GVT, in order to reclaim state space which is no longer required. GVT is the least simulation time to which a process may roll back. Any state saved at a time prior to this time may be reclaimed[1]. GVT is also essential for commitment of output. There have been several algorithms proposed for computing GVT including [23], [24], [25].

As of now, a centralized GVT management algorithm, Samadi's algorithm is being used. We have chosen this algorithm because of the simplicity of its implementation. This algorithm presumes the existence of a central GVT manager which is responsible for broadcasting GVT computation requests, receiving responses, computing and broadcasting GVT periodically. This functionality has been encoded in the `UserInterface` class. It should be noted that the algorithm is not particularly efficient in terms of the message traffic it requires. This is because each message sent by a process must be acknowledged by the sender. On the other hand, it is very easy to compute, given the minima from each LP. Other distributed algorithms which are more efficient in terms of messages have been proposed [24], [25]. However, they are computationally more expensive than Samadi's algorithm. With the declining cost of communication (particularly on shared memory machines), this is a tradeoff which deserves some attention.

The algorithm is shown in Figure 6. The computation of GVT involves finding the minimum simulation time to

---

[1] In actual fact, one state before GVT is maintained to enable correct handling of rollbacks to GVT.

Procedure LocalMinimum:

mode = find;

min_1 = min. timestamp of unacked msgs;

min_2 = min. timestamp of tagged ack msg;

min_3 = local_time;

min_p = MIN (min_1, min_2, min_3);

report min_p to manager;

Figure 6: Samadi's Algorithm for GVT Computation used in ProperVHDL

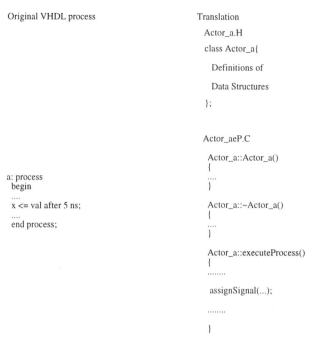

Figure 7: Code generation for a VHDL process.

which a process may rollback. Lin [24] has noted that the two primary difficulties in this computation are tracking transient messages and the simultaneous reporting problem. Samadi's algorithm solves the former by having message acknowledgement. The second problem is tackled by defining two states of execution of an LP – a normal state, and a state which is reached when a request arrives to compute GVT. The normal state is reached from the latter when a value of GVT is reported by the GVT Manager. Any acknowledgement sent out while a process is in the second state is tagged to denote this fact. Then, the local value of GVT reported is the minimum timestamp of an unacknowledged message, the minimum timestamp on a tagged acknowledgement and the local clock. Computation of the first value is accomplished by searching the output queue. The second quantity decreases monotonically, so it is sufficient to maintain a running minimum. The central manager computes GVT to be the minimum of all the local minima.

5.1.5 Other Time Warp Parameters

The simulator does not use bounded time windows to limit the optimistic execution. We utilize an aggressive cancellation policy to recover from rollbacks. State is saved after every event.

5.2 Code Generation

This section describes some aspects of C++ code generation from VHDL. The front end VHDL analyzer has been implemented using the PCCTS [26] tool for generation of LL(k) parsers. The output of the front end is an abstract syntax tree and a set of symbol tables. A code generator accepts these as input and traverses the tree to generate C++ code.

As mentioned briefly before, each VHDL process is translated into a C++ class. This involves generation of a

header file containing the data structures for each class. In addition a .C file containing the constructor, destructor and methods carrying out the behavior embodied in the original VHDL process is generated. This is shown in Figure 7.

VHDL constructs such as signal assignments, variable assignments and wait statements are made by calls to methods implementing their functionality in the VHDLActor base class. Conditional and looping constructs are directly translated into C++. In order to correctly handle VHDL code with wait statements arbitrarily interspersed in the source VHDL it was necessary to perform certain transformations which are described below.

Wait statements entail suspension of a process statement until a condition is satisfied, timeout occurs, or event [2] occurs on a signal. When the process is ready for resumption, it must begin executing code from the statement succeeding the wait statement. In our scenario, this means that the executeProcess() method can potentially be suspended and resumed from an arbitrary position in the code. However, the actor model precludes suspension and resumption of a thread from an arbitrary point within it [4].

Hence, we had to mimic this suspension and resumption by splitting up the executeProcess() method into a set of methods with each such method ending in a wait statement after enabling the method containing the code succeeding the wait statement, as in Figure 8. Resumption is then implemented simply by calling the enabled method. A simi-

---

[2]In VHDL, an event is a change in the value of a signal. The VHDL equivalent of an event or timestamped message as used in PDES terminology is *transaction*.

Source VHDL   Generated Code

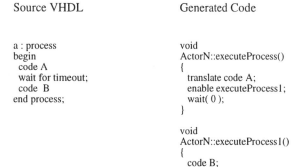

```
a : process                void
begin                      ActorN::executeProcess()
  code A                   {
  wait for timeout;          translate code A;
  code  B                    enable executeProcess1;
end process;                 wait( 0 );
                           }

                           void
                           ActorN::executeProcess1()
                           {
                             code B;
                           }
```

Figure 8: Translation of a VHDL process with a wait statement in the middle of the code

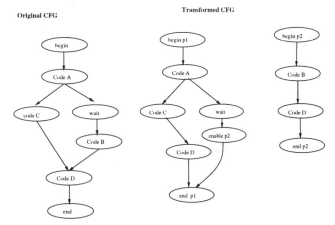

Figure 9: Generating code for a wait statement in a conditional construct.

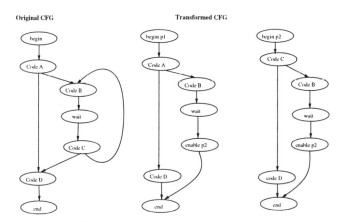

Figure 10: Generating code for a wait statement in a looping construct.

Table 1: Runtimes in seconds with default actor placement on SPARCServer 1000

circuit	1 proc	2 procs	4 procs	8 procs
8x8	11.3	6.1	3.9	5.3
16x16	48.6	25.6	16.2	15.2

Table 2: Runtimes in seconds with default actor placement on Intel Paragon

circuit	1 proc	2 procs	4 procs	8 procs	16 procs
8x8	10.6	10.3	8.6	7.2	-
16x16	411.9	440.1	31.22	20.1	14.1

lar notion was first reported in [27] where issues regarding compilation of message driven programs from conventional imperative programs were discussed.

We now consider handling wait statements appearing in a branch of the *if-then-else* construct. Figure 9 contains the original and transformed control flow graphs (CFG) for this case. All the code upto the wait statement, including the *if* statement is placed in the method p1 (code A). If the condition in the *if* statement evaluates to TRUE, then the wait statement is executed after enabling method p2. When the wait statement is satisfied, the method p2 is enabled. On the other hand, if the condition evaluates to FALSE, then execution of p1 continues in the appropriate manner.

The case of wait statements in a loop body is shown in Figure 10. The looping condition is evaluated in the method p1, and if the loop must be entered, then the wait statement is started after enabling p2. If the looping condition evaluates to FALSE then the code after the loop is executed. When the wait condition is fulfilled, the method p2 is invoked. On entry to p2, the remainder of the loop (Code C) is completed. Then the looping condition (Code B) is

reevaluated. If it is necessary to reenter the loop, the wait is executed after enabling p2 again. If Code B evaluates to FALSE, the remainder of the program (Code D) is evaluated.

6   Experimental Results

We now describe some experiments and preliminary results. Initial experiments were performed using two VHDL descriptions. These are an 8x8 bit array multiplier (with 71 VHDL processes) and a 16x16 bit array multiplier (with 271 processes). Each description is fed an input vector file of 100 vectors.

The simulations were run on a shared memory multiprocessor (8 processor SUN SPARCServer 1000) and a distributed memory machine (20 node Intel Paragon). Our initial experiments are shown in Tables 1 and 2 . The numbers show that on the SPARCserver, the runtimes scale well with increasing number of processors upto 4 processors and then a deterioration occurs. On the Paragon, however, the runtimes scale poorly upon increasing the number of pro-

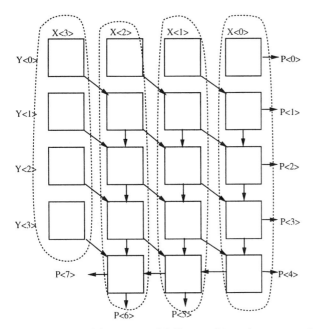

Figure 11: 4x4 bit array multiplier partitioned to run on 4 processors

cessors.

The ProperCAD II runtime environment assigns actors to processes randomly. It starts up the simulation using the desired number of heavyweight processes, but assignment of actors to these processes is entirely random. To gain speedups especially on distributed memory machines, it is essential to place actors in such a way that communication is kept as local as possible. Random assignment of actors will therefore not optimize the communication. Hence, our next step was to apply strings based partitioning [28] to the multipliers. This yielded the partition shown in Figure 11. The partitioning strategy also attempts to take care of load balance by assigning approximately equal numbers of actors to each partition. In this case, the actors have approximately equal computational grain size. We therefore did not assign weights (reflecting the computational grain size) to each of the actors prior to partitioning. In descriptions having actors of varying grain size, it will be necessary to do so, in order to obtain a reasonably balanced partition.

The results obtained with partitioning applied are shown in Tables 3 and 4. Clearly, placement of actors based on a circuit partitioning strategy improves the scalability of the simulation i.e. the overhead of communication does not overcome the benefits of utilizing additional processors.

It should be noticed that for the 16x16 multiplier, when 1 and 2 processors are used, the simulation is thrashing badly, but that the partitioning is able to produce a good result for 2 processors in spite of this. Using a larger number of processors relieves the thrashing problem.

Table 3: Runtimes in seconds with circuit partitioned actor placement on SPARCServer1000

circuit	1 proc	2 procs	4 procs	8 procs
8x8	12.8	6.1	3.9	2.93
16x16	48.7	24.8	14.1	8.8

Table 4: Runtimes in seconds with circuit partitioned actor placement on Intel Paragon

circuit	1 proc	2 procs	4 procs	8 procs	16 procs
8x8	11.1	9.8	7.7	6.4	-
16x16	411.7	289.2	17.4	12.7	10.4

Table 5: Runtimes in seconds for ISCAS benchmarks executing on SPARCserver

circuit	#actors	1 proc	2 proc	4 proc	8 proc
c17	7	250.8	145.6	72.8	109.3
c432	162	356.6	258.3	121.3	102.4
c499	204	637.63	310.7	188.3	-
s298	135	28.8	12.85	8.11	5.8
s344	177	52.55	40.58	14.84	10.03

We have also run some experiments with the ISCAS [29, 30] set of benchmarks, which are shown in Tables 5 and 6. The simulations on the Sparcserver show good scaling. However, serious memory difficulties prevented us from gathering more conclusive data on the Paragon.

7   Conclusions and Future Work

We have described the implementation of a VHDL simulator using the Time Warp algorithm in the context of Actor based parallelism. Furthermore, our preliminary results show that placement of processes based on a partition of the circuit topology leads to improvements in runtime and scalability. In the future, we intend to run simulations on a wider set of benchmark VHDL descriptions to see whether these partitioning strategies will continue to yield favorable results for less regular circuit structures.

Table 6: Runtimes in seconds for ISCAS benchmarks executing on Paragon

circuit	#actors	1 proc	2 proc	4 proc	8 proc	16 proc
c432	162	-	582.747	-	24.92	20.81
c499	204	-	-	-	-	-
s298	135	-	-	-	-	-
s344	177	-	-	-	-	-

References

[1] IEEE, New York, NY, *IEEE Standard VHDL Language Reference Manual*, 1988.

[2] D. Jefferson, "Virtual time," *ACM Transactions on Programming Languages and Systems*, vol. 7, no. 3, pp. 404–425, 1985.

[3] S. Parkes, J. A. Chandy, and P. Banerjee, "A library based approach to portable, parallel, object–oriented programming: Interface, implementation and application," in *Supercomputing '94*, November 1994.

[4] G. A. Agha, *Actors: A Model of Concurrent Computation in Distributed Systems*. The MIT Press, 1986.

[5] Jade Simulations Int. Co., "Implementation issues of Jade's VHDL simulator," tech. rep., Calgary, Alberta, Canada, 1989.

[6] T. J. McBrayer and P. A. Wilsey, "Process combination to increase event granularity in parallel logic simulation," in *Proceedings of Int. Parallel Processing Symposium*, April 1995.

[7] J. C. Willis and D. P. Siewiorek, "Optimizing VHDL compilation for parallel simulation," *IEEE Design and Test of Computers*, pp. 42 – 53, September 1992.

[8] K. L. Kapp, T. C. Hartrum, and T. S. Wailes, "An improved cost function for static partitioning of parallel circuit simulations using a conservative synchronization protocol," in *Proc. of 9th Workshop on Parallel and Distributed Simulation*, pp. 78 – 85, June 1995.

[9] K. M. Chandy and J. Misra, "Asynchronous distributed simulation via a sequence of parallel computations," *Communications of the ACM*, vol. 24, pp. 198 – 206, April 1981.

[10] B. Vellandi and M. Lightner, "Parallelism extraction and program restructuring of VHDL for parallel simulation," in *Proc. European Design Automation Conf. (EDAC-93)*, March 1993.

[11] C.-P. Wen and K. Yelick, "Portable runtime support for asynchrnous simulation," in *Proc. of the 1995 Int. Conf. on Parallel Processing*, vol. 2, pp. II–196 – II–204, The Pennsylvania State University, 1995.

[12] R. Bagrodia and W. Liao, "A language for design of efficient discrete event simulations," *IEEE Transactions on Software Engineering*, March 1994.

[13] J. Cong, Z. Li, and R. Bagrodia, "Acyclic multiway partitioning of boolean networks," in *31st ACM/IEEE Design Automation Conference*, pp. 670 – 675, June 1994.

[14] M. L. Bailey, J. V. Briner, and R. D. Chamberlain, "Parallel logic simulation of VLSI systems," *ACM Computing Surveys*, vol. 26, pp. 255–294, Sept. 1994.

[15] L. Soule and T. Blank, "Parallel logic simulation on general purpose machines," in *Proc. 26th Descign Automation Conf.*, pp. 81–86, June 1989.

[16] B. Ramkumar and P. Banerjee, "ProperCAD: A portable object-oriented parallel environment for VLSI CAD," *IEEE Trans. Computer-Aided Design*, vol. 13, pp. 829–842, July 1994.

[17] A. W. Appel, *Compiling with Continuations*. Cambridge: Cambridge University Press, 1992.

[18] B. Ramkumar and P. Banerjee, "ProperEXT: A portable parallel algorithm for VLSI circuit extraction," in *International Parallel Processing Symposium*, pp. 434 – 438, 1993.

[19] S. Parkes, P. Banerjee, and J. H. Patel, "ProperHITEC: A portable, parallel, object–oriented approach to sequential test generation," in *Proceedings of the Design Automation Conference*, pp. 717–721, june 1994.

[20] S. Parkes, P. Banerjee, and J. Patel, "A parallel algorithm for fault simulation based on proofs," in *International Conf. on Computer Design*, (Austin, TX), Oct 1995.

[21] S. Kim, J. A. Chandy, S. Parkes, B. Ramkumar, and P. Banerjee, "ProperPLACE: A portable parallel algorithm for cell placement," in *International Parallel Processing Symposium*, (Cancun, Mexico), pp. 932–941, April 1994.

[22] K. De, J. A. Chandy, S. Roy, S. Parkes, and P. Banerjee, "Portable parallel algorithms for logic synthesis using the MIS approach," in *International Parallel Processing Symposium*, (Santa Barbara, CA), pp. 579–585, April 1995.

[23] B. Samadi, *Distributed Simulation, Algorithms and Performance Analysis*. PhD thesis, UCLA, 1985.

[24] Y. B. Lin and E. D. Lazowska, "Determining the global virtual time in a distributed simulation.," in *Proceedings of International Conf. on Parallel Processing*, pp. 201 – 209, 1990.

[25] L. M. D'Souza, X. Fan, and P. A. Wilsey, "pGVT: An algorithm for accurate gvt estimation," in *Proc. of 8th Workshop on Parallel and Dist. Simulation*, pp. 102–109, June 1994.

[26] T. J. Parr and R. W. Quong, "ANTLR: A predicated-LL(k) parser generator," *Software, Practice and Experience*, vol. 25, p. 789, July 1995.

[27] J. G. Holm, A. Lain, and P. Banerjee, "Compilation of scientific programs into multithreaded and message driven computation," in *Proceedings of the 1994 Scalable High Performance Computing Conference*, (Knoxville, TN), pp. 518–525, May 1994.

[28] Y. Levendel, P. Menon, and S. Patel, "Special purpose computer for logic simulation using distributed processing," *Bell System Tech. J.*, vol. 61, pp. 2873–2910, Dec. 1982.

[29] F. Brglez and H. Fujiwara, "A Neutral Netlist of 10 Combinational Benchmark Circuits and a Target Translator in Fortran," *IEEE Intl. Symp. on Circuits and Systems*, vol. 3, June 1985.

[30] F. Brglez, D. Bryan, and K. Kozminski, "Combinational Profiles of Sequential Benchmark Circuits," *IEEE Intl. Symp. on Circuits and Systems*, pp. 1929–1934, May 1989.

Optimistic Simulation of Parallel Architectures Using Program Executables *

Sashikanth Chandrasekaran and Mark. D. Hill

Computer Sciences Department
University of Wisconsin–Madison
1210 West Dayton Street
Madison, WI 53706 USA
wwt@cs.wisc.edu

Abstract

A key tool of computer architects is computer simulation at the level of detail that can execute program executables. The time and memory requirements of such simulations can be enormous, especially when the machine under design—the target—*is a parallel machine. Thus, it is attractive to use parallel simulation, as successfully demonstrated by the* Wisconsin Wind Tunnel *(WWT). WWT uses a conservative simulation algorithm and eschews network simulation to make lookahead adequate. Nevertheless, we find most of WWT's slowdown to be due to the synchronization overhead in the conservative simulation algorithm.*

This paper examines the use of optimistic algorithms to perform parallel simulations of parallel machines. We first show that we can make optimistic algorithms work correctly even with WWT's direct execution of program executables. We checkpoint processor registers (integer, floating-point, and condition codes) and use executable editing to log the value of memory words just before they are overwritten by stores. Second, we consider the performance of two optimistic algorithms. The first executes programs optimistically, but performs protocol events (e.g., sending messages) conservatively. The second executes everything optimistically and is similar to Time Warp with lazy message cancellation. Unfortunately, both approaches make parallel simulation performance worse for the default WWT assumptions. We conclude by speculating on the performance of optimistic simulation when simulating (1) target network details, and (2) on hosts with high message latencies and no synchronization hardware.

1 Introduction

Simulation is a popular technique to study and evaluate proposed computer architectures. To simulate the complex interactions in the proposed design, researchers must be able to run applications (i.e., program executables) in addition to stochastic workloads. Unfortunately, the time and memory requirements of such simulations can be enormous, especially when the machine under design is a parallel machine. Therefore, researchers have begun using parallel simulation—i.e, using an existing parallel machine (the *host*) to simulate the parallel machine under study (the *target*). A technique known as *direct execution* [3] is used to execute program executables. With direct execution, the host simulates only those features in the target machine that it does not support (e.g., cache-coherence, synchronization operations). In this paper we use the term *event* only to refer to those actions that require simulation by the host. The common features, such as program instructions, are not simulated—instead, they are directly executed by the host. The Wisconsin Wind Tunnel (WWT) is a simulator that executes program executables on a Thinking Machines CM-5 host to simulate cache-coherent shared-memory computers [14]. WWT directly executes all instructions and memory references that hit in the target cache. Program executables are edited so that during WWT's direct execution they also keep track of target execution time (by incrementing a counter). WWT regains control on cache misses and simulates the target cache, directory, etc., by sending timestamped messages.

WWT uses the conservative *time bucket* synchronization mechanism [18] to coordinate simulation of the processor nodes. Simulation proceeds in parallel for quanta of duration Q. Each node must synchronize with all other nodes at the end of every quantum, after which all nodes proceed in parallel for another quantum Q. Without target network simulation, the minimum target time between events and the events that they can generate in remote nodes (also called the *lookahead*) is the *target network latency*. In order to have sufficient lookahead, WWT avoids network simulation and sets the quantum length to the fixed target network latency. Nevertheless, we find most

---
*This work is supported in part by NSF Grant MIP-9225097, Wright Laboratory Avionics Directorate, Air Force Material Command, USAF, under grant #F33615-94-1-1525 and ARPA order no. B550, Sun Microsystems and Thinking Machines Corporation, Our Thinking Machines CM-5 was purchased through NSF Institutional Infrastructure Grant No. CDA-9024618 with matching funding from the University of Wisconsin Graduate School. The U.S. Government is authorized to reproduce and distribute reprints for Governmental purposes notwithstanding any copyright notation thereon. The views and conclusions contained herein are those of the authors and should not be interpreted as necessarily representing the official policies or endorsements, either expressed or implied, of the Wright Laboratory Avionics Directorate or the U.S. Government.

Step	Time	% of total time
Direct Execution	131	3.99%
Protocol Simulation	740	22.55%
Quantum Synchronization	2338	71.26%
Barrier Synchronization	72	2.20%

Table 1: Breakdown of total simulation time with conservative simulation.
The table shows the breakdown of simulation time when simulating the program Ocean, on a target machine to be described in Section 2. *Time* is in millions of host cycles. Direct Execution refers to the time spent executing target instructions on the host node. Protocol simulation includes simulation of the target cache and target directory events. While quantum synchronization refers to the time spent by host nodes waiting for other nodes to reach the end of the quantum and for the messages to reach their destinations, barrier synchronization is the time taken for nodes to complete the barrier after the network has delivered all messages and the last node has entered the barrier. The target program was executed for 16 million target cycles.

of WWT's slowdown to be due to the synchronization overhead in the conservative simulation algorithm (Table 1).

In this paper, we examine the use of optimistic parallel simulation algorithms to simulate parallel machines using program executables. To the best of our knowledge, this is the first work to demonstrate how optimistic techniques can be used with directly executed programs. To correctly save the state of a target program, we checkpoint the processor state by copying the registers (integer and floating-point) and condition codes at the end of each quantum. Restoring the processor state only involves storing the values back into their respective registers. We incrementally save the target program's memory by editing the program executable to include instructions that log the value of memory words before every *store* instruction. To restore the memory state, we invoke a routine in the target program that replaces the old values in memory. Using these techniques, we study two optimistic approaches:

- A hybrid approach that optimistically executes target program instructions and memory references that hit in the target cache and conservatively simulates protocol events. We use Reynolds' terminology [15] and call this a *risk-free* optimistic approach.

- An aggressive Time Warp-like optimistic approach that executes all target program instructions, memory references (including those that miss in the target cache) and protocol events optimistically.

Optimistic approaches have been shown to perform better when simulating target systems such as queuing networks and when using stochastic workloads [12].

This paper, on the other hand, compares the performance of conservative and optimistic approaches by executing shared-memory applications. We find that for all the applications that we executed on a CM-5 host, the conservative technique performs better than either optimistic technique. The risk-free technique runs an average of 1.5 times slower than the conservative simulation. This technique improves the lookahead only by an average of 36 target machine cycles since shared-memory parallel programs spend significant time in communication and synchronization. The aggressive technique reduces the frequency of synchronization among the host nodes by up to 66%. However, rollback overheads dominate the execution and it is up to 2.5 times slower than the the conservative simulation.

We then speculate on simulation performance in two cases that could be more favorable to optimistic simulation: (1) Accurate simulation of the target network, which forces the lookahead to be much less than the constant network latency. At low lookaheads, synchronization overheads are exacerbated and optimistic techniques may yield better performance. (2) Simulation on hosts with high network latencies and no hardware support for synchronization. We speculate that the optimistic approaches would perform better on hosts where synchronization operations must be performed in software (at a higher cost).

The next section provides a brief background on our workloads. Sections 3 and 4 present the performance of the risk-free optimistic technique and the aggressive optimistic technique respectively. Section 5 presents the scenarios where optimistic techniques may offer better performance. Section 6 describes related work, Section 7 describes future work, and finally, Section 8 presents our conclusions.

2 Target Machines and Workloads

Our target machines are composed of nodes which contain a CPU, a 256KB 4-way set-associative data cache, and local memory. The nodes are connected by a network that has a fixed latency of Q (=100) cycles. An all-hardware directory-based coherence protocol is used to maintain a sequentially consistent view of shared-memory.

The three applications that we chose to present are *Ocean*, *Sparse*, and *Water*. Ocean and Water are from the SPLASH benchmark suite [17], and Sparse is a locally written shared-memory program. Ocean is a hydrodynamic simulation that models a two-dimensional cross-section of a cuboidal basin. The input data set used was a 98×98 grid. Sparse solves $AX = B$ in parallel for a sparse matrix A. The input matrix was a 256×256 dense matrix. Water is a water molecule simulation performed on 256 molecules for 10 iterations. We chose these benchmarks because they exhibit different computation/communication ratios and communication patterns. While Ocean has a very high communication overhead, Sparse has a moderate communication overhead and Water spends very little time in communication.

144

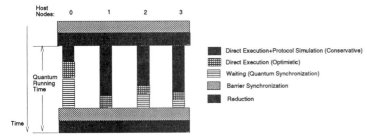

Figure 1: A pictorial view of the different steps in a quantum when using a risk-free optimistic technique.

3 A "Risk-Free" Optimistic Mechanism

In this section, we present the implementation and performance of a *hybrid* approach that adds optimism to the existing conservative mechanism. This strategy is similar to the Breathing Time Buckets strategy supported in SPEEDES [18]. Like the conservative technique, events are processed in quanta. However, these quanta do not have the constant length, Q. Instead, the *event horizon* determines the quantum length. The event horizon is the minimum event time of all events generated during optimistic simulation of the previous quantum plus the target network latency. We refer to the logical time of the event horizon as the *safe time*. The safe time is computed by performing a synchronous *min reduction* of the event times. Processing events beyond the safe time *may* cause time accidents, i.e., events processed beyond the safe time may have to be rolled back. Thus a quantum length is the logical time between two successive event horizons ($\geq Q$).

The conservative technique (combining direct execution and simulation of events) is used to process *safe* events—events with timestamp less than the safe time. When a host node has no events that it can safely process, it checkpoints the target processor state and optimistically executes target program instructions. However, to confine rollbacks to the local processor, cache misses and other events beyond the safe time that may cause communication are not processed optimistically. Instead, the node participates in the global synchronization to check for causality errors and to compute the next event horizon. The probability of optimistically executed instructions being incorrect tends to increase the further simulation proceeds beyond the safe time. To prevent such incorrect computations from proceeding too far ahead into the logical time and increasing the probability of a rollback, we insert a *mega-quantum* expiration event that puts an upper bound on the optimistic phase in each cycle. Scheduling the mega-quantum expiration event at $3 \times Q$ cycles gives the best performance. Figure 1 illustrates the different steps in a quantum when using a risk-free optimistic technique.

We now discuss the techniques needed to save and restore the state of a directly executed program (Sec-

tions 3.1 and 3.2). Directly executed programs can manipulate any part of a target node's state. However, since the risk-free mechanism prevents the target program from executing beyond an event, we only need to save and restore the target program's register and memory state.

3.1 Saving Processor State

WWT schedules a checkpoint event at the end of each quantum. Whenever the target program returns control to WWT (due to a quantum expiration, or an event), the executive interface to the CM-5 kernel [13] saves the target global registers (including the program counter) and the condition codes in a buffer. We only need to copy the buffer and save the floating-point registers and the floating-point status register to *partially* checkpoint the target processor state. On a machine with no register windows (e.g., a MIPS-like architecture) the *entire* processor state could be constructed by making a copy of all the registers. On a SPARC processor, we need to save the registers in all the active register windows that were used by the target program before starting optimistic execution of the target program. When a time accident is detected, we copy the global integer registers, floating-point registers and the condition codes from the checkpoint buffer into the host node's registers. The target register window is restored before returning to the target program for restarting direct-execution from the checkpoint.

3.2 Saving Memory State

The simplest solution to saving memory state is to copy the entire target address space; however this involves very high overhead. Instead, the target memory is saved incrementally by logging all changes to it. The target program changes the state of memory by executing *store* instructions. We use EEL [9], an executable editing library, to instrument the target store instructions with a small piece of code (e.g., four instructions before a *store-word*) that loads the old value from memory and saves it in a log in the target address space.[1] Note that stores to both private and shared memory locations are logged. When a time accident is detected, we invoke an unroll procedure in the target program that restores the values in the target memory starting from the end of the log. This unroll procedure is linked to the target program along with the instrumentation of the store instructions. An important concern in optimistic techniques is the memory required for saving state. Our technique uses 4K bytes (a page) for logging changes to memory and less than 300 bytes to save the processor state. This overhead is less than 1% of the memory required by a program that has a data set size of 1MB per node.

---

[1] Actually, stores to target memory during the conservative phase are also logged, since it is more expensive to detect the state of the simulation and avoid logging. When a checkpoint is taken the log pointer is reset to the start of the log.

Application	Procs	% Computation	Conservative Simulation Time (million cycles)	Risk-Free Optimistic Simulation		
				Time (million cycles)	Average Quantum Length (cycles)	Slowdown
Ocean	8	16	7097	9276	112	1.31
Ocean	16	14	4398	6127	107	1.39
Ocean	32	12	3245	4505	104	1.39
Sparse	8	67	1775	2880	136	1.62
Sparse	16	46	2098	2902	128	1.38
Sparse	32	25	3329	4249	120	1.28
Water	8	59	6733	10918	202	1.62
Water	16	51	5100	8800	170	1.73
Water	32	41	4029	7759	145	1.92

Table 2: Performance of conservative vs. risk-free optimistic simulation.

This table shows the percentage of time spent by the applications in computation, the simulation times, the average quantum length, and the slowdown of the optimistic technique when compared to the conservative simulation. The target network latency was set to 100 cycles. While the simulation times refer to the *host* cycles (in millions), the average quantum length refers to the *target* cycles.

3.3 Performance Evaluation

Table 2 compares the performance of the risk-free optimistic technique and the conservative simulation for the target system parameters described in Section 2. The average quantum length is the average number of target cycles simulated between barriers and indicates how often synchronization is performed between host nodes. The results clearly demonstrate that the risk-free optimistic technique fails to increase the lookahead and performs worse than the conservative simulation. Simulation of applications that have a significant communication overhead is mostly conservative since protocol events are simulated conservatively. The net result is that the average quantum length is only slightly greater than the lookahead in the conservative simulation (100 cycles). Synchronization is performed nearly as often and the additional overheads of saving and restoring state and computing the event horizons result in a slightly longer execution time. Water and Sparse have a significant computation component and accordingly, optimistic execution improves the lookahead. However, an increase in lookahead alone is not sufficient to speedup the execution. In particular, optimistic execution results in a higher load imbalance between the host nodes. For example, a node could be executing target instructions until the mega-quantum while all other nodes are waiting at the barrier. The increased lookahead (or parallelism) must outweigh the load imbalance and overheads to achieve speedups.

Table 3 presents the breakdown of the simulation time for Ocean. The results show that the overhead of restoring target state and computing the global event horizon is minimal (about 3% for Ocean and less than 10% for all the applications that we simulated). Saving target registers requires less than fifty instructions and accounts for about 2% of the simulation time. The overhead of saving target memory is harder to segregate since the target memory is incrementally saved as the program is directly executed. Although the time for direct execution has increased by 75 million cycles

Step	Time	% of total time
Conservative Execution	123	3.26%
Protocol Simulation	808	21.44%
Optimistic Execution	83	2.20%
Quantum Synchronization	2581	68.49%
Barrier Synchronization	64	1.72%
Reduction	92	2.44%
Undo	17	0.45%

Table 3: Breakdown of total simulation time with risk-free optimistic simulation.

The table shows the breakdown of simulation time when simulating Ocean. *Time* is in millions of host cycles. Conservative Execution refers to the direct execution of the target program instructions until the checkpoint. Optimistic execution refers to the direct execution of target program instructions beyond the checkpoint. Protocol simulation includes simulation of the target cache and target directory events. Quantum Synchronization refers to the time spent waiting for nodes to arrive at the barrier and for the the network to deliver all the messages at the end of each quantum. Barrier Synchronization is the time taken for nodes to complete the barrier after all messages have been delivered and the last node has entered the barrier. Reduction is the time spent in calculating the new event horizon and Undo refers to the time spent unrolling the target registers and memory. The target program was executed for 16 million target cycles.

(from 131 to 206 million cycles), it still accounts for less than 6% of the total simulation time.

4 A Time-Warp-like Optimistic Technique

In this section we present an aggressive technique that executes both target program instructions and protocol events optimistically. We call it Time-Warp-*like* since a few target synchronization operations such as *swap* are simulated conservatively.

4.1 Rolling Back Protocol State

Processing protocol events optimistically poses new problems: protocol events send host messages in order to simulate the parallel machine. Mechanisms would hence be required to undo incorrectly sent messages and incorrectly simulated protocol events. We implement the classical solution proposed by Jefferson [8] and send *anti-messages* that annihilate incorrectly sent messages.[2] All protocol events essentially perform one or more of the following actions:

- Modify the state of a block (either in the target cache or directory). For example, an invalidation event would mark a cache block *invalid*; a directory event could set a bit associated with the block to indicate that a target node has a cached copy.

- Send one or more messages to other host nodes. For example, an invalidation event would send an acknowledgement message to (the host node that simulates) the directory indicating that the block has been invalidated; a directory event could send a copy of a block to (the host node that simulates) the cache in response to a request.

- Update the logical clock of the hardware that services the event, i.e., cache or directory.

Since directly executed programs can modify any part of their virtual address space, copying the entire state of the cache or the directory would be prohibitively expensive. Protocol events, however, modify memory in block sizes (typically 32-128 bytes). It makes sense, therefore, to save the state of the target block that was modified by each optimistically simulated event. Analogously, restoring the target state is also done incrementally and is a four-step process:

1. Restore the state of each directory entry that was modified optimistically. For instance, this might result in sending an *anti-response* message to the node that requested a copy and clearing a bit to restore the bit vector of owners.

2. Restore the state of all optimistically modified cache blocks. For instance, this could involve marking a cache block as *valid* to undo an invalidation event.

3. Restore the state of the memory modified by directly executing the target (Section 3.2).

4. Copy the target program registers from the checkpoint buffer (Section 3.1).

This technique requires about 4K bytes of memory for saving protocol state in addition to the memory

---

[2]Although anti-messages are generated immediately, they are buffered and *sent* only when the logical clock sweeps past the timestamp of the incorrect message without regenerating the same message (i.e., we implement *lazy cancellation*).

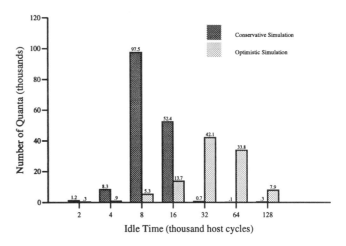

Figure 2: Histogram of idle times.

This figure shows a histogram of the average host idle time in each quantum when executing Ocean. The idle time is the time spent by a host node waiting for other nodes to synchronize. In the conservative scheme the average idle time is mostly between 8,000 and 16,000 cycles while the optimistic scheme results in an average idle time mostly between 32,000 and 64,000 cycles.

---

required to save target processor and memory state. The additional memory is still less than 1% of the memory used by an application that has a data set size of 1MB.

4.2 Performance

Table 4 compares the performance of the aggressive optimistic technique and the conservative simulation. For the sake of convenience, we reproduce the time taken for simulation using conservative simulation from Table 2. The results clearly demonstrate that the conservative simulation outperforms the aggressive simulation. The increase in average quantum length denotes that the aggressive simulation is able to synchronize less often. The performance of the aggressive simulation is sensitive to the mega-quantum length. Large optimistic windows increase the scope for useful work to be done before synchronization and hence allows the simulation to synchronize less often (up to 60% less often). However, this comes at a high cost; the probability of an event being simulated incorrectly increases greatly as nodes move further from the global virtual time. Undoing incorrectly processed events leads to an avalanche of anti-messages. For example, for Ocean and Sparse the message traffic increased by up to 66% due to the aggressive simulation. Computation-bound applications such as Water do not suffer from the effect of numerous anti-messages. Instead, such applications tend to rollback and redo their computations. For example, with Water the time spent in executing instructions in the target program increased by up to 300%. Figure 2 illustrates the difference in load imbalance using a histogram of idle times. The load imbalance could be reduced if a host node can detect that one or more host nodes are waiting at the barrier and stop optimistic simulation. Unfortunately the CM-5 does not

Application	Procs	Conservative Simulation	Aggressive Optimistic Simulation		
		Time (million cycles)	Time (million cycles)	Average Quantum Length (cycles)	Slowdown
Ocean	8	7097	14867	187	2.09
Ocean	16	4398	9951	173	2.26
Ocean	32	3245	8509	154	2.62
Sparse	8	1775	3406	195	1.92
Sparse	16	2098	4023	186	1.92
Sparse	32	3329	6012	193	1.80
Water	8	6733	11090	248	1.65
Water	16	5100	9876	244	1.93
Water	32	4029	8805	238	2.18

Table 4: Performance of conservative vs. aggressive optimistic simulation.
This table shows the simulation times, the average quantum length and the slowdown of the optimistic technique when compared to the conservative simulation. The mega-quantum length for Ocean and Sparse was set to 200 cycles while the mega-quantum length for Water was set to 300 cycles. While the simulation times refer to the *host* cycles (in millions), the average quantum length refers to the *target* cycles.

provide a fast broadcast mechanism that can enable all host nodes to synchronize as soon as the first node enters the barrier.

We performed experiments using four other shared-memory benchmarks (*Barnes*, *Cholesky* and *Mp3d* from the SPLASH benchmark suite [17] and a parallelized version of *Appbt* [1]) and obtained similar results. We restricted the presentation to three applications in the interest of brevity.

5 Scenarios Favorable to Optimistic Simulation

The results presented in the earlier sections demonstrate that for the default WWT assumptions (i.e., no target network simulation, constant target network latency of 100 cycles), the conservative technique has adequate lookahead to offer better performance than both optimistic techniques when executing our shared-memory applications on the CM-5. We now consider two scenarios that are more favorable to optimistic simulation.

Less Lookahead Due to Network Simulation: Without network simulation, the quantum length was equal to 100 cycles for the conservative algorithm and ≥ 100 cycles for optimistic algorithms. Depending on the desired accuracy of simulation of the target network contention and topology, the quantum length must be less than or equal to the message latency. The fixed network latency assumption results in an error of over 20% in several cases [2]. Reducing the quantum length results in a further increase in the synchronization cost. Since optimistic techniques improve the lookahead and reduce the frequency of synchronization, they may perform better if the network simulation messages are not rolled back frequently.

Greater Host Message Latencies: Parallel systems such as a network of workstations are becoming popular since they provide low-cost alternatives to the current generation of parallel machines (such as the CM-5). We expect many of these systems to have high latency messages (10-100s of μs) and little or no

hardware support for synchronization. The CM-5, on the other hand, provides fast messages and hardware support for fast barriers and reductions (the latencies of these operations are all less than 10μs on the CM-5). Hyder and Wood study the implications of latency and synchronization tradeoffs using a variety of applications [7].

How would high latency networks and no hardware synchronization affect the trade off between conservative and optimistic simulation? Both techniques must ensure that all messages sent during a quantum are received before the beginning of the next quantum. In the absence of synchronization hardware, each host node must send an acknowledgment message for each message that it receives and perform a simple software barrier once all acknowledgments have been received [7]. On a host with a network latency of 100μs, synchronization at the end of the quantum would be an order of magnitude more expensive than on the CM-5. This favors optimistic techniques since they need to incur the high cost of this software synchronization less often. Unfortunately, this saving does not come for free—the costs of rolling back incorrect messages also increases. Fortunately, this will not be a dominating factor in applications that do not communicate often. Figure 3 illustrates that for applications with a low communication overhead, optimistic techniques may be a better choice on future parallel systems.

6 Related Work

This paper presented techniques to integrate direct execution with optimistic simulation and studied the performance of three simulation techniques. Unger et al. [21] present an incremental state saving scheme in the Jade simulation environment. A state manager exports an interface to the application and calls this interface before each change of a block of state. The backtrace of memory snapshots are saved in a buffer that is unwound on rollback. Incremental state saving is performed in SPEEDES using two techniques [19].

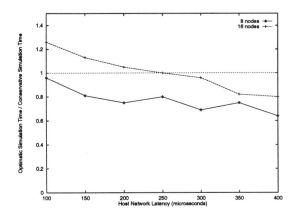

Figure 3: Effect of host network latency on simulation time.

This figure compares the performance of conservative and optimistic simulations as the host network latency is increased. All synchronization operations are performed in software. The application program was Water running on 8 and 16 host nodes. Points above 1 indicate that the conservative simulation is better while points below 1 indicate that the optimistic simulation performs better. With 8 nodes, optimistic simulation is always faster, while with 16 nodes it performs better when the latency is more than 250 μs.

In the delta exchange method event processing is divided into two steps —The first step does the basic event processing while the second step exchanges the new state values. In the rollback queue mechanism the C++ assignment operators are overloaded to automatically save state information.

Shah et al. [16] simulate a shared-memory target machine on a shared-memory host. Their technique is optimistic with respect to timing correctness and reconciliation is performed only at synchronization points. Rollback of the target program is never required because the underlying host machine keeps the memory consistent and only data-race-free programs are executed. However, only the target cache is simulated and the technique has been shown to scale only up to 8 processors. WWT models the parallel machine more accurately and could use the above techniques when the host is a shared-memory machine.

Falsafi and Wood [4] propose simulating multiple target nodes in a single host node. The advantage of this approach is that it reduces load imbalance. Unfortunately, less memory is available to each target node and architects may be restricted to using smaller input data sets.

7   Extensions and Future Work

The most important deficiency of our work is a precise understanding of why optimistic simulations performed worse than the conservative technique. This may enable us to refine optimistic schemes and eliminate the drawbacks of the two techniques that we studied. We have also not attempted to tradeoff accuracy in the simulation for performance. We find

that incorrect computations almost always affect the timing behavior of the system being simulated, but rarely affect the functional behavior. Introducing approximations may reduce rollbacks of target program execution and message sends.

We have used a simple algorithm for computing the global virtual time(GVT). This algorithm requires that all host nodes perform a barrier before the GVT can be computed. Researchers have recently proposed efficient algorithms to perform global synchronization with optimistic simulation [11]. Since a large fraction of the simulation time is spent in global synchronization, incorporating the new algorithms would improve the performance of optimistic simulation.

Finally, we are in the process of porting WWT to a cluster of workstations connected by a Myrinet switch. The network latency of this host system is about $100\mu s$ and it has no synchronization hardware. We expect that this implementation would give us new insights and help us better understand the performance of various parallel simulation techniques.

8   Conclusions

This paper presented new techniques to integrate direct execution of a parallel application and optimistic parallel simulation. We used checkpointing and incremental logging to correctly save and restore the state of directly executed program executables. We used these techniques to develop two optimistic strategies for parallel simulation that represent the ends of the spectrum of the degree of optimism. A risk-free technique executed only target program instructions optimistically and resorted to a global virtual time calculation before simulating protocol events. An aggressive technique used a Time-Warp-like algorithm to simulate protocol events and send messages optimistically.

We compared the performance of these techniques with the conservative simulation algorithm. We found that for the shared-memory applications that we executed on a CM-5 host, the conservative technique offered better performance. The behavior was similar for three different target system sizes—8, 16, and 32 nodes and three different application programs each having a different communication pattern. Optimistic simulations are plagued by two main problems when used for simulating parallel machines using program executables:

- Simple optimistic techniques that avoid the complexity of undoing protocol events and message sends are unable to improve the lookahead in the simulation. The additional overhead accompanied by little gains make them perform up to twice as slow as the conservative simulation.

- Aggressive optimistic techniques improve the lookahead and are able to reduce the frequency of synchronization. However, these gains come at a very high cost; lowering the costs by restricting the size of the optimistic window also relinquishes chances of increasing lookahead. We found that the Time Warp like technique performs up to 2.5 times slower than the conservative simulation.

Several researchers have reported successes with using optimistic simulation [5, 12, 22]. The two notable reasons for the sharp contrast in our conclusions are:

- Our workloads are directly executed programs. Previous studies of simulation strategies have been mostly performed using synthetic workloads, not program executables.

- Our target system is a parallel machine with an interconnection network that provides full connectivity. An implication of this is that a rollback in a node could potentially affect any other node in the system within a logical time equal to the latency of the target network.

We surmise that optimistic techniques may perform better when the host machine has a high network latency (100s of μs), no hardware support for synchronization and the parallel application being executed does not communicate often. Unfortunately, it is debatable whether parallel simulation itself is cost-effective with such host system parameters. Decreasing the quantum length for detailed simulation of the target network may also favor optimistic simulation when the network simulation messages are not rolled back frequently.

Acknowledgment

We thank Doug Burger, Babak Falsafi, Alain Kägi, Rahmat Hyder, Steve Reinhardt and David Wood for helping us understand WWT and for useful suggestions that improved this paper. David Wood contributed to the genesis of some of the optimistic techniques described in this paper. We thank James Larus for generously supporting EEL, Rahmat Hyder for providing code that simulates high latency host machines and the anonymous referees for comments on an earlier draft of this paper. We thank David Wood and Steve Reinhardt for pointing out an error in the network simulation experiments. We thank all the members of the Wisconsin Wind Tunnel project for technical support and encouragement that made this research possible.

References

[1] David Bailey, John Barton, Thomas Lasinski, and Horst Simon, *The NAS Parallel Benchmarks*, Technical Report RNR-91-002, Revision 2, Ames Research Center, August 1991.

[2] Doug Burger and David A. Wood, *Accuracy vs. Performance in Parallel Simulation of Interconnection Networks*, International Symposium on Parallel Processing, April 1995.

[3] Helen Davis, Stephen R. Goldschmidt, and John Hennessy, *Multiprocessor Simulation and Tracing Using Tango*, In Proceedings of the 1991 International Conference on Parallel Processing (Vol. II Software), pages II99–107, August 1991.

[4] Babak Falsafi and David A. Wood, *Cost/Performance of a Parallel Computer Simulator*, In Proceedings of PADS, 1994.

[5] Richard M. Fujimoto, *Performance of Time Warp Under Synthetic Workloads*, Proceedings of the SCS Multiconference on Distributed Simulation, January 1990.

[6] Richard M. Fujimoto, *Parallel Discrete Event Simulation*, Communications of the ACM, 33(10):30-53, October 1990.

[7] Rahmat Hyder and David A. Wood, *Synchronization Support for Networks of Workstations*, In Proceedings of the International Conference on Supercomputing (ICS), 1996.

[8] David R. Jefferson, *Virtual Time*, ACM Transactions on Programming Languages and Systems, 7(3):404–425, July 1985.

[9] James R. Larus and Eric Schnarr, *EEL: Machine-Independent Executable Editing*, Programming Languages Design and Implementation (PLDI), 1995.

[10] David Nicol, *Conservative Parallel Simulation of Priority Class Queuing Networks*, IEEE Transactions on Parallel and Distributed Systems, 3(3):398–412, May 1992.

[11] David Nicol, *Global Synchronization for Optimistic Parallel Discrete Event Simulation*, Proceedings of the seventh workshop on Parallel and Distributed Simulation, July 1993.

[12] Presley, M., Ebling, M., Wieland, F., and Jefferson, D. R., *Benchmarking the Time Warp Operating System with a computer network simulation*, In Proceedings of the SCS Multiconference on Distributed Simulation, 21, 2 (March 1989), pp. 8-13.

[13] Steven K. Reinhardt, Babak Falsafi, and David A. Wood, *Kernel Support for the Wisconsin Wind Tunnel*, Proceedings of the Second USENIX on Microkernels and Other Kernel Architectures, September 1993.

[14] Steven K. Reinhardt, Mark D. Hill, James R. Larus, Alvin R. Lebeck, James C. Lewis, and David A. Wood, *The Wisconsin Wind Tunnel: Virtual Prototyping of Parallel Computers*, ACM SIGMETRICS, 1993.

[15] P. Reynolds, *A Spectrum of Options for Parallel Simulation*, Proceedings of the 1988 Winter Simulation Conference, pages 325-332.

[16] Gautam Shah, Umakishore Ramachandran, and Richard Fujimoto, *Timepatch: A novel technique for the parallel simulation of multiprocessor caches*, TR-94-52, GIT, October 1994.

[17] Jaswinder Pal Singh, Wolf-Dietrich Weber, and Anoop Gupta, *SPLASH: Stanford Parallel Applications for Shared Memory*, Computer Architecture News, 20(1):5-44, March 1992.

[18] Jeff S. Steinman, *SPEEDES: A Multiple-Synchronization Environment for Parallel Discrete-Event Simulation*, International Journal in Computer Simulation, Vol. 2, Pages 251-286.

[19] Jeff S. Steinman, *Incremental State Saving in SPEEDES using C++*, In Proceeding of the 1993 Winter Simulation Conference, Pages 687-96.

[20] Thinking Machines Corporation, *The Connection Machine CM-5 Technical Summary*, 1991.

[21] Brian W. Unger, John G. Cleary, Alan Covington, and Darrin West, *An External State Management System for Optimistic Parallel Simulation*, In Proceedings of the 1993 Winter Simulation Conference.

[22] Wieland, F. et al., *Distributed combat simulation and Time Warp: The model and its performance*, In Proceedings of the SCS Multiconference on Distributed Simulation 21, 2 (March 1989), pp. 14-20.

Session 8

Work In Progress

Session Chair
Phil A. Wilsey, University of Cincinnati, USA

Session 9

Potpourri: Languages, Models, and Algorithms

Session Chair
Bruno R. Preiss, University of Waterloo, Canada

Design of High Level Modelling / High Performance Simulation Environments

Bernard P. Zeigler and Doohwan Kim

AI and Simulation Group
Department of Electrical and Computer Engineering
University of Arizona
Tucson, AZ 85721
zeigler@ece.arizona.edu
dhkim@ece.arizona.edu

Abstract

Advances in massively parallel platforms are increasing the prospects for high performance discrete event simulation. Still the difficulty in parallel programming persists and there is increasing demand for high level support for building discrete event models to execute on such platforms. We present a parallel DEVS-based (Discrete Event System Specification) simulation environment that can execute on distributed memory multicomputer systems with benchmarking results of a class of high resolution, large scale ecosystem models. Underlying the environment is a parallel container class library for hiding the details of message passing technology while providing high level abstractions for hierarchical, modular DEVS models. The C++ implementation working on the Thinking Machines CM-5 demonstrates that the desire for high level modeling support need not be irreconcilable with sustained high performance.

1 Introduction

The computing power of recent massively parallel supercomputers is rising to the challenge of exploding demands for speed and memory that can be dedicated to a single problem. In their quest for computation speed, designers of commercial supercomputers have often sacrificed generality and flexibility. As a consequence, conventional workstations offer much more comfortable platforms for model construction and simulation. Thus the need has emerged for high level "front ends" supporting model development for high performance platforms. Existing applications of parallel discrete-event simulations developed on distributed memory multicomputers are often highly architecture dependent. Synchronization protocols, whether conservative [3], optimistic [12], or application specific[10], must generally be adapted to a new application, making it difficult to migrate one system to another. Implementing intricate synchronization protocols in distributed memory multiprocessor systems is tedious because message passing incurs serious communication overhead and programming complexity[2]. Few tools exist to aid the programmer in debugging and verifying such protocols.

Thus our motivation in building a general purpose and portable discrete-event simulation environment is to shield the modeler from having to deal with the underlying message passing technology while exploiting the speed and memory advantages of high performance platforms. Nicol[16] has stressed the importance of developing parallel simulation environments that hide most synchronization protocols and automate a wide variety of simulation models.

We have developed a Heterogeneous Container Class Library (HCCL) that can be implemented in both sequential and parallel/distributed platforms. The objective is to provide convenient object-oriented primitives for utilizing a collection of distributed computing resources to solve large problems and to speed up computations[4]. Implemented in C++, these classes contrast with other concurrent portable C++ computing models [1] which compose distributed data structures with parallel execution semantics. HCCL provides concurrency and a parallel computing paradigm at a higher level of abstraction encapsulating the details of the underlying message passing mechanisms.

In particular, applied to discrete event simulation, HCCL abstractions support construction of deadlock-free, synchronous, parallel DEVS simulation environments. In this paper, we describe a conservative synchronization protocol, based on HCCL primitives, that has high processor utilization and achieves significant speedups relative to uniprocessor simulation of the same models. Concepcion[7] proposed a generic methodology for mapping DEVS hierarchical, modular simulation models to a tree structured multiprocessor architecture. Our C++-implemented DEVS simulation environment[25] is based on this methodology. However, the implementation manages simulation messages at any level of the hierarchy without the need for special hardware. This hardware independence enables it to be readily ported to a variety of distributed, multicomputer platforms. Our approach exploits closure under coupling of the DEVS formalism[22] to support automated model partitioning and mapping to a processor architecture. Other DEVS implementation on parallel/distributed platforms can be found in [6, 14].

The rest of the paper is organized as follows:

Section 2 introduces Parallel DEVS, a revision of the sequential DEVS formalism aimed at full exploitation of parallel execution. The parallel container class and its implementation on the Thinking Machines CM-5 are discussed in section 3. Section 4 presents the parallel DEVS/HCCL architecture for the parallel simulation. Section 5 presents benchmarking results obtained for parallel simulation execution time with a class of high resolution, large scale ecosystem models. Finally we draw conclusions from this research.

2 Background

In this section, we discuss why we based the simulation environment on the system-theoretically based formalism, DEVS.

2.1 The DEVS formalism

DEVS falls within the formalisms identified by Ho[11] for Discrete Event Dynamical Systems (DEDS). Because of its system theoretic basis, DEVS is a universal formalism for DEDS[23]. The universality claims of the DEVS are justified by characterizing the class of dynamical systems which can be represented by models. Praehofer and Zeigler[18] showed that any causal dynamical system which has piecewise constant input and output segments can be represented by DEVS. Viewed as dynamical systems, all

discrete event models expressed in logical process or similar formalisms, fit this condition. However, so do a great variety of event-based, continuous state-space systems. Closure under coupling is a desirable property for subclasses of dynamical systems since it guarantees that coupling of class instances results in a system in the same class. The class of DEVS-representable dynamical systems is closed under coupling. This justifies hierarchical, modular construction of both DEVS models and the (continuous or discrete) counterpart systems they represent.

2.2 Parallel DEVS

Recently the DEVS formalism was revised to remove all vestiges of sequential processing and to enable full exploitation of parallel execution[5]. We now review this structure.

A DEVS basic model is a structure:

$$M = < X, S, Y, \delta_{int}, \delta_{ext}, \lambda, ta >$$

X: a set of input events.
S: a set of sequential states.
Y: a set of output events.
$\delta_{int} : S \to S$: internal transition function.
$\delta_{ext} : Q \times X^b \to S$: external transition function,
  where X^b is a set of bags over elements in X.
$\lambda : S \to Y^b$: output function.
$ta : S \to R_{0+\to\infty}$: time advance function,
  where $Q = \{(s, e) | s \in S, 0 < e < ta(s)\}$,
  (e is the elapsed time since last state transition).

DEVS models are constructed in hierarchical fashion by interconnecting components (which are DEVS models). The specification of interconnection, or coupling, is provided in the form of a coupled model. The structure of a *coupled model* is:

$$DN = < X, Y, D, \{M_i\}, \{I_i\}, \{Z_{i,j}\} >$$

X: a set of input events.
Y: a set of output events.
D: a set of component names.
for each i in D, M_i is a component.
for each i in $D \cup \{self\}$, I_i is the influencees of i.
for each j in I_i, $Z_{i,j}$ is a function, the i-to-j output translation.

The structure is subject to the constraints that for each i in D,
$M_i = < X_i, S_i, Y_i, \delta_{int i}, \delta_{ext i}, ta_i >$ is a DEVS basic structure,

I_i is a subset of $D \cup \{self\}$, i is not in I_i,
$Z_{self,j} : X_{self} \rightarrow X_j$,
$Z_{i,self} : Y_i \rightarrow Y_{self}$,
$Z_{i,j} : Y_i \rightarrow X_j$.

Here *self* refers to the coupled model itself and is a device for allowing specification of external input and external output couplings.

The behavior of a coupled model is constructed from the behaviors of its components and the coupling specification. The *resultant* of a coupled model is the formal expression of such behavior. Closure of the formalism under coupling is demonstrated by constructing the resultant and showing it to be a well defined DEVS. Such closure ensures that hierarchical construction is well defined since a coupled model (as represented by its resultant) is a DEVS model that can be coupled with other components in a larger model. Details of closure proof are given in [5].

3 Implementing the HCCL on the CM-5

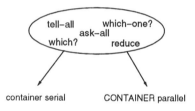

Figure 1: Five Primitives of Containers Classes

A *container* is an object used to allocate, and coordinate, the processing of objects transparently to the user[4]. The main features of object-oriented programming such as the concept of class, inheritance, information hiding, data abstraction, and polymorphism are needed to implement such class functionality. Due to its support of object-oriented programming and its widespread acceptance, the C++ language was used to implement the container classes.

HCCL contains a collection of *ensemble* methods to treat the items in a container as a unit. The five ensemble methods are enumerated as follows[25]:

- *tell-all* sends the same command to each object in a container.

- *ask-all* sends the same query to each object and returns a container holding the responses (which are also objects).

- *which?* returns the subcontainer of all objects whose response to a boolean query is TRUE.

- *which-one?* returns one of the objects in the container whose response to a boolean query is TRUE.

- *reduce* aggregates the responses of the objects in a container to a single object (e.g., taking the sum).

While *ensemble methods* are more parallel than sequential in nature, they have abstract specifications that are independent of how one chooses to implement them. Thus, using the polymorphism properties of C++ we define two classes for each abstract container class; one (lower-case) implementing the ensemble methods in serial form, the other (upper-case), implementing them in parallel form(Figure 1). The serial implementations run on any architecture that has a C++ compiler. In particular, if the nodes of a parallel or distributed system run C++, then the serial containers will work on them[25].

The distinction between serial *container* and parallel *CONTAINER* is the way message passing is accomplished. The implementation of parallel CONTAINERs must involve physical message passing among objects residing on different nodes. Such message passing must be implemented employing the communications primitives provided by the parallel/distributed system of interest. For example, our CM-5 implementation employs CMMD(CM-5 message passing library). Likewise, a network of workstations linked together under PVM [20] offers the communication primitives supplied by PVM. In a serial system, message passing is reduced eventually to subroutine invocation. For shared memory systems, system-specific synchronization primitives are provided and explicit message passing is not required.

Figure 2 sketches the construction of parallel CONTAINERs on the CM-5. The User Interface object sends ensemble method messages to a set of coordinators in a string format. These ensemble methods are employed to organize parallel objects and collect replies from containers by physical message passing. Thus, the User Interface provides a high level of control to coordinate all containers running on processing nodes. The coordinator and container are of the same parallel CONTAINER class, but they differ in the way each executes the commands or queries of the ensemble methods. For instance, multicast ensemble method messages are initiated by the coordinator, providing global information with its containers. The ordinary containers that are under the control of the coordinator are to receive and pass the messages. The coordi-

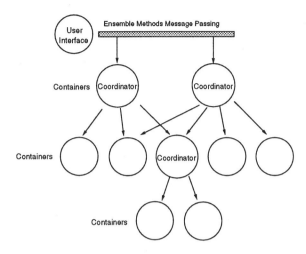

Figure 2: Construction of Parallel Containers on CM-5; one-to-one mapping objects to processing nodes

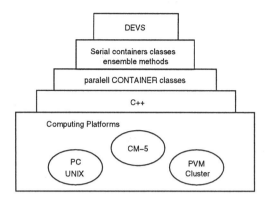

Figure 3: Implementation of DEVS using Containers Classes in C++

nator collects the returned values from its containers and uses them as more meaningful information for the coordination of its containers. Container entities can be organized into hierarchies using containers and co-ordinators at any number of levels appropriate to the application. Such structures can be dynamically configured during the application runtime as well as at initial setup using basic container operations(e.g., *add* and *remove*).

Both serial and parallel containers retain the data abstraction and modular construction critical to object-oriented programmability. In addition to the basic containers' behavior, the parallel CONTAINERs classes have to maintain concurrency and synchronization of the objects on multiple computing resources. Multicasting ensemble methods to container members can achieve a high degree of concurrency in a parallel architecture. Collection of responses from containers nodes that executed queries keeps them properly synchronized.

Using ensemble methods a collection of processors can be organized and managed by parallel CONTAINER class objects. So a user application program can be layered over such CONTAINERs without concern for coordination of underlying computing resources. In the next section, we illustrate parallel CONTAINERs serve as the supporting layer of the parallel DEVS simulation environment.

4   Parallel DEVS implementation over parallel CONTAINER

One of the key objectives in designing the DEVS-based high performance simulation environment is portability of models across platforms at a high level of abstraction. A DEVS model should not be rewritten or modified to run on serial, parallel or distributed environments[25]. Such portability would enable a model to be developed and verified in serial platform and then be easily ported to a parallel/distributed platform. DEVS implementation over container classes in an object-oriented form can achieve this portability goal. The DEVS formalism is expressed as a collection of objects and their interactions with the details of the implementation hidden within the objects. The user interacts with only those interfaces that manifest the DEVS constructs while being shielded from the ultimate execution environment. This approach is well illustrated in Figure 3. DEVS is implemented in terms of a collection of HCCL classes.

The parallel DEVS-C++ simulation environment is different from other efforts [19] to build a general and portable simulation environment, in that a higher level of control scheme, such as containers class is employed.

In Figure 4, a two-dimensional grid of atomic components called *cells* is partitioned into *blocks*. Each block is assigned to a processor node. The closure property of DEVS guarantees that each block can itself be regarded as a DEVS model which can now be considered as a component model for a larger configuration. These components are then grouped together to form a new DEVS model (shown as "top block") which is equivalent in behavior to the original composition of cells. Note that blocks function as containers whether they contain cells or (in the case of the top block) lower level blocks.

A cycle in a DEVS simulation can be implemented

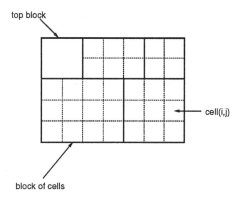

Figure 4: Hierarchical Construction of Block Models from Atomic Cell Models

in terms of ensemble methods. It is outlined as follows:

1. *Compute the next event time*: this is done by a reduction which gets the minimum of the component times to next event.

2. *Determine the imminent components*: these are the components whose next event times are minimal. They are identified by using the *which?* ensemble method.

3. *Tell all the imminent components to sort and distribute their output messages called the mail.*

4. *Tell all the imminent components to execute their internal transition functions.*

5. *Tell all components with incoming mail to execute their external transition functions with their mail as input.*

Figure 5 illustrates the mapping of top block and the nodal blocks on the processing nodes to implement the watershed models linked with GIS. The mapping corresponds to that of parallel CONTAINERs since the DEVS block models are embodied in the CONTAINER environment. The top block functions as a coordinator of the containers and the container on a processing node implements a DEVS block model. In other words, looking inside a node, we see it executing a DEVS simulation cycle in a block model based on serial containers. These serial blocks are coordinated at the next level by the DEVS simulation cycle using parallel CONTAINER ensemble methods on CM-5.

The parallel and synchronous nature of ensemble methods can construct the deadlock free synchronous parallel DEVS simulation environment. The User Interface block dictates each step of simulation to its container processors. In the current

DEVS/CONTAINER architecture, the User Interface block contains the global time of next internal event. This is determined as the minimum of the nodal blocks' times of next internal event. The nodal blocks whose next time of events are minimal will generate the output messages and execute their internal transitions. A sequential nodal block's time of next internal event is also the minimum of its components (ultimately) cells' times of next internal event. This conservative synchronization approach is guaranteed not to violate simulation time causality during simulation[22].

Mathematical reasoning in [16] shows that the statistical average performance difference of conservative and optimistic synchronization is a factor of 2. It is expected the overhead of rollback in the case of Time Warp on the CM-5 can significantly degrade the overall simulation performance in addition to the relatively low factor of speedup gain between two algorithms[8].

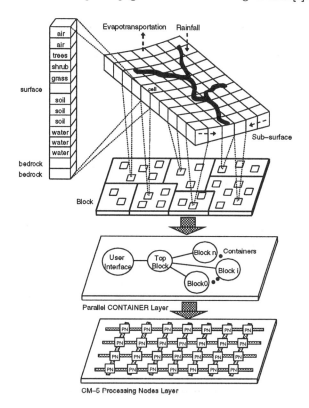

Figure 5: Mapping of Block Models to CM-5 Processing Nodes

The typical problem of conservative algorithms is low processor utilization. However, the sequential DEVS simulation on each node can achieve high processor utilization rates. Our approach to improving simulation performance is to employ hierarchical structure of DEVS models to find optimal mappings of model components to processor blocks[26].

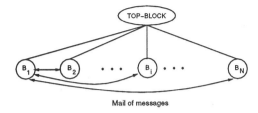

Figure 6: Mail Handling Scheme on CM-5: Localized sorting in source blocks and localized distribution

The output and input messages of a DEVS model are transferred in a form analogous to *mail* distribution. The mail approach has an advantage of treating messages as containers with specialized methods for assembling and disassembling a collection of contents (port,value,and address structures). Exchange of mail among nodal blocks occurs at every cycle during a simulation run. Since a major overhead in parallel simulation is physical communication, mail distribution algorithms should be designed to minimize communication time. Figure 6 shows mail sorting and distribution scheme for step 4 of the DEVS simulation cycle, shown to be the best in trial tests[25]. Each source block sorts the output mail locally and directly sends it to processing nodes containing the destination addresses. The efficiency of the scheme depends on the number of nodal blocks, the size of messages to be passed between blocks and the speed and topology of the communication network[17].

The overhead of parallel CONTAINER operations should be kept low as the number of processors used increases. Figure 7 shows the test results on the CM-5 for 500 iterations of DEVS simulation cycle. Initially we used a serial technique whose communication time increases rapidly as the number of processors increases. This was later replaced by a multicasting technique for ensemble methods which shows that a nearly flat dependence on number of processors can be obtained. This multicasting function sets up a tree-style asynchronous communication pattern with CMMD blocking message passing functions. This tree-style communication pattern can also be used to implement the reduce function minimizing the communication overhead. Using the multicasting technique, the major communication cost in a DEVS simulation cycle is due to the mail message exchange between the neighborhood block nodes. This overhead is shown by the dotted curve in Figure 7. Based on the experimental results to be discussed, the overhead

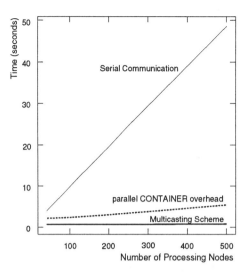

Figure 7: Multicasting Time of Ensemble Methods on CM-5

consumes less than 10% of the overall communication/computation cycle.

5 Example of Parallel DEVS Simulation; Watershed linked with GIS

Besides distributed simulation, direct access to GIS data bases is a major requirement for computing environment capable of addressing complex ecological questions. The linkage was achieved by implementing a data handler object in C++ which processes data requests from models. The data object allows the model to be developed without knowledge of how the data is stored. The models can request information at a specific geographic location and data is returned in the form that the model requires. This allows hierarchical GIS-based models expressed in DEVS to be developed on a serial workstation. After verification, they can be mapped to a parallel/distributed environment by recompiling with the parallel version of containers. We have demonstrated this methodology in the development and execution of a GIS-based watershed model. The GIS databases that drive the hydrology simulation contain thematic layers for elevation, slope, aspect, vegetation, soils and other essential parameters. As an atomic DEVS cell component, we employed a model for surface infiltration and runoff[24]. In contrast to other models where channels are "built in" using distinct functional components, our high resolution model enables channel flows to "emerge" from the underlying water dynamics and landscape topography.

Experiments on sequential machines consisted of running a single block containing different numbers of cells on each machine. The sequential execution results on the Sparc 2 processor and the SparcServer 1000 workstation show that the latter is twice as fast as the former. The CM-5 employs a Sparc 2 processor with 32 megabytes of memory. Initial results showed that the ratio of execution times became greater as the number of cells increased due to the dynamic memory management, which resulted in a superlinear speedup. Subsequently, the cell model was refined using an efficient memory management technique in the development process.

A GIS data set, with 509 × 509 cells, was simulated on the CM-5 with one level of hierarchical construction. Experiments consist of simulating subsets of the full data set. The number of processing nodes used on the CM-5 increases in proportion to the data set. That is, for an array of $N \times N$ cells, N processors are employed, each with a row of N cells.

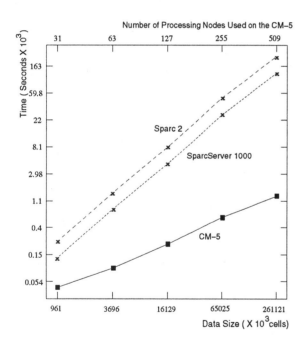

Figure 8: Experimental Results for large data size on CM-5

Figure 8 shows the parallel execution times on the CM-5 along with the sequential execution times on the Sparc 2 and SparcServer 1000 machine. It is shown that simulation of about a quarter million cells on the CM-5 takes less than 20 minutes while it takes more than 64 hours on the Sparc 2 workstation. This translates to a speedup of 192.

6 Conclusion

In this paper, we discuss a hierarchical, flexible and parallel simulation environment based on DEVS/containers abstractions. DEVS models' portability not only separates the behavior from implementation but supports the development of models on a serial platform which are relatively easy to translate to parallel simulation environments. Using object-oriented technology, the parallel simulation environment is built on top of parallel CONTAINER classes. As a result, a modeller is hidden from the parallel simulation synchronization protocol and is freed from the difficulty of writing and debugging such protocols. While the DEVS/containers architecture for parallel simulation was first implemented on a massively parallel platform (CM-5), the simulation architecture can be mapped to any heterogeneous and distributed computing environment such as the PVM-based network we have implemented[25].

Observed performance of the CM-5 implementation on high resolution real world problems demonstrates that high performance need not be sacrificed in providing high level abstractions to the discrete event modeller.

Acknowledgments

This research was supported by NSF HPCC Grand Challenge Application Group Grant ASC-9318169, Rome Labs Contract F30602-95-C-0230 and F30602-95-C-0250. It employed the CM-5 at NCSA under grant MCA94P02.

References

[1] F. Bodin, P. Beckman, D. Gannon, S. Narayana, and S. X. Yang, "Distributed pC++: Basic Ideas for an Object Parallel Language", Scientific Programming, Vol. 2, No. 3, pp 7-22, Fall 1993.

[2] A. Chien, "Concurrent Aggregates Supporting Modularity in Massively Parallel Programs", The MIT Press, 1993.

[3] K. M. Chandy and J. Misra, "A case study in design and verification of distributed programs", IEEE Trans. Software Engineering. SE-5, pp 440-452, Sept., 1979.

[4] Y. K. Cho, *Parallel Implementation of Container using Parallel Virtual Machine*, Master thesis, The University of Arizona, Tucson, AZ, 1995.

[5] A. Chow and B. P. Zeigler, "Revised DEVS: A Parallel, Hierarchical, Modular Modeling Formalism", Proc. Winter Simulation Conf., 1994.

[6] E. R. Christensen and B. P. Zeigler, "Hierarchical, Distributed, Object oriented and Knowledge based Simulation", In 8th Military Operations Research Society Symposium, 1990.

[7] A. I. Concepcion, "A hierarchical computer architecture for distributed simulation", IEEE Transactions on Computers, Feb. 1989.

[8] A. Ferscha, "Probabilistic Adaptive Direct Optimism Control in Time Warp", In Proc. of the 9th Workshop on Parallel and Distributed Simulation, 1995.

[9] R. M. Fujimoto, "Parallel discrete event simulation", CACM, vol. 33, pp. 30-53, 1990.

[10] A. Greenberg, B. Lubachevsky, D. Nicol, and P. Wright, "Efficient Massively Parallel Simulation of Dynamic Channel Assignment Schemes for Wireless Cellular Communications", Proceedings of 8Th Workshop on Parallel and Distributed Simulation, pp. 187-194, 1994.

[11] Y. C. Ho, "Special issue on discrete event dynamic systems", Proceedings of the IEEE, 77(1), 1989.

[12] D. R. Jefferson, "Virtual Time", ACM Trans. Programming Languages Systems, 7(3) pp. 404-425, July 1985.

[13] V. Jha and R. L. Bargodia, "A Unified Framework for Conservative and Optimistic Distributed Simulation", 8th Workshop on Parallel and Distributed Simulation, 1994.

[14] C. Liao, A. Motaabbed, D. Kim, and B. P. Zeigler, "Distributed Simulation Algorithm for Sparce Output DEVS", In Proc. of AI, Simulation and Planning in High-Autonomy Systems, Sept. 1993.

[15] Y. B. Lin, "Special Issue on Parallel Discrete Event Simulation", Journal of Parallel and Distributed Computing, vol. 18, pp. 391-394, 1993.

[16] D. Nicol, R. M. Fujimoto, "Parallel Simulation Today", Annals of Operations Research vol.53 pp. 249-285, Nov. 1994.

[17] R. Ponnusamy, R. Thakur, A. Choudhary, K. Velamakanni, Z. Bozkus, and G. Fox, "Experimental Performance Evaluation of the CM-5", Journal of Parallel and Distributed Computing, vol. 19, pp. 192-202, 1993.

[18] H. Praehofer and B. P. Zeigler, "Automatic abstraction of event-based control models from continuous base models", submitted to IEEE Trans. Systems, Man and Cybernetics, 1995.

[19] Jeff S. Steinman, "SPEEDES: Synchronous Parallel Environment for Emulation and Discrete Event Simulation", Advances in Parallel and Distributed Simulation, Proceedings of the SCS Multiconference, pp. 95-103, 1990.

[20] V. S. Sunderam and *et. al.*, "The PVM Concurrent Computing System: Evolution, Experience, and Trends", Parallel Computing, vol. 20, no. 4, pp. 531-545, 1994.

[21] B. P. Zeigler, "DEVS representation of dynamical systems: Event-based intelligent control", Proceedings of the IEEE, 77(1):72–80, 1989.

[22] B. P. Zeigler, *Object-Oriented Simulation with Hierarchical, Modular Models: Intelligent Agents and Endomorphic Systems*, Academic press, San Diego, CA, 1990.

[23] B. P. Zeigler and W. H. Sanders, "Preface to special issue on environments for discrete event dynamic systems", Discrete Event Dynamic Systems: Theory and Application, 3(2):110–119, 1993.

[24] B. P. Zeigler, Y. Moon, V. L. Lopes and J. Kim, "DEVS Approximation of Infiltration Using Genetic Algorithm Optimization of a Fuzzy System", submitted to Journal of Mathematical and Computer Modeling, 1995.

[25] B. P. Zeigler, Y. Moon, D. Kim, and J. G. Kim, "C++DEVS: A High Performance Modelling and Simulation Environment", 29th Hawaii International Conference on System Sciences, Jan. 1996.

[26] B. P. Zeigler and Guoqing Zhang, "Mapping Hierarchical Discrete Event Models to Multiprocessor Systems: Concepts, Algorithm, and Simulation", Journal of Parallel and Distributed Computing, vol. 9, pp. 271-281, 1990.

Queueing Models and Stability of Message Flows in Distributed Simulators of Open Queueing Networks

Manish Gupta, Anurag Kumar, Rajeev Shorey
Electrical Communication Engineering
Indian Institute of Science, Bangalore
Bangalore, INDIA, 560 012
e-mail: manish, anurag, shorey@ece.iisc.ernet.in

Abstract

In this paper we study message flow processes in distributed simulators of open queueing networks. We develop and study queueing models for distributed simulators with maximum lookahead sequencing. We characterize the "external" arrival process, and the message feedback process in the simulator of a simple queueing network with feedback. We show that a certain "natural" modelling construct for the arrival process is exactly correct, whereas an "obvious" model for the feedback process is wrong; we then show how to develop the correct model. Our analysis throws light on the stability of distributed simulators of queueing networks with feedback. We show how the stability of such simulators depends on the parameters of the queueing network.

1 Introduction

In a *distributed discrete-event simulation* (DDES), each process can be viewed as receiving time-stamped messages over several sequential channels; i.e., on each channel the messages arrive in time-stamp order. The aggregate message stream arriving at the process is, however, not in time-stamp order. The purpose of the synchronization mechanism (optimistic [3] [2], conservative [7], or variations of these) is to produce a message stream that is in time-stamp order, for further processing by the event processor. Obviously, the complication in the sequencing procedure arises when a channel is empty, for then the sequencer does not know what to do with the messages in the non-empty channels. Suppose, however, the sequencer is told the time-stamp of the next message to arrive in all the empty channels. This is all the information the sequencer needs to sequence the messages that can be sequenced at this time (no additional

information about future arrivals will help). Such information if available at each channel is called *maximum lookahead* [4], and is, in general, not practically obtainable. Maximum lookahead is, of course, an upper bound to any practical lookahead, and is hence expected to yield an upper bound on simulator performance. With this in mind, in this paper we study distributed simulators with maximum lookahead sequencing.

In this paper we are interested in message flow processes in distributed simulators of open queueing networks. Our objective is two fold. The simulation makes progress when event processors correctly process event messages; thus the rate of flow of correctly processed messages is indicative of the performance of the distributed simulator (e.g., speed-up). Further, the study of message flow processes yields an understanding of issues such as stability and boundedness of message queues. Note that it has been shown in [4] that in distributed simulation of feedforward networks the message queues are unstable. Our emphasis in this paper is on the second objective. The first objective is dealt with in a companion paper [5].

Our approach is via *queueing models of distributed simulators* with maximum lookahead. The "customers" in these queueing models are the event messages and the servers are the event processors. Obviously the throughput of correct messages in such a queueing model relates to the rate of progress of the simulation. Owing to the synchronization problem, these queueing models have features that do not appear in the usual queueing models in the literature. In this paper we develop and study such queueing models for distributed simulators of queueing networks with feedback. Maximum lookahead simulators are found to be the simplest to model. We show that a certain "natural" modelling construct for arrival processes in the simulator is, in fact, exactly correct, whereas an "obvious" model for the feedback

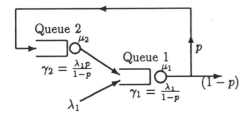

Figure 1: A Queueing Network with Feedback

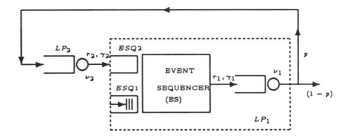

Figure 2: Simulator of the Queueing Network with Feedback

processes is wrong; we show how to develop the exact feedback model. Our analysis in this paper throws light on the stability of distributed simulators of queueing networks with feedback. We show how the performance of simulators of queueing networks with feedback depends on the parameters of the queueing network.

The paper is organized as follows. In Section 2, we consider a queueing model with two queues with feedback. We develop the queueing model of a simulator in which each queue is simulated by a process on separate processors. External arrivals into each queue are shown to result in arrivals of batch event messages into each process. In Section 3, we characterize these "external" batch arrival processes in the simulator of the queueing network. Section 4 is devoted to characterizing the message feedback process. We show the incorrectness of the Bernoulli feedback model, and demonstrate the exact feedback model for a limiting case of the original 2 queue model. Finally, in Section 5 we develop an exact model for the feedback process in a more general case. Analysis of this model suggests how the stability of the message queues depends on the parameters of the original queueing network. Section 6 has the conclusions. Appendix contains the details of some mathematical derivations.

2 Development of the Queueing Model of the Simulator

In this section, we consider a queueing network with two queues and feedback. We begin to develop the model of the distributed simulator of the queueing network. Some nonstandard modelling constructs arise, which we proceed to develop in subsequent sections.

As usual, we call the simulation processes running on the simulator processors as logical processes (LPs) and the queueing (sub)networks they simulate as physical processes (PPs). If the queueing network is mapped onto m logical processes (each on a separate processor) these are denoted $LP_1, LP_2, \ldots, LP_m$.

2.1 A Queueing Network with Feedback

Consider a network with two queues and a feedback shown in Figure 1. The distributed simulator for this network is shown in Figure 2. The simulation of each queue is assigned to a separate LP. Denote by μ_i, $i = 1, 2$, the service (exponential) rate of queue i in the queueing network with feedback. λ_1 is the external arrival (Poisson) rate of customers to Queue 1 in the queueing network. $\nu_i, i \in \{1, 2\}$ is the service (exponential) rate of the event processor queue in LP_i. The event sequencer (ES) has two message queues ESQ1 and ESQ2. Queue ESQ2 is fed by LP_2. Note that since Queue 1 in the PP has external arrivals generated within LP_1, the corresponding event sequencer queue (ESQ1) will always have a backlog of messages.

Denote by γ_i the throughput of queue i $(i = 1, 2)$ in the queueing network, and by r_i the throughput of LP_i $(i = 1, 2)$ in the simulator. We assume that the queues of the queueing network (PP) are stable. Thus, $\gamma_2 = \frac{\lambda_1 p}{1-p} < \mu_2$, $\gamma_1 = \frac{\lambda_1}{1-p} < \mu_1$.

In this problem, owing to the feedback loop, the conservative event sequencer will deadlock; a deadlock occuring each time queues LP_2, ESQ2, and the event processor of LP_1 in the simulator are empty. With a maximum lookahead sequencer, however, it is clear that in this situation the lookahead in queue ESQ2 is ahead with probability (w.p.) 1, of the time-stamp of the first message in queue ESQ1, and hence this message can be allowed to enter and the simulator progresses. This can be argued as follows. Suppose that the first message in queue ESQ1 is fed back, then the maximum lookahead in queue ESQ2 will be equal to the sum of three terms: the time-stamp of the first message in queue ESQ1, a sample of an exponential random variable with rate μ_1, and, a sample of an exponential random variable with rate μ_2. Note that an exponentially distributed random variable (corresponding to the service time) is zero w.p. 0, thus the lookahead in queue ESQ2 is ahead (w.p. 1) of the time-stamp of the first message in queue ESQ1. If the first message in queue ESQ1 is not fed back, essentially the same arguments hold as above along with the fact that the time-stamps of messages in queue ESQ1

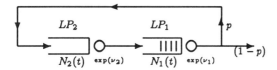

Figure 3: Equivalent Queueing Model of the Simulator in Figure 2

are monotonically increasing. *Thus the simulator with maximum lookahead sequencing does not deadlock.* Note also that *with maximum lookahead sequencing all event messages are correctly processed exactly once.*

We study the distributed simulator of Figure 2 with the maximum lookahead algorithm. Whenever a message leaves queue ESQ2 of the simulator, the timestamp of the next message to arrive at queue ESQ2 is provided to the sequencer (i.e., maximum lookahead operates), and all messages from queue ESQ1 with timestamp less than this lookahead time are moved to the event processor. Therefore, after each departure from queue ESQ2, a batch of messages arrive at the event processor in LP_1. This batch consists of the message that leaves queue ESQ2 plus some arrival messages from queue ESQ1. It is easy to show [6] that the mean batch size is $1 + \frac{\lambda_1}{\gamma_2} = \frac{1}{p}$. In the queueing model of Figure 1, if we have no feedback, the resulting network is a feedforward network. It can be proved [4] that in the distributed simulator of a feedforward network, if the timestamp processes are Poisson, then the batches departing from the event sequencer are geometrically distributed. No such claim can be immediately made about the batch size distribution in simulators of networks with feedback (as in Figure 1). In Section 3, we will investigate the distribution of the batch size in this model.

2.2 Queueing Model of the Distributed Simulator

A queueing model of the distributed simulator is shown in Figure 3. In this model no event sequencer is shown; instead, a departure from LP_2 brings a batch of messages to the event processor of LP_1. The mean batch size is given by $\frac{1}{p}$. As in the queueing model in the simulator, a fraction $(1-p)$ of the events processed by LP_1 depart from the system, and the rest are fed back. Note that this is not to claim that the *feedback process* is Bernoulli, i.e., independent and identically distributed (i.i.d.) feedbacks with probability (w.p.) p.

Our aim is to analyse the event message processes in this queueing model. We would like to obtain the simulator throughput, by which we mean the rate at which processed events *leave* the simulator after event processing at LP_1. We may be interested in the system sojourn time of customers entering Queue 1 in the

queueing network model. Each departure from the simulator will yield a sample of sojourn time, and hence simulator throughput is a meaningful quantity.

Before steady-state throughput can be determined, however, stability of the message queues needs to be established. Analysis of the queueing model in Figure 3 can only proceed after we characterize the batch arrival process at LP_1 and the feedback process from LP_1 to LP_2. This we now proceed to do in Sections 3 and 4.

3 Characterization of the "External" Arrival Process in the Simulator

In the model in Figure 1, denote by ρ_i, $i = 1, 2$, the server utilization factor of queue i. Then, $\rho_1 = \frac{\lambda_1}{\mu_1(1-p)}$ and $\rho_2 = \frac{\lambda_1 p}{\mu_2(1-p)}$. For notational convenience $(1-p)$ is written as $\bar{p}$ in the analysis.

Now observe that the external arrival batches that arrive following a departure from LP_2 into LP_1 (see Figure 3) are just the batches of external arrivals between successive departures from Queue 2 to Queue 1 in Figure 1.

We prove that the batches of customers arriving between departures from Queue 2 to Queue 1 in Figure 1 are i.i.d. and geometrically distributed with mean equal to $\frac{1}{p}$.

3.1 Analysis for the Two Queue Model

Consider a departure from Queue 2 to Queue 1 (Figure 1) in the stationary regime. Let the number of customers in queue i, $i = 1, 2$, just *after* this departure be denoted by X_i. By the Arrival Theorem [8] we know that

$$P(X_1 = k_1, X_2 = k_2) = \rho_1^{k_1 - 1}(1 - \rho_1)\, \rho_2^{k_2}(1 - \rho_2),$$

$$k_1 \geq 1, k_2 \geq 0$$

Let

Y_i = the number of customers in queue i, $i = 1, 2$, just *after* the next departure from Queue 2 to Queue 1

A = the number of external arrivals to Queue 1 *until* the next departure from Queue 2 to Queue 1

We are interested in calculating the joint generating function

$$\tilde{b}(w_1, w_2, z) \quad := \quad E\left(w_1^{Y_1} w_2^{Y_2} z^A\right)$$

164

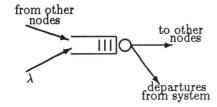

Figure 4: A Node in a Jackson Network

$$= \sum_{k_1=1}^{\infty} \sum_{k_2=0}^{\infty} P(X_1 = k_1, X_2 = k_2) \cdot$$
$$\cdot E\left(w_1^{Y_1} w_2^{Y_2} z^A | X_1 = k_1, X_2 = k_2\right)$$

It is easily shown that [6]

$$\tilde{b}(w_1, w_2, z) = \frac{p}{(1 - \bar{p}z)} \tilde{g}(w_1, w_2) \qquad (1)$$

where, $\tilde{g}(w_1, w_2) := \sum_{k_1'=1}^{\infty} \sum_{k_2'=0}^{\infty} \rho_1^{k_1'-1}(1-\rho_1)\rho_2^{k_2'}(1-\rho_2)w_1^{k_1'}w_2^{k_2'}$.

Observe from Equation 1 that $\tilde{b}(w_1, w_2, z)$ factors into two generating functions, one in z and the other in (w_1, w_2). It follows that after a stationary departure (Y_1, Y_2) and A are independent. Further $P(A = k) = (1-p)^k p$ for $k \geq 0$, and $P(Y_1 = \ell_1, Y_2 = \ell_2) = \rho_1^{\ell_1-1}(1-\rho_1)\rho_2^{\ell_2}(1-\rho_2)$ for $\ell_1 \geq 1, \ell_2 \geq 0$, Since the number of external arrivals until the next departure after the one which left behind (Y_1, Y_2) depends only on (Y_1, Y_2), it follows that the numbers of external arrivals between successive departures from Queue 2 to Queue 1 form an i.i.d. sequence with a geometric distribution.

It follows that in the queueing model of the maximum lookahead simulator, shown in Figure 3, *each event arriving from LP_2 to LP_1 is immediately followed by a geometrically distributed number of external arrival events. The successive such batches are i.i.d..*

3.2 A Generalization Using Time Reversal Arguments

In this section, we extend the results of the last section. For a Jackson Network [8], we prove that the sequence of number of external arrivals at a node between successive arrivals from other nodes is a geometrically distributed i.i.d. process.

Consider a typical node of a stationary Jackson Network. This is shown in Figure 4. λ is the external arrival rate of customers to the node. Customers arrive at this node from various other nodes also. Now consider the reversal of the stationary Jackson Network. In the reversed network, a transition from state j to state

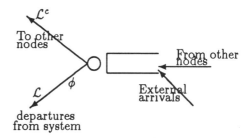

Figure 5: Reversal of the Node in Figure 4

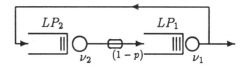

Figure 6: Queueing Model for the Simulator in Figure 2 showing Batch Arrivals into LP_1.

i corresponds to the transition from state i to state j in the original network. The reversal of the node in the stationary Jackson Network in Figure 4 is shown in Figure 5. In the reversed network, the customers that leave the system correspond to the external arrivals in the original network. Therefore, we need to find the distribution of the customers that leave along link $\mathcal{L}$ in the reversed node.

We denote by ϕ, the probability of a customer leaving the node in the reversed network. Then, between two departures that join any of the other nodes (along $\mathcal{L}^c$ in Figure 5), the number of departures that leave on link $\mathcal{L}$ is geometrically distributed, and is equal to n with probability $\phi^n(1-\phi)$. Further the sequence of the number of such departures along $\mathcal{L}$, between successive departures along $\mathcal{L}^c$ is i.i.d. But the reversal of this process is precisely the number of external arrivals between successive arrivals from other nodes.

Thus, we have shown that at any node in a stationary Jackson Network, the number of external arrivals between two arrivals from other nodes is geometrically distributed, and the sequence of such numbers is i.i.d.

It follows that in the model of a distributed simulator of a Jackson Network, in the stationary regime, *the successive external arrival batches triggered by a departure from one queue to another are i.i.d and geometrically distributed.* Note that an LP simulates a single *Queue.*

4 Characterization of Message Feedback Process

From the analysis in Section 3, we conclude that the model for the maximum lookahead simulator in Figure 2

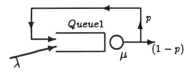

Figure 7: Limit of the Queueing Network in Figure 1 when $\mu_2 \to \infty$, and $\mu_1 = \mu$.

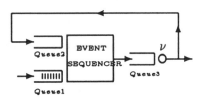

Figure 8: Limit of the Simulator in Figure 2 with $\nu_2 \to \infty$, and $\nu_1 = \nu$.

will have the form shown in Figure 6 where the $(1 - p)$ next to the arrow entering LP_1 denotes that each departure message that moves from LP_2 to LP_1 actually brings in a batch of $k \geq 1$ customers with probability $(1 - p)^{k-1}p$, and the successive such batches are i.i.d.

In Figure 7 is shown the limit of the queueing model of Figure 1 as $\mu_2 \to \infty$, and in Figure 8 is shown the limit of the simulator of Figure 2 as $\nu_2 \to \infty$. Note that we have replaced the symbols μ_1 by μ and ν_1 by ν. The queueing model for Figure 8 with maximum lookahead will have the form shown in Figure 9.

Due to the difficulty in characterizing the message feedback process from queue 1 to queue 2 in the model shown in Figure 6, we initially study the simpler model in Figure 9.

Observe that each message departure from the event processor corresponds to the departure of a customer from Queue 1 in the PP of Figure 7. If the customer is fed back in the original queueing network then the corresponding message is fed back in the simulator, otherwise the message corresponds to a customer leaving the system. Thus a fraction p of the message departures from the event processor are fed back (and subsequently carry with them i.i.d. geometrically distributed batches of external arrival messages into the event processor).

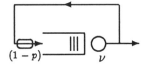

Figure 9: Partially Developed Model for the Simulator in Figure 8

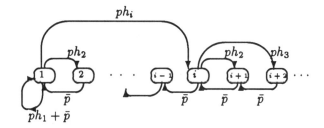

Figure 10: Transition Probability Diagram of the Message Queue Length Process in the Event Processor in Figure 8, using the Bernoulli Feedback Model

It remains to characterize the process by which messages are selected for feedback. We first show that the Bernoulli feedback model is wrong. We do this by assuming the Bernoulli feedback model and then analysing the resulting Markov chain of messages queued in the event processor; this Markov chain is found to be not positive recurrent. This is in disagreement with simulations, however, since we observe that, in simulations, message queue lengths remain stable. Also the Bernoulli feedback model predicts instability in cases where stability of the model is obvious(we shall demonstrate the source of the problem in section 4.2).

4.1 Incorrectness of the Bernoulli Feedback Model

With the Bernoulli feedback assumption, the i.i.d. geometric batch feedback model (Figure 9), and exponential event processing times, it is clear that $X(t)$, the number of messages in the event processor at time t, is a Continuous Time Markov Chain whose transitions occur at the epochs of a Poisson process of rate ν. Hence we can just as well study $\{X_n\}$ the queue length process embedded at these Poisson epochs. Further, nothing is lost in assuming $\nu = 1$. Letting, for $k \geq 1$, $h_k = (1 - p)^{k-1}p$, the transition probability diagram of $\{X_k\}$ is depicted in Figure 10. For notational convenience $(1 - p)$ is written as $\bar{p}$ in this figure and subsequent analysis.

Observe that when maximum lookahead synchronization is used, the simulation will never deadlock. Hence when just 1 message is present in the event processor and this message leaves, owing to the available maximum lookahead, the next arrival message can be generated and inserted into the event processor, thus avoiding deadlock. The Markov chain transition diagram in Figure 10 depicts this self transition from 1 to 1.

Thus, we obtain the transition probability matrix P, which has the well known structure of the embedded

Markov chain in an $M/G/1$ queue:

$$P = \begin{bmatrix} 1 - p(1 - h_1) & ph_2 & ph_3 & \cdots & ph_i & \cdots \\ \bar{p} & ph_1 & ph_2 & \cdots & ph_{i-1} & \cdots \\ 0 & \bar{p} & ph_1 & \cdots & ph_{i-2} & \cdots \end{bmatrix}$$

This is clearly an irreducible and aperiodic Markov chain. To study its positive recurrence, we attempt to find a solution for $\pi = \pi P$, $\sum_{i \in S} \pi_i = 1$. A little algebra shows that any solution to $\pi = \pi P$ will be of the form $\pi_i = p\pi_1$ for $i \geq 2$. Thus, $\sum_{i \in S} \pi_i = 1$ cannot be satisfied and the Markov chain is not positive recurrent. Therefore the message queue is unstable.

In addition, it can be shown by standard analysis that all the states of the Markov chain are recurrent. This implies that the Markov chain is null recurrent.

This analysis shows that the Bernoulli feedback model yields unstable message queues in the simulator of Figure 8. However, no instability is seen from a simulation study of the simulator.

We now refine the queueing model of the simulator in order to capture the stability of the event processor queue. This is done in the next subsection.

4.2 Refinement of the Queueing Model of the Simulator

We first demonstrate the source of the problem by studying the simulator in Figure 8 with infinite service rate in the PP of Figure 7, i.e., $\mu = \infty$ but finite service rate ν in the simulation. Consider now a feedback epoch τ in the PP. In the simulator (Figure 8) the corresponding feedback message is immediately followed by a geometrically distributed batch of messages corresponding to external arrivals *until the next feedback*. In the PP this (next) feedback must come from among the queued messages at the epoch τ^+ or the external arrival messages until the next feedback. Since the service time in the PP is infinite, however, each arrival always sees an empty PP queue, and hence the next feedback after τ must be due to the *last* arrival that arrives between the two feedbacks. Thus, in the simulator model, the feedback probability of the *last* arrival in the batch is 1 and for others it is zero, and not p for every message as asserted by the Bernoulli feedback model. Observe that the mean number of customers that will be fed back from each arriving batch (including the feedback that preceded the batch) is 1 in both models.

Then for $\mu = \infty$ we get the following CTMC model. When there are $n \geq 1$ messages in the event processor queue, messages depart after i.i.d. exponential(ν) service until 1 message is left. This message *must* be fed back after its service. There is thus always at least one message in the event processor queue. Again embedding

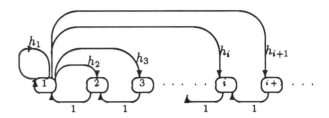

Figure 11: Transition Probability Diagram of the Message Queue Length Process in the Event Processor in Figure 8, with $\mu = \infty$, using the Correct Feedback Model

at service completion epochs (which form a Poisson process of rate ν) we get a Markov chain with the transition probability diagram shown in Figure 11; h_k, $k \geq 1$ is as defined in Section 4.1. In this Markov chain the mean time to return to state 1 is $\sum_{i=1}^{\infty} ih_i < \infty$. We conclude that the simulator is stable. Note that we have the exact model for the simulator when $\mu = \infty$ and event processor service times are i.i.d. exponential(ν).

We conclude that the feedback processes in the distributed simulator model need to be modelled carefully, otherwise erroneous conclusions arise. Further for the simple queueing model and its distributed simulator studied above, *the stability of the simulator message queues is independent of ν*, the processor speed. Also observe that, whereas in a serial simulation of the model of Figure 7 there will be at most 2 pending events, *the number of unprocessed messages in the event processor in the distributed simulator is unbounded*, as is clear from the Markov chain model (Figure 11).

5 Queueing Network with Two Queues and Feedback: Revisited

A little thought shows that in the simple model of Figure 7 and the model of its maximum lookahead simulator in Figure 8, there is a close correspondence between customer queues in the PP and message queues in the LP. Hence stability of the PP implying stability of the LP is hardly surprising. A similar result is not at all obvious, in general, for the PP in Figure 1 and its simulator model of Figure 6. If ν_2 is, for example, very large (say ∞) then the message queue in LP_1 of the simulator model in Figure 6 can grow to very large values, and will have little correspondence to the queue lengths in Queue 1 of the PP. We therefore turn now to the more difficult problem of analysing the feedback process in

Figure 6 and a study of the stability of the consequent queueing model.

We consider the situation in which μ_1 and μ_2 in Figure 1 are finite, but in Figure 6 (the simulator model) $\nu_2 = \infty$, while $\nu_1 < \infty$. In this situation each feedback from LP_1 (Figure 6) instantaneously enters LP_1 again, bringing with it a batch of arrivals. Thus the LP model is as in Figure 9, except that feedback events have their time-stamps incremented owing to the nonzero service time in Queue 2 of the PP. We change our point of view slightly by associating with each departure from LP_2 to LP_1 those arrivals that immediately precede this departure (i.e., this departure was the lookahead event, based on which the batch of arrivals was "taken in"). Observe that, with maximum lookahead, LP_1 will never become empty, so we consider an arrival from LP_2 and its associated arrival batch as *one customer* with exponential service time distribution with rate $\nu_1 p$; this is an exactly correct model which follows from the results in Section 3.

Now let $\{X_n, n \geq 0\}$ be the queue length process in the event processor in LP_1, embedded at batch service completion epochs, i.e., at Poisson epochs with rate $\nu_1 p$. Each batch of events, upon being serviced, yields events that get fed back into LP_1. The feedback events correspond to those customers who come in the batch in the PP but get fed back to Queue 2 after service at Queue 1. Let this sequence of feedback batches in the PP be $\{F_k\}$; for a stationary and ergodic PP, the sequence $\{F_k\}$ is also stationary and ergodic. Then clearly (recall $\nu_2 = \infty$), for $X_0 \geq 1$, $X_{n+1} = \max(X_n - 1 + F_n, 1)$. It is well known ([1], [8]) that $\{X_n\}$ converges in distribution to a proper random variable if, with probability 1, $\lim_{n \to \infty} \frac{1}{n} \sum_{k=1}^{n} F_n = E(F) < 1$. In Appendix, it is established that $E(F) < 1$ if $\rho_1 < 1$ and $\rho_2 < 1$ in the PP.

Now let $\tau_1, \tau_2, \dots$ be the epochs of service completions at LP_1 with $\nu_2 < \infty$. Observe that for any $\nu_2 \in (0, \infty]$, the nth service completion at LP_1 corresponds to the same event in the PP. If $(X_{\tau_n}^{(2)}, X_{\tau_n}^{(1)})$ is the state of the system with $\nu_2 < \infty$ at the epochs τ_n then it can be shown by induction on n that $X_{\tau_n}^{(1)} + X_{\tau_n}^{(2)} = X_n$. Intuitively, the only way the customers can leave the system (with or without $\nu_2 < \infty$) is at a service completion at LP_1. Also the only way the customers enter LP_2 is when there is a service completion at LP_1, i.e., at service completion at LP_2 (with $\nu_2 < \infty$) the total number in the system is invariant.

For other transitions between τ_n and τ_{n+1} (these correspond to jumps from LP_2 to LP_1) we have the number in the system equal to X_n. Thus, letting $n = 0, 1, \dots$ index all the jumps in the uniformized chain, if $(X_n^{(2)}, X_n^{(1)})$ is the state of the system ($\nu_2 < \infty$)

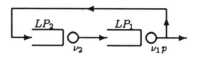

Figure 12: Queueing Model for the Simulator in Figure 2, obtained from Figure 6, by Dilating the Service Time at LP_1.

then $\{X_n^{(2)} + X_n^{(1)}\}$ also converges in distribution to the proper random variable.

Thus we find that the simulator is stable if the original queueing model is stable. The processing rates in the simulator do not play a role in the stability of the simulator. Of course, the rate of simulation progress is more if the simulator processes are faster.

6 Conclusions

In this paper we have developed models for message flows in distributed simulators of queueing networks with maximum lookahead sequencing, with a view towards stability analysis of event processor queues.

We characterized the "external" arrival processes in the simulator of an open Jackson Network, and proved that the batches of customers arriving between departures from one queue to another are i.i.d. and geometrically distributed.

We demonstrated the difficulty in characterizing the message feedback processes in the simulator model. We showed that the Bernoulli feedback model is wrong, and developed the feedback process model for a two queue example.

Analysis of the resulting models showed that *the stability of message queues in the simulator depends on the stability of the queueing model being simulated*; thus *faster processors in the distributed simulators do not yield a stable simulation of an unstable queueing model.* This is quite in contrast with serial simulation; observe that serial simulation of an unstable M/M/1 queue requires an event list with at most 2 pending events.

This paper is just an initial effort on what is obviously a hard problem. Further work should help to show how the throughput of the simulator depends on parameters of the queueing model and the processing speeds in the simulator.

Appendix: Proof that $E(F) < 1$

Let Γ denote a customer (recall that each such customer models a batch of events) that has just finished service at LP_1 in the simulator model of Figure 12 (obtained from Figure 6 by dilating the service time at LP_1). To determine $E(F)$, i.e., the expected number of customers that are fed back when Γ finishes service, we look at the original queueing network (in Figure 1). Recall that Γ corresponds to a customer C that jumps from Queue 2 to Queue 1 in the PP (the queueing network). When the customer C is in the midst of jumping from Queue 2 to Queue 1 in the PP, it sees some number n_2 in Queue 2 and some number n_1 in Queue 1 in the PP. Observe that all the external arrivals that are implicitly associated with Γ in the simulator model have already entered Queue 1 of the PP before the epoch at which C jumps from Queue 2 to Queue 1. Let the number of these external arrivals associated with C be given by A. If $n_1 \geq A$, it means that all the A arrivals are candidates for feedback to Queue 2 in the PP. In this situation, the expected number of feedbacks that are put in LP_2, upon the service completion of Γ in LP_1, is Ap. (Note that since $\nu_2 = \infty$, all the feedbacks to LP_2 arrive instantaneously to LP_1). Now consider the case when $n_1 < A$; without further analysis, we can only infer that the expected number of arrivals in A that are fed back to Queue 2 is at least $n_1 p$. We show below that the expected number of feedbacks to Queue 2 is $n_1 p + \min(A - n_1, n_2) p_1$, where $p_1 := \left(\frac{\mu_2}{\mu_2 + \lambda}\right)$. Note that C can be fed back with probability p.

When $n_1 < A$ then consider the queueing system in Figure 1 at the instant when C makes a transition from Queue 2 to Queue 1 in "forward" time. Now we look at "reversed" time. In the reversal of the system, C jumps from Queue 1 to Queue 2 and A is the number of external departures from Queue 1 that follow C but precede the next jump from Queue 1 to Queue 2. Further F is the number of these departures that resulted from customers that came to Queue 1 from Queue 2. When $n_1 < A$ then we know that $E(F) \geq n_1 p$. Given that Queue 2 is nonempty, the probability that an arrival to Queue 1 came from Queue 2 is $p_1 = \left(\frac{\mu_2}{\mu_2 + \lambda}\right)$. Obviously, no more than $\min(A - n_1, n_2)$ can come from Queue 2 in the reversed network. It can be easily shown that the expected additional number that came from Queue 2 is $(\min(A - n_1, n_2)) p_1$.

Thus we can write $E(F)$ as follows, ($\bar{p} := 1 - p$)

$$E(F) = \sum_{n_1, n_2} \pi(n_1, n_2) \left\{ \sum_{k=0}^{n_1} \bar{p}^k p k p \right.$$
$$+ \sum_{k=n_1+1}^{n_1+n_2} (n_1 p + (k - n_1) p_1) \bar{p}^k p$$
$$\left. + \sum_{k=n_1+n_2+1}^{\infty} (n_1 p + n_2 p_1) \bar{p}^k p \right\} + p$$

where, for $\rho_1 < 1$ and $\rho_2 < 1$, by Arrival theorem [8],

$\pi(n_1, n_2) = (1 - \rho_1)\rho_1^{n_1}(1 - \rho_2)\rho_2^{n_2}$, and $p_1 := \left(\frac{\mu_2}{\mu_2 + \lambda}\right)$.

The explanation of the above expression is the following. We first condition on what C sees in Queue 1 and Queue 2 in the PP when it is making a jump from Queue 2 to Queue 1. Then we condition on the number A in the arrival batch that precedes it. The first term in the curly brackets in the expression above corresponds to the case when $n_1 \geq A$; the second term corresponds to the case when $n_1 < A$ but $n_2 \geq (A - n_1)$; and the third term corresponds to the case when $n_1 < A$, $n_2 < A - n_1$. The last term (p) in the expression for $E(F)$ corresponds to the fact that the customer C corresponding to the batch Γ that has just finished service at LP_1 can also be fed back with probability p.

Finally, note that $E(F) - 1$ simplifies to

$$\frac{(1 - \rho_1)\bar{p}}{(1 - \bar{p}\rho_2)(1 - \bar{p}\rho_1)} \left\{ -1 + \rho_2 \left(1 - p_1\bar{p} - p\bar{p}_1\right) \right\}$$

which is < 0 when $\rho_1 < 1$ and $\rho_2 < 1$.

References

[1] Borovkov, A. A., *Stochastic Processes in Queueing Theory*, Springer-Verlag, 1976.

[2] Fujimoto, R.M., "Parallel discrete event simulation", *Commun. ACM 33*, 10 (October 1990), 30-53.

[3] Jefferson, D.R., "Virtual time", *ACM Trans. Prog. Lang. and Syst.*, 7, 3 (July 1985), 404-425.

[4] Kumar, A. and Shorey, R., "Stability of Event Synchronisation in Distributed Discrete Event Simulation", In *Proceedings of 8th Workshop on Parallel and Distributed Simulation (PADS '94)*, July 6-8, 1994, Edinburgh, Scotland, U.K.

[5] Shorey, R., Kumar, A., Manish, G., *"Throughput Bounds and Optimal Mappings for Distributed Simulation of Queueing Networks"*. Submitted.

[6] Shorey, R., *"Modelling and Analysis of Event Message Flows in Distributed Discrete Event Simulators of Queueing Networks"*, PhD Thesis, Submitted Jan. 1996, Deptt. of ECE, Indian Institute of Science, Bangalore, India.

[7] Misra, J., "Distributed discrete event simulation", *ACM Comput. Surv. 18*, 1 (March 1986), 39-65.

[8] Walrand, J., *An Introduction to Queueing Networks*, Prentice Hall, 1988.

[9] Wolff, R. W., *Stochastic Modelling and the Theory of Queues*, Prentice Hall, 1989.

Discrete-Event Simulation and the Event Horizon
Part 2: Event List Management

Jeffrey S. Steinman

Metron, Incorporated
512 Via De La Valle, Suite 301
Solana Beach, CA 92075
steinman@ca.metsci.com

Abstract

The event horizon is a very important concept that applies to both parallel and sequential discrete-event simulations. By exploiting the event horizon, parallel simulations can processes events optimistically in a risk-free manner (i.e., without requiring antimessages) using adaptable "breathing" time cycles with variable time widths. Additionally, by exploiting the event horizon, one can significantly reduce the overhead of event list management that is common to virtually every discrete-event simulation.

This paper is a continuation of work previously reported at PADS94. In that report, a complete mathematical formulation of the event horizon was derived under equilibrium conditions using the hold model. Various forms of the beta density function were consequently used to verify the predicted results of the analytic model.

This second report describes how the concept of the event horizon can also be applied to event list management. By exploiting the event horizon, the performance of several priority queue data structures are improved including: linked lists, various binary trees, and heaps. A somewhat detailed description of these modified data structures along with other relevant background information is provided for completeness. Performance results for each priority queue data structure is presented.

Introduction

Discrete-event simulations are built upon two fundamental building blocks. First, there are *simulation objects*. Discrete-event simulations normally simulate many objects which frequently map to real world objects in the simulated system. Each simulated object contains an encapsulated set of variables that describe its state.

Second, there are *events*. All interactions between objects in a logically correct discrete-event simulation occur through time-tagged events which must be processed for each simulation object in their correct time order to preserve logical correctness. Logically correct parallel discrete-event simulations usually require an event to be associated with a single simulation object. However, sequential simulations do not always enforce this requirement.

Events can potentially do two things: (1) Events can modify the state of their corresponding simulation object, and (2) events may schedule new events to occur in the future (causality forbids events to ever be scheduled in the past).

During the course of a simulation, a list of pending events waiting to be processed must be maintained by the simulation machinery. If the event list ever becomes empty then by definition, the simulation has reached its end time and is therefore terminated. In sequential simulations, the pending event with the earliest time tag is always the next event to be processed (parallel simulations, especially optimistic ones, can be more complicated) [11, 14].

Two basic operations are required for sequential event list management. The *remove* operation removes the event with the earliest time tag from the list of pending events so that it can be processed. The *insert* operation inserts a newly scheduled event back into the list of pending events. These two operations are essentially the same operations that are required by priority queue data structures.

The Event Horizon

The event horizon is a fundamental concept in parallel simulation and has been used to support a number of risk-free optimistic simulation studies [1,6,17,18]. In order to exploit the event horizon for event list management algorithms, it is assumed that as new events are generated, they are not immediately fed back into the main priority queue data structure, but instead are collected in an unsorted temporary holding queue. The event with the earliest time tag in this temporary queue is tracked. When the next event to be processed happens to be in the temporary queue (i.e., the event horizon has been crossed), the queue is sorted (a binary merge sort algorithm is easily performed on linked lists) and then merged back into the main priority queue data structure.

Because all new events are put in the temporary holding queue, the insert operation is always accomplished in constant time with very low overhead since it simply involves adding another item to the bottom of an unsorted linked list. However, when the list must be sorted (this occurs after the event horizon is crossed), it is sometimes tricky to merge its sorted events with the main priority queue data structure. Keep in mind that the main priority queue itself may be a very complicated data structure. In all of the discussions, the following definitions are used (see [19] for further details):

N = Number of processing nodes
n = Number of pending events
m = Average number of events per event horizon
B = Event insertion bias (from top of list)

Finally, unless otherwise stated, this paper assumes that the simulation is under equilibrium conditions (i.e., one new event is generated per event processed; this is the basis of the hold model) [3,8].

Priority Queues and the Event Horizon

A number of well known priority queue data structures have been discussed in the literature [7,9,12,15]. This section gives an overview of various priority queues as well as performance analysis and measurements. Techniques for applying the event horizon to each of these data structures are outlined.

Nine different beta-density functions were used to measure the performance of the different event-list data structures [19]. The beta function was chosen because of its flexibility in providing a wide variety of shapes. The beta density function is given below as [10],

$$\beta^{n_1 n_2}(t) = \frac{(n_1 + n_2 + 1)}{n_1! \, n_2!} t^{n_1} (1-t)^{n_2} \qquad (1)$$

A two hump distribution was generated by combining two equally weighted near and far future beta distributions. These distributions are specified below in Table 1. The Bias represents the average fraction of events required for traversal in a linked list starting from the top of the list.

Table 1: Nine beta functions

Description	n_1	n_2	Bias
Flat	0	0	0.667
Triangle Up	1	0	0.800
Triangle Down	0	1	0.600
Bell Shaped	20	20	0.913
Asym. Near Future	2	18	0.710
Asym. Far Future	18	2	0.954
Far Future	20	0	0.977
Near Future	0	20	0.512
Two Hump	0,20	20,0	0.523

Figure 1 shows a plot of the nine beta-density functions used for analysis in this paper. These nine different beta functions represent a wide spectrum of event generation statistics and are comparable to many of the distributions used by other measurements [2,4,5,8,13,14].

Figure 2 plots the average number of new events collected in the temporary queue (assuming the hold model) per event horizon as a function of the number of pending events for each of these nine beta functions.

All measurements were obtained using an HP9000/715 75 MHz workstation. The results were repeatable to within several microseconds. The HP C++ compiler was used with the optimizer enabled. For all measurements taken, each event generated a single new event distributed into the future according to the nine different beta distributions (i.e., the hold model).

All of the overheads (everything other than removing events from, and inserting new events into the list) were carefully measured and subtracted from the timing measurements by first running dummy loops that mimicked

those operations. Furthermore, steps were taken to keep the overhead small. Free lists were chosen to reuse event data structures in order to minimize memory-management overhead. Random numbers were pregenerated and stored in large arrays to reduce random-number-generation overheads.

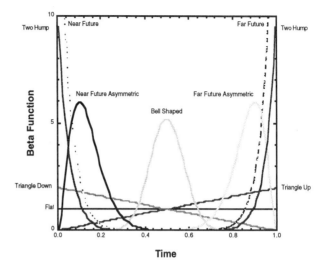

Figure 1: The nine beta-density functions used in this paper.

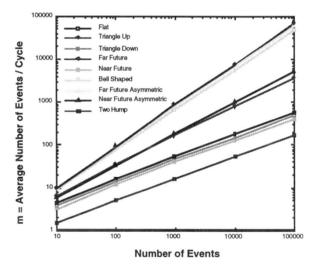

Figure 2: The average number of events processed per event horizon cycle.

The result of these efforts to minimize the overhead was that 0.0029 ms per event was subtracted from each of the measurements. This amount of overhead was small compared to the amount of time it typically took to manage the event lists for large (n > 1,000) data structures. Enough events were processed for each data structure to become stable. Finally, the initial density of events as a function of time was correctly generated using the results derived by the previous event horizon paper [19].

171

Linked Lists

The simplest priority queue data structure is a sorted linked list. Inserting an event into this data structure requires traversing the list until the proper slot is found for the event. Removing an event from the list is performed in constant time because the list is always sorted. The time for inserting an event and removing an event is given by:

$$T_{list} = C_1 Bn + C_2 \qquad (2)$$

Where C_1 represents the overhead for traversing a linked list, C_2 represents the overhead for removal, and B is the event insertion bias [8,19]. Performance results for linked list priority queues are given below in Table 2.

Table 2: Performance in milliseconds for linked lists.

Dist. \ n	10	10^2	10^3	10^4	10^5
Flat	0.00130	0.01009	0.10626	4.79610	84.3564
Tri. Up	0.00187	0.01214	0.12988	6.01976	97.8821
Tri. Down	0.00166	0.01017	0.09735	4.28571	73.3466
Bell Shaped	0.00187	0.01426	0.14734	6.94305	113.168
Asym. Near	0.00185	0.01245	0.11435	5.11578	88.4158
Asym. Far	0.00127	0.01273	0.14534	7.17282	117.524
Near Future	0.00130	0.00908	0.15098	3.52737	63.8613
Far Future	0.00128	0.01047	0.13425	7.01388	118.910
Two Hump	0.00155	0.00597	0.12154	3.67722	62.8712

It is very easy to apply the event horizon principle to linked list priority queues. The temporary list is sorted at each event horizon boundary and then merged back into the main list of pending events. This data structure is called the SPEEDES Queue and was used in the early versions of the SPEEDES operating system [17].

Merging m sorted events into a list of $n-m$ sorted events can be done in worst case $O(n)$ time. Because sorting m events can be done in $O(Log_2(m))$ time, and because the sort and merge operations are only required every m events, the following expression relates the overhead for event list management per event.

$$T_{SPEEDESQueue} = C_1 + C_2 \log_2(m) + C_3 \frac{n}{m} \qquad (3)$$

Here, C_1 represents the constant overhead for inserting and removing an event under normal circumstances, C_2 represents the overhead for sorting m items using the binary merge sort algorithm on lists, and C_3 represents the overhead for merging m events in the temporary list back into the main list that contains $n-m$ events.

It is easy to derive the value for m that minimizes the overhead of the SPEEDES Queue by taking the derivative of the above expression with respect to m and setting it to zero. The result is given below.

$$m_{optimal} = \frac{C_3}{C_2} n \log_e(2) \qquad (4)$$

This expression shows that the optimal value for m is related to the overheads required by the merge and sort operations. Normally, one would expect the merge operation

to require less overhead than the sort operation. This means that the optimal value for m should be somewhat less than 0.693 times the number of total pending events (depending on the implementation). It is also interesting to note that the best performance one can expect from the SPEEDES Queue (obtained when plugging the optimal value for m back into equation 2) is logarithmic behavior with a very small coefficient.

While the SPEEDES Queue has exceptionally good performance when m is close to its optimal value, the SPEEDES Queue can also have very poor performance when m is close to one. In fact, when m is equal to one, the SPEEDES Queue degenerates back into a linked list. Because of this fact, the SPEEDES Queue is not recommended for general discrete-event simulation systems although it almost always is a better alternative to plain linked lists. There may be some exceptions, however, when the SPEEDES Queue is an excellent choice, especially when applications have enough lookahead to provide large event horizon cycles. Performance results of the SPEEDES Queue are given in Table 3.

Table 3: Performance in milliseconds for the SPEEDES Queue.

Dist. \ n	10	10^2	10^3	10^4	10^5
Flat	0.00182	0.00278	0.00724	0.06199	0.24959
Tri. Up	0.00154	0.00296	0.00409	0.01940	0.04338
Tri. Down	0.00199	0.00306	0.00848	0.06959	0.28825
Bell Shaped	0.00208	0.00204	0.00343	0.01117	0.01915
Asym. Near	0.00181	0.00251	0.00429	0.01653	0.03860
Asym. Far	0.00152	0.00204	0.00305	0.01028	0.01771
Near Future	0.00194	0.00304	0.01362	0.08391	0.33714
Far Future	0.00162	0.00241	0.00285	0.00880	0.01648
Two Hump	0.00222	0.00449	0.02764	0.18375	0.75607

Binary Trees

Binary trees and their many variants are frequently used to support priority queue data structures [5]. Each node in a binary tree has three pointers: a pointer to its parent, a pointer to its left child, and a pointer to its right child. The root node, of course, is unique because it has no parent since it is at the top of the tree. Leaf nodes (which are at the bottom of the tree) have no children. It is possible for a node that is not a leaf to be missing either a left or right child. Each node in a binary tree also has a time tag value that is used for sorting. By definition, all of the elements in the left subtree below a node have time tags less than or equal to the node's time tag. Similarly, all of the elements in the right subtree below a node have values greater than or equal to the node's time tag.

When using binary trees to support priority queues, it is possible to maintain a special pointer to the leftmost element (i.e., the event with the smallest time tag). As an event is removed from the tree, the event with the next smallest time tag can be found in constant time by locally traversing the tree from the point where the most recent event was removed. This is faster than always starting at the top of the tree and traversing downward to the left until the leftmost leaf node is found. Thus, most of the overhead involved when using binary tree data structures as priority queues comes from inserting events, not from removing events. Events are inserted by traversing down the tree, moving left or right until a leaf node is reached. The event is then added as either a left or right child of the leaf node.

Table 4 shows how inserting events can be very inefficient for "vanilla" binary trees. Because events are always removed from the left side of the tree and because new events are inserted somewhat randomly with typical event insertion biases larger than 1/2, trees almost always become skewed to the right[1]. For example, it is possible for the tree to degenerate into a linked list if events are scheduled with a constant lookahead value (FIFO event scheduling). Various techniques have been developed to help this skewing problem. Some of these approaches are discussed below. Before describing them, however, it is important to define the basic tree rotation operation used by all of the tree data structures described in this paper.

Table 4: Performance in milliseconds for binary trees.

Dist. \ n	10	10^2	10^3	10^4	10^5
Flat	0.00498	0.00784	0.01540	0.06468	0.29739
Tri. Up	0.00506	0.00940	0.02025	0.10505	0.50757
Tri. Down	0.00478	0.00691	0.01133	0.02605	0.05333
Bell Shaped	0.00588	0.00840	0.01291	0.03518	0.04759
Asym. Near	0.00506	0.00718	0.01009	0.02290	0.03906
Asym. Far	0.00552	0.01307	0.02537	0.06131	0.23754
Near Future	0.00506	0.00709	0.01153	0.0231	0.03983
Far Future	0.00589	0.0186	0.05720	0.36440	2.26619
Two Hump	0.00505	0.01178	0.04015	0.21838	1.17882

Tree rotations permit the structure of a binary tree (or subtree) to change while preserving the tree's integrity (i.e., the elements in the tree remain sorted). The easiest way to explain the tree rotation operation is with a figure. Notice how, in Figure 3, a right rotation about the Y node still preserves the B subtree so that it is between X and Y. A left rotation about the X node restores the tree back to its original shape.

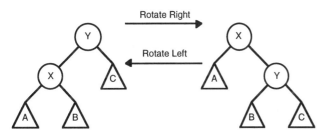

Figure 3: Tree rotations

Balanced Binary Trees

One very well known technique for managing binary sorted trees was developed by Adelson, Velsky, and Landis (AVL Trees) [5]. Their approach ensures (with much overhead) that the tree is always perfectly balanced. Because of the large amounts of overhead involved, and because it is not necessary for the tree to be perfectly balanced, another approach with

---

less overhead is described below called the SPEEDES Balancing Heuristic Tree.

The SPEEDES Balancing Heuristic and the SPEEDES Tree

The SPEEDES Balancing Heuristic keeps trees in rough balance with little overhead. To support this data structure, two more pieces of information are required by each node of the tree. The number of descendants to the left and the number of descendants to the right. Note that for a given node,

$$N_{left} + N_{right} + 1 = N_{subtree} \qquad (5)$$

Keeping this balancing information intact is fairly straight-forward. As events are removed or inserted, the tree is traversed downward starting from the root. The N_{left} and N_{right} values are modified at each node visited along the traversed path until the event is either removed or inserted. When inserting a new event, a balancing heuristic is applied at each node along the traversed path that tests if the subtrees below are grossly out of balance. This check first determines if the following expression is true (note, the factor of 3 was chosen empirically).

$$\left| N_{left} - N_{right} \right| > 3 \left(N_{left} + N_{right} \right) \qquad (6)$$

If this condition is true, then a second check is made to determine if there are enough events in the subtrees below to make it worthwhile to rotate its structure. A reasonable number to use is 20 (i.e., if there are less than 20 events in the combined subtrees of a given node, then it is not worth the effort to perform tree rotation operations). If there are enough events to warrant a rotation, the tree is rotated either left or right in order to hopefully improve its balance before moving downward.

Because the rotations are done only when needed, it is possible for portions of the tree to become out of balance. That is not a problem. While it might take some work to bring the tree into balance, it is amortized over time. No proof is offered in this paper to guarantee the worst case performance of this heuristic. However, all of the measurements made to date show that this balancing heuristic appears to keep the tree in nearly perfect balance with relatively low overheads. Performance is provided in Table 5.

Table 5: Performance in milliseconds for balancing heuristic tree.

Dist. \ n	10	10^2	10^3	10^4	10^5
Flat	0.00364	0.00952	0.01843	0.03216	0.04941
Tri. Up	0.00384	0.01007	0.01829	0.03175	0.04865
Tri. Down	0.00339	0.00951	0.01722	0.03236	0.04969
Bell Shaped	0.00385	0.01008	0.01674	0.02986	0.04648
Asym. Near	0.00357	0.00924	0.01701	0.03162	0.04948
Asym. Far	0.00495	0.01074	0.01750	0.02838	0.04470
Near Future	0.00366	0.00896	0.01820	0.03271	0.04922
Far Future	0.00478	0.01232	0.01866	0.02887	0.04240
Two Hump	0.00353	0.01002	0.01792	0.02935	0.04541

This balancing heuristic tree approach has been extended to take advantage of the event horizon. First of all, events are not added to the tree one at a time, but instead are collected in a temporary holding queue. When the next event to be

---

processed is in the temporary queue, it is sorted, the top event is removed (because it is the next event to be processed) and then the rest of the list is merged into the binary tree. In order to accomplish this merge operation, one more piece of information is required by each node of the tree. Each node tracks the maximum possible time tag, T_{max}, allowed in its subtree. This information permits the tree to be locally traversed as the sorted list is merged instead of forcing each event in the list to start at the top of the tree the way normal insertion is usually performed.

When a node is inserted into the tree as a left descendent, its value for T_{max} is the time tag of its parent. If the event is a right descendent, its value for T_{max} is the same as its parent's value for T_{max}. Figure 4 shows an example of such a binary tree.

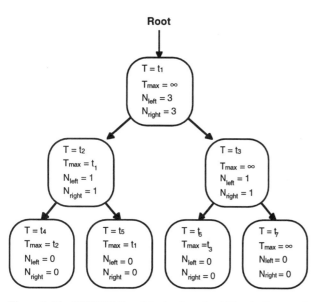

Root

T = t_1
$T_{max} = \infty$
$N_{left} = 3$
$N_{right} = 3$

T = t_2
$T_{max} = t_1$
$N_{left} = 1$
$N_{right} = 1$

T = t_3
$T_{max} = \infty$
$N_{left} = 1$
$N_{right} = 1$

T = t_4
$T_{max} = t_2$
$N_{left} = 0$
$N_{right} = 0$

T = t_5
$T_{max} = t_1$
$N_{left} = 0$
$N_{right} = 0$

T = t_6
$T_{max} = t_3$
$N_{left} = 0$
$N_{right} = 0$

T = t_7
$T_{max} = \infty$
$N_{left} = 0$
$N_{right} = 0$

Figure 4: The SPEEDES Tree data structure. In addition to the normal pointers in a binary tree, and the time tag value required for sorting, nodes also maintain T_{max}, N_{left}, and N_{right} values. The SPEEDES Tree also maintains a single pointer to the root of the tree and to the current event (i.e., the node with the smallest time tag).

In the SPEEDES Tree, a pointer always designates the event with the earliest time tag in the tree. As events are popped out of the tree to be processed, this pointer is updated locally. In other words, popping events out of the tree doesn't require starting at the top of the tree and then working downward until the left-most node is found (this would take logarithmic time). Instead, the next event is obtained from the tree in constant time.

While popping events out of the tree, the balancing information (N_{left} and N_{right}) is ignored. Thus, by the time the event horizon is about to be crossed, the tree balancing information is not correct. However, it can be corrected by working from the left-most event in the tree back up the tree until the root is reached, updating N_{left} on each node visited in the process. The number of steps is less than $log_2(n)$ because the tree will tend to be skewed to the right. Furthermore, updating the tree-balancing information only occurs after m events are processed. Therefore, restoring the balancing

information in the tree normally involves a negligible amount of overhead.

Merging the sorted list of new events into the tree is a complex process. The first event to be processed at the start of the next cycle will be the first event in the sorted secondary list, not the next event in the tree (this is part of the definition of the event horizon). Therefore, the pointer to the next event will be the first event in the secondary list. This first event is inserted as the left child of what was previously thought of in the tree as being the next event.

Now, the rest of the list must be merged into the tree. The tree is traversed left to right as events from the sorted secondary list are inserted into the SPEEDES Tree. After an event is inserted, the tree must be traversed upward until a node is reached that has T_{max} greater than the time tag of the next event to be inserted. Only then is it safe to insert the next event into the current subtree. As the tree is ascended, the tree-balancing information is updated. Then, the subtree is traversed downward left and right, until the bottom of the tree (where the event is to be inserted) is reached. As the subtree is descended, the balancing heuristic operation is performed, to keep the tree from becoming unbalanced.

One way to further optimize event insertion is to track the most recent node that passes the T_{max} test. Inserting the next event can start from that node instead of from the bottom of the tree where the previous event was inserted. This reduces the overhead for going up the tree as events from the secondary list are merged with the tree.

Once all of the events in the secondary list are merged into the tree, a final step is required. Starting from the last merged event, the tree must be ascended to the root, updating the tree balancing information along the way. After this step has been completed, the balancing information at each node of the tree is correct.

While this paper does not prove this fact, measurements have shown that the worst case time for insertion is logarithmic for all of the event generation distributions studied to date. However, if many events are collected in the secondary list, then the number of traversal steps for insertion is comparable to $log_2(n/m)$. Thus, the SPEEDES Tree performs better than logarithmic time for tree insertion (of course, at the expense of sorting the secondary list of m events). The average SPEEDES Tree overhead per event can be written as,

$$T_{SPEEDESTree} = C_1 + C_2 \log_2(m) + C_3 \log_2(n/m) \qquad (7)$$

Here, C_1, C_2, and C_3 are the respective overhead coefficients for removing, sorting, and merging events. Note that if $C_2 = C_3$, there is no advantage to using the SPEEDES Tree over the plain Balancing Heuristic Tree described above. However, measurements have shown that typically $C_2 \ll C_3$. For example, sorting 10,000 events on an IRIS4D SGI workstation using a binary merge sort algorithm was measured to take about 0.004 ms per event, while inserting events generated by a flat distribution into a Balancing Heuristic Tree of size 10,000 took about 0.032 ms per event.

The SPEEDES Tree is a very good data structure for managing events and is a significant improvement over the SPEEDES Queue since it exhibits worst case logarithmic behavior. However, it is too complicated for wide-spread general use. As a note, this data structure was used for several years in SPEEDES until the SPEEDES Qheap (described later) was developed. The SPEEDES Tree is not recommended for general use although it does present some interesting concepts. Performance is provided in Table 6.

Table 6: Performance in milliseconds for the SPEEDES tree.

Dist. \ n	10	10^2	10^3	10^4	10^5
Flat	0.00440	0.00653	0.01353	0.02625	0.04217
Tri. Up	0.00421	0.00578	0.01046	0.02514	0.04264
Tri. Down	0.00459	0.00690	0.01285	0.02699	0.04396
Bell Shaped	0.00412	0.00588	0.00951	0.01838	0.03468
Asym. Near	0.00440	0.00672	0.01350	0.02792	0.04327
Asym. Far	0.00339	0.00457	0.00676	0.01691	0.02607
Near Future	0.00395	0.00746	0.01555	0.0288	0.04510
Far Future	0.00339	0.00493	0.00610	0.01401	0.02247
Two Hump	0.00450	0.00718	0.01554	0.01896	0.03315

Splay Trees

Before leaving the topic of trees altogether and discussing heaps, it is important to consider one final binary tree data structure, the Splay Tree [16], that has been sometimes quoted as the fastest tree-based priority queue data structure [8]. The results obtained in this study do not confirm this claim.

The main idea behind Splay Trees is to use a two-step rotation operation, called the "splay operation", to bring elements inserted or removed back to the top of the tree. This heuristic keeps the parts of the tree that have been recently accessed near the top of the tree in order to reduce future access times. This heuristic works very well when inserting a large number of events into the tree with the same (or similar) time tags. However, it does not work so well when events are somewhat randomly inserted into the tree because of the large number of expensive rotations that are involved (often worse than $log_2(n)$).

The splay operation on a node promotes that node to the top of the tree through a sequence of two-step rotations. There are four cases to consider when applying the splay operation to a node in the tree. In the first case, if the node is the root, then nothing needs to be done. In the second case, if the parent of the node is the root, then a rotation about the root is performed to make the node the new root. In the third case, the Zig-Zig (or Zag-Zag) case, the node and its parent are either both left descendants or are both right descendants. For this case, the grandparent is rotated first, then the parent is rotated (see Figure 5). The fourth case is the Zig-Zag (or Zag-Zig) case, where the node and its parent are either left-right or right-left descendants. In this case, the parent is rotated first, then the grandparent is rotated (see Figure 6). These steps are repeated until the node has been promoted to the top of the tree and becomes the root.

Normally, the splay operation is performed whenever an event is inserted into or removed from the tree. However, by continually tracking the left-most node, events can be removed from the tree in constant time without applying the splay operation. While the heuristic of splaying may appear to have good amortized properties, it can involve an enormous amount of overhead since the number of rotations required can be very high. Table 7 shows the performance of Splay Trees. It is interesting to see how the splay operation, in fact, does help reduce the number of operations for the Far Future and Two Hump distributions (which have a large

amount of locality for event insertion) but it is also interesting to see how poorly it performs for the Flat and Near Future distributions (where events have very little locality during event insertion).

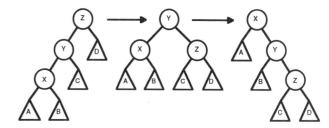

Figure 5: Zig-Zig rotations for Splay Trees. The node and its parents are either both left descendants or are both right descendants.

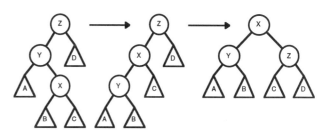

Figure 6: Zig-Zag rotations for Splay Trees. The node and its parent are either left-right descendants or right-left descendants.

Table 7: Performance in milliseconds for Splay trees.

Dist. \ n	10	10^2	10^3	10^4	10^5
Flat	0.00588	0.01111	0.01832	0.03351	0.05461
Tri. Up	0.00579	0.01018	0.01531	0.03079	0.05123
Tri. Down	0.00608	0.01157	0.01805	0.03449	0.05642
Bell Shaped	0.00422	0.00830	0.01389	0.02560	0.04555
Asym. Near	0.00616	0.01083	0.01683	0.03283	0.05479
Asym. Far	0.00376	0.00747	0.01180	0.02282	0.04002
Near Future	0.00617	0.01148	0.01948	0.03514	0.05694
Far Future	0.00357	0.00578	0.01041	0.01911	0.03365
Two Hump	0.00533	0.00841	0.01434	0.02548	0.04406

It is not too difficult to apply the event horizon concept to Splay Trees. Events are simply inserted into a temporary queue in order to provide constant insertion times. Removing events from the Splay tree can also be performed in constant time if the event horizon has not yet been crossed, and if the leftmost event is tracked in the Splay Tree without applying the splay operation. All of the real overhead in using the event horizon for Splay Trees comes when the event horizon is crossed.

When the event horizon is crossed, the events are sorted in the temporary list and then one at a time inserted into the Splay Tree using the splay operation. By sorting the events first, better locality is preserved as the events are inserted into the Splay Tree. One problem with this approach is that the splay tree can become grossly skewed to the left. This is because of the predominance of left rotations required as sorted events are inserted into the tree. However, this is normally not a problem since all of the rotations are amortized over time.

Because of the large overheads involved in Splay Trees, this paper does not recommend this data structure for event list management. The SPEEDES Tree outperformed the Splay Tree in almost every case. Furthermore, the SPEEDES Qheap (described later) is generally much faster anyway and has no worst case scenarios. Performances results for the SPEEDES Splay Tree are shown in Table 8. These results show that applying the event horizon to Splay Trees does improve performance.

Table 8: Performance in milliseconds for the SPEEDES Splay tree.

Dist. \ n	10	10^2	10^3	10^4	10^5
Flat	0.00653	0.01083	0.01735	0.03024	0.04824
Tri. Up	0.00552	0.00942	0.01247	0.02459	0.04213
Tri. Down	0.00682	0.01203	0.01692	0.03143	0.05024
Bell Shaped	0.00468	0.00625	0.00856	0.02000	0.05803
Asym. Near	0.00580	0.01026	0.01360	0.02718	0.04517
Asym. Far	0.00440	0.00550	0.00696	0.01356	0.03959
Near Future	0.00718	0.01131	0.01875	0.0322	0.05106
Far Future	0.00404	0.00513	0.00633	0.01328	0.02822
Two Hump	0.00681	0.00924	0.01441	0.02437	0.04057

Heaps and the SPEEDES Qheap

Heaps are normally implemented as binary trees with the property that each node is at least as small as the value of its children nodes (if they exist) [7,9,12,15]. Figure 7 shows a typical heap stored in a binary tree structure. Although it is not necessary, heaps are almost always implemented using fixed arrays for storing pointers to their tree nodes. Modular arithmetic allows tree nodes to be directly accessed and manipulated, thereby allowing the normal tree traversal operations to be bypassed.

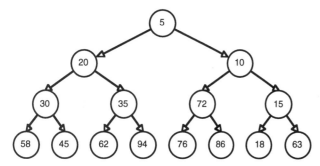

Figure 7: An example of elements stored in a heap using a tree representation.

Instead of describing heaps using binary trees and exploiting modular arithmetic schemes with fixed arrays, this paper describes a novel implementation of a heap using only linked lists. This new data structure is called the Qheap. The benefits of this approach are very low overheads (typical of linked list manipulations), freedom from fixed array data structures, and simplicity.

Fundamental to the Qheap is a sorted linked list, denoted by Q, that is never allowed to have more elements than a fixed size, denoted by S. The size, S, should roughly be chosen as the point where straight event insertion into an already sorted linked list outperforms traditional logarithmic techniques. If S is chosen to be 2, then the Qheap simply performs as a binary heap. However, just as divide and conquer sorting

algorithms perform better when using straight insertion-sort techniques for small sublists, so does the Qheap by choosing S to be a reasonable value. Typical ranges for S might be somewhere between 20 and 80[2].

As elements are added to the Qheap, they are directly inserted into Q. However, if the number of elements in Q is equal to S, the list is first *metasized* into a single *metaitem* with its sort value determined by the first element of Q. Metasizing Q into a single metaitem is done prior to the insertion of the new element. As further elements are added to Q, the same procedure is repeated. It is therefore possible for Q to contain metaitems mixed with real event items. Furthermore, when metasizing Q into a single metaitem, it is possible for the new metaitem to also contain metaitems which in turn might contain other metaitems, etc.. In this manner, the Qheap is actually a recursive linked list data structure that closely relates to the heap property (although it is not necessarily a binary heap). Examples of inserting elements into the Qheap are shown in Figure 8.

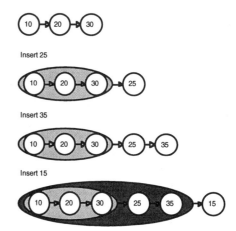

Figure 8: Inserting items into the Qheap with $S = 3$. Assume that Q already contains 3 items. In the first step, an item with value 25 is inserted. Because there are already 3 items in Q, the items in Q are metasized into a single metaitem with value 10 and then the item with value 25 is inserted. Q now contains two items. In the second step, an item with value 35 is inserted directly into Q. In the third step, an item with value 15 is inserted. Once again, since there are already 3 items in Q, the items are metasized into a single item and then the item with value 15 is inserted. Q ends up with 2 items, one of which is a complex metaitem.

Removing items from the Qheap is more difficult than inserting items because it is possible that the item removed from the top of Q is actually a metaitem itself. If this is so, then the metaitem must be *untangled* by removing its top item, redefining the rest of the metaitem's list as a new metaitem, making sure that Q does not have more than S elements (if it does, then the elements in Q are turned into a single metaitem and placed back into Q as its only element), and then inserting this new metaitem back into Q. The untangling procedure is repeated until a single element is found. Figure 9 shows an example of removing an item from the Qheap. Performance results for the Qheap are provided in

---

[2] Our measurements showed only about a 10% difference in performance for $20 < S < 80$. We used S=40 for our final results.

Table 9. These results were obtained using the value of 40 for S.

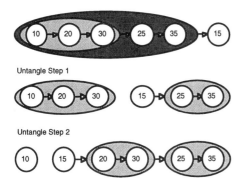

Untangle Step 1

Untangle Step 2

Figure 9: Removing an item from the Qheap with $S = 3$. Assume that Q initially has two items (see previous Figure). In the first step, the metaitem with value 10 is removed from Q. Since it is a metaitem, the top metaitem (containing 10,20,30) is removed and the rest (25,35) is redefined as a new metaitem and inserted back into Q with value 25. In the second step, the item with value 10 is removed from the metaitem (containing 10,20,30). The rest of the items (20,30) are redefined as a new metaitem and inserted back into Q with value 20. Since the remaining item (10) is a single item (not a metaitem), the untangling procedure is finished. The item (10) is then returned from the remove operation.

Table 9: Performance in milliseconds for the Qheap.

Dist. \ n	10	10^2	10^3	10^4	10^5
Flat	0.00328	0.00636	0.01131	0.01829	0.02913
Tri. Up	0.00302	0.00652	0.01084	0.01746	0.02848
Tri. Down	0.00311	0.00689	0.01196	0.01801	0.02928
Bell Shaped	0.00320	0.00662	0.01007	0.01644	0.02655
Asym. Near	0.00329	0.00672	0.01123	0.01847	0.02967
Asym. Far	0.00283	0.00634	0.00811	0.01496	0.02371
Near Future	0.00324	0.00671	0.01136	0.01793	0.02943
Far Future	0.00289	0.00606	0.00701	0.01323	0.02134
Two Hump	0.00286	0.00497	0.00836	0.01470	0.02314

It is very easy to apply the event horizon principle to the Qheap. Instead of directly inserting events into Q, they are added to Q_{temp}. When the event horizon is crossed, Q_{temp} is sorted, the top item is removed as the next event, the rest of the list is metasized, and then inserted into Q. The obvious advantage of using $Qtemp$ is to provide for larger numbers of events to be in a single metaitem, thereby reducing the average number of untangling steps. This new data structure is called the SPEEDES Qheap and is currently used in the SPEEDES operating system.

Because heaps are known to have worst case $log_2(n)$ amortized behavior, this data structure should never break down. Also, because it is composed from linked lists, it should have very low overheads. There are no complicated rotation operations or funny balancing heuristics to apply. This data structure does not require fixed sized arrays or modular arithmetic. The only (slightly) complicated part of this data structure is the untangling procedure (which is actually very straight-forward). Performance results for the SPEEDES Qheap are provided in Table 10.

Table 10: Performance in milliseconds for the SPEEDES Qheap.

Dist. \ n	10	10^2	10^3	10^4	10^5
Flat	0.00275	0.00472	0.00778	0.01156	0.01627
Tri. Up	0.00319	0.00484	0.00627	0.00996	0.01588
Tri. Down	0.00273	0.00512	0.00791	0.01208	0.01664
Bell Shaped	0.00274	0.00447	0.00563	0.0107	0.01918
Asym. Near	0.00283	0.00464	0.00647	0.01014	0.01691
Asym. Far	0.00301	0.00466	0.00552	0.00967	0.01818
Near Future	0.00279	0.00482	0.00853	0.01255	0.01697
Far Future	0.00244	0.00440	0.00510	0.01024	0.01713
Two Hump	0.00282	0.00412	0.00619	0.01035	0.01425

Because of its nice properties, the SPEEDES Qheap data structure is highly recommended for general event list management in discrete-event simulations. Provided below is a step-by-step procedure for supporting the SPEEDES Qheap.

SPEEDES Qheap Insertion

1. Place the item to be inserted at the end of the Q_{temp}.
2. Update T_{min} if this item has the smallest time tag out of all the items in Q_{temp}.

SPEEDES Qheap Removal

1. Check if the event horizon is crossed (i.e., if T_{min} is less than the time tag of the next item in Q). If so, perform steps a through f and then return. Otherwise, go on to step 2.
   a. Sort Q_{temp} and then set T_{min} to infinity.
   b. Remove the top element (this is what is returned as the next event) and call it *NextEvent*.
   c. Metasize the rest of the elements from Q_{temp} into a new metaitem called $Meta_{temp}$.
   d. Check if Q already contains S elements. If it does, metasize all of its elements into a new metaitem and place it back into Q as its only element.
   e. Insert $Meta_{temp}$ into Q.
   f. Return *NextEvent*.
2. Remove the top item from Q and call it *NextItem*. Then loop over steps a through e below until *NextItem* is not a metaitem.
   a. Check if *NextItem* is a metaitem. If not, then break out of the loop and return *NextItem* as the *NextEvent*. Otherwise, we know that *NextItem* is a metaitem which must be untangled in the steps b-e below.
   b. Remove the top element from *NextItem* and call it *NewItem*. *NextItem* now contains one less item. If *NextItem* has only a single element, then unmetasize it so that *NextItem* is a regular item.
   c. Check if Q already contains S elements. If it does, metasize all of its elements into a new metaitem and place it back into Q as its only element.
   d. Insert *NextItem* into Q.
   e. Set *NextItem* = *NewItem* and then go back to a.

177

Summary and Conclusions

This paper discussed various priority queue data structures and how their performance is enhanced by exploiting the event horizon. The results of this study show that the SPEEDES Qheap easily outperformed the other data structures without any "worst-case" problems. The SPEEDES Qheap is not a binary heap, but instead is recursively constructed from linked lists. Thus, it has low overheads that are typical of linked lists.

Future work in this area might involve studying how the SPEEDES Qheap can be applied to Calendar Queues. One idea would be to use the SPEEDES Qheap instead of linked lists for each time bucket. The benefits of this approach may provide significant improvements in worst-case Calendar Queue performance.

Acknowledgments

The research described in this paper was carried out by Metron Incorporated and by the Jet Propulsion Laboratory, California Institute of Technology. The work was sponsored by NCCOSC RDTE Division and through Innovative Science & Technology at the Pentagon by agreement with the National Aeronautics and Space Administration. Reference herein to any specific commercial product, process, or service by trade name, trademark, manufacturer, or otherwise, does not constitute or imply its endorsement by the United States Government or the Jet Propulsion Laboratory, California Institute of Technology

Biography

Jeff Steinman received B.S. degrees in computer science and in mathematical physics from California State University Northridge in 1980. He then worked at Hughes Aircraft Company in the Radar Systems Group for four years while studying physics at UCLA. In 1988, he received his Ph.D. in experimental high-energy particle physics from UCLA, where he measured the quark content of virtual photons generated at the Stanford Linear Accelerator Center. He then joined the technical staff at the Jet Propulsion Laboratory (JPL) where he designed and developed simulations for strategic missile and air defense. Jeff Steinman was the principle developer of the Synchronous Parallel Environment for Emulation and Discrete-Event Simulation (SPEEDES) operating system and has nearly 20 publications in the field of parallel simulation technologies. He has received several achievement awards from NASA for his research in parallel simulation. Jeff Steinman joined the staff at Metron Inc. in 1996 as a Senior Analyst where he is continuing his work in parallel and distributed simulation.

References

[1] Bellenot, S. 1993, "Performance of a Riskfree Time Warp Operating System." In proceedings of the *7th Workshop on Parallel and Distributed Simulation (PADS93)*. Pages 155-158.

[2] Brown R., 1988. "Calendar Queues: A Fast O(1) priority Queue Implementation for the Simulation Event Set Problem." *Communications of the ACM.* Vol. 31, No. 10, Pages 1220-1227.

[3] Chou C., Bruell S., and Jones D., 1993. "A Generalized Hold Model." In Proceedings of the *1993 Winter Simulation Conference.* Pages 756-761.

[4] Chung, Sang, and Rego 1993. "A Performance Comparison of Event Calendar Algorithms: an Empirical Approach." Software-Practice and Experience. Vol. 23, No. 10, Pages 1107-1138.

[5] Crane C., 1972. "Linear Lists and Priority Queues as Balanced Binary Trees." STAN-CS-72-259, Computer Science Department, Stanford University.

[6] Damitio M., et. al., 1994. "Comparing the Breathing Time Buckets Algorithm and the Time Warp Operating System on a Transputer Architecture." In proceedings of the *SCS European Simulation Multiconference.* Pages 141-145.

[7] Horowitz E. and Sahni S., 1976. "Fundamentals of Data Structures." Computer Science Press, Inc.

[8] Jones D., 1986. "An Empirical Comparison of Priority-Queue and Event-Set Implementations." *Communications of the ACM.* Vol. 29, No. 4., Pages 300-311.

[9] Lewis T. and Smith M., 1976. "Applying Data Structures." Houghton Mifflin Company, Boston.

[10] Papoulis A. 1965. "Probability, Random Variables, and Stochastic Processes." McGraw-Hill Series in System Science, New York, pages 104, 147.

[11] Prasad S. and Naqib B., 1995. "Effectiveness of Global Event Queues in Rollback Reduction and Load Balancing." In proceedings of the *9'h Workshop on Parallel and Distributed Simulation (PADS'95).* Pages 187-190.

[12] Press W., et. al., 1988. "Numerical Recipes in C: The Art of Scientific Computing." Cambridge University Press.

[13] Rongren R., Riboe J., and Ayani R., 1991, "Lazy Queue: An Efficient Implementation of the Pending-event Set." In proceedings of *The 24th Annual Simulation Symposium.* Pages 194-204.

[14] Rongren R., et. al. 1993. "Efficient Implementation of Event Sets in Time Warp." In proceedings of the *7th Workshop on Parallel and Distributed Simulation (PADS93).* Pages 101-108.

[15] Sengupta S. and Korobkin C., 1994. "C++: Object-Oriented Data Structures." Springer-Verlag.

[16] Sleator D., and Tarjan R. 1985. "Self Adjusting Binary Search Trees." *Journal of the ACM.* Vol. 32, No. 3, pages 652-686.

[17] Steinman J., 1992. "SPEEDES: A Multiple-Synchronization Environment for Parallel Discrete-Event Simulation." *International Journal in Computer Simulation.* Vol. 2, No. 3, Pages 251-286.

[18] Steinman J. 1993. "Breathing Time Warp." In Proceedings of the *7'th Workshop on Parallel and Distributed Simulation* (PADS93). Vol. 23, No. 1, July 1993, Pages 109-118.

[19] Steinman J., 1994. "Discrete-Event Simulation and the Event Horizon." In Proceedings of the *8th Workshop on Parallel and Distributed Simulation (PADS'94).* Pages 39-49.

Session 10

Short Papers

Session Chair
John G. Cleary, University of Waikato, New Zealand

A Performance Evaluation Methodology for Parallel Simulation Protocols

Vikas Jha   Rajive Bagrodia

Computer Science Department
UCLA
Los Angeles, CA 90024

Abstract

Most experimental studies of the performance of parallel simulation protocols use speedup or number of events processed per unit time as the performance metric. Although helpful in evaluating the usefulness of parallel simulation for a given simulation model, these metrics tell us little about the efficiency of the simulation protocol used. In this paper, we describe an Ideal Simulation Protocol (ISP), based on the concept of critical path, which experimentally computes the best possible execution time for a simulation model on a given parallel architecture. Since ISP computes the bound by actually executing the model on the given parallel architecture, it is much more realistic than that computed by a uniprocessor critical path analysis. The paper illustrates, using parameterized synthetic benchmarks, how an ISP-based performance evaluation can lead to much better insights into the performance of parallel simulation protocols than what would be gained from speedup graphs alone.

1   Introduction

Parallel simulation refers to the execution of a discrete event simulation program on parallel computers (see [7] for a survey). Most of the experimental performance studies of parallel simulation protocols have used speedup or number of events executed per unit time as the performance metric. While both these metrics are appropriate for evaluating the usefulness of parallel simulation for a particular simulation application, they tell us little about the efficiency of the parallel simulation protocol used. It is well known that the execution time for most simulation protocols is bound by the critical path time [3] of the simulation model (there exist protocols, called supercritical protocols[9], that are theoretically capable of beating the critical path time. For the rest of the paper, we limit our attention to non-supercritical simulation protocols). While evaluating and comparing performances of such protocols, therefore, it is more meaningful to use the relative execution time with respect to the critical path time as a performance metric. Critical paths have been used in the past to prove theoretical bounds and properties[11, 1] of parallel simulation protocols.

We describe the design and implementation of an

Ideal Simulation Protocol(ISP), based on the concept of critical path, that computes the best possible (non-supercritical) execution time for a simulation model by actually executing it on the given parallel architecture. The primary contributions of this paper are:

- ISP computes the best possible parallel execution time by actually *executing* the model on the parallel architecture, rather than a uniprocessor trace analysis of the critical path[6]. Therefore, it computes a more realistic bound that takes into account all the overheads associated with the parallel simulation of the model on the given architecture, except those specific to different simulation protocols. Also, theoretical or uniprocessor critical path analyses, almost always assume an arbitrary number of processors. In our implementation, both ISP and the simulation protocol, whose performance is being evaluated, execute on the same number of processors.

- We illustrate the usefulness of the proposed methodology with a performance evaluation of the null message protocol[4] on a set of parameterized synthetic benchmarks. We show that using ISP gives us better insights into the performance of the null message protocol than using speedup figures alone.

ISP has been implemented as one of the available simulation protocols in the Maisie simulation environment[2]. Besides serving as a reference point for computing the efficiency of a given simulation protocol, a representative pre-simulation with ISP can also give a realistic prediction of the available parallelism in a simulation model (which is different from the parallelism in the system being simulated [12]). If the speedup potential is found to be low, the user can change the model, which may include changing the partitioning of the system into logical processes (LPs), or their mapping to the processors, in order to improve the parallelism in the model.

The rest of the paper is organized as follows: section 2 describes the protocol and its implementation. Section 3 describes some experiments and results, and conclusions are discussed in section 4.

2 Protocol and Implementation

We assume a general familiarity with the message-based approach to discrete event simulation, and optimistic and conservative parallel simulation protocols (see [7] for an overview).

We classify the factors that affect the execution time of a parallel simulation protocol on a given architecture into two categories - *protocol-independent* factors and *protocol-specific* factors. The protocol-independent factors include the parallelism in the simulation model, computation speed of the processor, communication latency, event queue management and context switching overheads etc. Some of these factors may be *indirectly* affected by the choice of protocol e.g. the rate at which a protocol executes messages may affect the average size of the unprocessed message queue, thus affecting the queue management overhead. We ignore such secondary effects, since they are typically small. The *protocol-specific* overheads depend on the choice of the simulation protocol. For the conservative protocols, they may include the overhead of processing and propagating the null messages[4] or conditional event messages[5], and the idle time spent by a processor when one of its LPs *has its next message to be processed in the message queue, but cannot process it* because the information that no earlier message will be delivered to the LP has not reached the LP yet. In case of optimistic protocols, the *protocol-specific* overheads may include the state saving overheads, the rollback overhead, and the Global Virtual Time (GVT) computation overhead.

We want the Ideal Simulation Protocol (ISP) to include all the *protocol-independent* factors, but exclude the *protocol-specific* overheads. We can eliminate the *protocol-specific* overheads if at all times, each LP *knew the identity of the next message it is going to execute*. This knowledge can be provided to each LP through a pre-existing *event trace* of the simulation.

Ideal Simulation Protocol(ISP): (a) It performs the protocol-independent activities like receiving a message, enqueueing it, picking the earliest unprocessed message, processing it if appropriate, and sending out any resulting outputs. (b) An LP processes the earliest available unprocessed message *only if* it is the same as the *next message* to be processed, as determined from the event trace (this check is performed every time a new message arrives at the LP). Thus, an LP waits for the next message, if not yet received, and ignores future messages that arrive early.

Implementation: In order to keep the ISP execution time close to optimal, we try to minimize the overhead corresponding to reading and matching the event trace. The entire trace is read into a linked list at the beginning of the simulation in order to exclude the trace reading time. Every message is assigned a globally unique numeric identifier, which is the same in the trace and the ISP execution, so that comparison of messages during ISP execution is a simple numeric operation. Assigning such identifiers is simple if the trace is produced by a uniprocessor execution. However, if the simulation is too large to be executed sequentially, the trace can be produced by a parallel simulation, and then post-processed to assign globally unique identifiers.

Assuming each processor has at most one LP mapped to it, the execution time of the ISP is a very close approximation to the best possible execution time for any non-supercritical simulation protocol on the given architecture.

However, *if more than one LP are mapped to any processor*, the execution time of the ISP on n processors may not be a lower bound on the execution time of the simulation model on n processors. This is illustrated by the following example: assume two LPs A and B are mapped to the same processor p, and both have their *next events*, m1 and m2, respectively, available at some point during execution. LP C, mapped on a different processor, is idle, waiting for its *next event* that is going to come from LP A, after it finishes executing m1. Clearly, scheduling A before B on the processor p will result in a faster overall execution. However, it is not possible to detect at run-time, without considerable extra overhead, the optimal schedule for each processor. A static analysis of the trace cannot help either because the optimal schedule is a function of message execution times, communication overheads, and other overheads, which cannot be accurately predicted statically.

Extending ISP to allow more than one LPs on a processor: Using ISP, we can still compute the optimal execution time of a simulation model *for a given schedule*. Thus, if we ensure that ISP uses the *same* schedule that was used by the simulation protocol (whose performance we are trying to evaluate) during its execution, the ISP execution time would give a fair reference point. Such a trace can only be produced by the actual parallel run which would record the event sequence for each *processor* rather than each *LP*.

3 Experiments and Results

In order to illustrate the usefulness of an ISP-based performance evaluation methodology, we carry out a performance evaluation of a null message[4] based conservative implementation of the Maisie simulation language, using a set of parameterized synthetic benchmarks written in Maisie. The details of the implementation and its performance on different benchmarks are described elsewhere [10].

Benchmarks: The parameterized synthetic benchmark is a closed network of N FCFS servers (with shifted-exponential service time), arranged in a circular fashion, with J messages circulating between them. The number of LPs mapped to each processor, E, is 1. An LP sends its outputs to any of its C neighbors to the right with equal probability. Thus, C=1 corresponds to a ring topology, whereas C=16 represents a completely connected network. All models are simulated up to H time units. COMP represents the computation associated with the processing of every message (each unit of COMP represents 0.16 microsecond of computation).

The experiments were carried out on the IBM SP supercomputer each of whose nodes is an RS/6000 processor with 128 MB of main memory. The speedups for parallel execution were computed with respect to an efficient, splay tree based, global event list sequential implementation executing on one node of IBM SP.

In this section, we study the effect of changing four model characteristics, namely, lookahead, communication topology, message density, and computation granularity on the performance of the null message protocol. Using ISP, we attempt to quantitatively break down the change in the overall performance (speedup) of the protocol into two components: change in the amount of parallelism inherent in the model, and change in the efficiency of the protocol in exploiting that parallelism.

For each experiment, we plot three graphs. The first graph plots the *speedup* for both - the null message protocol and the ISP. The second graph plots the *efficiency*, defined as the ratio of the execution time of ISP to the execution time of the null message protocol. The third graph plots the overall Null Message Ratio (NMR), ratio of the number of null messages sent to the number of regular messages sent, traditionally used as an indicator of the simulation overhead for null message based simulation protocols[8].

3.1 Lookahead

Lookahead of an LP at simulation time t is defined to be l, if after processing all the inputs with timestamp t or less, it can predict all its outputs until time $t + l$ or less. It is well known that a higher lookahead generally means better performance for the null message protocol[8]. We program the FCFS servers as lazy servers[8] i.e. we do not exploit their non pre-emptive nature. The only source of lookahead in our servers is the pre-computed service time of the next job to depart. In order to control the amount of lookahead in the system, we introduce a Lookahead Factor(LAF) whose value can range in $[0.1, 1.0]$. If S is the precomputed service time for the next job, then the LP only expresses $LAF * S$ as its lookahead. Thus, a value of 1.0 for LAF for all LPs represents a good lookahead system, whereas a value 0.1 represents a poor lookahead system (we do not set LAF to 0.0 since the null message protocol needs a minimum lookahead to guarantee progress).

The experiments are carried out with a ring topology (C=1). Figure 1 shows how the speedup varies with the value of LAF for null message protocol and the ISP. The speedup of ISP remains unaffected, since LAF only effects the *efficiency* of the null message protocol, and not the degree of parallelism in the simulation model. As would be expected, the efficiency improves dramatically as we increase LAF from 0.1 to 1.0 (Figure 2). This is also confirmed by the NMR graph (Figure 3). However, even when the LAF is equal to 1.0, the null message protocol is considerably slower than the ISP (efficiency = 0.65). This is explained as follows: Consider two servers A and B. A sends a job j at simulation time t to B. Before sending j, A precomputes the service time, s_A of the next job that will depart from A. Along with j, A also piggybacks a null message with timestamp $t + s_A$ which implies that A will not send any more messages to B with timestamp smaller than $t + s_A$. Upon processing

j, B computes its departure time to be $t + s_B$, where s_B is the service time for job j at B. Clearly, job j will leave as soon as it arrives i.e. will experience zero blocking overhead *only if $s_B < s_A$*, which will be true only half the time. In the ISP execution, however, jobs never experience any blocking, since every LP has only one source.

3.2 Communication Topology

We study the effect of changing communication topology by changing the value of connectivity, C, for each LP. We choose the value of J to be 16 i.e. each LP starts with 1 job initially. As seen in Figure 4, the parallelism in the model drops as C is increased. This is because of a greater load imbalance in the model: consider the execution of ISP with C=1. Given fixed computation and communication costs, there is always one unprocessed job at every LP at the end of each iteration. Thus, the load is equally balanced. Now, if the connectivity is increased to 2, at the end of the first iteration, there is a 0.25 probability that an LP will have 2 unprocessed jobs, and a 0.25 probability that it will have no unprocessed jobs. This causes load imbalance, and the speedup for ISP drops The drop is maximum when C changes from 1 to 2, and gradually levels off.

Increasing C also makes the protocol less efficient. An increase in connectivity means that each LP has to wait for (synchronize with) a higher number of LPs, thus increasing the blocking time for each message. Also, a higher number of null messages have to be sent because there are more output channels. This results in a decrease in efficiency (Figure 5), and an increase in NMR (Figure 6).

3.3 Message Density

The experiments in this section were carried out with C equal to 2. As shown in Figure 7, an increase in message density (J) improves the speedup of ISP. This is because it *improves* the *parallelism* in the model by distributing the load better; if the message density is high, chances that each LP has some jobs to process at any given time are high. The improvement levels off eventually when each server has a job to process at all times.

Figure 8, however, shows what may initially seem to be a counter-intuitive behavior: the efficiency of null message protocol *degrades* as the message density increases. The graphs show that for low message densities, despite a high NMR (Figure 9), the protocol has very good efficiency. This is because the null messages are sent when the LP would otherwise be idle. Whereas, for high message densities, even though the relative null message overhead (NMR) is low, the efficiency is not very high because these null messages are sent when the LP could otherwise be processing regular jobs.

Note that it is still desirable to have a high message density in the application, since it improves the overall speedup for the null message protocol. The fact that efficiency degrades as the message density increases simply points to the fact that the protocol is not able to take full advantage of the increased parallelism. Perhaps a different protocol, or the same protocol with different values for its tunable parameters, may perform better.

3.4 Computation Granularity

The experiments in this section were conducted with C=1, J=16, and LAF=1.0. Lets briefly analyze how the ideal speedup would change with granularity. If each message incurs a fixed overhead of c time units (this includes the communication latency and message receiving overheads etc.) at each LP, and has a computation granularity of p time units, a simple expression for the "ideal" speedup would be $N/(1+c/p)$. Increasing the value of p would, therefore, improve the speedup, until it saturates at a value close to N. Figure 10 confirms this behavior. Note, however, that the speedup saturates at a value less than N. This is because on the IBM SP machine that we used, some of the allocated processors could be up to 30% slower than the rest (user has no control over the allocation of nodes). In case of the sequential runs, several runs were performed and one that executed on the faster node was chosen.

The NMR is almost completely independent of the computation granularity (Figure 12). This seems consistent with a similar analytical result derived in [11], although our assumptions are slightly different from theirs. Despite the fact that the NMR is almost constant, the *efficiency* of the protocol *improves* with an increase in computation granularity (Figure 11). This is because the execution time spent on processing null messages, *relative to total execution time* decreases as the computation granularity increases, even though the *number* of null messages relative to the total number of regular messages remains the same.

4 Conclusion

We described Ideal Simulation Protocol (ISP), an experimental analog of critical path analysis, which computes the best speedup possible for a simulation model on a given parallel architecture. Using several benchmarks, we show that ISP gives us much better insights into the performance of simulation protocols than using speedup graphs alone. To summarize, using ISP offers the following advantages :

- Before spending effort into *tuning* a parallel simulation for a new application, a smaller pre-simulation can be executed using ISP to estimate the best possible speedup. If that is found to be small, a different partitioning/mapping of the system may be tried.

- While comparing speedups on different benchmarks, or different parameter values for the same benchmark, ISP helps us breakdown the change in speedup into two parts: the part due to changed parallelism in the model, and the part due to changed efficiency of the simulation protocol.

- A comparison with ISP provides a more consistent comparison of simulation performance results from different sources, since it is able to factor out many of the differences in architectures, programming styles etc.

Acknowledgments

This research was partially supported by ARPA/CSTO, under contract DABT-63-94-C-0080, and NSF PYI award ASC9157610. We would like to thank Office of Academic Computing, UCLA, and Argonne National Labs for the use of their IBM SP system.

References

[1] Kumar A. and R. Shorey. Stability of event synchronisation in distributed discrete event simulation. In *1994 Workshop on Parallel and Distributed Simulation*, Edinburgh, July 1994.

[2] R. Bagrodia and W. Liao. Maisie: A language for design of efficient discrete-event simulations. *IEEE Transactions on Software Engineering*, April 1994.

[3] O. Berry and D. Jefferson. Critical path analysis of distributed simulation. In *Proceedings of 1985 SCS Multiconference on Distributed Simulation*, pages 57–60, January 1985.

[4] K.M. Chandy and J. Misra. Asynchronous distributed simulation via a sequence of parallel computations. *Communications of the ACM*, 24(11):198–206, August 1981.

[5] K.M. Chandy and R. Sherman. The conditional event approach to distributed simulation. In *Distributed Simulation Conference*, Miami, 1989.

[6] D. Conklin, J. Cleary, and B. Unger. The sharks world: A study in distributed simulation. In *1990 Simulation Multiconference: Distributed Simulation*, San Diego, California, January 1990.

[7] R. Fujimoto. Parallel discrete event simulation. *Communications of the ACM*, 33(10):30–53, October 1990.

[8] R. M. Fujimoto. Performance measurements of distributed simulation strategies. Technical Report Tech. Rep. UUCS-87-026a, University of Utah, Salt Lake City, 1987.

[9] D. Jefferson and P. Reiher. Supercritical speedup. In *Annual Simulation Symposium*, April 1991.

[10] Vikas Jha and Rajive Bagrodia. Transparent implementation of conservative algorithms in parallel simulation languages. In *Winter Simulation Conference*, December 1993.

[11] Yi-Bing Lin. *Understanding the Limits of Optimistic and Conservative Parallel Simulation*. PhD thesis, University of Washington, Seattle, August 1990.

[12] D.B. Wagner and E.D. Lazoska. Parallel simulation of queueing networks: Limitations and potentials. Technical report 88-09-05, Dept. of Computer Science, University of Washington, Seattle 98195, September 1988.

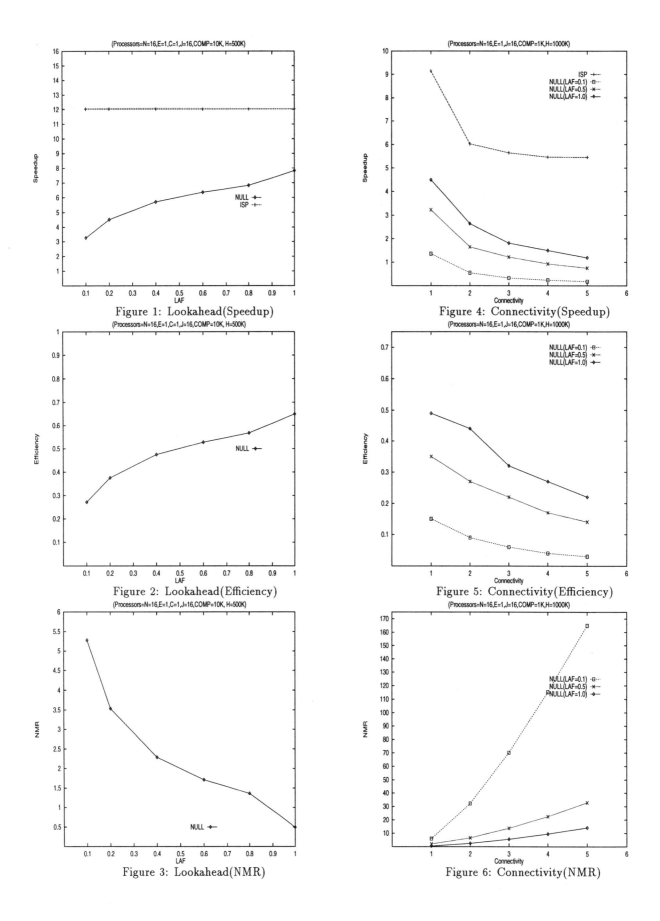

Figure 1: Lookahead(Speedup)

Figure 2: Lookahead(Efficiency)

Figure 3: Lookahead(NMR)

Figure 4: Connectivity(Speedup)

Figure 5: Connectivity(Efficiency)

Figure 6: Connectivity(NMR)

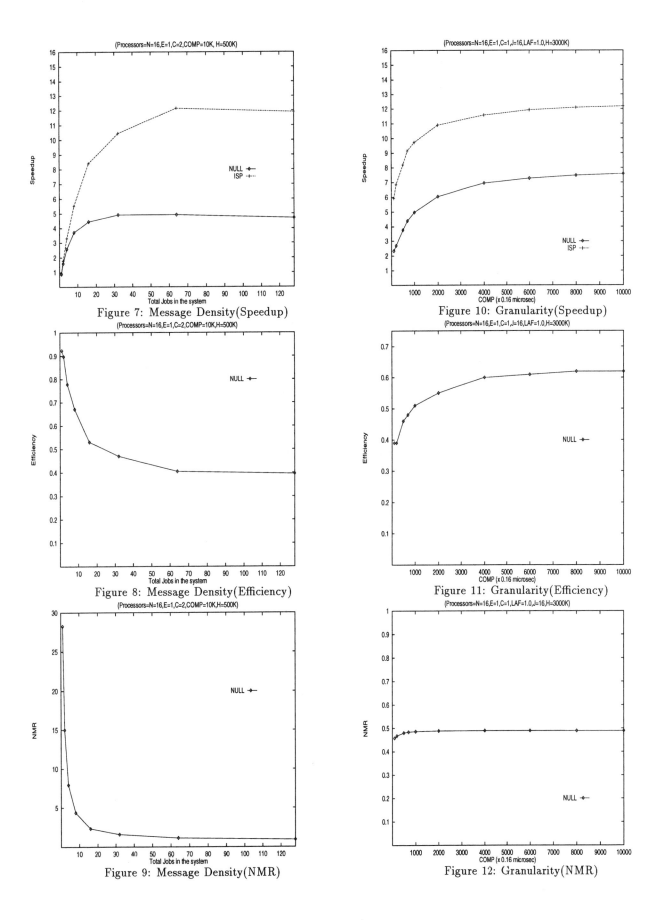

Figure 7: Message Density(Speedup)

Figure 8: Message Density(Efficiency)

Figure 9: Message Density(NMR)

Figure 10: Granularity(Speedup)

Figure 11: Granularity(Efficiency)

Figure 12: Granularity(NMR)

Estimating the Cost of Throttled Execution in Time Warp

Samir R. Das

Division of Computer Science

The University of Texas at San Antonio

San Antonio TX 78249-0667

Abstract

Over-optimistic execution has long been identified as a major performance bottleneck in Time Warp based parallel simulation systems. An appropriate throttle or control of optimism can improve performance by reducing the number of rollbacks. However, the design of an appropriate throttle is a difficult task, as correct computations on the critical path may be blocked, thus increasing the overall execution time. In this paper we build a cost model for throttled execution that involves both rollback probability and probability for an event computation being on the critical path. The model can estimate an appropriate size of time window for a throttled execution using statistics collected from the purely optimistic execution. The model is validated by an experimental study with a set of synthetic workloads.

1 Introduction

The Time Warp [11] protocol for parallel discrete event simulation (PDES) has shown a lot of promise to exploit the parallelism in a simulation model without requiring intricate model specific information. However, it is prone to inefficient execution in many situations due to over-optimistic behavior [4], when some logical processes (LPs) operate at a much larger simulation time than others. Over-optimism may cause long and/or cascaded rollbacks [12] and the Time Warp system may spend a considerable amount of time in rolling back incorrect computation. Over-optimism may lead to other performance problems as well. For example, over-optimistic LPs may consume memory resources at an uncontrollable rate, making it impossible to complete the simulation with a finite amount of memory. Even if sufficient memory can be provided, memory management overheads may dominate [3, 4].

Thus, a conventional wisdom in PDES community has been to study mechanisms that exhibit a "controlled" form of optimism, and exploit the advantages of the optimistic execution without its liabilities. In the past, several mechanisms to *throttle* Time Warp have been suggested Important examples include, (i) limiting all event computations within a simulated time window above the global virtual time (GVT) [14, 19], (ii) rolling back all processes to GVT (or close to GVT) at stochastically selected intervals in real time [13], (iii)

not sending messages unless they are guaranteed to be correct, thereby eliminating the need for anti-messages [5, 17] (this is also known as *risk-free* computation), (iv) bounding the total amount of memory that can be allocated to the Time Warp system using memory management protocols like cancelback [3, 4], (v) limiting the number of events each LP may execute beyond GVT [18]. All these mechanisms have been shown perform better than the "purely optimistic" Time Warp for certain simulation models. In general, it is believed that an appropriate throttling of Time Warp execution (i.e., blocking one or more LPs even if they have unprocessed events in their future event list) has a strong potential for improved performance. However, the throttle must be applied with caution. As observed in [15], both purely optimistic Time Warp and Time Warp with an adaptive throttle can arbitrarily outperform each other under specific circumstances. Thus it is imperative to study the appropriateness and amount of throttle required for the best possible performance.

With this goal, we develop a cost model for estimating the benefits of throttling, which can be used to design time window based throttling. The model uses monitored statistics about the rollback and event commitment behavior and computes estimates for the rollback probability and the critical path. These estimates are used to construct an appropriate size of the time window to throttle the execution. The rest of the paper is organized as follows. In Section 2, we provide a background of the problem and relate our approach to other work in this direction. Section 3 describes the cost model. Section 4 validates the model using an experimental study. Section 5 concludes the research and points to future work.

2 Background and Related Work

Limiting optimism (or throttled execution) can be beneficial as it can potentially reduce rollbacks, and hence, rollback related costs (state restoration, sending antimessages, message cancellations at destinations). It can also reduce costs related to virtual memory management [4]. On the other hand, limited optimism can be potentially harmful in case it blocks correct computations that may affect the *critical path*[1] of the sim-

---

[1] Informally, an event is on the critical path if any delay in executing it increases the total time to complete the parallel

ulation. This tradeoff must be balanced properly to achieve the best performance.

There has been a considerable amount of work demonstrating the effectiveness of different throttling schemes as mentioned in the previous section. However, comparatively little attention has been paid in designing adaptive schemes that *automatically* computes the appropriate amount of throttle (e.g., the size of the time window). Notable exceptions are described in the following. Ball and Hyot's adaptive concurrency control scheme [1] adjusts a blocking window according to the minimum of a function that describes the cpu cycles lost due to blocking and due to rollback recovery. Das and Fujimoto's adaptive memory management protocol [4] takes an indirect approach and controls the memory allocation to adjust the throttle. Ferscha and Lüthi [7] uses a probabilistic cost model to evaluate the tradeoff between optimistically processing and conservatively blocking the simulation engine. Their model computes an optimal real time delay interval to minimize the rollback overhead. Ferscha in another work [6] suggests probabilistic throttling of logical processes based on time-series forecasting. Hamnes and Tripathi [10] proposes a local adaptive protocol, where real time blocking windows are computed based on inter-arrival times (both real and virtual) of messages in each input channel. Srinivasan and Reynolds promotes the use of near perfect state information (NPSI) (such as, a good estimate of GVT) to compute the *error potential* for logical processes and to throttle the processes with higher error potential [16].

Our present work has similarity to some of the above in that it also estimates the rollback probability based on the past behavior. We, however, use the notion of *degree of optimism* (virtual time difference from the GVT) rather than any notion of real time. It focuses on using a direct, time window based approach and relies on a good estimate of GVT[2]. Also, we attempt to design a more aggressive throttle than the above approaches by involving estimates of the critical path of the computation. Only those computations are blocked that have a high probability of being either incorrect, or correct but off critical path.

3 A Cost Model for Controlled Optimism

In Time Warp, the optimism of an logical process (LP) can be quantified as the virtual time difference between the LVT (local virtual time) of that LP and the current value of GVT. We call this the *degree of optimism*. Thus every event execution, correct or incorrect, takes place at certain degree of optimism. Each event execution can meet with one of the two possible eventualities — (i) the execution can roll back, or (ii) the execution can commit (i.e., GVT sweeps past the timestamp of the event). If the degree of optimism

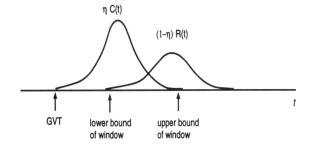

Figure 1: Normalized distribution for degrees of optimism for correct (to be committed, $C(t)$) and incorrect (to be rolled back, $R(t)$) event computations.

is recorded as a part of the event state for each event execution, a frequency distribution for committed or rolled back executions on a scale of optimism can be computed. This can be done by noting the degree of optimism (which is a part of the event state) each time an event is rolled back or fossil collected.

Let $C(t)$ denote the fraction of events committed with degree of optimism t (as a fraction of total number of events committed), and $R(t)$ denote the fraction of events rolled back with degree of optimism t (as a fraction of total number of events rolled back). Thus $C(t)$ and $R(t)$ have the property of probability density functions (see Figure 1). An upper and a lower bound of the time window used for throttling can be easily constructed by noting the optimism values where $C(t)$ and $R(t)$ become close to zero (see Figure 1). If η be the Time Warp efficiency (fraction of total number of events committed and total number of event executions), the following function $p(t)$ denotes the probability that an event execution at optimism level t will be rolled back:

$$p(t) = \frac{(1-\eta)R(t)}{\eta C(t) + (1-\eta)R(t)}. \qquad (1)$$

We ignore the mathematical technicality that the concept of probability mass at a single point for a continuous distribution is meaningless. In essence the functions $p(t)$, $R(t)$ and $C(t)$ denote the probability mass within a very small window of virtual time around t, i.e., $[t - \delta t, t + \delta t]$. In practice, statistical data is collected with a discretized virtual time scale, where the width of each discrete step can be thought to be $2\delta t$. We also note that, in principle, it should be possible to construct the functions $R(t)$ and $C(t)$ analytically for simple simulation models (such as simple closed queueing networks) using the knowledge of the underlying timestamp increment distribution. However, such analytical modeling is beyond the scope of this paper. We primarily focus on using empirical estimates of the above distributions from statistics gathered from the execution.

---

simulation. For a more formal definition see [9].

[2]Thus it is more suitable for shared memory systems with continuous GVT update mechanisms [20].

3.1 Estimating the benefits of throttling

As a first step to construct a cost estimate for blocking event executions at high degrees of optimism , we observe that an event execution with a high degree of optimism is very unlikely to control the critical path. On the other hand, an event execution at the least optimism level (i.e., at or near GVT) is very likely to affect the critical path. Thus, in the absence of a better knowledge about the critical path, it is reasonable to model the probability of a correct event execution being on the critical path, by a monotonically decreasing function, say $\chi(t)$: $\chi(t) \approx 1$ for $t \approx 0$, and $\chi(t) \to 0$ for $t \to \infty$ ($t \geq 0$). Thus the optimal width of the time window is the value of t minimizing the cost function:

$$\text{cost}(t) = rp(t) + \chi(t)(1 - p(t)), \qquad (2)$$

where r is the amortized cost of rolling back a single event execution (expressed in units of average event execution time), taking into account cost of state restoration, sending of antimessages and event cancellation at the destination. Note that in formulating the equation (2), we have ignored all second order effects. For example, we have assumed that (i) number of rollbacks do not affect the speed of rollbacks and (ii) delay in processing an event on the critical path can increase the completion time of the parallel simulation only by the average event execution time.

At present we rely on heuristic methods to estimate $\chi(t)$. In our experiments, we estimate $\chi(t)$ by $(1 - \int_0^t C(t) dt)$. This function represents the probability that a correct event is executed at optimism degree higher than t. This hypothesizes that a higher fraction of events committing with a degree of optimism beyond t indicates a greater probability that the events committing at degree t are critical.

4 Model Evaluation

We use experiments on an operational Time Warp system [2] to validate the cost model. The experiments have been carried out on a four processor Sparc-Station20 with 64MB main memory and 1MB cache per processor. Each processor is a 50MHz Super-Sparc. The simulation application is a PHOLD workload model [8]. In PHOLD each LP, upon executing an event forwards it to another randomly chosen LP with a timestamp increment. The timestamp increment may come from a probability distribution (a biased distribution with mean 1.0 is chosen for the experiments). The system is initialized with a set of events (called the *message population*, which is 1024 in our experiments). A total of 16 LPs are used, 4 on each processor. Intuitively, PHOLD is similar to a closed queueing network simulation where each queue has an infinite number of servers. The timestamp increment is same as the service time at the servers, and the message population is the same as the job population.

Hot-spots are created in the PHOLD model to introduce asymmetry, which in turn increases rollbacks.

Three versions of the model are used: (i) symmetric model (no hot-spots), (ii) 10% hot-spot (i.e., 10% of all message traffic is directed to one single LP and the rest are uniformly distributed among all LPs) and (iii) 40% hot-spot.

Figure 2(a) and (b) show normalized $C(t)$ and $R(t)$ (i.e., $\eta C(t)$ and $(1 - \eta) R(t)$) as a function of t (degree of optimism). To conserve space only the symmetric model and the 40% hot-spot model are shown. Note the respective position and size of the normalized $C(t)$ and $(R(t)$ envelops. A large size of the $R(t)$ envelop indicates a large number of rollbacks. A shifted $R(t)$ envelop with respect to $C(t)$ indicates a severe over-optimistic behavior. Figure 2(c) shows the cost(t) function computed using the equation (2) for all three models. These data were collected using a purely optimistic Time Warp kernel. The same models were then executed on a Time Warp kernel with a time window based throttle. Figure 2(d) shows the speed of simulation in committed events/sec on this kernel for different time window sizes. It is observed that the optimal size of the time window (i.e., corresponding to the fastest execution) has a close correspondence to the minima of the cost function in Figure 2(c).

5 Conclusions

We have developed a cost model for throttled execution of Time Warp that can be used to construct an adaptive throttle. The cost model uses rollback probability and estimates of the critical path behavior to construct a cost function whose minima describes an optimal width of a time window. The model dictates that an event is computed *only* when there is a high probability that it is correct as well as on the critical path, and this combined probability overwhelms the probability that it may be incorrect. Though only the rollback and critical path costs are included in the model, such an aggressive design is expected to minimize the overall memory usage.

Our model estimates an appropriate size of the time window based on a "purely optimistic" execution. It can be integrated as a part of an adaptive throttling policy that releases throttle occasionally to renew the estimate for the appropriate size of the time window. Our future work includes (i) refining both the cost model and the function used for estimating the critical path, and (ii) developing an adaptive throttle based on this cost model.

References

[1] D. Ball and S. Hoyt. The adaptive Time-Warp concurrency control algorithm. *Proceedings of the SCS Multiconference on Distributed Simulation*, 22(1):174–177, January 1990.

[2] S. R. Das, R. Fujimoto, K. Panesar, D. Allison, and M. Hybinette. GTW: A Time Warp system for shared memory multiprocessors. In *1994 Winter Simulation Conference Proceedings*, pages 1332–1339, December 1994.

[3] S. R. Das and R. M. Fujimoto. A performance study of the cancelback protocol for Time Warp. *Proceedings of*

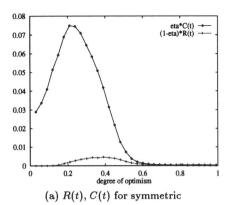

(a) $R(t)$, $C(t)$ for symmetric

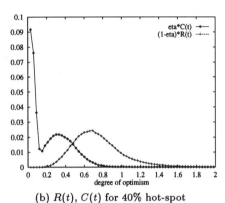

(b) $R(t)$, $C(t)$ for 40% hot-spot

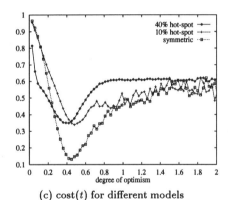

(c) cost(t) for different models

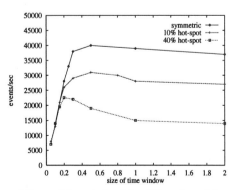

(d) speed (events/sec) for different models

Figure 2: Experimental Results

the 7th Workshop on Parallel and Distributed Simulation, 23(1):135–142, May 1993.

[4] S. R. Das and R. M. Fujimoto. An adaptive memory management protocol for Time Warp parallel simulation. In Proceedings of the 1994 ACM SIGMETRICS Conference on Measurement and Modeling of Computer Systems, pages 201–210, May 1994.

[5] P. M. Dickens and P. F. Reynolds, Jr. SRADS with local rollback. Proceedings of the SCS Multiconference on Distributed Simulation, 22(1):161–164, January 1990.

[6] A. Ferscha. Probabilistic adaptive direct optimism control in Time Warp. In Proceedings of the 9th Workshop on Parallel and Distributed Simulation, pages 120–129, 1995.

[7] A. Ferscha and J. Lüthi. Estimating rollback overhead for optimism control in Time Warp. In Proceedings of the 28th Annual Simulation Symposium, 1995.

[8] R. M. Fujimoto. Performance of Time Warp under synthetic workloads. Proceedings of the SCS Multiconference on Distributed Simulation, 22(1):23–28, January 1990.

[9] M. A. Gunter. Understanding supercritical speedup. In Proceedings of the 8th Workshop on Parallel and Distributed Simulation, pages 81–87, 1994.

[10] D. O. Hamnes and A. Tripathi. Evaluation of a local adaptive protocol for distributed discrete event simulation. In Proceedings of the 1994 International Conference on Parallel Processing, pages III:127–134, August 1994.

[11] D. R. Jefferson. Virtual time. ACM Transactions on Programming Languages and Systems, 7(3):404–425, July 1985.

[12] B. D. Lubachevsky, A. Shwartz, and A. Weiss. An analysis of rollback-based simulation. ACM Transaction on Modeling and Computer Simulation, 1(2):154–193, April 1991.

[13] V. K. Madisetti, D. A. Hardaker, and R. M. Fujimoto. The MIMDIX operating system for parallel simulation and supercomputing. Journal of Parallel and Distributed Computing, 18(4):473–483, August 1993.

[14] L. M. Sokol and B. K. Stucky. MTW: experimental results for a constrained optimistic scheduling paradigm. Proceedings of the SCS Multiconference on Distributed Simulation, 22(1):169–173, January 1990.

[15] S. Srinivasan and P. F. Reynolds. Adaptive algorithms vs. Time Warp: An analytical comparison. In 1995 Winter Simulation Proceedings, 1995. To appear.

[16] S. Srinivasan and P. F. Reynolds. NPSI adaptive synchronization algorithms for PDES. In 1995 Winter Simulation Proceedings, 1995. To appear.

[17] J. Steinman. SPEEDES: A unified approach to parallel simulation. In 6th Workshop on Parallel and Distributed Simulation, pages 75–84, Jan. 1992.

[18] J. S. Steinman. Breathing Time Warp. In Proceedings of the 7th Workshop on Parallel and Distributed Simulation, pages 109–118, May 1993.

[19] S. J. Turner and M. Q. Xu. Performance evaluation of the bounded Time Warp algorithm. Proceedings of the SCS Multiconference on Parallel and Distributed Simulation, 24(3):117–126, January 1992.

[20] Z. Xiao, F. Gomes, B. Unger, and J. Cleary. A fast asynchronous GVT algorithm for shared memory multiprocessor architectures. In Proceedings of the 9th Workshop on Parallel and Distributed Simulation, pages 203–208, 1995.

Parallel Simulation of Billiard Balls using Shared Variables

Peter A. MacKenzie and Carl Tropper
School of Computer Science
McGill University, Montreal, Canada H3A 2A7

Abstract

We present, in this paper, a conservative algorithm for the parallel simulation of billiard balls. It is common to employ a spatial approach to these simulations, in which the billiard table is partitioned into segments which are simulated by different processors. It differs from previous approaches in that it makes use of shared variables to enable processors to ascertain the state of the computation at neighboring processors. The shared variable corresponds to a region at the boundary of the table segments (the so-called critical region). By making use of shared variables a significant speed-up over the execution time of a purely conservative approach is obtained. The algorithm was implemented on a BBN Butterfly, as was a purely conservative algorithm. In the conservative algorithm, a processor wishing to process a ball in the critical region waits until the neighboring processors simulation time is greater then the time of the event it wishes to process. In our experiments, we examined three population levels of balls-2400, 4800 and 7200. These populations were chosen to reflect a low, medium and high population of balls. The shared-variable approach resulted in a 30 to 50 percent decrease in the execution time of the purely conservative approach.

1 Introduction

Many systems can be viewed as collections of objects moving around a defined space and interacting with each other. The objects can range from atoms and molecules to inter-planetary objects acting under the influence of gravity. Such problems intuitively lend themselves to a parallel simulation algorithm in which the physical space in which the objects interact is divided up into regions and each processor on a multi-computer simulates those objects within a region.

The difficulty in simulating such a model is that each processor must simulate an object in its own region although the objects behavior may be influenced by an object in another processor's neighboring region. This system can be modelled as the classic network of logical processes communicating via message passing in which the messages contain information pertaining to the behavior of objects in each processor's region. The two classical approaches to parallel simulation, conservative and optimistic deal with this problem in a manner consistent with their paradigms.

The algorithms described in this paper are conservative in nature and make use of shared variables in order to allow a processor to access the state of its neighbor's objects. If the dynamics of the objects being simulated are understood, it is then possible for the algorithm to make inferences on whether it can safely proceed, whereas a conservative approach [3] would have to block.

As a paradigm of the problem we are interested in simulating, we chose a billiard ball simulation [2]. We simulate billiard balls travelling around a table, bouncing off the boundaries and colliding with one another. The balls are represented in our model by

190

velocity and position at a given time. We simplify the problem by allowing for a frictionless table and ignoring the rotation of the balls.

The remainder of this paper is organized as follows. Section 2 contains a summary of previous work on the problem. In section 3 our parallel algorithm, making use of shared variables, is described. Section 4 contains the performance results realized from this algorithm.

2 Previous Work

In this section we briefly summarize previous work on parallel billiard ball simulation. A more detailed summary may be found in [6].

In [2] an efficient serial algorithm is described, which is made use of in the algorithm described in [3] as well as the algorithm described in this paper.

Parallelizing the billiard ball simulation requires that the table be divided up into separate regions which are distributed among the processors and that each processor simulates the balls in its assigned region. Each processor "shares" a border with two or more other processors and has to pass balls back and forth across these borders. This interdependency between the processors requires that an algorithm maintain causality when the processor's simulation times are different.

In [3] the serial algorithm of [2] is parallelized. The algorithm rests upon the assumption that there is an upper bound on event propagation speeds, the consequence of which is that two balls which are sufficiently far apart can be processed concurrently. The bounded lag algorithm [1] is employed to synchronize the simulation. A portion of the region in each processor adjacent to the boundary, referred to as the insulation layer, is defined in order to control er-

rors that may occur from balls crossing the boundary from an adjacent processor. Balls in the interior of the region surrounded by the insulation layers can be simulated without the possibility of an error. However, in order to simulate an event in the insulation layer, the time stamp of the event must be smaller than the time stamps of the events in all of the adjacent processor's insulation layers. Otherwise, the processor must block.

Unfortunately, causality errors can still occur due to balls gaining sufficient speed to travel across the insulation layer in time less than the maximum (assumed) time or as a result of a propagation of collisions through a chain of balls located close together. To deal with such errors, a checkpointing strategy is employed in which states are saved when the floor of the bounded lag restriction [1] exceeds some incremental value. When an error is detected the algorithm redoes the simulation from the most recent checkpoint. The parallel algorithm was emulated on a serial machine. Execution times were not reported. Instead, results centered about the frequency of rollbacks.

Finally, in [5], a version of the billiard balls simulation referred to as colliding pucks was used as a test case for Time Warp

3 The Shared Variable Algorithm

Parallelism exists in the billiard ball simulation because events in one region can be processed independently of those in other regions. However, balls close to the boundary between two regions do not share this luxury. Causality may be violated when two events on opposite sides of a border between two processors are processed out of sequence.

The method used to process balls serially within each processor is the algorithm found in [2].

It is the way in which balls are simulated inside the critical regions that distinguishes the shared variable approach from that of [3] and which results in substantial performance improvements. In each processor a portion of the simulation region adjacent to the boundary of the region with another processor is designated as a *critical region*, similar to the insulation layer of [3]. Each processor maintains, along with its event heap, a list of events which take place in the critical region. These lists are shared by all neighboring processors and are used to determine when a ball will cross the border and to determine whether a processor may safely proceed without error. The algorithm avoids the severe blocking restrictions for processing events close to the border encountered in [3],the consequence of which is the serializing of event execution in the insulation layer.

The algorithm has a different processing regime depending on whether an event occurs inside or outside of the critical region. The algorithm first determines if the current ball A_1 being processed at $current-timeP_a$ is in the critical region. If A_1 is not in the critical region then the processor must wait only if $current-timeP_a > current-timeP_i + B$ for any processor P_i which shares a border with P_a (B is the distance from the edge of the critical region to the border divided by an estimated maximum velocity).. By restricting the processing of balls to when $time(e) < current-timeP_{neigh} + B$, a ball from another processor cannot cause a violation of causality.

If the current ball A is inside the critical region, a ball directly across the border can affect it in time less than B. It is at this point that a strictly conservative approach blocks whereas the shared variable algorithm tries to determine if it may proceed. There are two conditions that must be satisfied in order for the shared variables to be utilized. First, $current-timeP_a > current-timeP_i$ for some neighboring processor P_i-this indicates that there is a ball in P_i that can affect A and the algorithm needs to determine if it may proceed. The second condition is the same as if the ball is outside the critical region; $current-timeP_a < current-timeP_i + B$. If $current-timeP_a > current-timeP_i$ then the processor needs to know if any of the balls in the critical list of P_i can affect ball A. This is not helpful if $current-timeP_a > current-timeP_i + B$ since a ball outside of P_i's critical region could affect P_a. Hence looking at the balls in the critical region would not be enough, and in this case the processor must block.

In figure 1, processor P_a's current-time P_a is 2.0 when it tries to process A_1 at time $A_1 = 2.0$. At the same real time processor P_b's $current-timeP_b$ is 1.75 when it tries to process a ball outside of the critical region. Under "strict conservatism" processor P_a would have to wait since $current-timeP_a < current-timeP_b$. Using shared variables processor P_a can look "inside" of P_b and determine the state of balls near the border. Since the earliest time which a ball could cross the border from P_b is $timeB_2 > current-timeP_a$, P_a can safely proceed.

It is important to recognize that with a densely populated critical region, balls may be involved in more than one collision on their way towards a border between two processors. As the algorithm bases its lower bound only upon the next event , it is possible to miss a collision that may cause an error as an unexpected ball crosses the border. It is also possible for balls to reach velocities that exceed the estimated maximum velocity or to form chains across the criti-

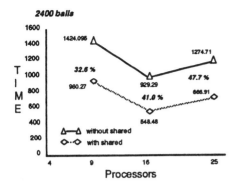

Figure 2: **Shared Variables vs Without Shared-2400 balls**

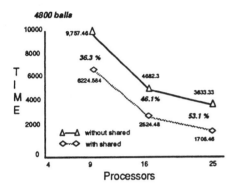

Figure 3: **Shared Variables vs Without Shared-4800 balls**

balls are bounced back and forth across the boundary. The processors are forced to simulate in lock step as they share these balls - no method to reduce the amount of time spent waiting can completely overcome this. As can be seen from table 1, the number of occasions when the algorithm with shared variables is able to avoid waiting with 7200 balls is less than number of occasions with 4800 balls.

As the number of processors increases the improvement in execution times increases for the shared variable method over the non-shared variable method. With more processors "dividing" the table space, the percentage of space near borders between two processors increases, causing dependencies between the processors.

Fundamentally, the purpose of using shared vari-

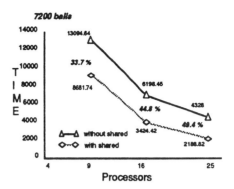

Figure 4: **Shared Variables vs Without Shared-7200 balls**

		shared	not shared
processors	9	1341	6376.2
	16	683.26	3379.3
	25	383.08	2258.8
7200 balls			
		shared	not shared
processors	9	2593	4940.3
	16	604.04	2824.3
	25	357.08	1847.1
4800 balls			
		shared	not shared
processors	9	232.01	752.68
	16	102.74	425.02
	25	83.82	342.69
2400 balls			

Table 1: **Time Spent Waiting**

ables is to reduce the amount of waiting time. As can be seen from table 2, the amount of time a processor wastes waiting for other processors is greatly reduced using shared variables. Figures 2,3 and 4 show this improvement in execution time. With 2400 balls and 9 processors the time of the shared variable approach is 32.6% less than that of the algorithm without shared variables. Those improvements rise

		number of balls		
		2400	4800	7200
processors	9	53.11	131	104.4
	16	49.75	149.5	137.31
	25	50.24	152	126.52

Table 2: **Blocking Avoidance**

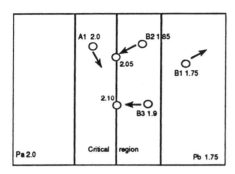

Figure 1: **Shared Variables in the Critical Region**

cal region that could result in causality errors. As in [3] a state recovery mechanism would be necessary to correct these errors. This remains a project for future work.

Although the current implementation was done on a shared memory machine the shared variables can be implemented on a distributed memory machine as was done, for example, in [7].[4] contains a general discussion of the use of shared variables in distributed simulation. Details of the shared variable algorithm may be found in [6].

4 Experiments

The experiments were run on an BBN butterfly, a shared memory multiprocessor based on the 68200 microporocessor in which each processor accesses shared memory using a shared bus.

The simulations were done with a 200X200 square unit table and with 1 unit diameter balls. The experiments were run with 1200, 2400 and 7200 balls on the table. Their initial position and velocities vectors were randomly generated using the C library rand() function. The balls were allowed to occupy any position on the board provided that a ball was not touching or overlapping with another ball. The x and y coordinates of the velocity vectors were between the range of -4 and +4 units per second. The number of processors used were 4, 9, 16 and 25.

We compare our algorithm to a conservative algorithm which doesn't use shared variables. In this algorithm, when a processor needs to process a ball in the critical region it must wait until each of the neighboring processor's simulation time is greater than the time of the event it wishes to process. The algorithm makes use of the serial algorithm of [2] within each processor.

As can be seen in the graphs in figures 2,3 and 4,significant speed-ups occur relative to a simulation without shared variables for each of the populations. When we go from a low density population of 2400 to higher density population of 4800 the time saved with the shared variables increases by a modest amount. Without shared variables, as the density increases there are more balls in the critical region to simulate, forcing a processor to move in lock step with its neighbors. However, with shared variables there is more opportunity to use this shared data to recognize opportunities in which it is possible to avoid blocking. Table 2 shows that there were more occasions with 4800 and 7200 balls than with 2400 balls when the shared variable algorithm could determine that it could safely proceed.

The percentage decrease in execution time gained through the use of shared variables begins to level off at a population of 7200 balls, although there are still impressive reductions in execution time. The shared variable method's time is between 35% less with 9 processors and 50% less with 25 processors. These improvements are comparable to those obtained with 4800 balls, which are comparatively 37% and 53.1%

With more balls in the critical regions there is a greater dependency between the processors as the to 41% with 16 processors and 48% with 25 processors. Similar results occur with the other simulation sizes. With 4800 balls and 9 processors there is a 37% reduction in execution time, with 16 processors there is a 46% reduction and with 25 processors there is a 43% reduction. Note that with a population size of 2400 balls the increase in execution time from 16 processors to 25 processors results from the number of balls per processor being too small- the simulation is overwhelmed by the overhead of passing messages.

References

[1] Lubachevsky,B., "Bounded Lag Distributed Discrete Event Simulation", Distributed Simulation, SCS Simulation Series,1988, pp 183-191

[2] Lubachevsky,B."How to Simulate Billiards and Similar Systems", Journal of Computational Physics 94, 1991, pp 255-283

[3] Lubachevsky,B. "Simulating Colliding Rigid Disks in Parallel Using Bounded Lag Without Time Warp", Distributed Simulation, SCS Simulation Series,vol 22, no 1,pp 194-202

[4] Mehl,H and Hammes,S, "Shared Variables in Distributed Simulation", Proc.7th Workshop on Parallel and Distributed Simulation (PADS93),1993,IEEE Computer Society Press, vol. 23, no. 1, pp 68-76

[5] Hontalas,P.,et al. "Performance of the Colliding Pucks Simulation"on the Time Warp Operating Systems",Distributed Simulation, SCS Simulation Series, vo 21, no 2, pp 3-9

[6] MacKenzie, P., "Parallel Simulation of Billiard Balls using Shared Variables", Technical Report SOCS-96, M.Sc. thesis, McGill University, Montreal, Canada

[7] Tropper, C. and Boukerche, A., "Parallel Simulation of Communicating Finite State machines", Proc. 7th Workshop on Parallel and Distributed Simulation (PADS93), 1993, IEEE Computer Society Press, vol. 23, no.1, pp. 143-151

Improving Conservative VHDL Simulation Performance
by
Reduction of Feedback*

Joel F. Hurford and Thomas C. Hartrum
Department of Electrical and Computer Engineering
School of Engineering
Air Force Institute of Technology

Abstract

This paper describes two forms of feedback in the simulation runtime of VHDL circuits that greatly influences performance. While circuit feedback and strongly connected components have been observed and documented as detrimental influences to conservative parallel discrete event simulation (PDES) efficiency, that influence has never been quantified. Moreover, in this study, the phenomenon of induced feedback [1] was observed to diminish speedup to the same degree as explicit feedback. In this paper the influence of feedback on simulation runtime is analyzed and an $O(n)$ algorithm for its elimination is presented. In addition, a metric for the quantification of feedback is introduced. By measuring feedback, it is possible to balance its influence on simulation runtime with that of other factors (e.g. load balance, number of processors, machine granularity, etc.) through the use of a cost-based partitioning approach. This paper reports significant improvements in runtime for three circuits due to the prevention of feedback using the partitioning algorithm presented. In addition, strong correlation between the feedback metric and conservative parallel simulation overhead is demonstrated.

1 Introduction

In the design of digital circuits using a hardware description language such as VHDL (VHSIC Hardware Description Language), simulation provides an effective way to test designs at an efficiency of time and resources. However, the rapid growth of circuit complexity (doubling every three years) creates an overwhelming computational demand on sequential simulators. Parallel simulations seek to surpass sequential performance by scaling to the problem with additional processors. Parallel simulation performance, however, is bounded by the communication demands between simulation entities and the overhead involved to maintain causality [2]. This overhead can be minimized by carefully partitioning the circuit components and mapping them to the physical processors. This assignment of tasks to processors to optimize performance is known to be NP-Complete. To further complicate the difficulty of partitioning, the optimization criterion, runtime, is only measureable by executing the simu-

lation. Since the goal is to partition the circuit *before* executing the simulation, the optimization criterion must be estimated by the available *a priori* parameters.

This paper studies the effect of feedback between the parallel processors on the performance of parallel discrete event simulations which utilize the Chandy-Misra [3] conservative synchronization protocol. A unique graph-based partitioning algorithm is developed for static dependency graphs of VHDL circuits which generates a feedback-free partition. Furthermore, a feedback metric is developed for use in a cost-based partitioning strategy which demonstrates high correlation to observed null message volume, a key indicator of protocol overhead. This allows the reduction of feedback to be included in the optimization strategy when it is not feasible or possible to eliminate it altogether.

2 Graph-Based Partitioning
2.1 General Graph Partitioning Model

One approach to partitioning circuits is to use a Task Precedence Graph (TPG), where each node in the TPG represents a single VHDL process and each arc represents a signal flow between two behaviors. The TPG is then partitioned into Logical Partitions (LPs) which are assigned to processors, one LP per processor. This results in a Processor Graph (PG), where the nodes represent processors.

2.2 Previous and Related Work

Two general techniques used to accomplish partitioning are heuristic based and cost based. Heuristic techniques allocate tasks to processors by adhering to a rule or pattern of behavior without attempting to assess the quality of the partition. Cost-based techniques assess the relative quality of partition decisions using some cost model that correlates to the optimization criterion.

2.3 Heuristic Based

Heuristic techniques are computationally efficient, but fail to capture the complex relationships inherent in the system under study. Examples of heuristic approaches include random and simple search partitioning. Boukerche groups strongly connected components

196

based on depth first search in order to reduce the possibility of deadlocks by eliminating loops between processors [4]. When more detailed cost based methods are used, these heuristic methods are often employed to find a starting partition for the cost method.

2.4 Cost Based

Cost based techniques search for an optimal (or "good") mapping by moving TPG nodes between LPs based on whether or not the move improves a cost function [5]. There are three problems to be solved here. The first is to identify those parameters of the partitioning that are correlated to the actual runtime of the partitioned program. The second problem is to find the proper form of equation relating those parameters to a cost value that is a good estimate of the runtime. The third problem is finding an efficient way of reaching the optimal value of the cost function. An exhaustive search of all possible partitions is computationally impossible for most circuits of interest. Typical greedy techniques such as hill-climbing tend to converge to a local optimum, and may miss better or global optima. One approach to the efficiency problem is through *simulated annealing*, where "wrong" moves are accepted probabalistically in order to avoid being trapped at a local extreme point. *Genetic algorithms* also provide a method of searching around the entire mapping space.

3 Feedback

Feedback is the presence of a cycle in the Processor Graph which results from partitioning the Task Precedence Graph. In conservative simulation, the presence of feedback causes increased NULL message traffic and decreased parallelism due to blocking. In order to prevent deadlock, NULL messages will circulate around such a loop, each cycle increasing the safe simulation time by the sum of delays through all LPs in the loop until the time of an executable event is reached. The effect of feedback is therefore particularly destructive for conservative simulations due to this "spinning up" of clock values of cycle members [6].

Feedback can be caused one of two ways. *Inherent feedback* refers to the existence of cycles in the Task Precedence Graph, that is, feedback loops in the circuit itself. If nodes within this loop are assigned to different processors, then a loop will be formed in the Processor Graph as well.

The second form of feedback, *induced feedback*, can result from the partitioning of the TPG. Even if no circular dependency exists in the TPG, a loop in the PG can be formed as nodes are grouped into sets (LPs).

In either case, feedback is destructive due to the effect of generating potentially large numbers of NULL messages. The remainder of this paper considers two approaches to reducing the effect of feedback: eliminating it altogether and quantifying it as a factor in a cost function.

4 Feedback Prevention

Feedback is caused by the formation of a circular dependency between processors. Both inherent feedback and induced feedback must be addressed to eliminate the problem. Inherent feedback can be addressed by identifying strongly connected components (SCCs) of the TPG which are then assigned to LPs as indivisible components (see Figure 1). If no part of an SCC crosses LP boundaries, then there will be no inherent feedback in the processor graph. Care must be taken to avoid a potential computational imbalance between the processors.

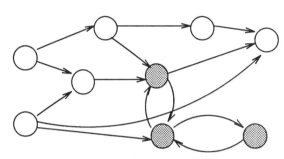

Task Precedence Graph

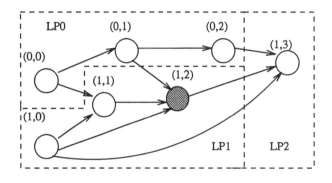

SCC Graph

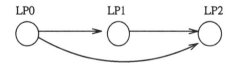

Processor Graph

Figure 1: Feedback Free Contraction of TPG by Breadth-by-Source Algorithm

The heuristic compromise between feedback prevention and load balance presented here depends on the distance or *depth* of each behavioral SCC from its source. A source and all its descendant behavioral SCCs form a set. These sets are the basis of allocation to LPs. Behavioral SCCs with more than one source are exclusively grouped with the source that has the fewest total descendents. This helps to balance the sizes of these "source sets". Depth of a node can be defined as follows.

Let

G be the acyclic behavioral SCC graph;
S be the set of source vertices in G;
v, w be vertices in G;
$desc(v, w) = true$ if a path exists from v to w;
$weight(v) =$ number of behaviors in v;
$size(v) = \sum_{\forall w \bullet desc(v,w)} weight(w)$;
$lpath(v, w) =$ number of arcs in longest path
  between v and w.

Then
$depth[s_z] = (z, 0) \qquad \forall s_z \in S$
$depth[v] = (x, lpath(s_x, v)) \quad \forall v \notin S$
where
$\exists s_x \in S | desc(s_x, v)$
$\land (\forall s_y \in S | desc(s_y, v) \Rightarrow size(s_x) \le size(s_y))$

It then follows that
if $depth[v] = (x, lpath(s_x, v))$ and
  $depth[w] = (y, lpath(s_y, w))$
then $depth[v] < depth[w]$ if and only if
$x < y$ or $x = y \land lpath(s_x, v) \le lpath(s_y, w)$

Source sets are considered in decreasing order of size (i.e. total number of behaviors). By allocating source sets to LPs in this manner, source nodes are more likely to be spread over multiple LPs mitigating pipelining effects [7]. Each source set is considered by traversing the set with a modified Breadth-First-Search (BFS). The BFS navigates considering a single depth incrementally. As a node is visited, its depth is interrogated. Only if it is at the current depth of consideration will it be allocated to the "current" LP. If some other path causes its depth to be greater than current consideration, its allocation is deferred. This technique combs dependency arcs between LPs into a single direction of increasing depth. Dependent behavioral SCCs will always be allocated after the nodes on which they depend. In other words, nodes in LP_y will only depend on LP_x if LP_x is constructed before LP_y. The BBS Algorithm (Figure 2) guarantees no feedback will exist in the Processor Graph while encouraging gate-level computational balance and a distribution of source nodes over all LPs.

5 Quantifying Feedback

Eliminating feedback is not the ultimate solution to the partitioning problem for several reasons. A circuit with a large SCC (or that consists of a single SCC) cannot take advantage of a large number of processors with anything approaching load balance. Also, partitions have been observed that contain feedback yet outperform equivalent no-feedback partitions [7]. There are many influences on simulation runtime, of which feedback is one. The cost-based partitioning approach takes into account these factors in its cost function. For feedback to be included in such a cost function, it is necessary to quantify the feedback by defining a metric. Ideally the metric would be based on directly measureable dependency graph parameters before executing the simulation, and would correlate

Algorithm 1 *BBS (Breadth-by-Source)*

Contract TPG to SCC Graph G.
Let S be the set of all sources ordered by decreasing number of total descendants.
Let $Adj[v]$ be the set of vertices adjacent to v in G
Let Q be a FIFO queue
Determine the *depth* of each SCC node.

$AvgLoad \leftarrow \frac{TotalNumberOfBehaviors}{NumberOfProcessors}$
$id \leftarrow 0$
For each $s_x \in S$
  $CurrentSearchDepth \leftarrow 0$
  $Q \leftarrow \{s_x\}$
  While $Q \ne \emptyset$
    $u \leftarrow head[Q]$
    $Dequeue(Q)$
    Allocate u to LP_{id}
    if $Load(LP_{id}) > AvgLoad$ then
      $id \leftarrow id + 1$
    end
    $CurrentSearchDepth \leftarrow depth[u] + 1$
    For each $v \in Adj[u]$
      if v is unmarked and $depth[v] = (s_x, CurrentSearchDepth)$ then
        Mark v
        $Enqueue(Q, v)$
      end
    end
  end
end

end

Figure 2: Breadth-by-Source Algorithm

well with runtime of the resulting simulation. Since many factors contribute to the runtime, showing direct runtime correlation with any metric is difficult. Another indication of the metric's usefulness would be to demonstrate its correlation to overhead incurred by the presence and degree of feedback, such as the volume of NULL messages observed in the executing simulation.

The feedback metric presented in this section was developed by analysis of how NULL messages are generated in the presence of a loop. The load, size and number of strongly connected components in the PG are indicative of the amount of feedback present and should be reflected in the metric. Moreover, Nicol [8] observed that fanout is important in conservative discrete event simulation since arcs tend to chain the progression of descendant LPs. Thus it is expected that descendants of an SCC will be inhibited by the inefficient progression of their predecessors. Using these influences, the feedback metric (ϕ) is defined by Equation 1. A Processor Graph (PG) of N LPs contains a number of LP level strongly connected components SCC_i. It is important to distinguish between the behavioral SCCs constructed as part of the previous algorithm and the SCCs that may participate in a Processor Graph. In this case, SCCs are composed of LPs and must have at least two members. For each LP that participates in an SCC, sum itself and all descendants (which includes other members of the SCC). This sum represents the size and influence of SCCs within the PG.

$$\phi = \frac{\sum_{\forall SCC_i}(size(SCC_i)\sum_{\forall LP_j \in SCC_i \cup DESC_i} Load(LP_i))}{N \sum_{\forall LP_i} Load(LP_i)}$$

(1)

Example applications of this metric are presented in Figure 3. The denominator of Equation 1 normalizes the metric for all circuits over all LP configurations. The metric ranges from 0.0 to 1.0 where 0.0 represents the absence of feedback and 1.0 is characteristic of a PG where all LPs are members of a single SCC.

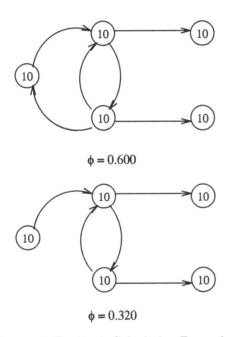

$\phi = 0.600$

$\phi = 0.320$

Figure 3: Feedback Calculation Examples

6 Experimental Results

6.1 Simulation Environment

Simulations were conducted on an Intel iPSC/2 hypercube with 8 processors. The parallel VHDL simulator VSIM [9] executes a SPMD processing model. VHDL simulations were conducted for an 8-bit Carry Lookahead Adder (CLA), an 8-bit Wallace Tree Multiplier, and a 16-bit x 16-bit Associative Memory Array. The CLA circuit has 77 behaviors and 152 interbehavior arcs. The Wallace Tree multiplier uses 1,050 behaviors and 1,770 inter-behavior arcs. The largest

circuit is the Associative Memory with 4,243 behaviors and 9,312 arcs. The circuits represent different application granularities and functional behavior.

6.2 Eliminating Feedback

Tests compare no-feedback partitions with the results of previous research in three categories: speedup, blocking time, and null message volume. *Speedup* is the ratio of sequential simulation runtime to parallel simulation runtime. Speedup is biased in these experiments since an unoptimized sequential simulator is used. *Blocking time* sums the time over all LPs that an LP suspends processing[1] in accordance with conservative blocking rules. *Null message volume* is a simple count of all NULLs sent during the simulation.

Figures 4 through 6 demonstrate significant speedup improvements achieved with the elimination of feedback. While the fine granularity of the CLA circuit limits the benefit of parallelization, it still demonstrates the superiority of the no-feedback partition. As seen in Figures 7 through 9, the increase in performance directly corresponds to reductions in null message volume. Similar observations can be made regarding processor blocking time. The BBS partitioning demonstrates consistent efficiency for all three circuits over all LP configurations.

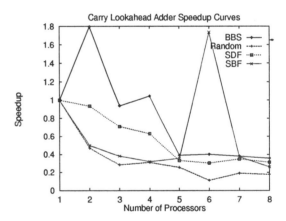

Figure 4: Speedup Curves for Carry Lookahead Adder

6.3 Validating the Metric

In order for the metric to be legitimate, it must correlate with the overhead induced by the presence (or absence) of feedback. Ideally, ϕ would negatively correlate with speedup directly. Unfortunately, it has been repeatedly shown that partitioning is a complex, perhaps combinatoric, problem that will not be predicted by a single parameter. Moreover, samples collected using various partitioning techniques (e.g. BFS, DFS, Annealing, Random, etc.) do not vary ϕ in isolation of other terms. Thus it becomes difficult to assess the behavior of the criterion in relation to ϕ when so many other terms are also changing. In addition

---

[1]During blocking, an LP still sends and receives messages, however, no events are processed.

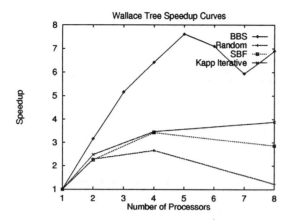

Figure 5: Speedup Curves for Wallace Tree Multiplier

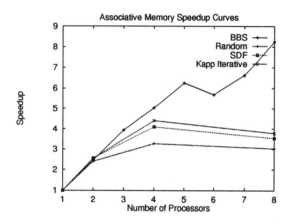

Figure 6: Speedup Curves for Associative Memory

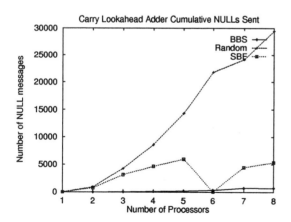

Figure 7: NULLs Sent for Carry Lookahead Adder

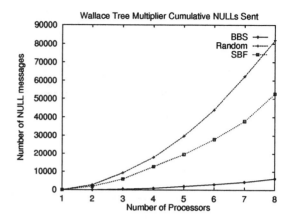

Figure 8: NULLs Sent for Wallace Tree Multiplier

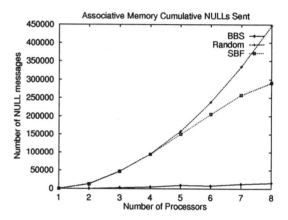

Figure 9: NULLs Sent for Associative Memory

to an original sample set of 525 partitions of various techniques, 651 additional samples were collected that sought to modify ϕ in isolation. Each partition of the second sample set began with a BBS solution which was modified to induce some feedback. Each partition of a circuit–LP configuration in the restricted set differs by the placement of only two behaviors. Consequently, most graph parameters are relatively unaffected by the difference. Unfortunately, correlation data in this restricted portion of the general search space showed no stronger a relationship to speedup or blocking time than that in the initial sample set. One relationship that did persist in both samples sets was a strong correlation with NULL message volume. Although not as definitive as a relationship with runtime, ϕ strongly correlates to a pertinent indicator of protocol overhead. Actual statistics of both sample sets are presented in Table 1. While high correlations were observed for *speedup* and t_{Block} in some cases, only the correlation with *NullsSent* was consistent across circuits, partitioning schemes, and LP configurations. It

Dataset	Circuit	Criterion	Correlation over LP Configurations	
			Avg	Std
General	CLA	*speedup*	-0.406	0.417
		t_{Block}	0.662	0.159
		NullsSent	0.823	0.088
	Wallace	*speedup*	-0.904	0.039
		t_{Block}	0.868	0.050
		NullsSent	0.792	0.091
	Associative Memory	*speedup*	-0.101	0.206
		t_{Block}	0.201	0.168
		NullsSent	0.881	0.056
Restricted	CLA	*speedup*	-0.524	0.376
		t_{Block}	0.802	0.102
		NullsSent	0.683	0.086
	Wallace	*speedup*	-0.722	0.096
		t_{Block}	0.919	0.058
		NullsSent	0.792	0.118
	Associative Memory	*speedup*	0.188	0.368
		t_{Block}	0.249	0.408
		NullsSent	0.821	0.121

Table 1: Validation of Feedback Metric

is this correlation with a pertinent protocol indicator that validates ϕ as a legitimate metric for feedback.

7 Summary and Future Work

The following conclusions can be made about feedback in conservative simulations based on this research:

- *Feedback is a pertinent influence to protocol efficiency.* For three different circuits, NULL message volume and time spent in conservative blocking drastically increased in the presence of feedback. No-feedback partitions had reduced overhead and correspondlingly lower runtimes.

- *The proposed feedback metric (ϕ) succeeds in indicating the detrimental influence of feedback to conservative protocol efficiency.* For all three tested circuits, ϕ had a consistent, strong correlation with NULL message volume for over 1100 samples.

- *The BBS algorithm is an efficient technique for intelligent partitioning.* Demonstrating superior performance for all circuits, the BBS algorithm is only of $O(n)$ complexity. Cost model based techniques will be challenged to exceed the performance of the BBS algorithm sufficiently to justify the additional computational expense of those methods.

Despite the success in improving speedup for the circuits analyzed, the BBS algorithm requires additional validation on more circuits and LP configurations. More important than the BBS algorithm is continued evaluation and improvement of the feedback metric. Cost based techniques require accurate models as their first priority. Identifying and validating feedback as an accurate parameter in conservative simulation will benefit all cost based research.

References

[1] D. L. Mannix, "Distributed discrete-event simulation using variants of the chandy-misra algorithm on the intel hypercube," Master's thesis, Air Force Institute of Technology (AU), Wright-Patterson AFB, OH, December 1988. AFIT/GCS/ENG/88D-14.

[2] R. M. Fujimoto, "Parallel discrete event simulation," in *Proceedings of the 1989 Winter Simulation Conference*, pp. 34–41, 1989.

[3] K. Chandy and J. Misra, "Asynchronous distributed simulation via a sequence of parallel computation," *Communications of the ACM*, vol. 24, pp. 198–206, April 1981.

[4] A. Boukerche and C. Tropper, "Sgtne: Semi-global time of the next event algorithm," in *Proceedings of the 9th Workshop on Parallel and Distributed Simulation*, pp. 68–77, 1995.

[5] K. L. Kapp, T. C. Hartrum, and T. S. Wailes, "An improved cost function for static partitioning of parallel circuit simulations using a conservative synchronization protocol," in *Proceedings of the 9th Workshop on Parallel and Distributed Simulation*, pp. 78–85, 1995.

[6] D. B. Wagner and E. D. Lazowska, "Parallel simulation of queuing networks: Limitations and potentials," *Performance Evaluation Review*, vol. 17, pp. 146–155, May 1989.

[7] J. F. Hurford, "Accelerating conservative parallel vhdl simulation," Master's thesis, Air Force Institute of Technology (AU), Wright-Patterson AFB, OH, December 1994. AFIT/GCS/ENG/94D-10.

[8] D. M. Nicol, "The cost of conservative synchronization in parallel discrete event simulations," *Communications of the ACM*, vol. 40, pp. 304–333, April 1993.

[9] T. A. Breeden, "Parallel simulation of vhdl circuits on intel hypercubes," Master's thesis, Air Force Institute of Technology (AU), Wright-Patterson AFB, OH, December 1992. AFIT/GCE/ENG/92D-1.

On Extending More Parallelism to Serial Simulators

David Nicol*
Department of Computer Science
The College of William and Mary
Williamsburg, VA 23185

Philip Heidelberger
IBM T.J. Watson Research Center
P.O. Box 704
Yorktown Heights, NY 10598

Abstract

The Utilitarian Parallel Simulator (U.P.S.) extends parallelism to the CSIM sequential simulation tool by providing several new modeling constructs. Using conservative synchronization techniques, these constructs automatically support time-synchronized communications between CSIM submodels running on different processors. This paper describes extensions to U.P.S. that allow the user to assist U.P.S. by providing additional "process lookahead," thereby reducing the frequency of synchronizations. The use and effect on performance of process lookahead is described for several models. In a mobile cellular communications model, the use of process lookahead results in up to a 60% improvement in speedup on 32 nodes of the IBM SP2. A factor of 3 improvement is obtained on a closed queueing network simulation running on 32 nodes of the Intel Paragon.

1 Introduction

In an earlier paper [8], the *Utilitarian Parallel Simulator* (U.P.S.) was described. U.P.S. extends parallelism to the CSIM [12] sequential simulation package. Parallelism is provided by defining several new, but natural, modeling constructs to the CSIM language. These language extensions automatically support time-synchronized communications between CSIM submodels running on different processors. In particular, one CSIM submodel communicates a message to another CSIM submodel by delivering the message to a *carrier*, a U.P.S. construct responsible for delivering CSIM messages across processor boundaries. From there the synchronization and communication are automatic. U.P.S. implements several conservative synchronization protocols. The lookahead required by these protocols is determined entirely by information generated and kept internally by the U.P.S. *carriers*. As such, the lookahead calculations and implementation of the synchronization protocols are completely hidden from the user. This relieves the user of the particularly tricky details of synchronization and message passing, thereby easing the burden of parallel model development.

However, U.P.S. performance is sensitive to the amount of lookahead available inside the carriers. Furthermore, since U.P.S. uses only information generated by the carriers and not any model-specific knowledge, the lookahead calculation is unnecessarily conservative. In particular, the lookahead generated and used by carriers essentially accounts for when a CSIM message may affect another processor's state, assuming that a message has already been delivered to the carrier. If the arrival times of messages to the carriers can be pre-determined, or lower-bounded, then this additional lookahead can be used to reduce synchronization frequency.

This paper explores the possibility and effect of providing the U.P.S. carriers with additional, model-dependent lookahead for the purpose of improving performance. There are two approaches to this problem:

1. *Automatically* provide the additional lookahead by either modifying CSIM or, for example, further extending U.P.S. to analyze the model and automatically extract lookahead.

2. Providing an interface through which users can (optionally) *manually* declare additional lookahead to U.P.S. , which then incorporates this information into its internal algorithms for determining synchronization times.

The first approach is the more attractive one from an ease of modeling point of view. However, as CSIM is a commercial tool that was not written by the U.P.S. developers, modification of CSIM is not a viable option. In addition, CSIM provides rich simulation capabilities that would make automatic extraction of lookahead very challenging (e.g.,

pre-emptive queues and the arbitrary program flow control provided by a general purpose programming language such as C). The second approach places an additional burden on the modeler; however in certain instances, the user can easily determine lookahead even though the model structure is fairly complex. In this paper, we explore the second option, of "process lookahead" where lookahead is computed by CSIM processes and is communicated to U.P.S. through function calls.

In Section 2, we briefly review relevant background material on CSIM and U.P.S. Section 3 describes the details of incorporating process lookahead into an overall synchronization scheme. Section 4 explores the effect of process lookahead on simulator performance for two different models: a mobile cellular communications network model and a closed queueing network model. (Initial performance results using process lookahead were presented in [9].) Use of process lookahead can dramatically improve speedups. The improvement in speedup is highest in situations when it is most needed: on models with low intra-carrier lookahead running on a large number of processors. For example, in the mobile cellular model, speedups were increased by up to 60% when run on 32 nodes of the IBM SP2. Conclusions are given in Section 5.

2 CSIM and U.P.S.

CSIM is a C language-based function library that implements a process-oriented view of simulations. In ordinary CSIM, processes can interact with one another in several ways. Two of the primary interactions are:

1. Queueing for a *facility* that represents a multi-server queue.

2. Sending a *message* to a *mailbox*, and waiting for a message to arrive at a mailbox, i.e. posting a *receive* at the mailbox.

The U.P.S. extensions combine and extend the above two mechanisms by permitting a process to *ship* a *package* to a *remote mailbox* residing on another processor using a *carrier*. Associated with the carrier is a multi-server facility, with non-zero, state-independent service times. Shipping a package (a message) involves queueing for the facility associated with the carrier and sending the message across processor boundaries. The *carrier* abstraction naturally models different types of communication channels—the communication delay across the channel provides the lookahead U.P.S. exploits. When a package is shipped, U.P.S. ensures that the message will appear in the remote mailbox at precisely the same simulation time that the carrier's facility is released, i.e., the arrival time of the package is the queueing plus service time at the carrier's facility. The definitions and use of CSIM and U.P.S. constructs are similar. For example, a CSIM mailbox is defined by a *mailbox(name)* call where *name* is mailbox's name. In U.P.S. , a remote mailbox is defined by a *remote_mailbox(name,processor)* call where *processor* gives the identity of the processor on which the remote mailbox exists. CSIM messages are sent using a *send(mb,msg)* call where *mb* is the identity of the mailbox and *msg* is a memory pointer to the message (or an integer valued message). In U.P.S. , packages are sent using a *ship(c,msg,len,rbox)* call where *c* is the carrier, *msg* and *len* are the package's starting address and length, respectively, and *rbox* is the identity of the remote mailbox.

U.P.S. currently supports three synchronization protocols: YAWNS – a window-based algorithm [10, 11], WHOA – a pairwise appointments algorithm within a global window [3, 5], and PUCS – an algorithm exploiting Markovian structure, if present [4]. In this paper, we will only consider the YAWNS protocol. U.P.S. pre-samples service times from the carrier's service time distribution function to obtain the lookahead required for synchronization. In this way, even though it may not know when next it must send a package to another processor, it knows the difference between the package's "send" time and "receive" times. In particular, in a single server carrier, if the current simulation time is t and the pre-sampled next service time is

*This work is supported in part by NSF grant CCR-9201195. It is also supported in part by NASA contract number NAS1-19480 while the author was a consultant at the Institute for Computer Applications in Science and Engineering (ICASE), NASA Langley Research Center, Hampton, VA, 23681.

s, no processor will receive an as-yet-unsent package from this carrier with a receive time of less than $t + s$.) Each processor's local lookahead (i.e., a lower bound on the minimum next receive time on any package this processor has yet to send) is fed into a global reduction to determine the window length: the end of the window corresponds to the first possible time that a package from *any* processor arrives at *any another* processor. In this way, any package generated in a window won't arrive during that same window. Each processor then simulates until the end of the window, picks up any packages generated for it during this window, calculates the next window and continues. The local lookahead is simply the sum of:

1. The time of the next event on CSIM's event list - this is a lower bound on the earliest time at which a package can arrive at (i.e., deliver a package to) a carrier and makes no other assumptions on model structure.

2. The minimum off-processor package arrival time, assuming that a package has just arrived at the carrier. This minimum is taken over all carriers on the processor.

The carrier service times are assumed to take the form $k + R > 0$ where k is a known non-negative constant and R is a (possibly) random part that is returned by a service time sampling function provided by the user. If the carrier has an infinite number of servers, then we require $k > 0$, since an infinite number of service times cannot be pre-sampled by the carrier. In this case, part 2 of the above local lookahead calculation is simply k. (Infinite server carriers naturally arise in applications, e.g., to model propagation delays down a fiber link.)

If either contribution to the local lookahead is small, then the window will be small and performance may suffer. Thus there are several situations in which there is an opportunity to improve the lookahead:

1. The carrier's utilization is low because arrivals to the carrier are infrequent. The local lookahead calculation conservatively assumes that the next event *might* be an arrival to the carrier.

2. The carrier has an infinite number of servers but $k \ll E[R]$. The local lookahead calculation conservatively assumes that the next pre-sampled service time *might* actually attain its minimum possible value k.

Process lookahead is designed to overcome the performance bottleneck that arises in the above situations.

We note in passing that the issue of providing language mechanisms to convey lookahead information to conservative synchronization schemes is not much studied. Some techniques look at how lookahead may be automatically derived from a model [6, 1, 7], but among these only Maisie allows a modeler to convey lookahead information. This accomplished by Maisie's provision of a function called *lookahead*. The extensions we describe in this paper serve much the same role as does Maisie's function call. The differences are based on the essentially different points of view of the simulation model, and the different underlying synchronization techniques. Maisie uses the "Logical Process" view, where LPs exchange messages. A call to *lookahead* with argument δ at time t is a promise that the LP will not send a message with time-stamp less than $t + \delta$. Our calls are semantically similar, but the basis of our tool is a process-oriented framework complicates matters somewhat. Under Maisie, a single LP thread of control is responsible for calling *lookahead*. In U.P.S. there are potentially many threads of control, each of which has a different notion of lookahead. In U.P.S. then we have each individual thread report its lookahead, and have U.P.S. manage all of the lookahead declarations and transform them into information that can be used by YAWNS.

3 Process Lookahead

Increasing the width of the YAWNS windows using process lookahead involves providing bounds on the arrival times of packages to carriers. In queueing network models, packages often represent jobs in the network. Such bounds can be sometimes determined by pre-sampling both the route (i.e., sequence of queues to be visited) and the service times at the queues. As a job experiences queueing delays along its route, the arrival time at the carrier can be increased by the queueing delays. We will give several examples of this in Section 4. For the moment, we assume that it is possible to compute such bounds. We first describe how lookahead is declared to U.P.S. , a user responsibility. Next, we describe how U.P.S. (internally) uses the declared process lookahead.

3.1 Declaring Process Lookahead

When the YAWNS window calculation begins, there are three types of CSIM processes that may eventually generate a package that will arrive at a carrier. First, there are processes that already exist on the processor (type 1 processes), e.g., a process representing an existing job in the queueing subnetwork assigned to that processor. Second, there are processes that have not yet been created on the processor, but may be spawned as a direct result of receiving an incoming package (in the next or future window) from another processor (type 2 pro-

processes). Third, there are processes that have not yet been created on the processor, but may be spawned by an already existing process, e.g., a future job arrival in an open queueing network (type 3 processes). As any of these process types may determine the upper limit of the window, all three must be dealt with.

If the U.P.S. process lookahead option is turned on, an existing process must register its lookahead with U.P.S. if there is a possibility that the process will generate an off-processor package. This is done by issuing a $h = register\_arrival()$ call which returns a handle h that can be used in $bound\_arrival\_time(h,t)$ calls that serve to declare time t to be the process lookahead corresponding to the process with handle h, i.e., by making this call a process is promising not to arrive at *any* carrier before time t. (These two actions may be combined in a single $h = register\_and\_bound\_arrival\_time(t)$ call and processes can issue a $deregister\_arrival(h)$ before they terminate.) As processes learn more about their lookahead, additional $bound\_arrival\_time(h,s)$ calls can be made, however, we require that $s \geq t$ for the subsequent calls, i.e., a process can never decrease its lookahead.

Now consider a type 2 process, i.e., a process that will be spawned due to a package receipt. Suppose a window calculation is entered at simulation time T and there is a package sent during the previous window with arrival time $A \geq T$. This package will be picked up by U.P.S. at time T and deposited in the appropriate mailbox (called a *station* on the receiving processor) at time A. The lookahead for this package is at least A, however often some package arrival time corresponds to the end of the previous window, i.e., $A = T$ for some package. Thus using package arrival times as lookahead for the next window will, in general, not be of much help. To get around this problem, a station may have a *lookahead handler* associated with it. The handler is a user written function that is called at window boundaries, when the message associated with the package is physically received by U.P.S. (at time T). The handler is passed the package's actual arrival time (A) and a pointer to the package. Based on this information, the handler can then compute the lookahead for the process that will be created (at time A) and declare this lookahead via a $register\_and\_bound\_arrival\_time$ call. With this mechanism, we can compute lookahead corresponding to every in-coming package at the beginning of the window.

For type 3 processes, i.e., uncreated processes, $new\_process\_arrival(t)$ call serves to declare t as the earliest time at which a process eventually destined for a carrier is created. The reason why type 3 processes need to be handled slightly differently will be explained shortly.

3.2 Using Process Lookahead

As processes declare lookahead, a lookahead heap is maintained by U.P.S. These will be combined with the pre-sampled service times at carriers and fed into a global reduction to determine the length of the next window. Let us focus on a particular carrier C with $C < \infty$ servers and let $S[i]$ denote the pre-sampled service time that will be used by the i-th arriving process to the carrier $(1 \leq i \leq C)$. For the moment we assume there are no type 3 processes. Let $A[i]$ be the i-th smallest value on the lookahead heap and suppose there are H elements on the heap. Then the earliest time that the package corresponding to the arriving i-th process can arrive at another processor is $A[i] + S[i]$. Note that since the lookahead heap orders arrivals to *all* carriers, the process defining $A[i]$ may not ever send a package to carrier C—use of $A[i]$ for C's lookahead is a conservative lower bound. Since both type 1 and type 2 processes have all declared their lookahead by the time the window calculation begins, the types 1 and 2 lookahead for the carrier is

$$L_{12} = \min_{1 \leq i \leq M} \{A[i] + S[i]\} \qquad (1)$$

where $M = \min(H, C)$. Equation 1 represents the earliest time that a package from a type 1 or type 2 process can reach another processor. Note that Equation 1 does not include the effects of queueing at the carrier. The reason for this is that a U.P.S. package can contain information generated at the time the package enters service at the carrier. This prevents pre-sending the package when it arrives at the carrier. Thus the usual method of incorporating queueing delays into lookahead calculations at queues [5] must be modified.

Now suppose there is a lower bound S on the arrival time of any type 3 process to the carrier. Since there might be an arbitrary number of arrivals of type 3 processes just after time S, we cannot associate pre-sampled service times with type 3 processes. Therefore, the type 3 lookahead for the carrier is simply $L_3 = S + k$ where k is the minimum service time at the carrier. The overall lookahead for the carrier is then $L = \min(L_{12}, L_3)$.

If there are an infinite number of servers at the carrier, Equation 1 needs to be modified to reflect the fact that an infinite number of service times cannot be pre-sampled; in fact, in the original version of U.P.S. , no service times were pre-sampled at an infinite server carrier. Suppose that C service times have been pre-sampled, then

$$L_{12} = \min \left\{ \min_{1 \leq i \leq M-1} \{A[i] + S[i]\}, A[M] + k \right\}. \qquad (2)$$

The additional term $A[M] + k$ that appears in Equation 2 but not in Equation 1 represents the possibility that additional arrivals may occur just after time $A[M]$ and that any such arrival may experience a minimum service time. The equation for L_3 remains unchanged in this case. Examining Equation 2, we see that the minimum carrier service time is only directly combined with the arrival farthest into the future and that typical service times are combined with potential arrivals closest into the future. Without process lookahead, the minimum service time is only combined with the next event into the future.

At window calculation times, U.P.S. determines the ordered times $\{A[i]\}$ and then computes the lookahead equations for each carrier on the processor; it then feeds the minimum carrier lookahead into the reduction. The primary overhead in implementing process lookahead is maintenance of the lookahead heap. This involves logarithmic time (in the number of entries on the heap) per insertion. At window times, a cost of order $M \log(M)$ is incurred (amortized over all carriers) since M entries are removed from the heap, are sorted, used in the lookahead equations, and then reinserted onto the heap.

4 Experimental Results

In this section, we describe the use and effect of process lookahead for two different models. In particular, we describe how the structure of the U.P.S. model had to be changed in order to accommodate process lookahead.

4.1 Mobile Cellular Network

The first model is a mobile cellular communications network, described in more detail in [9], and similar to that discussed in [2]. In this particular model there are 1024 hexagonally shaped cells with a fixed number of frequencies (20) per cell. With probability p (= 0.25) a call travels to a new cell. The travel time is $k + R$ minutes where R is exponentially distributed with mean $(6 - k)$; the carriers have an infinite number of servers with this service time distribution. We consider two cases corresponding to low and moderate amounts of carrier service time lookahead, $k = 0.1$ and $k = 1.0$, respectively. If a call does not travel, it stays in the current cell for an exponentially distributed amount of time with mean 3 minutes. The (Poisson) arrival rate is 3 calls/minute/cell. With these parameters an average of approximately 14 frequencies/cell are occupied in steady state.

The U.P.S. model without process lookahead samples the decisions as to whether or not to terminate or travel to a new cell (and if so, to which cell) as the call progresses through the model. In addition, there is a single arrival process per processor which always has 1 arrival pending. The model with process lookahead pre-samples N call arrivals into the future. Only one of these, the next arrival, is put on CSIM's future event list; the rest are used for process lookahead as follows. The complete route of each call is computed when the call arrives. For each cell along this route, the holding or travel time of the call in the cell is also pre-sampled (except for cells where the call travels across processor boundaries; these travel times are sampled by U.P.S.). From this information, it is easy to determine when a call might enter a carrier, if ever, and if so, to place the call on the lookahead heap. The last (N-th) arrival time serves as the type 3 process lookahead time. A simple circular buffer was used to implement the N pre-sampled calls. The packages for the process lookahead version of this model are larger than the version without process lookahead, since the complete route and service times need to be sent. The lookahead handler, invoked when packages are received, simply scans through the list of cells to be visited accumulating service times until a cell on another processor is identified.

We first investigate the sensitivity of performance to two parameters that control the amount of process lookahead: C, the number of pre-sampled service times at the carrier, and N, the number of pre-sampled calls per processor. For these experiments, we fix $k = 0.1$ (low carrier service time lookahead) and the number of processors at 8. The model without process lookahead exhibited a speedup of 4.4 on 8 nodes of the IBM SP2 (compared to a strictly serial CSIM model). Figure 1 shows that, for fixed N, the efficiency of the process lookahead model increases as C increases. However, for low C, the process lookahead model is somewhat slower since the cost of heap maintenance more than off-sets the slight increase in window length that is obtained when only a few carrier service times are pre-sampled. For example, with $N = 10$ and $C = 2$, the average window length is 0.12 minutes compared to 0.10 minutes without process lookahead. With low values of C, only a few carrier service times are pre-sampled and thus the window length is determined by the the minimum carrier service time plus a future arrival time near the top of the heap. By similar reasoning, for fixed C, there is little benefit to increasing N beyond a certain point. In fact, if N is made too large, then heap maintenance costs will begin to dominate and execution times will decrease. Similarly, for a fixed value of N, the effectiveness of process lookahead increases as C increases since then the minimum service time gets added to a carrier arrival time that is farther into the future. For example, with $N = 200$ and $C = 20$, the average window length increases to 0.41, more than 4 times its length without process lookahead. The maximum benefit of process lookahead observed in this example is to increase speedup by 15%, from 4.4 to 5.1. We next perform speedups studies on up to 32 nodes of the SP2. For these runs, we fix $C = 20$ and $N = 200$ and consider both low ($k = 0.1$) and moderate ($k = 1.0$) carrier service time lookahead. Results with

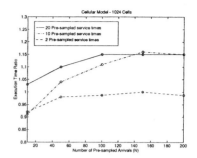

Figure 1: Ratio of execution times on 8 nodes of the SP2 (time without process lookahead / time with process lookahead)

low carrier service time lookahead case are shown on the left side of Figure 2. The figure displays speedups both both with and without process lookahead. For small numbers of processors, the model without process lookahead runs slightly faster. This is due to a number of factors, including heap maintenance costs, longer message sizes, and a limited increase in window length. For example the 2 processor speedups are 1.6 and 1.7 for the model with, respectively without, process lookahead. The respective average window lengths are 0.22 and 0.1 minutes. On two processors, there are 512 cells/processor and pre-sampling $N = 200$ arrivals per processor yields an expected arrival time of the N-th arrival of only 0.26 minutes into the future (= $200/(3 \times 512)$), which corresponds to the expected type three lookahead L_3 (per processor). Increasing N to 400 increases the average window to 0.35 minutes, but only marginally increases speedup to 1.63. For a small numbers of processors, the number of cells/processor is high leading to a relatively high computation/communication ratio, and window calculation is not the performance bottleneck. For a large number of processors, the computation/communication decreases and windows become more expensive operations, so the benefit of using process lookahead increases. On 32 processors, the speedup increases from 6.5 to 10.6, an increase of about 60%, when using process lookahead and the average window length increases by a factor of 3.

Results with moderate carrier service time lookahead case are shown on the right side of Figure 2. Here, the process lookahead model runs slightly slower than the model without process lookahead until 32 processors when there is a slight improvement. In this model, the windows are relatively large to begin with, and the process lookahead does not increase them by much. For example, on 16 and 32 processors the average window lengths increase by factors of only 1.25 and 1.2, respectively. Only on 32 processors, where window calculation costs are highest, this does translate into improved speedup, from 15.3 to 15.9.

4.2 Closed Queueing Network

Next we consider performance on a simply parameterized model of a closed queueing network. The network consists of N "clusters", each cluster consists of Q identical central server (one CPU and 5 IO devices) stations. The network is initially seeded with J jobs per cluster. The service time received at a cluster station is random, with mean S (this service mean is split between the CPU and IO servers). On entering a cluster, a job is given S/p total service ($0 < p < 1$) to be received within the cluster before being routed to a network link device, and be routed elsewhere. On exiting, a destination cluster is chosen uniformly at random from among all clusters. Each time service is received by the job, its observed service time is subtracted from the preassigned service sum. The random time required to transfer

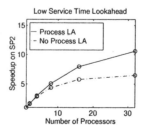 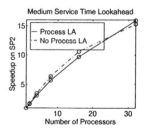

Figure 2: Speedups on SP2 for cellular model with 1024 cells.

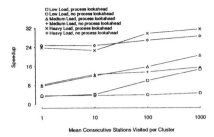

Figure 3: Speedup of closed queueing network model, using 32 nodes of the Intel Paragon

a job between clusters is taken to be $S/2$ plus an exponential with mean $S/2$.

As part of a job's receipt at a processor, it is assigned a handle using the $register\_arrival()$ call. Later, when its receive time is reached, the job is processed by cluster-entry code. There the job's initial cluster station is chosen, and its intra-cluster service total (S/p) is assigned. At that point $bound\_arrival\_time()$ is called, passing in this service total. To receive service at a station, the service time is randomly sampled (or is measured), so that upon completing service, the received service can be subtracted from the job's remaining service time. That remanent is then passed again to U.P.S. through the $bound\_arrival\_time()$ call. This call is not redundant. If the job encountered any queueing at this station, its ultimate cluster departure time is delayed by the amount of time in queue. This additional delay is implicitly conveyed to U.P.S. by the post-service call to $bound\_arrival\_time()$.

The magnitude of process lookahead is parametrically controlled by p; $1/p$ is the mean number of consecutive cluster stations visited by a job before exiting. We have seen earlier that the overall workload has a large influence on the performance gain available by using process-lookahead. The same is true for this model. We ran experiments where $Q = 20$ and $N = 32$, on 32 processors of the Intel Paragon, with each processor hosting one cluster. The experiments varied p so that the mean number of consecutive stations visited by a job at a cluster varied between 1, 10, 100, and 1000. The experiments vary J between 1 (low load), 10 (medium load), and 100 (heavy load). Figure 3 presents the speedups from these experiments. The raw processing rates represented by these speedups range from about 3000 job completions (at a server) per second to 45000 job completions per second. Speedups are measured against one-processor versions of the parallel code, but there is very little difference between the parallel code's behavior on one processor (with process lookahead disabled) and that of a specifically serial model. The data in this model confirms the trends observed in the previous model. The benefits of process lookahead are substantial when lookahead is good and workload is light. In the specific case of light workload and extremely good process lookahead, a factor of 3 improvement is observed. For that same level of lookahead, a 30% performance gain is observed under medium load, and a 10% gain is observed in heavy load. As before there is a cross-over point (in lookahead) before which using process lookahead is slightly detrimental to performance, owing to heap overhead costs. The magnitude of this degradation is not large; our understanding of it as being logarithmic in the heap size is borne out by our data (the workload designations "low", "medium", and "high" vary the lookahead heap size by increasing orders of magnitude).

5 Conclusions

This paper considers extensions to the U.P.S. parallel simulation system. U.P.S. automatically handles the message passing and time synchronization, leaving only the model partitioning aspects of parallelism to the user. Earlier studies indicated situations in which speedup was limited using this approach. The extensions considered in this paper allow the user to assist U.P.S. by providing additional model-dependent "process lookahead" to U.P.S. A simple interface for providing this lookahead was described; essentially the user needs to lower bound the arrival times of processes to U.P.S. carriers, which deliver packages across processor boundaries.

The details of how process lookahead can be incorporated within the YAWNS synchronization algorithm were described. Because YAWNS uses a global window, processors need only be concerned with determining the time the next synchronization event (the end of the next window). Integrating process lookahead with the other U.P.S. synchronization algorithms, which are based on pairwise appointments, appears more challenging.

Examples were given describing how model structure needs to be changed in order to exploit process lookahead. When using this feature, the user must be more aware of the fact that the simulation is running in parallel. This makes model development more challenging, but can result in significant increases in speedup precisely when such improvements are most needed: on a large number of processors in otherwise low lookahead models. This approach resulted in speedup improvements of up to 60% for a mobile cellular communications model running on 32 nodes of the IBM SP2, and a factor of 3 improvement on a closed queueing network model running on 32 nodes of the Intel Paragon. For the benchmark models considered in this paper, determining process lookahead was straightforward. Further experience with complex models will help to increase our understanding of the utility of the approach.

The approach we describe is somewhat more conservative than it needs to be, in two ways. The arrival times heap aggregates all arrival times for all carriers; it is possible to restructure the lookahead interface so that lookahead to specific carriers is is declared, and carriers manage their own lookahead heaps. The overhead of providing this refinement is higher; only experiments will show whether the benefits it provides are worthwhile. A second way of improving lookahead is to more fully exploit the FCFS property in a carrier by presending (when possible) a package at the instant it is delivered at the carrier. Presently U.P.S. waits to presend the package until the point at which it enters service; this is necessary only when the contents of the message depend on the carrier state at that point.

Further work will examine these optimizations and explore the utility of process lookahead on other models.

References

[1] R.L. Bagrodia and W.T. Liao. Maisie: A language for the design of efficient discrete-event simulations. *IEEE Transactions on Software Engineering*, vol. 20, no. 4, 225–238, April 1994.

[2] C.D. Carothers, R.M. Fujimoto and Y.-B. Lin. A case study in simulating PCS networks using Time Warp. In *Proceedings of the 9th Workshop on Parallel and Distributed Simulation (PADS '95)*, 87-94, IEEE Computer Society Press, 1995.

[3] P.M. Dickens, P. Heidelberger and D.M. Nicol. A distributed memory LAPSE: Parallel simulation of message-passing programs. In *Proceedings of the 8th Workshop on Parallel and Distributed Simulation (PADS)*, 32-38, IEEE Computer Society Press, 1994.

[4] P. Heidelberger and D.M. Nicol. Conservative parallel simulation of continuous time Markov chains using uniformization. *IEEE Transactions on Parallel and Distributed Systems*, vol. 4, no. 8, 906–921, 1993.

[5] D.M. Nicol. Parallel discrete-event simulation of FCFS stochastic queueing networks. In *Proceedings ACM/SIGPLAN PPEALS 1988: Experiences with Applications, Languages and Systems*, 124–137. ACM Press, 1988.

[6] GTU, Inc., Arlington, VA. *CPSim 1.0 User's Guide and Reference Manual*, June 1994.

[7] V. Jha and R. Bagrodia. Transparent Implementation of Conservative Algorithms in Parallel Simulation Languages. In *Proceedings of the 1993 Winter Simulation Conference*, Los Angles, CA., Dec. 1993, 677–686.

[8] D.M. Nicol and P. Heidelberger. On extending parallelism to serial simulators. In *Proceedings of the 9th Workshop on Parallel and Distributed Simulation (PADS '95)*, 60-67, IEEE Computer Society Press, 1995.

[9] D.M. Nicol and P. Heidelberger. Parallel execution for serial simulators. IBM Research Report RC-20205, Yorktown Heights, New York, 1995.

[10] D.M. Nicol, C. Micheal, and P. Inouye. Efficient aggregation of multiple LP's in distributed memory parallel simulations. In *Proceedings of the 1989 Winter Simulation Conference*, 680–685, IEEE Computer Society Press, 1989.

[11] D.M. Nicol, The cost of conservative synchronization in parallel discrete-event simulations. *Journal of the ACM*, vol. 40, no. 2, 304–333, April 1993.

[12] H. Schwetman. CSIM : A C-based, process oriented simulation language. In *Proceedings of the 1986 Winter Simulation Conference*, 387–396, IEEE Computer Society Press, 1986.

Author Index

Notes

Notes

Notes

Notes

Notes

Notes

3/21/96